A HISTORY OF THE ENGLISH LANGUAGE

Also by N. F. Blake

AN INTRODUCTION TO ENGLISH LANGUAGE
(with Jean Moorhead)

AN INTRODUCTION TO THE LANGUAGE OF LITERATURE

THE LANGUAGE OF SHAKESPEARE

A History of the English Language

N. F. BLAKE
Professor of English Language
University of Sheffield

NEW YORK UNIVERSITY PRESS
Washington Square, New York

First published in the U.S.A. in 1996 by
NEW YORK UNIVERSITY PRESS
Washington Square
New York, N.Y. 10003

Library of Congress Cataloging-in-Publication Data
Blake, N. F. (Norman Francis)
A history of the English language / N. F. Blake.
p.   cm.
Includes bibliographical references and index.
ISBN 0–8147–1292–4
1. English language—Grammar, Historical.   2. English language–
–History.   I. Title.
PE1075.B45   1996
420'.9—dc20   96–12951
                                                        CIP

Printed in Hong Kong

Contents

Preface		vi
List of Abbreviations		viii
List of Maps		x
List of Figures		xi
1	What is a History of English?	1
2	Background Survey	24
3	Before Alfred	47
4	The First English Standard	75
5	The Aftermath of the First Standard	105
6	Interregnum: Fragmentation and Regrouping	132
7	Political, Social and Pedagogical Background to the New Standard	172
8	Language Change from 1400 to 1660	203
9	Establishing the Standard within Social Norms	236
10	Emancipation, Education and Empire	272
11	World Domination and Growing Variation	303
Notes		333
Suggested Further Reading		339
Appendix		
	Glossary of technical terms	341
	Phonetic script	350
Index		
	General	353
	English words	371

Preface

When I was asked to write a history of the English language in one volume for undergraduates and the general public, I was in the middle of editing the second volume of the *Cambridge History of the English Language*. The work I was doing on that volume prompted me to reconsider the appropriate way to organise a single-volume history of English. I came to the conclusion that it was better to focus on the development of standard English in order to give the volume cohesion and to prevent it from trying to achieve too much. I realise that such a decision makes the resulting work more restricted in its approach in that those who live in Australia might well feel that the contributions that their country had made to the development of English have been overlooked. But my own knowledge of varieties like Australian is limited and the impact of Australian on British English is something that might be better tackled by an Australian. However, the contribution made by and the form of English found in other countries cannot be overlooked and I hope I have made that clear in the final chapter of this present book. In particular, American English has had a considerable influence on British English over the years and so more attention is given to that variety in this book. But even it is seen from the viewpoint of how it has influenced the development of British English. As an editor of one volume of the *Cambridge History* I have also acted as part of the editorial team for all volumes, and I have gained immeasurably from being immersed in that work. Writers for the *Cambridge History* have helped me focus my ideas and understand the history of English more clearly. This book is the better for the work done for the *Cambridge History* and I am grateful to the various contributors to all the volumes who have, unknown to them, made my task with this book easier. I am also grateful to various colleagues in Sheffield, particularly David Burnley and Geoff Lester, for their help with many aspects of this book, and to Dr Robert McNamee for checking some references. Parts of the book have been given as lectures to the International Conferences on English Historical Linguistics and elsewhere, and I am indebted to my audiences for their comments.

The strategy I have adopted involves abandoning the traditional framework of Old, Middle, Early Modern and Late Modern English in favour of a more flexible format for the book as a whole. However, the concepts Old and Middle English are so ingrained that I have used them where I thought it would make the sense easier for the reader.

It may be appreciated that the approach adopted in this book is my own and I alone am responsible for its overall shape and contents. I hope it will prove stimulating for those who use it, and that it will help to develop that growing interest in the history of the language which has been manifest over the last few years. It is even a topic which is now more taught in schools because of the development of English Language A-levels and the National Curriculum.

N.F. BLAKE

List of Abbreviations

A	adjunct, adverbial
acc	accusative
adj	adjective
aux	auxiliary
dat	dative
e	early (e.g. eWS = Early West Saxon)
fem	feminine
gen	genitive
Gmc	(Proto-)Germanic
Goth.	Gothic
imp	imperative
ind	indicative
inf	infinitive
instr	instrumental
l	late (e.g. lWS = Late West Saxon)
Lat.	Latin
masc	masculine
ME	Middle English
ModE	Modern English
ModG	Modern German
n	noun
neut	neuter
nom	nominative
O	object
obl	oblique
OE	Old English
OED	*Oxford English Dictionary*
ON	Old Norse
perf	perfect
pers	person
PIE	Proto-Indo-European
pl	plural
pres	present
S	subject
sg	singular

V	verb
WGmc	West Germanic
WS	West Saxon
*	a reconstructed or hypothetical form
**	an unacceptable form or construction
Ø	a zero form, an empty slot in the grammatical system
/ /	a phonemic form
[ ]	a phonetic form
< >	a graph, i.e. a letter form
<	is developed from (as one sound may be developed from another)
>	develops into (as one sound may change to another)
(:)	a sound with or without length (e.g. *e(:)* means long and/or short *e*)

List of Maps

1   Anglo-Saxon dialect areas   xii

2   Dialects in the Interregnum   xiii

3   English in the world today: countries where   xiv
English is or has recently been an official language

List of Figures

4.1	*Cura Pastoralis*, King Alfred's preface	85
6.1	*The Canterbury Tales*, General Prologue (*c*.1405)	163
7.1	Letter from Margaret Paston to John Paston (1465)	183
7.2	*Love's Labour's Lost*, First Folio (1623)	193
7.3	Robert Cawdrey, *A Table Alphabeticall* (1604)	197
8.1	Edmund Coote, *The English Schoolemaister* (1596)	231
9.1	Dr Johnson, *A Dictionary of the English Language* (1755)	253
10.1	J. A. H. Murray, *A New English Dictionary on Historical Principles* (1888)	289

MAP 1 Anglo-Saxon dialect areas

MAP 2 Dialects in the Interregnum

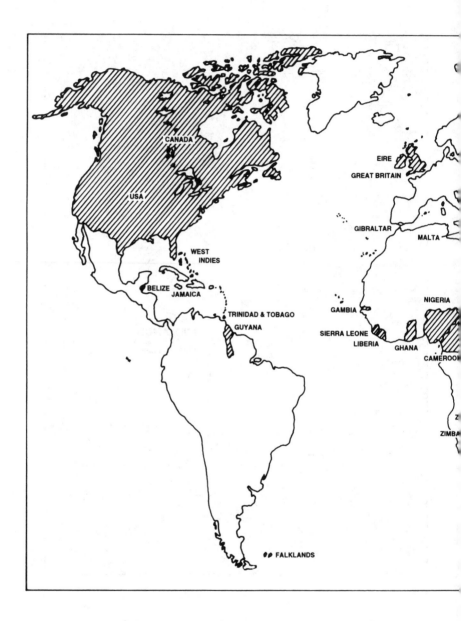

MAP 3 English in the world today: countries where English is or has recently been an official language

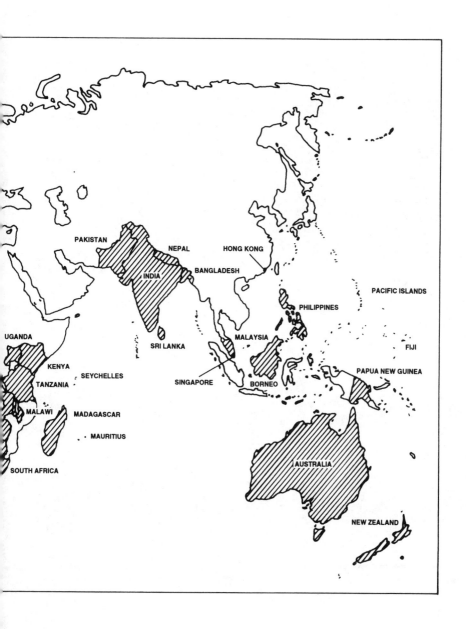

PAKISTAN
NEPAL
HONG KONG
BANGLADESH
INDIA
PACIFIC ISLANDS
PHILIPPINES
UGANDA
SRI LANKA
MALAYSIA
FIJI
KENYA
SEYCHELLES
TANZANIA
PAPUA NEW GUINEA
SINGAPORE
BORNEO
MALAWI
MADAGASCAR
MAURITIUS
AUSTRALIA
SOUTH AFRICA
NEW ZEALAND

1

What is a History of English?

To many people it might seem a relatively straightforward matter to write a history of the English language, for one simply starts at the beginning and carries through until the modern day. A history of the English language, however, does raise the questions of what one means by 'English' and what a history of it should seek to accomplish. Let us consider the first of these questions.

To most people today 'English' indicates the variety of the language known as Standard English – a variety characterised by the written form which is highly regulated. If one was seeking to learn English today, the appropriate goal would be to aim at a mastery of this variety. Consequently, a history of the English language might be thought to explain how Standard English arose and has developed since then. But in addition to this standard there are many varieties of English. In England itself there are numerous regional dialects, both rural and urban. There are also varieties found in Wales, Scotland and Ireland. When one looks abroad, one finds a whole range of other Englishes. The Standard American variety differs from Standard British English in various aspects, and within the United States there are many regional varieties. Most countries which were settled from or colonised by the English use English as their first language or as an approved, sometimes an official, variety. Even outside these countries, English is used widely as a *lingua franca* for purposes of commerce and science, because English has virtually achieved the status of a world language. For those who want to learn a second language, English is often their first choice. The result is not only that English is spoken in a plethora of different countries, but also that the differences among the speakers of English extend over an enormous range. In addition, each speaker of English has a number of different registers or forms of the language which are used for

1

various social occasions. The English one uses for an interview will differ in vocabulary, pronunciation and syntax from the English that person might use in a more intimate social situation. It is clear that a history of English could not encompass the development of all varieties and registers of the language which have existed and which still exist. Many of these are in any case not well documented, because until recently the information which survived was available only in written English and that meant in practice in a standard form.

There is the additional difficulty of deciding when 'English' began. English is a branch of the West Germanic family of languages which was brought to these islands from the fifth century AD onwards by the Germanic people known collectively as the Anglo-Saxons. When they arrived in England, they consisted of a number of tribes and tribal groupings, each of which probably spoke a different variety of their language even if the varieties were mutually intelligible. The previous occupants of the country were Romanised Celts and it was many years before the Anglo-Saxons conquered the country and established their own political system. It was several centuries before the various tribal groups, each with their own dialect, united politically under a single monarch, and even longer before they could be said to have accepted that there was a single language variety for the country as a whole. Indeed, some people might think this position has not been reached even today. The concept 'English' is to a large extent a political and educational one. People speak their own variety if that is sufficient for their day-to-day affairs, as it would often be if almost all the people they came into contact with were speakers of their own variety or could be understood without too much difficulty if they spoke a different variety. The development of a standard is often the result of increased education and mobility among the speakers, together with the need to communicate with others over space and time. A necessary precondition for the concept of a national standard language is writing, and in most cases this will be supported by the model of some outside language. A standardised form of English would have to wait for the introduction of writing into England and for the model of Latin to provide a guide as to what a standardised variety of a language might be like. The benefits of a standardised language become more obvious in the written form, for it promotes better communication and intelligibility. Hence, it would be difficult to claim that 'English' by this definition had begun before the introduction of writing and Latin through the conversion of the

Anglo-Saxons to Christianity following the arrival of St Augustine at the end of the sixth century AD. Although we could pretend that English began as soon as the first Angle or Saxon set foot in England, this would plainly be ridiculous. He or she spoke a variety of West Germanic and that variety may have contributed to the amalgam which would ultimately develop into the English language, but it would not be appropriate to suggest that a language which we could call English existed at that time. This, however, only brings us back to the question of when English began. It is probably impossible to answer that question with any accuracy, though we might date the beginning of English from the establishment of the first standard language in England. It is my contention that this did not happen until the time of King Alfred in the ninth century. Before his time various varieties which were to merge into English existed, but not English itself. Naturally, a history of English must take account of the varieties which contributed to the formation of this language, just as it must take account of all the other languages, such as Old French and Old Scandinavian, which have had major inputs into its development.

Knowledge of a language before the development of tape-recorders has to be gained from written sources and this makes writing of paramount importance to our understanding of the history. This point is worth emphasising because today linguists claim that speech is the primary medium of language and that writing is a development from speech. Although this may be true, writing and speech are not the same thing. It is difficult to disentangle the development of speech from written documents, because not only is writing by its nature conservative, but also it is used for different ends, particularly for communication in situations where the parties are separated over space and time. The possibility of asking for clarification in a face-to-face conversation is not available in writing, and so different structures need to be employed to minimise the risk of misunderstanding. Often it will appear as though writing makes periodic adjustments to catch up with the development of the spoken language, particularly in pronunciation. Once writing becomes fully standardised and ceases to change to reflect developments in pronunciation, changes in the latter must be detected by other means than through changes in the writing system. The methods and sources available for this type of enquiry will be explained briefly later in this chapter.

The other question raised at the beginning of this chapter was what a history devoted to the English language should contain. As already suggested, it cannot contain details of the history of all the varieties which generally go under the umbrella description of English today. For the most part it must focus on the development of that variety known as Standard English, though it must look outside that variety from time to time, if for no other reason than that other varieties have had some influence on the standard. But one should not expect to find in a book of this sort detailed information about the history of the Somerset dialect or of the New Zealand variety of English except in so far as they impinge on the nature and status of Standard British English itself. A concentration on the standard variety means considering how the system of the standard was formed and how it was modified under different pressures and influences. Often the changes in the standard will seem arbitrary and irrational, because they will often involve the replacement of one form by another taken from some other variety or register. Although change in the standard may be relatively easy to trace, explanations for such changes are more difficult to provide.

Traditionally histories of the English language have divided their account into three major periods: Old English (sometimes referred to as Anglo-Saxon), Middle English and Modern English. The last period is sometimes divided into two to give Early Modern English and Late Modern English. The reasons for this division are as much political as linguistic. Old differs from Middle English in that the Norman Conquest of 1066 introduced new settlers who spoke a variety of Old French and thus changed the nature of English. But there was an equally important series of invasions by Scandinavians (the so-called Viking invasions and settlements) from the end of the eighth century onwards, though this has not contributed to a similar division of the language by modern historians. Middle English differs from Early Modern English, and the transition from one to the other is traditionally dated at 1485 when the Tudors replaced the Yorkists after the Battle of Bosworth. Both 1066 and 1485 are political dates whose familiarity has forced historians of the language to accept them as significant for the development of the language as well. Most people have heard of the Anglo-Saxons and probably recognise that the medieval period came to an end in the fifteenth century; they do not find it difficult to accept that a history of the language should reflect these important political changes. The division into Early and Late Modern English is more contentious and has never been a matter of agreement. There are many possible political events, such as the restoration of the monarchy in 1660, or purely arbitrary dates, such as 1700, which have been put forward as marking this transition. Although politics and language are closely related, it may be that we have been looking at the wrong kind of political event to formulate our historical periods. Before we suggest alternatives to those outlined here, we should consider the possible linguistic reasons for thinking of historical periods in the language.

It had been accepted in the past, though not everyone today agrees, that changes in language, especially sound changes, happen slowly over a period of time. The reasons for change in language are complex, but in many cases it is possible to see that a change takes place gradually in the sense that it is accepted into the standard over a period of time. A new usage is first adopted by some people on some occasions. From there it spreads to other people and to a greater frequency among those who had already started to use it. At some stage it becomes used so frequently by a large number of people, or at least by a large number of those people who are thought to set the standard for the language, that the change is accepted as having occurred and is recognised by grammarians and others as acceptable in the standard language. This process can take place over a few years or possibly over a hundred years. Even when a change has been accepted into the standard, it does not follow that all speakers or users of the standard will adopt it. This type of change can be seen most clearly in syntax and lexis, for the position of change in sounds is more contentious. Consider, for example, the adjective *different*, which may be followed by one of three prepositions, *from, to* or *than*. Grammarians in the nineteenth and early twentieth centuries demanded that the correct preposition to use after this adjective was *from*, because it was more logical to use *from* in view of Latin usage and etymology, though their insistence suggests that this 'rule' was not always observed, particularly in speech. Today it is regular for people, particularly those under forty, to use *to* after *different*, and it would not be usual now for a schoolteacher to correct a pupil who used this preposition rather than *from*. Many older people, however, continue to use *from*, though it is not unreasonable to suppose that this usage will die out over the next twenty years. Some people use *than* after *different*, though its use is frowned on in Britain as an Americanism and because some consider it 'illogical'. But this change is a change in the system which is the standard, for it is clear that all forms may be heard in speech. Individual users of the language may on different occasions use all three. What can be seen is that a change is taking place and that it is only gradually accepted into the standard. It is important to bear this state of affairs in mind when considering the question of how far changes in the language can be used to act as boundaries to mark one historical period from another.

The usual division of the history of the language into three major periods – Old, Middle and Modern – was first proposed by Henry Sweet in a lecture on the history of sounds to the Philological Society in 1873. In the written version he wrote:

> I propose, therefore, to start with the three main divisions of *Old*, *Middle* and *Modern*, based mainly on the inflectional characteristics of each stage. Old English is the period of *full* inflections (*nama, gifan, caru*), Middle English of *levelled* inflections (*naame, given, caare*), and Modern English of *lost* inflections (*naam, giv, caar*).[1]

Although Sweet's article was concerned with the history of sound, his division into these three periods seemed so acceptable that they were taken over by other scholars without more ado. After all, we write about Anglo-Saxon history and we teach courses on Anglo-Saxon (or Old English) language and literature. Similarly there are courses on Middle English language and literature in universities and other institutions. To most people this division into three periods seemed natural and right. Sweet's argument is based on a morphological feature, namely the levelling and fall of inflections, where the former involves different inflectional endings being levelled under a single form and the latter the total disappearance of the inflections. This is why Sweet in his examples has all the Middle English unstressed vowels as *e* (the levelled form of *-a/u*) and has no unstressed vowels in the Modern English forms he has invented in a pseudo-phonetic representation. A moment's reflection will make clear that this principle of division is flawed. Today it may be true that most inflections have fallen, but some still exist. The plural of most nouns is formed by adding *-s*, so the plural of *stone* is *stones*. The third-person singular of the present indicative of most verbs also ends in *-s* so that there is a distinction between *I come* and *he comes*, just as the preterite of many verbs is formed by adding the inflection *-(e)d* so that there is a distinction between

I walk and *I walked*. In the Old English period there are many examples of the levelling of inflections in some of the extant texts, just as in Middle English certain texts show the fall of most inflections. The position is not unlike that outlined in the previous paragraph in that various changes are adopted by writers at different times and so there appear to be long periods in which the available evidence could be used to justify either the retention or the levelling of inflections at the presumed change-over from Old to Middle English, and either the levelling or the fall of inflections in the change-over from Middle to Modern English. Whatever linguistic phenomenon is chosen the same problem will recur. Changes in the language cannot be dated so specifically that we can use them to provide precise dates for the end of one period and the beginning of another. The levelling of inflections has been dated anywhere between approximately 900 and 1200. It all depends on what data are used and which texts are selected to provide the evidence. There is also the further problem of what particular linguistic feature should be chosen to provide the framework for dating the periods. Sweet chose the development of inflections, but other scholars have chosen other phenomena. Various features in the language undergo changes at different times and at different rates, and it is difficult to justify choosing one feature to the exclusion of others. In the change-over from Middle to Modern English, for instance, is the fall of inflections a more significant feature of the language than, for instance, the Great Vowel Shift?

Although we have courses in universities devoted to Old English language and literature and Middle English language and literature, it does not follow that this is the appropriate division to follow in a history of English. If a history of the English language should confine itself principally to the history of the standard language, we need to adopt an alternative division which reflects changes in and attitudes towards the standard. In this respect we need to distinguish between a 'standard' language and a 'standardised' language. The difference is largely political and educational. A standard language will develop into a standardised language, but the reverse is not true. By 'standardised' I mean a language which has achieved a reasonable measure of regularity in its written form. In earlier periods this may well mean that a teacher or master of a scriptorium imposed a set of preferred writing forms on those who were subject to his authority so that they wrote manuscripts using those forms fairly consistently.

Sometimes an individual may have achieved his own standardised writing, but have had no pupils to whom to pass it on. In later periods, printed material conforms to the house style of the publisher or whoever is responsible for the final document. Personal documents in any period will not necessarily conform to this standard because they are 'private' and thus intended only for a limited circulation. Usually these standardised languages are restricted geographically to a small locality that reflects the extent of the influence of the teacher. A standard language, on the other hand, is the written form which is either imposed or promoted over a wider geographical area than where it originated with the aim of making it the principal or sole written form in the country as a whole. Inevitably in the earlier periods of English, the standard was not as standardised as it became in later periods. The characterising feature is the political and educational will to impose a standard on the country as a whole by one means or another. A standardised language remains either regional or personal; a standard language has been adopted more widely throughout the country. The standard language remains standard only in writing; and even in writing it has been easier to impose a standard on spelling than on syntax or lexis. New words and new constructions continue to be accepted into the standard, as suggested above with *different from/to/than*. Sounds, on the other hand, remain outside the standard language. It is true that there is a form of spoken English referred to as Received Pronunciation, and it is this form which is taught to non-native speakers who wish to learn English. But most non-native speakers rarely achieve mastery of this variety, and of those who are native speakers, perhaps only 5 per cent in England use it with any frequency. Although the development of sounds within English is an important part of its history, it is difficult to make it a determining factor in deciding what periods to divide the language into.

In view of the considerations outlined above, this book divides the history of English into episodes which more accurately reflect the shifting attitudes to and developments within the standard. I provide a brief outline here of the 'periods' which I deal with in this book, but fuller justification for each division will be found in the respective chapters. It is only in the time of King Alfred that Anglo-Saxon England began to think of itself as a political entity, though unity was not to be achieved until the tenth century. The conquest of the north and east of the country by the Vikings provided the motivation for the gradual reconquest of these areas by the Wessex kings from Alfred onwards. To accompany this reconquest he provided copies of books which he distributed throughout his enlarged kingdom. He also helped to re-establish learning in the country as a whole. This meant extending the influence of what had been the dialect of one region more widely throughout the country, even if that regional variety was not as yet as standardised as later varieties were to be. Before the time of Alfred 'English' as an entity did not exist; a number of varieties existed, any one of which could have provided the basis for a future standard. That the standard turned out to be basically West Saxon was the result of political events and had nothing to do with the advantages or disadvantages of that dialect. Indeed, one could reasonably argue that culturally and educationally Wessex was not as advanced as some other parts of England before the Vikings arrived. Before Alfred's time we have a prehistory of English. After his time it is the West Saxon variety which provides the standard, though control over this form of English was never very secure until the end of the tenth century when attempts were made at Winchester to standardise this variety of English more thoroughly. The concept of a standard was established, even if the reality did not always match up with the ideal. A standard writing helped to provide support for political unity.

The Norman Conquest created a new situation as many of the principal officers of church and state were no longer English or English-speaking. The invaders brought with them their own version of French as well as the motivation to reinvigorate the educational system in England by incorporating it more firmly within the West European tradition. This meant that England experienced a renaissance of Latin learning which had already got under way in other parts of Europe. This did not happen immediately. Three languages became available for use in England: Latin, French and English. From the twelfth century onwards it was Latin that was in most respects the standard language of the country, and where Latin was not appropriate French was used. The pull of Old English was still strong and at first survived as an ideal. Many Old English manuscripts were copied in the twelfth and thirteenth centuries, and the concept of Old English must have been the inspiration behind the development of the local standardised forms of English that we find at this time. Gradually, however, the idea that England should have a standard English as distinct from a standard language which could be either Latin or French disappeared. We enter a period which has no concept of a standard English, and that may be dated to the middle of the thirteenth century or slightly earlier. The period from the time of Alfred until sometime about the middle of the thirteenth century may be regarded as one when an ideal of standard English modelled on some form of West Saxon or a development of it had some influence. The breakdown of this ideal, leading to what I have called later in this book the 'Interregnum', was provoked by the political circumstances of the Norman Conquest and the replacement of English by Latin and/or French. This hiatus in the history of standard English meant that when there were attempts to create a new standard, that standard would not necessarily model itself upon the original West Saxon variety which had formed the previous one. The new standard would be influenced by the varieties available in London which had become the largest English city and the centre of political power. In this intervening period England remained a single political unit and the concept of Englishness remained alive. The foundation for the re-creation of a standard existed, even though there was no standard at the time. Political unity and the memories of a past English greatness and standard remained possible potent forces. This period was, therefore, different in nature from the pre-Alfredian period which had never known what a standard language was within England. This intermediate period, the Interregnum, may be dated from approximately 1250 to 1400.

About 1400 the importance of French and Latin began to wane, and the need for a new standard in England emerged. Even in the fourteenth century various standardised forms of English are found in the London area so that the framework for the creation of a standard was there, since any of these standardised forms could be developed and extended over a wider area. The end of this Interregnum when no standard English form existed may be placed about 1400, for that is when the idea of using English in different activities, such as teaching, bureaucracy and trade, begins to manifest itself, though it should not be thought that the written language was itself as yet highly standardised. The important feature is the concern to use English as a national language rather than the achievement of a high degree of standardisation throughout the country. It is increasingly suggested by contemporary scholars that this process was promoted, if not initiated, by the

Lancastrian royal house. When Henry, Duke of Lancaster deposed his cousin Richard II, he became Henry IV, even though his claim to the throne was contrary to contemporary custom. Henry IV experienced several rebellions by disaffected aristocrats during the first years of his reign, and it cannot be said that he ever sat comfortably on his throne. The Lancastrians achieved respectability with the conquests in France gained by Henry V, particularly through his victory at Agincourt in 1415. Some scholars believe that the Lancastrians actively promoted the cause of English in order to increase their appeal to merchants and commoners against the aristocrats who were the leaders of the rebellions against them. Even if this is true, it is not likely that the kings would actively promote a standard as such. At best they would encourage the use of English as the national language, but this in turn would enhance the prospects of a standardised variety of London English being adopted as the variety to be used nationally. In order to follow this policy, the kings would have to rely on the forms of language most accessible to them, and that meant using one of the standardised forms of English used in the Chancery or some other government agency. From 1400 onwards the idea that there should be a single form of 'English' based upon the language of London and its environs became predominant. It was hardly surprising that this should lead writers and scholars to urge the further standardisation and in some cases the total reform of this variety. At first most of their energies were devoted to developing a uniform spelling system for English, and the main arguments centred on whether the system should reflect etymology or current pronunciation. The result was a unified spelling system, whose main lines were in place by the end of the seventeenth century, though absolute consistency was not established – and indeed has not even been achieved today. But that tolerance of variation which is found at the beginning of the seventeenth century, as in the first Folio of Shakespeare's works (1623), was severely reduced by its end. So this first period of the standard may be regarded as establishing a spelling system in writing for the country as a whole – a spelling system which was then promoted partly through education, but mainly through the publications of the printing press. It might be regarded as a standard spelling in printed English, because private writing, such as letters and diaries, continue to use a less regular spelling. The date at which this system was sufficiently standardised to provide an end-date for this period is difficult to establish, and we may need to fall back upon political events to provide us with such a date. The most attractive is perhaps 1660, the year in which the monarchy was restored in England after the revolution that had resulted in the beheading of Charles I and the exile of his family. When Charles II returned to England, he brought back with him French ideas and influences, including the whole question of regulating the vocabulary and syntax of the language. The onset of the so-called Age of Reason demanded a more prescriptive attitude to language, which forms a reasonable focus for a different period in the language's development.

The period from 1400 to 1660 was concerned with the establishment of a written standard throughout the country, though this took the form of worrying about the best spelling system to be adopted for the language and the nature of the English vocabulary. The latter found expression through a debate about the benefits of a Latinate vocabulary against a Saxon one and constant emphasis on the need to improve the rhetorical nature of the language to make it an expressive vehicle for literature. There were no attempts at codification of different features of the language, since most of the discussion was concerned with what might be best for the language rather than attempts to produce practical and authoritative guides for its use. The period which followed, which I start in 1660, was much more concerned with the regulation of the language and produced numerous books and pamphlets about what was 'correct' English. This is the age which saw the rise of the dictionary, culminating in Dr Johnson's dictionary of 1755. Many dictionary compilers were obsessed with the idea of producing lists of acceptable words for the language; they wanted to prescribe what words were acceptable and what were not. Although Dr Johnson started out with this idea as well, his experience in compiling his dictionary taught him that this was an impossible, even an undesirable, aim. But others were much more prescriptive than he was, and the existence of dictionaries which purported to list all the words in the language promoted the idea that what was not recorded in a dictionary could not be an acceptable English word. If it was acceptable, surely it would have been recorded in the dictionaries. This was also the age when grammars were produced with elaborate rules for what was acceptable usage in English syntax. These books, of which that by Bishop Lowth was perhaps the best known, often proceeded on the basis of what was not allowable in the language, for they tended to exhibit examples of bad usage which they proscribed. The basis for much of what they proposed was a comparison of English with Latin, so that what they considered the rules of Latin grammar were often transferred into English without any concern for whether it was appropriate to English or not. The focus of this period was on regulating the variety which had been established as the standard and making it conform to the dictates of reason and rational language as they were understood. We might date this period as continuing until the end of the eighteenth century, and perhaps 1798, which saw the publication of the *Lyrical Ballads*, could be regarded as a symbolic end-date. This collection of poetry attacked the idea of a pre-scriptive language for poetry and raised the concept that it should deal with 'the real language of men'. It was inspired in part by the French Revolution of 1789, which had called into question the very bases of the old order and its assumptions of regulation and conformity. This attitude gradually spilled over into language as well, for there seemed to be a profound attack on the nature of authority and the assumption that those at the top could dictate what was right and acceptable to the rest of society. While such attitudes did not change overnight, we can accept that there was a new spirit abroad which provides us with a convenient boundary in 1798.

The next period we shall consider covers mainly the nineteenth century, but the dates I will propose as its boundaries are 1798 and 1914. Both dates are symbolic, for the first marks the publication of the *Lyrical Ballads* and the second records the outbreak of the First World War. This latter date suggests the breakdown of old attitudes caused by the horrors of that war and how that breakdown affected all aspects of society, including attitudes to language. This period is unusual in that it appears to reinforce the attitudes prevalent in the previous period while also promoting attitudes that undermine them. It is an age of great imperial expansion which saw many young men from Britain going overseas to administer distant lands to bring their inhabitants the benefits of British civilisation. Many of these administrators came from public schools, which flourished as a result, and they were indoctrinated with certain attitudes to language. The language had to be regulated in order to serve as an administrative vehicle for the empire as a whole so that the English of India could be the same as the English of Jamaica. And so it was in theory, though the practice was naturally different. New words and new pronunciations were characteristic of different parts of the empire, and many of the administrators were influenced by them. However, education was recognised as an important stepping stone to success, not only for those who were to be trained as future administrators, but also for the indigenous people in different parts of the empire who wanted to reach high office under their imperial rulers. And education meant instruction in the standard language. At the same time poets like Wordsworth attacked the use of a formal variety like the standard for poetry and encouraged a quite different approach to poetry. Later nineteenth-century poets like Browning would write poems which reflected the thoughts and idioms of individualised people rather than reproducing a stereotype. The development of the novel increasingly promoted experiment with a wider range of linguistic usage.

It is also important to note that significant changes took place in the study of language itself. Two aspects may be highlighted. Firstly, the previous age had been concerned with regulating language and discovering the principles which underlined all language on the assumption that all languages followed the same structure. The nineteenth century was interested in the diversity of languages and varieties of language. The growth of the empire promoted interest in a whole range of languages other than the classical languages which had hitherto been the model for all linguistic structure. And scholars in England began to record the various regional dialects found in the United Kingdom. Whereas before these dialects may have been considered provincial and little more than barbarous, their use in poetry and the novel and the collections and studies based on these forms gradually meant that they were seen as real means of communication, even if they were not as socially acceptable as the standard. The respect for non-standard varieties increased, though this was a gradual process which even today has not made these dialects socially acceptable. One problem that such varieties faced, and still face, is that they do not usually exist in a regulated written form and thus may be regarded as inferior. Secondly, the nineteenth century saw an enormous growth in the historical study of language. Many of the changes in English and its ancestors which will be outlined in this book were discovered in the nineteenth century. The development of the concept of a family tree for languages and the recognition that English was a Germanic language which belonged to the

Proto-Indo-European family of languages (also known simply as Indo-European) were among the advances made at this time. Not unnaturally this put English and the classical languages into a different perspective. Their nature was not different from that of other languages, and English dialects could be regarded as closely related to standard English in origin and development; they had simply not been chosen to form the standard. Historical accident and natural selection did not mean that standard English was necessarily better than other varieties. So that while on the one hand the standard seemed to be reinforced by education and its spread through the empire, its position was being challenged by the acceptance of the nature of other varieties in relation to it. The challenge would become more significant in the final period of our story.

The last period of our history of the language extends from 1914 to the present day and may be characterised by fragmentation and uncertainty. The First World War saw many of the social certainties of the preceding age shattered. It also heralded the imminent demise of the empire and the rise of a new superpower, namely the United States of America. Americans, as we somewhat inappropriately call the citizens of the United States, use English as their native language in principle, but in practice many Americans who had come from different parts of the world to settle there may have had another language as their first language. Today Spanish is as important a language as English for many Americans. But the English spoken in America is different from that spoken in Britain and even the written form of their language differs in spelling, lexis and syntax. For some Americans such as Webster – whose name is still used for the standard American dictionary – it was important for American English to be seen to be different from British English. Where Americans had in the past accepted British English as their English, their own growing self-confidence meant that they were no longer willing to accept this position of inferiority, as they saw it, and struck out on an independent language path. American English is today at least as important as, if not more than, British English, and non-native speakers of English have to decide whether they will learn the American or the British variety. What is true of America has also become true of other varieties of English. As former colonial countries gained their independence they have wanted to promote their own native languages and to have their own form of English, where English is still retained as an official language. Dictionaries of local varieties of English have appeared with increasing frequency.

The growth in self-esteem of these countries has been paralleled by a decrease in self-confidence in England. Changes in attitudes to colonialism have made England re-evaluate its past and accept that independent countries have a right to develop their own linguistic strategies. At the same time the growth in the subject now known broadly as 'linguistics' has encouraged a quite different attitude to the study of language. Every language or variety of language is recognised as a suitable vehicle for communication and no one variety is considered better than another. The emphasis that linguistics has put on speech has undermined the pre-eminent position of the standard, which is essentially a written variety. The growing emphasis on encouraging people to use their own variety of language for communicative and educational purposes so that those who have been taught the standard are not automatically given a privileged position because of their language has given these varieties greater exposure and standing. Local radio and television encourage the use of their own local varieties of English in order to develop a group identity locally and to distance themselves from the suffocating embrace of the south-east. And a general revolt against authority and conformity has often taken the form among young men in particular in taking a pride in their own language, which is often the only characteristic which helps to distinguish them from those from other parts of the country. Naturally there are those who have not welcomed these developments and the Conservative governments of the 1980s and 1990s have tried to re-establish the role of the standard language now enshrined in the National Curriculum.

Those are the periods into which I shall divide the history of the language in this book. It may be time now to review briefly the sources available for a history and their interpretation. A history of the language must cover not only the changes within the elements which make up a sentence – the sounds, the inflections, the vocabulary and the syntax – but also the wider changes which are reflected in attitudes to the language and how the language is used for literary and other purposes. As most of our records until the twentieth century are written, it is difficult to gain a coherent idea of what speech was like at earlier periods. Any spoken forms are always reproduced in writing and the written form has a rather special relationship to speech. Speech in writing always reflects the restrictions which that medium imposes and the attitudes and prejudices of those who use the written medium. This is a particular problem for representing the sounds of the language at any period. The sounds have to be expressed in written forms and our writing system has never contained sufficient characters to be able to represent all the sounds that have been and are made by speakers of the language. Yet it is the history of sounds which has attracted the most attention among scholars if only because a limited number of sounds exist in any language and consequently sound is often considered to be that trait which can most easily be described fully in any language. Although syntax, vocabulary and morphology vary in the spoken and written varieties, these differences have not attracted so much attention, because the evidence is difficult to interpret in view of the potential mass of data, often conflicting, which could be used. Thus it is accepted that if a word is found in the twelfth century which is of Germanic origin and conforms to the changes that Germanic words under-went in English, it is possible to accept that the word existed in the period before the Norman Conquest. But no dictionary of Old English would include the word because the evidence for its existence is assumed rather than attested. Sounds are different in that the history of sounds presupposes certain developments, which therefore have to be accepted as part of the language at a given time, and as there are a restricted number of sounds in a language it is always possible to attest the presence of any individual one.

The Anglo-Saxons came from various parts of north-west Europe to settle in England from the fifth century onwards. As far as we are aware they brought no writing system with them, though it is possible that they brought the runic alphabet known as the *futhark*. This script was known only to a few people and was used for brief inscriptions on small pieces of wood or bone, which easily perished or disappeared, as well as on stone. There are few surviving monuments with runic inscriptions. When Christianity was re-introduced into England at the end of the sixth century, for it was known among the Romanised Celts, the monks brought the Latin writing system with them. They took it for granted that they would teach and use Latin, which was the language of the church used throughout Western Europe. Although the monks may have learned English and later recruited members from the Anglo-Saxon community, there would be little reason to produce a written form of the language at first. What they would require would be at most a form of written English which could help them to learn and teach Latin. This did mean that they had to develop a written English which was inevitably modelled on the only written language most of the monks knew, namely Latin. The sounds of English had to be transcribed in letters found in the Roman alphabet with one or two adjustments. Many of the early sources in this period are Latin texts with English names, which can give us some idea of the sounds of individual dialects, and Latin texts with English glosses. Most of these texts are religious ones such as psalters or gospels, which naturally have a specialised vocabulary. Texts written in a variety of English include charters and laws, which again have a specialised language. Although there may have been some form of oral poetry among the Anglo-Saxons, the only poetry which can probably be dated to this early period and which survives in an early form of the language are parts of *The Dream of the Rood* inscribed in runes on the Ruthwell Cross and short poems like 'Cædmon's Hymn' copied into the margin of Latin texts. It was only at the time of King Alfred, who sought to revive learning in England and felt that it had to be done through the medium of English, that we find a large number of texts. Many of these are translations from Latin, though a few native texts like *The Anglo-Saxon Chronicle* are also extant. Alfred's example was followed in the tenth century and numerous sermon collections and other texts, including four codices of poetry, some of which may date from a much earlier period than the actual manuscripts in which they survive, are found. All these texts are either literary or specialised, dealing with religion, the law or some branch of science. There are no texts which give us information about the English language, though Ælfric wrote a Latin grammar in English. It is difficult to read through these texts to understand what the language was like on a day-to-day basis and how people actually used it.

Since all these sources are handwritten, as they continued to be until the introduction of printing into England in 1476, it raises the problems of interpretation of the symbols used. A manuscript may be written, for example, in 1000, but be a copy of another manuscript written a few years or even more than a hundred years earlier. The surviving manuscript may be in the standard language of the time, but the text it was being copied from may have been written in a different dialect. Scribes were likely to adopt some forms from their copy as well as imposing their own variety upon the text they were copying. The result is likely to be what is today known as a *Mischsprache*, a mixture of different varieties both regionally and chronologically. Even if a manuscript can be localised and dated with a reasonable degree of accuracy, it does not follow that the language of the manuscript will reflect adequately that place and time. As with all standard languages, texts will be influenced by the standard to the amount that the scribe is familiar with it and feels he has to reflect its characteristics. Because a written language tends to be conservative, and the more standardised it is the more conservative it will be, developments in the spoken language do not readily find expression in the written language at first or even sometimes at all. Many texts containing Old English which were copied after the Norman Conquest will not necessarily show the changes which had taken place in the language partly as a result of that Conquest. Equally the influence of the Scandinavian languages, which may have been considerable in the aftermath of the Viking invasions, do not find much expression in tenth-century English texts, probably because they were considered alien to the standard that was then dominant.

These problems of interpretation have to be taken into account for all aspects of language, but with sounds there is the additional problem of trying to interpret what the actual symbols represent at the phonemic level. It is not possible to be certain about the precise pronunciation of any sound represented in writing even after descriptions of sounds start to appear in English in the sixteenth century. At best one can try to reconstruct the phonemic system operative in certain parts of England. In so far as standardisation took place, it was a standardisation of the written language and there were, as far as we can tell, no attempts to alter people's pronunciation, though it would not be surprising in view of human nature if some pronunciations were regarded as less elegant or even less acceptable than others. And certainly present dialect evidence suggests that regional pronunciations differed considerably throughout the country, though whether they also differed on a class basis we cannot tell for this early period. For the periods up until the beginning of the sixteenth century we must reconstruct the phonemic system without help from any descriptions of how sounds were made at the time. The evidence we use may be briefly described as follows. The sounds in English were represented by Latin letters, and we know from other sources what the rough phonetic representations of these letters were and can naturally assume that the English sounds must have been those that were similar to, if not identical with, the sounds represented by these Latin letters in Latin and other languages. The discipline of phonetics provides us with general rules which are applicable to any language. We know how sounds behave and how they are likely to change, for such changes follow known patterns. Where a text uses rhyme or other sound effects, we can accept that the words in question contained sounds that were either identical or could be taken to be so by the speakers of the variety, though if the text was copied into a different variety it would not follow that the rhyme would remain a perfect one. It is also possible to work backwards from our knowledge of present-day pronunciation not only of Received Pronunciation, but also of all the dialects known today. We can also work back from descriptions of sounds and attempts to reform English spelling on the basis of pronunciation which are found from the sixteenth century onwards. It is true that such descriptions may sometimes contain an element of idealisation, but they can never have been too far away from reality as far as the overall phonemic system is concerned. The history of English pronunciation can never take account of the pronunciations of all individual users of the language. It can only outline what the phonemic system of the most influential variety was, and illustrate how that system underwent changes either as a result of internal development or of external influences. Naturally changes in the writing system itself often provide clues as to what has happened in the development of sounds in the language, because new writing systems will tend to bear more relation to current pronunciation than the traditional one.

Changes of this sort were introduced after the Norman Conquest as a result of the influx of French speakers and scribes who had been brought up in a different spelling environment. Although many English texts written after the Conquest continue to be written in the Old English standard, gradually some new symbols are introduced and old ones displaced. Many of the texts which survive after the Conquest come from the West Midlands, an area which was among the last to be affected by the influence of the conquerors and where as a result English could still be written. With the growing use of Latin after the twelfth century, there is a period when English texts are found only sporadically and turn up in quite different places. Often the reason for the appearance of a text is hard to explain, as for example the appearance of a sophisticated poem like *The Owl and the Nightingale*, which was written at the beginning of the thirteenth century, probably in the Surrey/Kent area. Two attempts at producing a standardised language are found in this post-Conquest period. One associated with the West Midlands is a series of texts linked with the *Ancrene Wisse* from the early thirteenth century, in which there were clearly several scribes who had been trained to replicate a standardised language. The other is associated only with a single man, who calls himself either Orm or Ormin and was an Augustinian canon. His single text, the *Ormulum*, a poem of some 10,000 lines, is an English version of the Gospels and has been located as being written at Bourne, Lincolnshire. Other texts occur sporadically and attempts were made to encourage the use of English from time to time. Laʒamon's *Brut*, a thirteenth-century West Midlands text, and a manuscript known as the Auchinleck manuscript, from the London area in the early fourteenth century, both promote the use of English. Increasingly English was used, particularly in the London area, during the fourteenth century, and at the end of that century the writing of poetry in English becomes established with Chaucer and Gower. But most manuscripts of their work date from the fifteenth century.

From the fifteenth century, writing in English becomes increasingly common, and whereas hitherto it had been mostly of a literary or religious nature, from this time onwards correspondence and official writing becomes more common. Most of this writing still reflects restricted registers, though some indication of colloquial usage begins to appear in poetry, as for example in Chaucer's fabliaux. But the fifteenth and sixteenth centuries witness a change in the sources available. The introduction of printing means that published work increasingly reflects the tendency towards standardisation in spelling. Yet at the same time more informal sources start to make their appearance and, more importantly, writings about the English language and the relation of the standard form to other varieties are important sources of evidence. The growing standardisation of spelling leads to discussions about what is the most appropriate spelling to use, and in these discussions the relation of pronunciation to spelling forms a major concern. Grammars and dictionaries of English become available, but the grammars are at first strongly influenced by Latin grammars, and the dictionaries are at first collections of specialised vocabularies, particularly the so-called 'hard words', that is words borrowed from Latin or Greek, some of which may never have got beyond the pages of the dictionaries in which they are found. Interest is now shown in other varieties of language, such as the language of vagabonds and those at the periphery of society. It becomes easier to get some understanding of the range of usage outside the standard itself. In addition, letters and diaries begin to give us some understanding of informal English and the gap that exists between informal and formal varieties.

From this period onwards there are numerous books and discussions about various aspects of the English language. The eighteenth century contains books about syntax and grammar, spelling lists, and ever more comprehensive dictionaries. Comments about usage increase in frequency and comparisons between what usages are preferred and those that are actually used are found. The complaints about modern usage are often inspired by the assumption of a Golden Age of usage in the past or by the need to establish an Academy on the French model to correct abuses. Novels exhibit a wide range of styles and varieties. But the formalisation of the standard means that the evidence has to be interpreted from the comments made or the examples quoted rather than from direct evidence itself, for writing in varieties outside the standard is less and less common. The nineteenth century provides other sources as amateurs and scholars collect information about different varieties of English both at home and overseas. The standard language is now so well established that it can itself provide evidence only of changes in vocabulary with some indication of syntax and morphology. The evidence for sounds and other aspects of language has to be drawn from writings about the language and from the growing interest in the historical study of the language. This pattern continues into the twentieth century until the development of machines to record the spoken language and of the discipline of linguistics provides the impetus to study the spoken variety and the whole range of language use beyond the standard itself. This information also provides the means to work backwards. The growth of historical dialect study and the provision of dictionaries and word maps enable scholars to get a much better understanding of how individual dialects within the language developed, and this in turn provides more information about the standard variety. Details of some of these sources will be found in the following chapters, but it is important that readers have some idea about the various possible sources at this stage, how the sources differ from one age to the next and how the information they provide differs and has to be interpreted.

2

Background Survey

In this chapter I survey the results of major changes in English (for in individual chapters the overall effect of the changes may be lost sight of in the discussion of links in a longer chain), in order to detail some of the influences which may have promoted change and to consider how the advent of modern linguistic approaches has affected the way in which we have reappraised language change, with especial reference to English. I should perhaps stress at this point that although this book is informed by the methodology and theories associated with modern linguistics, readers are not assumed to be familiar with linguistics and a glossary at the end of the book provides an overall list with explanations of the linguistic and other technical terms used.

Within the sound system of English it is the long vowels and diphthongs which have changed most during its history. Whereas at its start English had a relatively homogeneous sound system in which long and short vowels differed principally in their length and in which there were very few diphthongs, the developments during the course of its history upset this coherent arrangement so that now there is a marked difference between long and short vowels in their quality as well as in their length. Long and short vowels do not necessarily pair together as they used to. In this respect English differs from many other West European languages, and it is one reason why many non-native speakers find English a difficult language to pronounce. Furthermore, because of its facility for borrowing from other languages, English has also taken over some sounds from different languages. Although the tendency has been to adapt foreign sounds to native English ones, this has not always proved possible – or has at least not always happened. In particular, certain new diphthongs, such as <oi, oy> usually pronounced /ɔi/, have been introduced into the language so that the inventory of diphthongs bears little relation to the long and short vowels. Many of these changes took place in the period from about 1200 to 1600 and have been a major cause of the difficulties of relating the spelling system to the pronunciation. This is partly because the spelling system of English was being established from the fifteenth century and many elements in it were stabilised before the changes within the phonological system had worked themselves through. Thus in Modern English the spelling <i> can represent the short vowel /i/ as well as the diphthong /ai/, which was developed from the original long vowel /iː/. Another aspect of present English spelling and its relation to the sounds of Received Pronunciation is that the London dialect was a mixed dialect using pronunciations from a variety of dialect areas. Some of these sounds from different areas have survived even though they are not represented in the spelling, or the spellings have survived even though the pronunciation reflects that of a dialect. This explains why a word like *merry* rhymes with a word like *bury*.

Germanic languages tend to stress the first syllable of a word unless that syllable is a prefix. In English this has resulted in a constant levelling of unstressed syllables. Since most unstressed syllables come towards the end of a word, this may have been an influence on the fall of inflections. At first many unstressed syllables were reduced to that sound known as *schwa*, represented as [ə] in the phonetic alphabet. This is still true today and many of the unstressed syllables in Modern English have this sound, as in *China* and *observer*; but unstressed syllables also occur at the beginning of words, as in *appeal* and *explain*. At earlier stages of the language the levelling of different vowel or diphthongal sounds to schwa often led to the loss of the syllable with this schwa sound altogether, and this naturally led to the disappearance of many inflectional endings, particularly those that had consisted solely of a vowel or a vowel plus nasal consonant.

It is more difficult to decide whether the nature of English word order has changed, partly because there is dispute as to whether the ancestor of English was a verb-second or verb-final language. Certainly in Modern English the position of the verb is essentially after the subject, but in earlier English the verb usually came second in main clauses and last in subordinate clauses, as is still largely true of Modern German. If this system still persisted in English, one might expect sentences like **When he his wife abandoned, lived he with his mother again* instead of our *When he abandoned his wife, he lived with his mother again*. The word-order patterns within English have changed so that the standard modern order is SVO(A).

In part this change has been expedited through the fall of inflections. Early varieties of English could be said to be a synthetic language, because the relationship among the words within a sentence was indicated as much through their inflectional endings as through their word order. Modern English, on the other hand, is an analytic language in which most inflections have either disappeared or have ceased to be important for distinguishing meaning. Although we still say *He comes*, the final -*s* is not significant because it is obligatory to include the subject *He* and because there is no other form ****He come with which it could be confused. If we all said and wrote **He come instead of *He comes*, there would be no confusion and no loss of meaning. After all, in the preterite we are perfectly happy to say *He came* where the verb has the same form in the third-person singular as in all the other persons. The relationship of the words in a sentence in Modern English is determined by their order and not by their endings. This has meant that the subjects of verbs must be expressed, unlike other languages which maintain verbal inflections through which the subject can be understood. Julius Cæsar could write in Latin *Veni, vidi, vici*, in which the subject is understood from the verb form; and although in some modern Romance languages like Italian or Spanish it is possible to do the same thing, in English we cannot imitate him by adopting an equivalent expression ***Came, saw, conquered*, since we must write *I came, I saw, I conquered*. In Modern English the subject, the verb and the object have specific positions, and it is through their positions in a clause that we can tell what function individual words have. Although poets may alter the order in which words occur, they run the risk of being mis-understood, either because we cannot tell which is the subject and object, or even in some cases because we cannot decide whether a word is a verb or a noun. In Shakespeare's *Timon of Athens* (IV.iii.23) there is a clause 'Destruction phang mankinde' which has caused commentators problems because of the word *phang*. The natural assumption is that here we have SVO, but some have thought on the basis of other examples in Shakespeare that the order is VSO with the sense 'May fangs destroy mankind'. While this interpreta-tion may seem far-fetched, there are many parallels in Shakespeare that make it possible. The freedom that existed in English word order has gradually been restricted so that any variation, such as one finds in some modern poetry, brings problems of interpretation with it.

An advantage that the fall of inflections has brought is the ease with which we can now use functional shift, the process by which one part of speech may be used as a different part of speech. When the language had a relatively well-developed set of inflections, the individual endings would indicate not only that a word belonged to a particular part of speech, but also what function within the sentence that word carried. Once word order replaced inflections to indicate the function of a word, it became possible to use any word in a given function because the word order would clarify the function of the word. Thus in principle, if not in practice, any word which is by derivation a noun can be used as a verb or an adjective or even an adverb, for it is principally the words which convey lexical meaning as distinct from those that have some grammatical function which have this freedom. To go back to the example from Shakespeare in the previous paragraph, the reason that *destruction* can be taken to be a verb is that, although it has the form of a noun, it can function as a verb, and in imperative clauses it is possible to put verbs at the beginning, as in *Help me heaven*. If we consider a noun like *radio*, it is perfectly easy to let it function as a verb, *He did not radio for help*, or as an adjective or, as it might more appropriately be called, a pre-modifier, *He is a radio operator*. This flexibility in allocating functions to words is one that has been exploited by poets, and it is often a mark of bureaucratic language or officialese, which is one reason why it often seems so dense to readers. It is a freedom also exploited by newspapers in their headlines and which at first sight can lead to ambiguity, as in the famous example from the Second World War: FIFTH ARMY PUSH BOTTLES UP GERMANS.

That example also shows another new feature of English, the use of what are sometimes called phrasal verbs, that is a verb which is made up of the verb element itself, in this case *bottles,* and a preposition acting adverbially, in this case *up*, with a meaning which is different from that of the constituent parts. In this instance *bottles up* must mean something like 'surrounds, prevents from moving or taking any action'. In earlier English this type of verb was very rare, since the use of prefixes was the norm. The meaning of a verb element was modified by the use of a prefix, which came before the verb and was attached to it, not by the addition of an adverbial proposition after it. Hence in Old English the verb *slēan* 'to strike' could be modified as *ofslēan* 'to kill' or *toslēan* 'to destroy completely'. This development of phrasal verbs can be considered alongside the fall of inflections which influenced how nouns and verbs function in English. In Modern English it is possible to have an inflectional ending -s to indicate possession, but that feature can also be expressed through a preposition, normally *of*. Thus *the boy's mother* can just as readily be expressed as *the mother of the boy*. Equally the indirect object may be indicated through word order by coming immediately after the verb or it may be expressed through the preposition *to*. The sentence *Give the boy the sandwich* can as readily be represented by *Give the sandwich to the boy*. This has meant that there has been a considerable growth in both the number and use of prepositions. Where earlier varieties of English could make do with fewer grammatical words, such as prepositions, Modern English has a high proportion of such words. This has in its turn altered the general stress pattern of the language. Where there originally existed longer words which contained stress near the front and one or more unstressed syllables afterwards, there now exist many monosyllabic words which may be preceded by one or more grammatical words. The effect has been to convert a falling rhythm into a rising one.

This development could also be associated with the growth in the number and use of conjunctions in English, though perhaps a greater influence in this regard has been that of translation into English from other languages, particularly Latin and French. The increase in the number of conjunctions is largely a feature of the written language because the spoken language is much simpler in its constructions. It is characteristic of the earlier stage of the language that there was a high level of paratactic structures, those that consist predominantly of clauses containing main verbs which are linked together by co-ordinating conjunctions like *and* or *but*. Writing in and translation from Latin and French encouraged hypotaxis, which is the use of a large number of subordinate clauses introduced by subordinating conjunctions like *when* or *because*, with the result that sentences are longer and more complicated structurally. Such hypotactic sentences are particularly characteristic of Latin, and attempts to enhance the literary quality of English have often resulted in the use of subordinate clauses in much longer sentences. This has in its turn promoted the development of new conjunctions, particularly those that might be termed phrasal conjunctions which consist of more than a single word. Such new conjunctions embrace forms like *in order that* and *considering that*. Thus four short sentences such as *They arrived at the field. The other army was encamped there. It started to rain heavily. Nevertheless, the battle commenced immediately.* could be transformed into a single sentence through using subordinating conjunctions as follows: *When they arrived at the field where the other army was encamped, the battle commenced immediately even though it started to rain heavily.* One can argue whether the hypotactic sentence means exactly the same as the four short sentences, but the single sentence is much more characteristic of the written language. It would, of course, be possible to link the four short sentences together paratactically by joining them all by *and* or *but*: *They arrived at the field and the other army was encamped there and it started to rain heavily, but nevertheless the battle commenced immediately.* This last sentence is much more characteristic of the spoken language.

We saw a moment ago that simple verbs with a prefix have tended to give way to phrasal verbs with a postposed adverbial proposition. It is also true to note that there has been a great increase in the use of auxiliary verbs in English, those verbs like *will* or *may* which come before the main lexical verb and indicate some aspect of the lexical verb. In part this development may be attributed to the fall of inflections which destroyed the old subjunctive mood, which could express such concepts as uncertainty or expectation, and to the influence of Latin in particular which had a much wider range of tenses than existed in English. Thus Latin had an inflectional ending to indicate the future tense. This tense does not exist in English and futurity was indicated through the present tense together with, if necessary, an adverbial, as is still possible in Modern English: *The plane arrives tomorrow morning.* But the auxiliary *will* has been recruited to express futurity, though that is not the only sense it carries: *The plane will arrive tomorrow morning.* At first it was unusual to have more than one auxiliary in front of a lexical verb, but in the written language it has been increasingly common to have more, partly since auxiliaries are often thought to make one's style rather more literary. Although the maximum number of auxiliaries which can be found together is six, such examples are extremely rare, not to say bizarre. Even sentences with only four auxiliaries are still relatively uncommon: *He would have been being coming now if he had not mixed up the dates.* The extension in the function of auxiliaries is also a factor in the development of the passive, which was a mood that did not exist in early English. This form, in which the object of the active clause becomes the subject of the passive clause so that the real subject after the verb need not be expressed, was promoted by its occurrence in Latin and is again particularly associated with the written language. In my own department in the university I would never put up a notice with the form *I forbid students to . . .*; I would always start a notice in the passive mood by adopting the formula *Students are forbidden to . . .*. The passive has the advantage that, as the subject need not be expressed, the notice seems more authoritative because the precise person who is doing the forbidding is not indicated.

An important aspect of the history of the language has been the change in the make-up and size of the vocabulary. English is a Germanic language and at first it contained a relatively restricted number of words, but it could expand its vocabulary through compounding and through borrowing. The number of borrowings in the early stages of the language was relatively restricted and many were inspired by trade with Latin-speaking countries or, a little later, by the need to develop new words to express the concepts found in the Christian religion. Compounding remained the principal method of word formation, and it was particularly associated with Old English poetry. Gradually the introduction of new words from other languages, principally Latin and French, but also Scandinavian and other European and non-European languages, led to a change not only in the composition of the English lexicon, but also in the connotations of and attitudes towards different types of word. Whereas originally Old English might have expressed the concept of a collection of words through *wordhord* or of an invader by sea as *særinc*, literally 'sea-warrior', these words were later replaced by *dictionary* and *pirate*, even though their connotations are rather different. What strikes one immediately about the modern forms is that they destroy any link with *word* and *sea* that existed with the older words. There is nothing in English to link *dictionary* with *word* or *pirate* with *sea*, whereas the compound forms contain these words as their first element. The transparency which existed in the older vocabulary was lost as more words were borrowed from other languages. The links which bound a compound word with the words from which it was formed were cut and English vocabulary became increasingly opaque. Many words were set adrift in form from those words with which they are closely related in meaning. There is no way that anyone can tell that *urban*, for example, is the adjective for *town*; the link in meaning is opaque and not transparent. There is no adjective formed from *town* such as *townish* or *towny* which would preserve that transparency. At the same time the introduction of many words from other languages, particularly at first from the prestige languages like Latin, French and to some extent Greek, meant that the English lexicon could be divided into two major categories, which are sometimes referred to as Anglo-Saxon and Latinate. Many Anglo-Saxon words are monosyllabic and refer to everyday things, whereas Latinate ones are more likely to be polysyllabic and to refer to concepts as much as to items of a more intellectual nature. The Anglo-Saxon word *see* differs not only in length but also in meaning and connotation from the Latinate *perceive*. Speakers of the language regard the latter as more elegant and learned, and its range of reference is restricted to mental and intellectual perception rather than to physical sight. The introduction of these words from other languages has also meant that there are subtle shades of meaning and often quite important differences in connotation between English words which have roughly the same meaning. In this respect the English vocabulary is much wider than that found in most other European languages. Although a word like *perceive* may have been introduced at first as a learned alternative to *see*, the fact that both words existed in the language led to a gradual separation in meaning and use. The latter can still refer to intellectual and emotional perception, but is less frequently found in that sense; the former is increasingly restricted to the intellectual sense and is rarely used for the concept of seeing physically with the eyes. Sometimes there may be little difference in meaning among the various words now found in English, but they differ pragmatically in when and with what other words they may be used, as can be seen by considering the usage of such words as *bodily, physical* and *corporal*.

As noted on several occasions already, English is a Germanic language and in any family tree of languages it would be placed with Dutch and German as descendants of the West Germanic branch of that family. But the effect of the various changes which have been briefly sketched in the previous paragraphs has been to change the nature of English so that it has lost many of its features of 'Germanicness'. While it may have adopted some features of the Romance languages, it has not become, nor could it become, a Romance language. Its basic structure remains that of a Germanic language and many people could probably carry on their day-to-day existence without using many Latinate words at all. But the more educated you are and the larger the vocabulary you have, the more likely you are to increase the Latinate section of your language.

During the previous paragraphs reference has been made in passing to some influences which have promoted change in English, but it is now time to review these more systematically. One important aspect of Britain is that it is a small island and thus has clearly defined boundaries. The island was populated by the Celts when the Anglo-Saxons arrived, though many of them may also have spoken a form of Latin. Although Celts continued to live on the island, they were gradually pushed to its outer western and northern fringes and had little impact on the development of English itself because for the most part the English were attuned to receiving influences from the south and east. Unlike many countries with fluctuating boundaries, English has not had to contend with many linguistic influences from neighbouring tribes or countries because of a shared land boundary. The fact that Britain is a relatively small island may have contributed to the early establishment of political unity in England and its maintenance more or less ever since. Political unity is an important feature in the development of a standard language. It meant that a standard could be developed in England relatively early and the role of dialects within the country accordingly diminished as influences on that standard. Here a comparison with Germany is instructive, for the modern country that we know as Germany did not exist until the nineteenth century. For most of the preceding period Germany consisted of a number of semi-independent states under a type of federal organisation. This delayed the introduction of a standard language until the sixteenth century and allowed the various dialects of German to have a status and a written form that made them quite different from the dialects found in England. Within Britain itself, the fact that Scotland was an independent kingdom until the union under a single monarchy after Elizabeth's death meant that although Scotland used English as its national language, it could develop its own written variety even if that variety was always subject to influence from the English one. The absence of land boundaries, especially with other Germanic-speaking countries, meant that English could develop in a relatively homogeneous way. At the same time, it differs from Latin-based languages like French or Spanish, since Latin was a standardised language and provided the model against which the new Romance languages could be measured. There was no ready-made standard that English could build on; it had to develop a standard from within its own resources by choosing a variety around which to establish the norm. This situation naturally allows for variety to creep in, for without continued strong political direction in the establishment and maintenance of the standard, other varieties will be able to make some impact.

Although England has had political unity for hundreds of years, it has never established an academy to regulate language. Hence standardisation has always been a somewhat haphazard affair. Although kings or political leaders may favour a standard, they have never set up any apparatus to enforce one. The result has been a kind of free for all in which consistency has never been aspired to, let alone achieved. There is no body which declares what is standard English, though there are many individuals who abrogate that responsibility to themselves. Thus although English has had a standard for a long time, that standard exhibits considerable flexibility and has been subject to constant change. It is in spelling that standardisation has been accomplished most successfully, because printers and publishers have developed their approved systems. But even in this area newspapers and others are happy to emend the standard spelling to suit their own convenience, and individuals in private correspondence are not too concerned about it. At least as important has been the influence of education: a standard language is a taught language. Since English spelling contains so many anomalies, the influence of education is more important than in some other languages because there must be an insistence on 'correct' spelling for people to spend the time necessary to learn the intricacies of the system. Although syntax and pronunciation may also be taught through the educational system, it is more difficult to control these because the number of items in syntax is potentially so large and because pronunciation is so much part of everyday language, which lies outside the control of educators.

An important influence on change in English has been conquest, which may be seen both as the conquest of England by other peoples as well as conquest of other countries by the English. There have been two important conquests of England itself. From the eighth century the Vikings raided England and ultimately settled here; and in the eleventh century England was incorporated into the Scandinavian empire under King Canute. Most of the invaders were Danish, though there were also Norwegians among them. The variety of Old Danish which most of them spoke was possibly mutually intelligible to the Anglo-Saxons, though the two languages contained important differences which may have influenced the development of Old English. It is often claimed, for example, that the difference in inflectional endings between English and Danish would have expedited the fall of inflections in English because speakers would need to adopt alternative linguistic strategies to make themselves mutually intelligible. These strategies would include word order at the expense of inflections. The Danes also brought with them many vocabulary items, idioms and syntactic structures which were adopted into different varieties of English. Since the principal areas of settlement by Danes and Norwegians were the north and east of the country, the dialects spoken in these parts of the country exhibit specialised features. One important feature that spread from these dialects to the rest of the country was the use of the plural forms of the third person of the personal pronoun to give Modern English _they_, _their_ and _them_. The second invasion of importance is the Norman Conquest of 1066. Not only was this more permanent, but also it was carried out by those who spoke a variety of a language which has had more cultural prestige than the language of the Vikings. Most schoolchildren in England continue to learn French as their second language; probably none ever learn Danish. French was and remains a culturally significant language, and it is likely that it would have had an important influence on English even if the Norman Conquest had never taken place. But the Conquest has influenced almost every aspect of the language: sounds, syntax, spelling and vocabulary. It is difficult to decide how much of this influence sprang directly from the Conquest itself rather than from contacts which were maintained afterwards. The kings of England claimed parts of France and even its throne for many periods in the Middle Ages, and thus there was a constant toing and froing between the two countries. The influence of French on English cannot be overemphasised, but it need not all be attributed to the Norman Conquest.

The conquest of other countries by the English started with the preliminary settlements in North America in the sixteenth century, but is also associated with the eighteenth-century colonisation of the Indian subcontinent and the eighteenth- and nineteenth-century colonisation of Africa and countries in the Pacific. For the most part the influence of these countries has been restricted to items of vocabulary, as travellers and administrators brought back new words which were adopted into English. Some of these influences have been strengthened in the twentieth century with the immigration into England of many people from former British colonies to supplement the workforce in England. They have introduced even more words, but have not affected the basic structure and pronunciation of the language.

Although conquest may be understood as the physical occupation of another country, in the exchange of linguistic items across languages the invasion of ideas and cultural attitudes is just as important, if not more so. The conquest of the country by Christianity from the end of the sixth century was as important as the conquest of the country by the Danes and the Normans. Christianity brought the Latin language and education to promote the teaching of Latin. It introduced writing and numerous books written in Latin. It promoted the concept of translation from one language into another and raised the whole idea of the relative standing of different languages. Since Latin had a long history and numerous works written in it, both classical and religious, it was clearly in most people's estimation a superior language to English. When translations were made from Latin into English, it was natural for the translators to take over not only vocabulary items but also syntactic structures. The so-called ablative absolute and the passive mood are examples of syntactic structures which were adopted relatively early. Attempts to reproduce the various tenses of Latin in English encouraged the development of auxiliaries in English. At first many of these features were found in the written language, but from there many passed into the spoken language as well. There is hardly an aspect of English which has not been touched by Latin. At a later date French also fulfilled much the same role as Latin; it was the language of culture and fashion. It was associated with good breeding and may have influenced notions of politeness among speakers of the language. Up to a point this may be little more than snobbery, but whatever it might be called there is no denying the significance it has had for language development and change. For example, the use of the plural form of the second person of the personal pronoun *you* as the polite form may have been motivated by the distinction between *tu* and *vous* in French; and this use of the plural ultimately led to the fall of the singular *thou* form in English. The role of French may be compared with other languages with less cultural status in England and elsewhere. Dutch has had some impact on English because Holland is just over the Channel from England and consequently trade between the two countries has flourished for hundreds of years. In the Middle Ages the Merchant Adventurers, the English fraternity of merchants, traded in Holland and at a later period Sir Philip Sidney died at Zutphen fighting against the Spaniards. The revolution of 1685 expelled James II and installed William and Mary on the English throne – and William was a Dutchman. The links between the two countries have existed for hundreds of years, but Holland is not held up as a model for the fashionable to imitate and consequently Dutch is a language which few English people learn. Hence, the influence of Dutch on English has been restricted to words dealing with trade and seafaring; other aspects of its culture have been disregarded as far as linguistic influence is concerned. The same applied to German, though over the years the links between England and Germany have been less intense than those between Holland and England. Germany has exerted an influence through music and philosophy on English taste and education, but it has hardly had much impact on the English language. To use a German word in English would not bring the same response from listeners as a word of French origin. Invasion and conquest are important, but the attitude of speakers of one language as to the status of other languages is just as important and is likely to have a more lasting impact on that language. Although trade may well bring languages into contact with one another, the resulting influence is likely to be less significant than the effect of fashion and what is little more than prejudice. Among the older languages this attitude has led to the idealisation of Latin and Greek, languages which most educated people would have been expected to have some familiarity with until the second half of the twentieth century, and among modern languages it has been French and to a lesser extent Italian that have always been regarded in England as languages which give expression to a culture worth emulating and responding to.

Once writing was introduced and standardised forms of English emerged, this fact alone influenced the development of the language. It is easier to influence the way people write than the way they talk, and standardisation in writing will constantly encourage the development of a more standardised and regulated language at both a written and a spoken level. With a standard writing system, people fall back on the written form as a guide to what the pronunciation should be. Anomalies will attract attention and lead to the possibility that they are eliminated. This is one reason why American spelling differs from English spelling, because there was an attempt to eradicate some anomalies as understood by Noah Webster in his work on that language. The written language helps to fossilise certain forms and will permit the reintroduction of archaic words which have dropped out of the language. The written language sets up attitudes towards education and usage so that divisions among various usages become rather more ossified. A good example is the case of initial /h/. For various reasons there is a tendency for this sound to fall, and we all in certain circumstances drop /h/. But because of writing, the retention of /h/ in pronunciation is considered a mark of education and many people take great care to pronounce it, even if the result may seem slightly ludicrous to others. Were it not for writing, there is much to suggest that initial /h/ would have fallen out of the language long ago. Those who are educated and know how to write and how to use the written language readily look down on those who do not possess these skills; that, in turn, may encourage others outside this educated circle to develop their own forms of language to exclude those who are in authority partly because of their command of the written form. Group identity can be established through language, as it is in the drug culture and in what is known as Black Vernacular English. Writing, of course, allows for the development of technology and science, which in their turn have a considerable impact upon the language.

Writing also creates need in the sense that it generates the need to enlarge the language, particularly the lexicon. Writing encourages variety of expression. It is considered possible to give expression to all basic human requirements by using a very small vocabulary; and this has been translated into the vocabulary associated with Basic English. This was a list of under a thousand words developed in the 1930s which were thought adequate for all day-to-day purposes. But no educated person would dream of restricting their writing or conversation to such a basic vocabulary, and all literature, particularly in its written form, encourages the development of new vocabulary. Equally the onset of new technologies and the production of new machines and labour-saving devices create the need for an enlarged vocabulary. Naturally at the other end, as it were, many words are no longer needed because what they expressed has been superseded. Many of the different expressions for agriculture and wildlife have disappeared. If barns are mass-produced or built to a standard pattern, all the old words for barn become obsolete and fall out of the language. Even fashion in language creates a need for new words because we all like to show that we are 'with it', but naturally as new words become fashionable the older ones drop out of the language – perhaps to be revived at some later date. Human interaction breeds the growth of societies and they in turn encourage the use of polite behaviour, which may in its turn influence changes in the language as certain forms are preferred to others.

Quite apart from these general pressures, linguists have shown that speakers of all languages readily adopt pronunciations which promote certain types of change, but changes in other parts of the language are also found. It is common in all languages for final consonants in words to be lost. This might be attributed to laziness, but is more an aspect of weak articulation at the end of words. To many people the spelling system encourages them to believe that all consonants at the end of words are pronounced – at least by educated speakers. One can naturally say *Alright* slowly so that the final /t/ is clearly heard, but in most dialogue it is pronounced weakly or not at all. This may depend on what environment the word occurs in. If, as usually happens, it is part of a longer sentence, as in *Alright we'll do it*, there is a good chance that most speakers of English would not pronounce the /t/ at all. Those that do are likely to sound formal, if not pretentious. As this happens in other words with a final consonant of the same type, in due course the nature of the consonants in this position will become blurred so that less educated people would not know what the correct spelling was and in languages which had not yet achieved a written form the final consonants might disappear altogether. At other times a different consonant from the one which is historically accurate may be introduced into writing and at other times hypercorrection may lead to the introduction of a consonant where one did not exist historically.

When two different consonants occur in the middle, or even at the end of a word, assimilation may take place and in the history of English this has been an important influence on the developments of consonants. A word like *Whitsun* is pronounced in many dialects as though it was spelt *Whissun*, which is indeed the spelling it receives in some representations of non-standard language in novels. When /l/ occurs in front of another consonant it regularly assimilates to the latter sound and thus disappears – think of the modern pronunciation of words like *salmon, should* and *half.* The assimilation does not always take the form of the first consonant being submerged in the second, for in the group /st/ the reverse happens, because in words with this group internally it is /t/ which disappears, as in *Christmas* and *castle.* But when /st/ comes at the end of a word, as in *Christ* and *cast,* the pronunciation may be retained except in fast speech when it is followed by another word. Thus in a sentence like *May Christ bless us,* it is likely that the /t/ in *Christ* would not be pronounced. More generally, it can be stated that as few languages like heavy consonantal groups, it is common to reduce them. In English this has certainly been true over the course of its history and is still operative today, whether a group is found in one word or is caused by consonants coming together at the end of one word and the beginning of another. With three consonants it is usually the middle one which will fall. In *landlady* and *handkerchief* the /d/ will not be pronounced except in very precise language. Similarly one would not expect to hear the /d/ of *grand* in a clause like *He's a grand lad.*

There are, however, some exceptions to this general principle. If two consonants are difficult to articulate together, then another may be inserted to ease the transition from one to the other. The verb *dream* has as its past tense the form *dreamt* (or *dreamed).* But this word is pronounced as if there is a group /mpt/ because the transition from the nasal /m/ to alveolar /t/ is difficult to articulate easily. This development can often follow the fall of a vowel sound which allows the two consonant sounds to occur together. We have seen early in this chapter that unstressed vowels become levelled under the schwa sound and may then disappear altogether. It was introduced earlier with reference to the unstressed syllables at the end of words, but they can also occur in the middle of words. When a three-syllable word has heavy first stress and medium final stress, the medial syllable will be unstressed and will fall out in pronunciation. When bisyllabic verbs like *fasten* occur with the ending *-ing,* they will lose the vowel of the second syllable to end up with a pronunciation like [faːsniŋ]. When this produces the consonant group /ml/, English speakers will often insert a /b/ between the two consonants. In the word *family* it is not unusual for the medial *i* to be dropped in pronunciation, and when that happens some speakers may insert a /b/ in the group

/ml/ which is formed through this dropping of the medial syllable. This development can be seen in words where this grouping arose a long time ago. The Modern English word *bramble* has as its equivalent Old English form *bræml* or *bræmel*, where the form without *e* may have arisen through oblique cases with a final inflection, such as *bræmles*. The obvious interpretation of this development is that speakers finding /ml/ difficult to pronounce inserted the /b/, which then became incorporated into the written form and accepted as standard.

A constant force within language change is that of analogy. Languages are systems which have to have a certain level of coherence to enable speakers to make themselves understood. Too much disturbance in the patterns can create problems of comprehension and these may often be counteracted by analogy. This means that when you have a predominant pattern in a language, forms which appear to belong to a weak or even to no pattern at all are attracted into the framework of the dominant pattern. This force affects all aspects of language from sound to syntax. It may be most easily seen in the morphology of English. Since Old English was an inflected language it had a variety of paradigms for nouns, each one of which had separate ways of forming the plural. Remnants of these are still found in Modern English, as may be appreciated by considering the pairs: *stone/stones*, *man/men*, *child/children* and *sheep/sheep*. The last three pairs have plurals which are not regular, but which have survived in certain words because they are so common that the force of analogy has not been able to alter them. Speakers of the language can tolerate exceptions to the dominant pattern when they occur frequently and when there are not too many of them. But most other nouns now form their plural by adding an *-(e)s* and that applies equally to nouns which existed in Old English and had a different ending (for example OE *word/word*, ModE *word/words*) or to words borrowed from classical or modern foreign languages (for example Lat. *formula/formulae*, now usually ModE *formula/formulas*). The same applies to verbs. In Modern English verbs can form their preterite either by adding *-ed/t* (for example *walk/walked*) or by changing the vowel of the stem (for example *ride/rode*). There were many different patterns of vowel alternation in Old English, many of which were disrupted by phonological changes in the language. The result has been that many of the latter type of verbs, known as strong verbs, have changed into the former type, known as weak verbs. Thus the present weak verb *climb/climbed* used to be a strong verb and can appear in Shakespeare as *climb/clomb*. All new verbs, whether formed by functional shift or from borrowing, tend to adopt the weak form which is now, and has been for some centuries, the dominant form.

Changes in syntax also tend to fall into certain patterns, but they are more difficult to characterise. When word order became the main method of indicating grammatical function, the order SVO became the dominant one for declarative sentences – those which make a statement rather than, for example, a command. In earlier forms of English there were a number of impersonal verbs which took the old dative form of the personal pronoun or noun which was placed before the verb itself. This survives in the now archaic *Methinks*, which could be interpreted as roughly 'To me [it] seems'. Once the pattern of SVO became established, an expression that had an oblique form before the verb became anomalous and was replaced. Today we can say either *It seems to me* or simply *I think*. Equally the word order pattern in English allows the adverbials to occupy a relatively free position, but this freedom has its limits. The pattern of putting the object as close to the verb as possible has grown stronger over the years and this has discouraged the placing of an adverbial between the verb and the object. A sentence like **I caught this morning the bus* is not generally acceptable except in poetry, because *this morning* could be understood as the object.

The causes and types of change within language outlined in the preceding paragraphs are both general and exemplary. They do not attempt to provide a complete inventory of all possible changes. They constitute some guide to the potential reasons and mechanisms for change so that readers of this book may understand that the changes which will be described in later chapters fall into recognised patterns, even if individual changes appear to be arbitrary and motiveless. It is not possible precisely to say why a change occurs. Often there are competing forms available within the language as a whole. These forms may exist in different registers or within different dialects. With mobility and the influence of speakers from other areas of the country or from abroad, the possibility that individuals would be exposed to different possible ways of saying the same thing was naturally considerable, even if they were not as extensive as they are today with radio and television. But from the beginning of the thirteenth century, if not earlier, London had established itself as a major city with considerable immigration from other parts of the country. As the seat of royal government it attracted people of all classes either to court or to seek advancement of one kind or another. The chances of hearing a range of speech in London must have been almost as great in, say, the fifteenth century as it is today. The variety was considerable. Ultimately language, particularly as it becomes standardised, makes a choice among the competing possibilities, though normally language cannot tolerate too much change at once. Why a particular form is preferred to another is often difficult to decide, though it is possible to offer explanations in some cases. I mentioned above that nouns in Modern English adopted -s as their standard plural. For a time it seemed that they might adopt -(e)n as the regular plural since this was characteristic of the southern dialects in the thirteenth century. But final *n* is less clear phonetically than final *s* and in many instances in English inflectional *n* has disappeared. This may have allowed the s-form to become the dominant form. As it happens, *s* was also the form more characteristic of the Midlands and the north, and the history of English shows that Standard English took over many northernisms, and that may have helped in the adoption of final *s* as against final *n*.

It is time now to turn to the different approaches to studying change in language. Generally speaking most attention has been given to phonology as distinct from other aspects. The reason for this is that changes in sound are more easily grasped: there are only a limited number of phonemes in any one language and consequently their study has natural parameters. With syntax and with vocabulary the number of possible items which might be available for study is in principle infinite. New words can be introduced at any time and syntax has many variables, which makes the study and regulation of syntax complicated. Furthermore, changes in vocabulary, and to a lesser extent in syntax, appear to be deliberate. New words are introduced because there is a need, either genuine or assumed, for them. Sounds, on the other hand, appear to change without motivation. There is no need to change the pronunciation of a word or group of words except perhaps in so far as the introduction of words from foreign languages might lead to the introduction of new sounds. There is no obvious advantage in changing the pronunciation of the vowel in a word like *stone* from its Old English /ɑː/ to its Modern English

/əʊ/. But the differences that have arisen in deciding how and why changes in sounds should be be studied can stand as an example for the overall question of how to analyse change.

In the nineteenth century it gradually became realised that many apparently unrelated languages came from the same family, and that the family relationship could be traced through the phonological development found in the individual languages. Words were more difficult to handle because they could so easily be borrowed from one language into another, and so one could not be certain at what stage a word came into the language – or rather one could not until the changes in phonology had been so clearly mapped that they provided the framework to make decisions of that sort. By comparing words in different languages, nineteenth-century scholars were able to isolate certain phonological patterns in these words which indicated that the words all came originally from common roots, which had been altered over time in regular patterns in the different languages. Unfortunately at first there seemed to be breakdowns in these patterns and so it was not possible to accept this evidence completely. Thus Jacob Grimm, who showed that certain Germanic consonants had different realisations from those found in Sanskrit, Greek and Latin, was puzzled by some apparent failures of these patterns. It was not until somewhat later in the nineteenth century that Karl Verner was able to provide a convincing explanation for the anomalies in what had become known as Grimm's Law. The actual form these changes took are explained in the next chapter. What is significant for this discussion is that this discovery led many at the time to accept that what had previously been regarded as inexplicable irregularity was subject to regular rules of change. At the same time developments in the theory of sounds, which showed how sounds were made and were related physiologically to one another, enabled scholars to appreciate that the changes they had discovered in the history of the Proto-Indo-European family of languages followed clear phonetic principles and were not arbitrary. The result was the statement postulated first in 1875 that 'The phonological changes which we can observe in documented linguistic history proceed according to fixed laws which suffer no disturbance save in accordance with other laws.'[1] In other words, sound changes followed immutable rules and any apparent flouting of such rules had to be explained through the formulation of additional rules, although it was also recognised that this did not apply to all varieties of a language because there could be local variations. The principle of rule-governed change allowed these scholars, who later became known as the neogrammarians, to make the discoveries they did, because they could rely on it to make the connections between the various languages. The implication of this principle was that sound change occurred by imperceptible degrees, often without the speakers of the language realising it, but its effects were lexically abrupt in that all words with that sound showed the change at one time.

In the early half of this century the linguists who became known as structuralists took a somewhat different view of language and change. They were interested in the system of any given language and many had studied languages such as the American Indian ones. They saw change in language as taking place within the systems that existed in a language from one synchronic period to the next. At each period a language consisted of a language system, and it was changes in the system which were significant and meaningful. Thus if there existed a series of voiced and voiceless consonants with a gap in the system because one of the voiced consonants was missing, there was a tendency for the system not to tolerate that gap and for it to be filled in some way. In this way they provided some understanding of why changes might happen in language. After the Second World War generative grammarians tried to understand how the rules which govern the transformations from the deep to the surface structure of a language may be modifed to produce a different surface structure. This approach is still developing and is not drawn upon in this book.

More important is the work of modern sociolinguists. Neogrammarians principally worked from older varieties of language; their studies were based on written documents and so seemed divorced from social or even human aspects of changes in language. Their laws tend to be clear-cut and unmessy since a rule implies that all examples of a particular sound develop into a different sound at the same time. There is one starting point and one finishing point, and these are the same for all examples in question. Sociolinguists today work with large databases of spoken language. They also rely on studies of bilingualism and multilingualism rather than the rather more simplistic studies of the neogrammarians who dealt with the development of a single language as though it was unaffected by social pressures or contact with other languages. The effect of much modern sociolinguistic research has been to suggest that sound change is the opposite of what the neogrammarians claimed, that it is in fact lexically gradual and phonetically abrupt. They also suggest that it is necessary to distinguish between innovation and change. Speakers may introduce many innovations into their own speech, but many or even most of these will never be accepted into the system of the language as a change. In other words, what may be significant in sound change is why out of the many innovations that individual speakers introduce into the language, only a few will be adopted as changes in the language system as a whole. Sound changes may represent the agreement of speakers of the language to accept certain innovations as changes to the norms which they had accepted hitherto. It has also been suggested that we should not refer to sound change, since for the most part the phenomenon is sound substitution; speakers of the language agree to replace one sound with another. For many speakers of the language this substitution may be quite abrupt because a new pronunciation has been accepted as the new norm. An understanding of this can be gained by considering the possible changes in stress that sometimes occur in Modern English. The word *controversy* has two possible stress patterns: *cóntroversy* or *contróversy* (where the accent indicates the syllable which is stressed). A change in stress can affect the quality of the vowels. Speakers deliberately choose one stress pattern or the other depending on what they understand or have been taught is the 'correct' way, and they may change what they have been used to saying if they decide that another pattern has acquired greater authority than the one they used before. In the end all speakers may agree on a single realisation of stress in this word so that a norm is established. It is this abrupt process which sociolinguists see as characteristic of sounds, for in words different pronunciations may be introduced by individual speakers as innovations and so such a change will spread slowly at a lexical level.

We may accept that this is a more human way of looking at sound change and probably at other changes which occur in language. Historically we can see that variety exists because there will be different realisations of a given word in spelling over a period of time. But we may not be able to understand the social pressures which caused innovations to become changes because the evidence is simply not available to us. The neogrammarian statement of sound changes is a useful shorthand method of highlighting what changes took place, even if we accept that they may not reflect social reality very closely. It is useful to note that one sound became another sound in the history of the language, even if this hides the many steps by which the change came about and the actual pronunciations represented by the written forms. Furthermore, historical linguistics has to make do with the evidence from writing since there is no evidence of real speech before the twentieth century. What is important to understand is that when it is claimed that /e:/ became /ei/, this is indicative of a change in the norm within the system which is to a large extent an idealisation of what actually happened. Within a historical account of the type found in this book, it is not possible to go into the precise circumstances of each change or even to outline the possible range of phonetic realisations of particular phonemes; it must suffice to provide the outlines of the historical development of the standard.

3

Before Alfred

On 2 February 1786 Sir William Jones, a British judge in India who had taken the trouble to learn Sanskrit during his residence there, delivered an address to the Asiatick Society in Calcutta about the relationship of Sanskrit to Latin and Greek. Latin and Greek were the languages which then formed a major part of the education of English schoolboys of a certain class, and so were well known to many of his audience. Of this relationship he claimed that Sanskrit bears

> a stronger affinity, both in the roots of verbs and in the forms of grammar, than could possibly have been produced by accident; so strong indeed, that no philologer could examine them all three, without believing them to have sprung from some common source, which, perhaps, no longer exists: there is a similar reason, though not quite so forcible, for supposing that both the *Gothick* and the *Celtick,* though blended with a very different idiom, had the same origin with *Sanscrit.*[1]

This quotation has become famous because it precipitated the nineteenth-century search for the links among those languages which together became described as the Proto-Indo-European family of languages. This family consists of all languages in Europe (except for Basque and the Finno-Ugric group, that is Finnish, Hungarian and some related languages), and many in Asia. However, some of the languages which used to belong to this family have died out leaving few remains, as is true of Hittite, or survive only in an ancient form in some restricted context such as religion, as is true of Sanskrit itself which remains a religious language in India. The earliest Sanskrit documents, the Vedic hymns, date from about 1000 BC, but their language reflects a much older poetic tradition. Classical Sanskrit appeared from about 500 BC, and in the following century an Indian grammarian called Panini wrote a grammar of Sanskrit which is remarkable for the information and methodology it contains. The written language was standardised by Panini and fellow grammarians, and their rules are still observed.

The Proto-Indo-European family is divided into two major groups, which geographically can be thought of as an eastern and a western group. They are usually known as the *satem* and the *centum* groups after the word for hundred in Avestan (an Old Iranian language) and Latin. Proto-Indo-European had both a palatal and a velar *k*, which were separate phonemes. In the eastern group these two phonemes remained distinct and the palatal sound developed into /s/, whereas in the western group the two phonemes merged under the velar /k/. The *satem* group, with which we shall no longer be concerned, contains such sub-groups as Indo-Iranian, Balto-Slavic, Armenian and Albanian. The main subgroups of the *centum* branch are Hellenic, which includes Greek and Mycenaean; Italic, which includes Latin and its descendants; Celtic, which includes two major subdivisions producing Welsh on the one hand and Gaelic on the other; and Germanic, to which English belongs. One important aspect of Proto-Indo-European is that it was an inflected language, that is it relied on changes at the end of words – inflections – to indicate grammatical functions in both nouns through case and number, and verbs through person, tense and mood. In all modern languages this inflectional system has broken down to a greater or lesser extent, and this is particularly true of English. The significant feature of Sanskrit is that the old Proto-Indo-European inflectional system is very well preserved so that it is from Sanskrit that we can understand what that system must have been like in the parent language. When we come to Old English, it needs to be remembered that the inflectional system which survived at that time is a pale shadow of the original system, and this is why it may seem both irregular and unstructured. It is not easy to put a date or place as to when and where the speakers of this Proto-Indo-European lived. Their existence is deduced from the comparison of the various modern languages and dead languages which have left traces rather than from archaeological remains. A comparison of the vocabularies of these different languages may give us some clues as to their homeland; for example, it has been suggested that, as there is no common word for 'sea' in the Proto-Indo-European languages, the speakers of this language did not live near a sea.

It is equally difficult to decide when the Proto-Germanic group of

Proto-Indo-European speakers emerged as a recognisable unit. The Germanic tribes are recognised as a distinct group of people by the Roman historians and by the end of the pre-Christian era they were settled in the north-west of Europe. As a linguistic grouping it was the treatment of certain consonants which nineteenth-century scholars used to recognise the Germanic tribes as a distinctive group. This movement in consonants is known as Grimm's Law, after Jacob Grimm who formulated it, or the First Consonant Shift. It consists of three major consonant changes. Firstly, the aspirated voiced stops appear in Latin as voiced fricatives and in Germanic as unaspirated voiced stops; secondly, the voiceless stops retained in Latin became voiceless fricatives; and thirdly, the voiced stops also retained in Latin became voiceless stops. These changes must have been happening at roughly the same time or else the voiceless stops created through the final change would have been subject to the second change. These changes produced the following differences between Latin and Germanic:

1. PIE aspirated voiced stops → voiced fricatives → Gmc voiced stops
   bh → f → b   cf. Lat. *frater* – ModE **b**rother
   dh → f → d   cf. Lat. *fingere* – ModE **d**ough
   gh → h → g   cf. Lat. **h**ortus – ModE **y**ard (cf. ON **g**arðr)
2. PIE voiceless stops → Gmc voiceless fricatives
   p → f   cf. Lat. **p**ater – ModE **f**ather
   t → th   cf. Lat. **t**res – ModE **th**ree
   k → h   cf. Lat. **c**ornu – ModE **h**orn
3. PIE voiced stops → Gmc voiceless stops
   b → p   cf. Lat. tur**b**a – ModE thor**p** [found in place names]
   d → t   cf. Lat. **d**ens/**d**entis – ModE **t**ooth
   g → k   cf. Lat. a**g**er – ModE a**c**re

This is a brief, schematised tabulation of the changes, but it does outline some correspondences between Latin and English. These correspondences are important in that English has over the years borrowed many words from Latin so that the same word etymologically may have come into English through two different channels, once through Germanic and a second time through Latin, with each form reflecting the changes detailed above. In the following pairs the first word is Germanic and the second Latin:

brother/fraternal; yard/horticulture; three/trinity; horn/cornucopia; tooth/dentist; and *acre/agriculture.*

Some of the changes outlined here were later modified through Verner's Law or the Second Consonant Shift, which arose through the rearrangement of stress in Proto-Germanic. A feature of Proto-Germanic as compared with Proto-Indo-European was that in the latter stress was variable and its position depended on a variety of factors, whereas in the Germanic languages there was a tendency to push the stress forward to the first syllable of a word. By Verner's Law the voiceless fricatives, some of which had developed through §2 above, became voiced when they were in a voiced environment and when the stress in Proto-Indo-European was not on the syllable which preceded this consonant. This resulted in the following changes: $f \rightarrow v$, $th \rightarrow d$ and $k \rightarrow g$. In addition the voiceless fricative /s/ became /z/ and then in North and West Germanic developed further to /r/. As it happens the effects of this change are not very visible in Modern English, because of various developments which have taken place subsequently. In Old English the variation between the original consonant and the new one can be seen most strikingly in the difference between the present and singular preterite tenses as compared with the preterite plural and past participle of the strong verbs. Thus OE *weorþan* has the preterite plural form *wurdon* and *forleosan* has the past participle *forloren.* The former does not survive in Modern English, but the latter has given us the verb *lose* and the adjective *forlorn*, which is based on the old past participle. The variation between *h* and *g* is not usually retained in English because *h* has fallen in voiced environments and *g* has often become diphthongised. Thus ModE *see* and *saw* originally showed this variation. In Old English the infinitive of this verb *sēon* is derived ultimately from a form **sehan.* The preterite plural was in Old English either *sāwon* or *sǣgon*, with the first form developing a diphthong from the original *ag.*

In addition to the two features mentioned in the previous paragraph, Grimm's Law and the establishment of stress on initial syllables, Germanic shows two further differences from other Proto-Indo-European languages. Firstly, in Proto-Indo-European the vowel system had both long and short forms of *a* and *o*, but in Germanic the long vowels were merged under long *o* and the short vowels under short *a*. In the consonant changes noted under §1 above Lat. *fráter* was compared with ModE *brother*, which had a long vowel in Old English, *brōþor*. This correspondence is explained by the retention in Latin of the original long vowel *a*, which in Germanic had been levelled under long *o*. On the other hand, Latin *octo* 'eight' is cognate with ModE *eight* originally from **aht-* (cf. ModG *acht*), because original Proto-Indo-European short *o* had been levelled under *a* in Germanic. Secondly, Germanic could form the preterite not only by modifying the root vowel like other Proto-Indo-European languages and as we still do in our so-called strong verbs like *see/saw*, but also by the use of an inflection added to the root. Several different forms of this inflection arose, but in Germanic they all had a dental or alveolar consonant, and have produced our so-called weak verbs. The Germanic languages share these four features which distinguish them from other Proto-Indo-European languages and provide the essential basis for regarding them as a separate group.

The group of languages forming the Proto-Germanic family can be broken down into three major subgroups, which are known as East Germanic, North Germanic and West Germanic. Although in the past these three groups were considered to be each independently derived from Proto-Germanic, many now think that the two latter subgroups should be considered as sharing a joint intermediate stage. In both North and West Germanic the *z* that had developed from PIE *s* through Verner's Law appeared as *r*, or sometimes in West Germanic disappeared. These two branches also shared a form of vowel development known as front mutation, though the change probably occurred independently in each branch. East Germanic is now extinct and is known from the Gothic language, which in the form of the Bible translated by Ulfilas in about 350 AD in a script of his own devising is the oldest surviving record of a Germanic language of any length, and from its descendant Crimean Gothic of which a few words were recorded in the sixteenth century. Because of its age Gothic is important in giving us information about early forms of Germanic. North Germanic differs from West Germanic in that it developed a suffixed article to express the meaning of the definite article and extended the inflection of the second-person singular of the present tense of verbs to the third person. This branch consists of the Scandinavian languages other than Finnish and Lappish. It is usually divided into an eastern and western branch, the former consisting of Swedish and Danish, the latter of Icelandic and West Norwegian (since in Norway the East Norwegian standard or *riksmål* is strongly modelled on Danish). North Germanic is important not only because there are extensive manuscript records of Old Icelandic and Old Norwegian (referred to jointly from now on as Old Norse) available from the twelfth century, together with runic inscriptions from the fourth century, but also because the Viking invasions in England led to many Scandinavian words being introduced into English. This is something to which we will return in the next chapter. The other branch of Proto-Germanic, West Germanic, consists of English, Frisian, Dutch and German and their descendants. Among these languages English and Frisian were originally closely linked, but naturally have tended to draw apart over the last fifteen hundred years.

West Germanic differs from North Germanic in being rather more conservative, but also in two major features. In Proto-Germanic there existed a *z* which appeared in Gothic as *s* and in Old Norse as *r*. In West Germanic this consonant fell in unstressed syllables and this had some important consequences for the development of nouns. Those nouns in Proto-Germanic which ended in -*z* in the nominative singular are represented in Goth. *dags* and ON *dagr* 'day'. In West Germanic this ending was lost, cf. OE *dæg*, ModE *day*, ModG *Tag*. This ending had originally distinguished the nominative or subject form from the accusative or object form of nouns (cf. ON nom *dagr*, acc *dag*), but in West Germanic languages this distinction was lost in those nouns which had originally had that ending. As this group contained a large number of nouns, it meant that the distinction between subject and object could no longer be expressed through the inflection. The other West Germanic feature is a phonological one, in that most consonants other than *r* were lengthened when they occurred between a short vowel and certain consonants, especially *j* but also *r, l, w, m* and *n*. Thus the Old English verb *lettan* 'to hinder' is parallel with Goth. *latjan* and ON *letja*. In this latter example both Old English and Old Norse show the development of Gmc *a* characteristic of North and West Germanic.

It is not certain where the Proto-Germanic people should be located geographically, but a reasonable guess is that they lived in the north of the area between the Elbe and the Oder and in parts of southern Scandinavia. Some time about 300 BC they began to occupy other lands and moved in all directions, ousting the existing inhabitants from their lands. It is at this stage that they also moved westwards along the coast of the North Sea towards the Rhine. As the Romans advanced north and the Germans migrated west, the two came into contact with each other. At the end of the first century AD Tacitus divided the Germanic people into three major groups, the Ingvæones, the Istvæones and the Erminones. What he meant by these is not clear, though it has usually been thought that the tribes who were to settle in England were part of the Ingvæones, who probably also included the Frisians and the Dutch. The Frisians are thought to be the people most closely related to the English from a linguistic point of view and many scholars refer to a sub-branch of West Germanic called Anglo-Frisian, which may be much the same thing as Ingvæonic. The Ingvæones can probably be located as living in Friesland, that is the North Sea coasts of Holland and Germany, and the southern part of the Jutish peninsula. They thus occupied an area where in what is now Schleswig-Holstein they shared a boundary with speakers of North Germanic. Before the Germanic peoples learned how to write and before the establishment of nation states, the intermingling of speakers of different linguistic backgrounds must have been common enough and it is difficult to think that any Germanic tribe was linguistically homogeneous.

In the eighth century the English historian Bede was to record in his *Historia ecclesiastica gentis Anglorum* (*Ecclesiastical History of the English Nation*) that England was colonised by three Germanic tribes which he labelled Angles, Saxons and Jutes. He reported that the Saxons had been invited over by Vortigern and the Romanised British to help them fight against their enemies from the north. Having settled in the east of England the newcomers invited others of their tribes over to settle here. This is recorded as happening in 450 AD. While there may be some element of truth in this, Saxons had been plundering the east coast of England for many years and the Romans had established a so-called Count of the Saxon Shore to defend the east coast against them. When the Roman armies were withdrawn in 410, Britain became more exposed to this kind of attack, and Vortigern or other leaders may well have tried to come to terms with these foreigners by inviting them in to fight with them against their enemies. It had been a well-tried Roman policy to employ one set of barbarians as auxiliaries to fight against another set, and the Romanised Britons may have adopted the same approach. This move to Britain by the Germanic tribes may be seen as part of their general migration and cannot be considered an invasion. It was probably not planned and at first permanent settlement may not have been intended. As the Saxons and others realised how attractive Britain was for occupation, more moved in. It is impossible to describe with any accuracy how this settlement proceeded or even which Germanic peoples were involved. Traditionally, it has been accepted that the Angles occupied the Midlands and north of the country, which is why the Midlands and northern dialects are referred to collectively as Anglian. The Saxons settled all of southern England except Kent and parts of Hampshire and the Isle of Wight. Their name survives in various county and regional names, such as *Sussex* 'South Saxons', *Wessex* 'West Saxons' and so on. Kent and the Isle of Wight with parts of neighbouring Hampshire were settled by the Jutes, though the dialect of Kent is referred to as Kentish rather than Jutish. Even if this overall settlement pattern is generally true, it does not account for which peoples undertook the settlement of large tracts of the country. Settlement in East Anglia and in the West Midlands may have been by other smaller tribal units. The settlement of England by the Germanic peoples is still part of prehistory and the evidence we have is archaeological and what later historians tell us. It is most likely that small groups of settlers came across from the Continent, some of whom may have belonged to recognised tribal groups, but others may well have been in more amorphous groupings, and gradually fanned out across England from east to west and from south to north.

Many might assume that the start of English dates from this migration from 450 AD onwards. But the tribes were only doing what they had done for many years: they were looking for new lands to settle as either population growth or the pressure of the movement of other peoples encouraged them to move on. The only difference this time was that they moved over a substantial area of water to their new lands. This need not be regarded as too significant as travel by water was often as easy as, if not easier than, travel by land. The new settlers in Britain almost certainly remained in touch with other Germanic peoples on the Continent through trade and other means, and the language spoken on both sides of the North Sea cannot have been too different at this stage. Moving to Britain did not in itself cut the new settlers off or create immediately the sense that they were different from those they had left behind. There was no sense of a national identity and no national language in these early centuries of settlement. The Anglo-Saxons, as we may call them, gradually settled the lands formerly occupied by the Celts. This also was in no way different from what had happened in north-west Europe, for as the Germanic peoples moved westwards it was usually to settle in the lands that had belonged to Celts. It seems very probable that the Anglo-Saxons had had some dealings with Celts before they came to Britain. But as they moved to settle the whole country, they appear not to have taken over many words belonging to the indigenous people. This is somewhat unusual, for the settlement extended over several centuries and was punctuated by periods of fierce resistance and some success by the Celts. Intercourse between the two sets of people must have been common enough and, although the Celts were increasingly driven back to the western and northern peripheries of the island, many pockets of Celtic settlement, such as the Elmet in Yorkshire, survived for a long period. The major impact of the Celtic language on English has been through the names of places and rivers. Places such as *London* and *Winchester* and rivers such as *Thames* and *Avon* are wholly or partly of Celtic origin. However, we should remember that many educated Celts may have been familiar with Latin through the long centuries of Roman colonisation and so the Celtic language may not have been regarded too highly by them. Also place and river names often had a Romanised form which could readily survive through a new settlement, and indeed such names often did survive invasions. Anyway, for whatever reason, Celtic has left little mark on English; quite apart from the vocabulary, there is little evidence of any influence on morphology, phonology or syntax. Nevertheless, intercourse between the two peoples carried on and the archaeological artefacts which have been discovered show that there was often a strong Celtic influence on the ornaments and household goods used by the Anglo-Saxons.

It is not possible to trace the precise path of the settlements, but one can assume that after initial settlements in the south-east and East Anglia, the Anglo-Saxons pushed along rivers and the Roman roads. By the end of the sixth century they had apparently occupied most of England except for the western fringes like Cornwall and may have encroached into what is now southern Scotland. However, this settlement was no doubt patchy to start with. The Anglo-Saxons preferred the river valleys with their heavier soils, whereas the Celts had tended to settle more on the chalk hills and other headlands. The country was still very wooded and travel cannot have been easy except along the arteries of the rivers and

Roman roads. At about the middle of the sixth century it was possible to recognise several distinct regions which had their own forms of government, and this gradually became recognised as the Heptarchy, or seven kingdoms – Wessex, Sussex, Kent, Essex, East Anglia, Mercia and Northumbria. These kingdoms were formed from other smaller subkingdoms and their unity may have been more apparent than real. Northumbria originally consisted of two kingdoms, Deira and Bernicia; Mercia included in the west a tribe known as the Hwicce, though its exact geographical situation is uncertain; among the Saxons there was a subgroup which gave its name to Middlesex or the Middle Saxons; and, as Bede noted, there were Jutes in southern Hampshire and the Isle of Wight. It is these seven kingdoms which provide the basis for most dialect study of this period, though written remains are not found until the beginning of the eighth century and even then some of these areas have left no trace from the pre-Alfredian period. In so far as their dialect can be traced it is often through working backwards from modern varieties. Politically, no one of these kingdoms was able to achieve supremacy over the others, though they did have some kind of loose federal structure and the principal ruler was known as the *Bretwalda*. Political ascendancy swung from one kingdom to the other. In the sixth century greater power lay in the south of the country, but in the next centuries it moved northwards, leading to confrontation between Mercia and Northumbria as their kings strove to achieve dominance over the other. Although some people may have been familiar with the runic alphabet, it was not well adapted to writing of any length and the Anglo-Saxons were essentially illiterate until the arrival of Christianity.

Compared with other West Germanic peoples, the Anglo-Saxons are exceptional in their early use of writing and in the large amount of writing that survives. The impetus for writing came from the conversion of the various kingdoms from 597 when St Augustine arrived in England. As it happens, Christianity had survived among the Celts of Ireland and missionaries also came to convert the Anglo-Saxons from there. They began their work in Northumbria, whereas Augustine landed in Kent and started his work in the south. The Celtic and the Roman churches differed in some of their practices and observances, though it was the Roman church which was to come out victorious in the seventh century at the Synod of Whitby. It was not surprising that Augustine should have gone to Kent, for Æthelberht, its king, had a Frankish wife who was already a Christian. Æthelberht agreed to become a Christian and his kingdom followed him in this, though for many the conversion may have been more apparent than real. Yet as soon as he had achieved this aim, Augustine was able to establish a new monastic foundation and commence producing manuscripts for liturgical use and educational purposes. Since no variety of the language or languages used by the Anglo-Saxons had yet been written down except in the runic script, it was necessary to produce a script to represent the variety of English used in Kent. This could then be adapted to other varieties as the need arose, though the correspondence between graphs and phonemes may well have been stable. Although royal charters and laws were written, writing remained very much the property of the church, and written texts were largely produced in monastic scriptoria during this period. Writing and Latin were largely synonymous for those who were educated, and the idea of producing extensive works in English could well have seemed a strange concept to them. If those who could read were familiar with Latin, why should there be any reason to produce works written in English? There was after all plenty of material written and available in Latin which would have been considered more significant than anything which might be written in English. Sermons could be delivered orally in English even if they were written down and survive in their written form in Latin.

Even so, some writing in English was needed. Names of English places and people had to be written down, and certain traditional features of Anglo-Saxon life, such as the law, would need to reflect the language in which it had been handed down in traditional form to maintain ancient legal practices. Consequently the different varieties of English had to be reduced to writing and we must now turn to the arrangements which were made as Latin was adapted for the native language. As far as vowels and diphthongs are concerned, the system which was adopted consisted of a single graph for the former and a combination of two graphs for the latter. The five graphs for vowels used in Latin were taken over to represent five long and short vowel sounds. No distinction was made in writing between long and short in the length of vowels so that long and short *a* were both represented by the graph <a>. Some writers do use accents, but they were not consistently employed to represent length. The Anglo-Saxons developed a fronted form of long and short *a* which was written as <æ> and a fronted version of long and short *u* which was written as <y>, a graph which was used in written varieties of early English only as a vowel. In some early texts <æ> may appear as a hooked *e* and a fronted form of *o* may appear as <œ>. The development of these different sounds will be discussed later in the chapter. As mentioned in a previous chapter, these vowel sounds were both long and short, and the difference in quality was essentially one of length. The two major diphthongs were written respectively <ea> and <eo> and they existed in both long and short forms, which were also not distinguished for length in writing. There were two additional diphthongs in some dialects and these took the form <ie> and <iu/io>. As for consonants, the Latin letters <j, q, v> were not used and <x> and <z> were used infrequently. Other letters were used, but many had a different shape in Old English or even a different realisation. Thus *w* could appear as <u> or <uu> or, more usually, with a special letter <ƿ> known as *wynn* derived from the runic futhark. The voiced and voiceless dental fricatives were represented by two symbols interchangeably; one was from the runic <þ>, and the other was a development of Lat. <d> with a stroke through the ascender <ð>. These two letters are known respectively as *thorn* and *eth*. In some documents there is a tendency to use thorn initially in a word and eth medially and finally. Some early documents also use <th> for either sound. The other letters were all employed at some time, but a few were not common. Thus Lat. *k* is found, but mostly <c> was used and it represented both /k/ as in *cuman* 'to come' and /tʃ/ as in *cirice* 'church'. Some early texts do use <k>, but it was not part of the later standard. The sound /ʃ/ as in ModE 'ship' was represented by <sc>, OE *scip*, and /dʒ/ as in ModE 'edge' was represented by <cʒ>, OE *ecʒ*. There was no distinction between palatal and velar *g* in writing, and both were represented by <ʒ> known as *yogh*. Both <c> and <ʒ> took on a different phonetic realisation according to the environment in which they occurred. Essentially in the neighbourhood of front vowels they were palatal and in the neighbourhood of back vowels they were velar. This did not apply to <sc> which was always palatal in words of Germanic origin. It was only in words introduced from other languages, notably Old Norse and Latin, that <sc> had a velar pronunciation. The reason that <v, z> were not or only rarely used and that there was no distinction between <ð> and <þ> is that these voiced and voiceless sounds were not distinguished phonemically. The symbol <s>, for example, could be pronounced /s/ initially and /z/ medially in voiced environments, but these sounds were in complementary distribution and were not phonemic. The same applies to the others. Initial <h> had much the same phonetic realisation as in Modern English, but medially and finally it was either the velar or palatal fricative /χ/ or /ç/. It should be remembered that when a double consonant occurs in writing it represents a pronunciation in which both are pronounced, as distinct from Modern English. Thus ModE *beginning* pronounces the <nn> as /n/, but in all forms of Old English a word like *winnan* would pronounce <nn> as we today pronounce the medial consonants in *penknife*.

During the time of the migration into England and the early settlements, a number of changes in the phonology of the various varieties of English took place which gradually made their pronunciation increasingly different from the varieties of Germanic which they had left behind on the Continent. These are often described as a series of sound laws, a term which it is convenient to use here as long as it is understood to represent an idealisation of the changes which occurred. These changes affected the vowels and diphthongs principally and so we may consider them first. The inventory of vowels in stressed syllables with which we are principally concerned and of diphthongs, which the future settlers had on the Continent, was probably made up of the following elements: short and long forms of the vowels *i, e, u* and *o*, short *a* and long *æ*, and the diphthongs *iu, eu, ai* and *au*, which were all long. A series of changes at about the time of the initial migration saw /ai/ monophthongised to /ɑ:/ so that there were now a series of five vowels with long and short forms and the long vowel /æ:/. By the change known as the First Fronting (or Anglo-Frisian Brightening) /ɑ(:)/, except when it occurred before a nasal, was fronted to /æ(:)/. This meant that there were now six vowels with long and short forms, though *æ*(:) and *a*(:) were in complementary distribution. Of the diphthongs, /au/ became /æu/, perhaps responding to the same fronting associated with the First Fronting, so that there were three diphthongs with a front vowel as initial element and /u/ as the second element. At a somewhat later date the final element in these diphthongs tended to take on the height of the first element, which was more dominant, to produce the diphthongs /iu, eo, æa/. Towards the ninth century *iu* and *eo* merged under *eo* in the West Saxon standard. The result was that after the start of the migration in the fifth century the vowel and diphthong system would have consisted of the long and short vowels *i, e, æ, u, o* and *a*, and the diphthongs *iu, eo* and *æa*, usually written <ea>.

Another early change known as Breaking or Fracture affected the front vowels /i(:), e(:), æ(:)/ when they occurred before *r* or *l* followed by another consonant or before *h*. The change is so called because the front vowels were 'broken' into diphthongs, *i(:)* → io/eo(:), e(:) → eo(:) and *æ(:)* → *æa(:)*. So **sehan*, for example, became **seohan* before at a later stage the *h* fell to leave the form *sēon* 'to see'; *sæh* → *seah* 'saw', and **erl* → *eorl* 'warrior'. Since *h* in medial or final position was originally a velar consonant, it would seem that the transition from a front vowel to a velar consonant was so great that a glide sound was introduced, which then formed a diphthong with the preceding vowel. The long diphthongs thus created were either identical with those developed from Germanic or accepted as the same, but the short diphthongs were completely new. The language now had matching long and short diphthongs *iu(:), eo(:)* and *æa(:)*, although this view has not been universally accepted because it has been suggested that the new short diphthongs were different in quality from those that existed already and may not have been diphthongs at all. At about the same time another sound change known as Retraction was operative by which the front vowel /æ/, when it occurred before a syllable with a back vowel, was retracted to /ɑ/. This created the situation that in some paradigms there was a contrast between *æ* and *a*; the noun *dæg* 'day' had as its plural forms *dagas* (nom, acc), *daga* (gen) and *dagum* (dat). This change was more operative with short *æ* than with the long vowel, though it does seem to have affected the long vowel sometimes.

It has already been noted that the symbols <c> and <ʒ> represented two sounds, a palatal and a velar, and Germanic /sk/ was palatalised in all environments to /ʃ/. An initial palatal /j/ had existed in Germanic in a variety of environments, including before front vowels, but even where Germanic had had /g/ this was palatalised in the environment of front vowels, though only where the front vowels were descended from West Germanic front vowels or had been created through the First Fronting. Germanic /k/ was palatised under the same conditions. When palatal /tʃ/ and /j/ occurred before a front vowel, that vowel tended to diphthongise with /e(:)/ becoming /ie(:)/ and /æ(:)/ becoming /æɑ(:)/. Thus *ʒieldan* is from earlier **ʒeldan*, a class V strong verb which had the preterite plural and past participle *ʒuldon/ʒolden*, where initial /g/ was retained. Similarly **ʒær*, **scæp*, **cæster* became *ʒēar*, *scēap* and *ceaster* (cf. ModG *Jahr*, *Schaffe* and Lat. *castra*). This palatalisation and diphthongisation did not occur in all varieties of early Old English and this accounts for the difference in the variation *-chester/-caster* in Modern English place-names. In some varieties of Old English where initial Germanic /j/ and the new English /ʃ/ occurred before back vowels, they developed a glide which was written as <i> or <e>, as in *sceop* 'poet' or *ʒiung/ʒeong* 'young'. Where there is an environment where *e* occurs after an initial palatal and before breaking consonants, *h* or *l/r* plus consonant, the result is usally *eo* rather than *ie*, which suggests that breaking occurred earlier than palatalisation after initial consonants. Thus we find *ceorl* 'man' rather than **cierl*, where the former arises from breaking and the latter would come from palatalisation.

Perhaps the most significant change in this prehistoric period, in so far as it is the one whose traces are still clearly visible in Modern English, was the one known as Front Mutation or i/mutation. The names reflect the two main elements of the change, namely that when an original /i/ or /j/ occurred in a syllable following one which contained a back vowel, then the back vowel of the preceding syllable was fronted to the equivalent front vowel. The following /i/ or /j/ mostly disappeared before the historical period, but it sometimes remains in writing as <i>. The new front vowels at first retained the rounding characteristic of /o/ and /u/, but the former lost its rounding fairly quickly. The mutation of the back vowels led to the following results:

/ɑ(:)/ → /æ(:)/
/o(:)/ → /œ(:)/ → /e(:)/
/u(:)/ → /y(:)/ [In Kentish this vowel developed
further to /e(:)/]

One important effect of this mutation was the creation of /y(:)/, a new, rounded front vowel. Another was that it created differences within the paradigms of both verbs and nouns. In verbs the second- and third-person singular of the present indicative had the West Germanic inflectional endings **-ist/-iþ*, which produced front mutation so that there was often a difference in the vowels of the infinitive and other persons of the present tense, as in *cuman/ cym(e)þ, faran/fær(e)þ*. In the nouns some paradigms had formed their plural with an *i/j* in the inflectional ending, and this led to a variation in the stem vowel between the singular and the plural, which is still found in some words such as *mouse/mice* (OE *mūs/mȳs*) and *man/men*. The latter example is explained because where the /æ(:)/ which arose from front mutation occurred before an *m* or *n*, it developed further to /e(:)/. The effect of this mutation on the diphthongs is more mixed. In the West Saxon dialect the mutation of both long and short *ea* and *eo*, whatever their origin, produced the diphthong written <ie>. In other dialects *ea* appeared as *e*, and *io/eo* remained unchanged. Thus Lat. *cáseum* was introduced into Germanic and would by fronting have given early OE **cæs-*, which after the development of an initial palatal would have produced the form **cēasi-*. This would then develop into eWS **cīese*, which is found in lWS as *cȳse*. At the same time as this change and possibly related to it, the /æ/ which had arisen from fronting was raised to /e/. The results of front mutation, as with so many other sound changes in early Old English, appear in the written documents of the historic period in a mixed state so that the precise operation of the change is often difficult to evaluate.

Towards the end of the prehistoric period of Old English a change, usually referred to as back mutation, occurred, whereby the short front vowels /æ, e, i/ were diphthongised when the back vowels /u/ or /ɑ/ were present in the following syllable, though the former often appears in later written texts as <o>. However, this change operated irregularly in the various dialects and its results are often affected by analogy. In some dialects it happened only when there was an intervening single consonant which was a labial or a liquid; in others it occurred through any intervening single consonant except /k, g/. In most dialects it did not occur when a consonant group came between the front and the back vowel. The result of this change is that *æ*, *e* and *i* become *ea*, *eo* and *io* respectively. The place-name for York appears in Latin as *Eburacum*, but in Old English as *Eoforwic*, where the original *e* has been affected by the following *u* to become *eo*. One can find examples of *spreocan* alongside *sprecan* 'to speak'.

In the previous paragraph it was noted that when /k/ or /g/ was the intervening consonant the operation of back mutation was often impeded. This may be explained because, particularly in the

Anglian dialects, the velar consonants /χ, k, g/ appear not to have tolerated immediately before them the typical early Old English diphthongs found in most dialects. When these consonants occurred either singly or in conjunction with the liquids /r, l/, they converted preceding diphthongs into monophthongs in a process usually referred to as smoothing. Long and short *ea, eo* and *io* were monophthongised respectively to *æ, e* and *i*, though the former often moved further to *e*. In those cases where /χ/ had fallen early, smoothing did not take place so that it is possible to find a contrast in Anglian between *nēh* (cf.WS *nēah*) and *nēolǣcan*. Anglian *liht* compares with West Saxon *leoht*, where early *io* appears as *eo*. Some varieties of the Anglian dialect also exhibit the change known as second fronting by which the /æ/ which arose through first fronting was raised to /e/, but the effects of this change were limited.

A significant change was the contraction of vowels leading to compensatory lengthening. This occurred particularly where *h* fell between vowels. We saw earlier that original **sehan* had lost its *h* because it occurred between vowels. This change probably reflects the unstable nature of /h/, particularly in the neighbourhood of vowels and liquids – a feature of English that is still clear today. In Old English there are many texts which do not indicate the presence of *h* in initial positions in particular, but also medially. Today words like *loaf* and *lord* come from Old English words with *h-, hlāf, hlāford*. When *h* fell between two vowels, it left the two vowels juxtaposed. This juxtaposition was not tolerated except where it produced *ua*; other groups either turned into diphthongs or, more usually, they coalesced into a single vowel or diphthong with compensatory lengthening if the prior vowels or diphthong + vowel had both been short. Thus **sehan* lost its *h* after it had caused breaking of *e* to *eo*; and this **seoan* developed into **sēon* with the short diphthong being lengthened. This would ultimately produce ModE *see*. Even where /h/ occurs between a liquid and a vowel or vice versa, the same thing would happen and lengthening could take place through the liquid. This gave rise to variation between long and short forms in certain noun paradigms where the nominative might have no ending and oblique cases had a vowel as the first element of the inflection. Thus *feorh* 'life' had the genitive *fēores*.

Proto-Indo-European had been an inflected language and its descendants had retained inflections to a greater or lesser extent.

There were still many inflections in the speech of the Anglo-Saxons when they came to England, but the system had already begun to break down. In Old English the system which operated was that nouns had four cases in singular and plural: nominative (or the subject case), accusative (or the object case), genitive (indicating possession) and dative (used after most prepositions and also as the indirect object). In many paradigms the nominative and accusative had fallen together in both singular and plural. In the plural all nouns had an identical ending for the genitive and another for the dative. So the distinctions between the various cases were becoming blurred, though they only broke down when Standard Old English itself ceased to be a dominant force. In nouns there were several paradigms depending on the principal vowel of the inflection in Germanic. The principal difference was between those nouns that had a vowel in the inflection and were formerly called strong nouns and those that had taken over the *-n* of the original stem and reinterpreted it as an inflection, which were formerly referred to as weak nouns. The latter group had *-n* in most oblique cases other than the nominative singular and the genitive and dative plural. The former group was more diverse. All nouns are characterised by different forms within each group and these have characteristically been called masculine, feminine and neuter. This distinction should be understood as purely formal and bears no relation to natural gender. It is important in that adjectives had to agree with the nouns they qualified in case, gender and number. It is not possible to give a complete list of the noun paradigms here, but it is important to mention some of the important differences which were significant for later developments.

Table 3.1 shows some examples of declensional paradigms. In these paradigms the *a-/u*-stem nouns are strong, whereas the *n*-stem nouns are weak. It must be stressed that the paradigms given are only examples and there were a number of other declensions, and even within individual groups the different genders may have had a slightly different realisation. The majority of masculine nouns were *a*-stem and the feminine ones *u*-stem except for those which were in the *n*-stem group, which contained nouns of all three genders. There were *i*-stem nouns which caused front mutation, such as *mann/menn, bōc/bēc*. In the neuter *a*-stem nouns, final *-u* in the nominative and accusative plural fell after a long syllable (a syllable with a long vowel or a short vowel followed by two consonants). Thus *word* was unchanged in the

TABLE 3.1

	a-stem		u-stem	n-stem
	Masculine	Neuter	Feminine	Masculine
Singular				
nom	stān	scip	ȝiefu	nama
acc	stān	scip	ȝiefe	naman
gen	stānes	scipes	ȝiefe	naman
dat	stāne	scipe	ȝiefe	naman
Plural				
nom/acc	stānas	scipu	ȝiefa	naman
gen	stāna	scipa	ȝiefa	namena
dat	stānum	scipum	ȝiefum	namum

plural because although it had short *o*, it was followed by the consonant group *rd*. This was the main feature in a group of words with uninflected plural, some of which survive today such as *sheep*.

Adjectives had much the same pattern as the nouns. They had three genders so they could agree with their nouns and they had the four cases in singular and plural. Their paradigms were very similar to, but not identical with, those for the nouns. The pronouns differed considerably from their Modern English equivalents. The first- and second-personal pronouns declined through the four cases in both singular and plural. The third-person personal pronoun had three genders, four cases and both singular and plural. In view of the changes that occurred in this pronoun, it is worth recording its forms in what became the West Saxon standard,

TABLE 3.2

	Singular			Plural
	Masculine	Feminine	Neuter	All genders
nom	hē	hēo	hit	hīe
acc	hine	hīe	hit	hī
gen	his	hire	his	hiera
dat	him	hire	him	him

as shown in Table 3.2. The features to be noted are that all forms of this pronoun begin with *h* in the singular and plural; there is no distinction of gender in the plural; and in the singular, masculine and neuter are closer together than either with the feminine. There also existed in Old English a dual pronoun, indicating the speaker or person spoken to and one other person, though this pronoun showed signs of disappearing from an early date. There was an interrogative pronoun which declined, but the masculine and feminine were identical and the neuter was distinguished only in the nominative and accusative *hwæt* as compared with the masculine/feminine *hwā*. There were also demonstrative pronouns which like the third person of the personal pronouns had three genders and five cases in the singular, and common forms for all genders, but only four cases, in the plural. The fifth case was an instrumental which was used mostly in certain grammatical constructions which survive today in expressions like 'The more the merrier' and in others rather like a Latin ablative. These cases should also be given in full (see Table 3.3). A second form of the demonstrative which occurred less commonly had the nominative singular forms *þes* (masc) and *þeos* (fem) and *þis* (neut) and nominative and accusative plural for all genders *þās*.

The verbs were divided into two major categories, the so-called weak and strong verbs. The weak verbs were a feature of Germanic and were formed by adding an inflectional ending that included a dental or alveolar consonant. Even from the earliest Old English period, this seems to have been the dominant verb pattern. The strong verbs were formed by changing the stem vowel, usually through the process known as ablaut (a form of vowel gradation) but sometimes through reduplication. The number of strong verbs inherited from Germanic probably amounted to little more than

TABLE 3.3

	Singular			Plural
	Masculine	Feminine	Neuter	All cases
nom	sē, se	sēo	þæt	þā
acc	þone	þā	þæt	þā
gen	þæs	þǣre	þæs	þāra
dat	þǣm	þǣre	þǣm	þǣm
instr	þȳ, þon, þē		þȳ, þon, þē	

300–400 and, although their number was constantly decreasing, this was not marked in the early Old English period. All verbs had two tenses, a present and a preterite, which as in Modern English expressed a non-past and a past. Other tenses had to be expressed through adverbs or had to be understood from the context. The verbs had an infinitive, and present and past participle, though the latter two had much stronger adjectival associations than today. In addition to the indicative mood, there was a subjunctive for both tenses. The subjunctive had a single inflectional ending for all singular persons and another one for all plural persons, and these endings were the same for both tenses. The indicative, on the other hand, had three separate endings for the singular, but a common one for the plural. The second and third persons of the present tense of the indicative showed front mutation under the appropriate conditions. There was also a singular and plural form of the imperative. There was no passive. The verbs that were to become auxiliary verbs were mostly full verbs in the earliest period, though traces of their development towards auxiliaries may be found, particularly in texts translated from or based on Latin. These verbs were mostly anomalous in structure because, as so-called preterite-present verbs, they had formed new present tense forms from old preterites and had formed new preterites. They did not normally exhibit all the forms that are found in other verbs.

The strong verbs fall into seven distinct patterns, though some of these patterns had themselves undergone change as a result of phonological developments in Proto-Germanic or English. The patterns are usually indicated through the forms of the infinitive, preterite singular (third person), preterite plural and past participle. The patterns are as follows:

I. **ī ā i i**
A stable pattern unaffected by other changes.

rīdan   rād   ridon   riden   'to ride'

II. **ēo/ū ēa u o**
Usually with a single consonant after the stem vowel, which could show the effects of Verner's Law.

crēopan   crēap   crupon   cropen   'to creep'
lēosan   lēas   luron   loren   'to lose'
scūfan   scēaf   scufon   scofen   'to shove'

III. **e æ u o**

This original pattern was frequently disturbed because the root vowel was followed by two consonants, the first of which was a liquid or nasal. The nasal caused the raising of *e* → *i* and *o* → *u*, and inhibited the fronting of *a* → *æ*. The liquids caused the breaking of *e* → *eo* and *æ* → *ea*, but not that of *e* before *l* + consonant. This resulted in a number of divergent patterns.

findan	fand	fundon	funden	'to find'
helpan	healp	hulpon	holpen	'to help'
ceorfan	cearf	curfon	corfen	'to carve'

IV. **e æ ǣ o**

This group had a single liquid or nasal after the root vowel; those examples with a nasal are few and often diverse in their final forms: they include *cuman* 'to come' and *niman* 'to take'.

| beran | bær | bǣron | boren | 'to bear' |

V. **e æ ǣ e**

These verbs have a single consonant other than a liquid or nasal after the root vowel. A palatal /j/ preceding the root vowel causes palatal diphthongisation where applicable.

| sprecan | spræc | sprǣcon | sprecen | 'to speak' |
| ʒiefan | ʒeaf | ʒēafon | ʒiefen | 'to give' |

VI. **a ō ō a**

| faran | fōr | fōron | faren | 'to go, travel' |

VII. This group shows different patterns because it originally consisted of reduplicating verbs; but the vowel or diphthong of the infinitive was repeated in the past participle, and both forms of the preterite had either *ē* or *ēo*.

| cnāwan | cnēow | cnēowon | cnāwen | 'to know' |
| hātan | hēt | hēton | hāten | 'to be called' |

This scheme contains only the standard verb forms, but there were many variants arising from various phonological developments within individual varieties.

There are three categories of weak verb, though the variation in these verbs is just as great as, if not greater than, that found in the strong verbs. Many show gemmination or the doubling of the consonant between the root and inflectional vowel, because they had originally had a *j* in their ending. This gemmination is not found when the root vowel is long, the intermediate consonant is an *r*, or a consonant group already exists. The major pattern is that of the first class. Since weak verbs form their preterite by adding an inflection which contains *d* or *t* in Old English, there is no need to distinguish the preterite singular from its plural, because they differ only in the ending indicating number.

I.	fremman	fremede	fremed	'to accomplish'
	cēpan	cēpte	cēped	'to keep'
	ferian	ferede	fered	'to carry'
II.	endian	endode	endod	'to end'
III.	habban	hæfde	hæfd	'to have'
	secʒan	sæʒde	sæʒd	'to say'

The verbs of the third category are among the commonest in the language, but they do show particular variety.

The different aspects of lexis and syntax found in Old English will be commented on in the next chapter, for it is only after the development of Standard Old English that sufficient writings are found to enable us to get some clear understanding of what these were like. Now it is time to introduce a short piece of early Old English to exhibit what the language was like in one of its early manifestations. The passage I have chosen is 'Cædmon's Hymn'. In his *Ecclesiastical History* from *c*.730 Bede reported the story of Cædmon who was attached to the monastery of Whitby at the end of the seventh century. Bede gave a Latin translation of this hymn in his narrative, but some early manuscripts contain what is a Northumbrian version of the original text added either in the margin or on a blank sheet. The Moore manuscript of the Latin *Historia* (Cambridge University Library MS Kk.5.16) is an eighth-century manuscript which contains the Northumbrian version in what appears to be a contemporary hand. This text reads with modern lineation and punctuation, though other manuscripts have slightly different spellings:

> Nu scylun herʒan hefaenricaes uard,
> metudæs maecti end his modʒidanc,
> uerc uuldurfadur, sue he uundra ʒihuaes,   3
> eci dryctin, or astelidæ.

> He aerist scop aelda barnum
> heben til hrofe, haleȝ scepen;   6
> tha middunȝeard moncynnæs uard,
> eci dryctin, æfter tiadæ
> firum foldu, frea allmectiȝ.[2]   9

This might be translated literally by each half-line as follows

'Now must [pl.] praise guardian of heavenly kingdom, might of
creator and his heart-thought, work(s) of glorious father, as he
of each wonder, eternal lord, ordained beginning. He first created
to children of men heaven as a roof, holy creator, then middle
earth, guardian of mankind, eternal lord, afterwards established,
earth for men, almighty lord.

This translation is deliberately literal so that points that need
explanation are not hidden under a more elegant translation.

Syntactically the poem is very simple consisting as it does of four
clauses divided into two groups (1–3 and 3–4; 5–6 and 7–9). These
groups are joined by what is either an adverb or a conjunction. In
line 7 *tha* is certainly an adverb. But *sue* in line 3 could be an adverb
with the sense 'so, thus' or a conjunction either with the sense 'how'
to tie in with Bede's Latin *quomodo* or with a causal meaning
'because, as'. The last of these options is perhaps the most
acceptable. This difficulty in deciding whether a word linking two
clauses together is an adverb or a conjunction is one that is
prominent in the early language, but is found right through the
history of English. Most clauses are relatively simple, consisting of
subject, verb and object with only an occasional indirect object or
adverb. The order is not always SVO, since in line 7 the object
middunȝeard comes before the subject, and where there are a
number of parallel phrases some of these are placed in different
parts of the clause. The parallels are all noun groups; the verbs are
not varied through parallelism. The result is somewhat ornate and
static; the piece is heavily descriptive like a hymn rather than
narrative. There are no articles, since the nouns are always
introduced as though the article is implied. Thus although I have
translated *hefaenricaes uard* as 'guardian of heavenly kingdom', we
would understand this phrase as implying today 'the guardian of
the heavenly kingdom'. However, the possessive pronoun *his* is

used, and *he* in both lines 3 and 5 is introduced as a subject although a noun group occurs as a subject later (*eci dryctin* and *haleg scepen*). The overall effect is that there are few grammatical words for the sense is expressed through the endings of the lexical words.

The understanding of the endings is not without problems. The second word *scylun* is the plural of the present tense of the preterite-present verb *sculan*, which normally has the meaning 'shall, must'. It is here operating as a kind of auxiliary, though the meaning is not entirely clear. More importantly, the subject of this verb is not expressed unless it is *uerc uuldurfadur* 'works of [the] glorious father', which would then have to be plural. Bede's Latin version has *debemus* and later versions of the hymn in Old English insert a *we* as subject; so *scylun* is normally taken by modern scholars to mean 'we must'. The 'we' is understood from the ending *-un* even though that is common to all three persons in the plural and is not specifically a first-person ending. As already implied, *uerc* could be either singular or plural. It is a neuter noun which had lost the original *-u* of its nominative and accusative plural so that these two cases were identical in singular and plural. It is most often understood as a singular. In line 9 *foldu* must be understood as accusative singular, but it is normally a *n*-stem noun which would end in *-an*; it is an example of the early loss of inflectional *-n* which was a characteristic feature of Northumbrian.

As far as spelling goes, the scribe of this manuscript uses <u> instead of <p> (wynn). Many inflectional endings have spellings which indicate early pronunciations such as *-æs* for later *-es* (gen sg) and *-i* for later *-e* (acc sg). In *haleʒ* the final syllable has <e> where later <i> would be normal. In *hefaen* and *heben* the second syllable, which presumably has only secondary stress, is represented through<ae> and <e> where one might have expected <u> or <o>. The *-ur* of *fadur* represents an older form of the genitive singular, more often written as *er* in later texts. The spelling *middunʒeard* has *un* as the inflected form of a weak noun rather than *an*; and in this it is similar to *foldu* which has <u> where *an* would be expected later. The form *tiadæ* has <ia> where one later expect to find <io> or even <eo>. In *heben* <b> represents the voiced form of the labial fricative which is more usually written in Old English as <f>, as it is in *hefaenricaes*, and the scribe uses <th> rather than <þ> in *tha*. In *allmectig*, *maecti* and *dryctin* the velar sound [χ] is represented by <c> rather than the more usual <h>, but that may be to indicate its nature as a velar rather than a palatal. The velar sound was much more characteristic of northern varieties. In *modʒidanc*, where later scribes would have used <þ>, this scribe uses <d> instead; and this together with *Tha* suggests that he did not use <þ> at all and preferred to use Latin characters. The symbol <ʒ> is used for the palatal /j/; there are no examples of a velar /g/ in the text. The vocabulary is all of Germanic origin; there are no words from Latin or Greek, even though the subject matter is Christian. This means that many of the words found in this hymn have since been replaced in the language. The creation of new words is achieved through compounding in such examples as *modʒidanc, uuldurfadur, middunʒeard, moncynnæs,* and through phrases consisting of a noun in the genitive and another noun, as in *hefaenricaes uard, metudæs maecti, uerc uuldurfadur, moncynnæs uard.* In other cases the two nouns are linked in some other way or there is an adjective with the noun. A feature of this hymn is the small number of prepositions. The use of the dative case explains the absence of a preposition like *to,* though it is interesting to note that there is an example of *til,* a word restricted to the northern varieties which has there the same sense as *to,* though it may in this context be slightly more emphatic.

The <y> in *dryctin* and *moncynnæs* represents the normal front mutation of /u/ from an original **druhtin* and **kuni.* The development of this front vowel by front mutation does not influence the velar nature of the preceding consonant which is /k/ rather than /tʃ/. The occurrence of <y> in *scylun* may be explained as a development of the diphthong found after initial palatals. Presumably original **sculun* developed a diphthong to give **sciulun* and this *iu* was later monophthongised and represented as <y>. Diphthongisation of *a* after palatal *sc* in **scapen* would have produced **sceapen,* which in the form *scepen* found in the poem must have arisen through smoothing, which is characteristic of Anglian. There is no evidence of the glide developing between the palatal and the back vowel in *scop,* since this was more characteristic of the southern varieties only. The operation of breaking is rather erratic. Breaking of *æ* before *rd* is found in *-ʒeard,* but not found in *uard* or before *-rn* in *barnum.* It is not found before *ld* as in *aelda.* Before *h* it occurred, but in *maecti* the original *ea* has been smoothed to *ae,* and in *-mectiʒ* the diphthong has been both fronted and smoothed. The breaking of *e* to *eo* presumably took place in *uerc,* though its operation was then countered by the smoothing of the diphthong *eo* to *e.* There are also no examples of the operation of back mutation. Perhaps the spellings of *hefaen-* and *heben* represent a weakening of the unstressed vowel so that back mutation was unlikely. Neither *metudæs* nor *-fadur* exhibit this mutation. The realisation of *a* before a nasal takes a variety of forms. Thus we have <a> in *-danc*, <e> in *end* and <o> in *mon-*. The form *end* arises from front mutation and raising before the nasal of a variant form **andi* of this word in Proto-Germanic, though it is not usual to find this mutation in English, possibly because of the weak stress of the conjunction. The variation between *o/a* in the other words is one that occurs throughout English and may indicate that the actual sound lay somewhere between /ɑ/ and /o/ and could thus be represented by either symbol. In *moncynnæs* we would expect the spelling <nn> in *mon-*, but when three consonants occur together as originally would have been true here with *-nnc-*, it is not uncommon for there to be a reduction of the middle one. The form *scepen* exhibits the loss of final *-d*; the loss of a final consonant, particularly in a consonant group, has been a feature of English almost throughout its history.

The points outlined in the previous paragraphs indicate some of the features of the language found in the north of England in the eighth century but are not intended to be exhaustive. They show how we can piece together the development of the language at this time. There are, however, very few texts from Northumbria in this period and so some explanations are naturally tentative. But through a knowledge of cognate languages like Gothic and Old Saxon, it is possible to get some idea of what the original form of the words may have been so that their representation in this text can be worked out. We shall examine a passage from what became Standard Old English in the next chapter, and this text and its language may be compared with the features to be explored there. Although this text is from Northumbria, there were also pre-Alfredian texts written in other dialect areas, particularly Mercia and Kent. Some of the writing produced in these areas will be considered at the beginning of the next chapter where the whole question of standardising a variety of Old English will be discussed. What is characteristic of this Northumbrian version of 'Cædmon's Hymn' is the different spelling system it exhibits, partly because it is earlier than other texts and partly because standard-isation had not been developed yet. Those used to the standard developed in Wessex later will regard this variety as somewhat erratic, but it has its own logic and inner coherence. It was only the incursion of the Danes which prevented a system like this from being converted into the written standard for the whole of England, for the north of England was much more developed culturally and educationally at this earlier period.

4

The First English Standard

In its entry for 793 the *Anglo-Saxon Chronicle* records the first major Viking raid against the north-east coast of England, for in that year the Danes ravaged the monastery at Lindisfarne. In the following year Jarrow, Bede's former home, was sacked, and in 795 the monastery at Iona, on the other side of Britain, was plundered. These raids were to become more frequent as the ninth century progressed and of all the English kingdoms it was Northumbria that initially bore the brunt of the attacks, because it had a long eastern coastline and perhaps also because it had many rich monastic foundations on or near the coast which provided tempting targets to the raiders from over the sea. To start with these attacks were no more than raids to win booty; it was only in the second half of the ninth century that the Danes and the Norwegians began to think seriously of conquest and settlement. However, these assaults undermined the power of Northumbria and they confirmed the growing strength of Mercia, which had already in the eighth century become the most powerful kingdom in England. The boundaries of any kingdom are difficult to define at this period, and how far Mercia extended in the eighth and ninth centuries is uncertain. Probably it included much of what we now delineate as the West Midlands and extended eastwards to include counties like Leicestershire, Northamptonshire, Derbyshire and Nottingham-shire. However, its centre appears to have been more in the west than the east, although this may partly be explained by the destruction of many eastern towns and monasteries by the Vikings. It is from the west that most of what sources which can be described as Mercian come.

During the eighth and first half of the ninth century there was a thriving cultural life in Mercia, most of which was based on the Christian religion. The most important poet of this time is Cynewulf, four of whose poems with runic signatures survive. His work gives no precise clues as to place and date of composition, though an early ninth-century Mercian origin seems most likely.[1] Since his poems survive only in tenth-century West Saxon copies, it is not possible to determine what the language they were composed in was like as far as sounds and spellings are concerned. There is no early copy such as we have for 'Cædmon's Hymn'. What is significant about the poems is their level of sophistication metrically and lexically, and the fact that Cynewulf should have used runic symbols for his signature since this implies that he composed his poems to be read rather than heard. Hence a written tradition had developed in Mercia, or at least its western parts, by the ninth century.

Other manuscripts containing prose texts in English, which are also later in date but whose contents seem to have originated at this time, are extant. Of these the most important is the *Life of St Chad*, found in a manuscript copied in the twelfth century but retaining many of the original spellings and words from the ninth. This life, a translation into Old English of a now lost Latin version, drew on Bede and other sources. In the twelfth century the manuscript was in Worcester and possibly it was written there, which may be why the scribe could acquire texts composed in the West Midlands in the ninth century. Two points about the *Life of St Chad* are significant. The first is that it is a translation, which suggests the need to provide works in English was already felt before the time of Alfred and that this was done through translation. Translations of such saints' lives as those of Chad may have been considered as a suitable complement to the poetic works by Cynewulf which all deal with religious topics. The second is that the language of this text in so far as it can be seen through the twelfth-century copy is relatively standardised. This suggests that the concept of standardisation also pre-dates the time of Alfred. What is less clear, because it is so difficult to localise the few texts that survive, is how far this standardisation influenced other works. At present there does not seem to be sufficient evidence to indicate that this standardisation had extended beyond the borders of Mercia. We can trace a number of other texts which have a similar spelling to that found in the *Life of St Chad*, but we cannot localise them with any accuracy.[2] What does need to be emphasised is that when Alfred began his programme of translation and regeneration of learning, he was able to call on help from scholars who came from Mercia, and he was to some extent building upon and perhaps imitating what had happened there in the first half of the ninth century. What may have been lacking in Mercia – and which was supplied by Alfred – was the political will on behalf of the monarchy to provide the necessary language and writings in a standardised form throughout the country. This may have seemed less necessary in the first half of the ninth century, and so whatever extension of this West Mercian standardised language took place was achieved sporadically through monastic contacts rather than through political direction. It was the decision by the Viking invaders to aim for permanent conquest in the second half of the ninth century which was to change that.

The Vikings who attacked Britain followed two main routes. Some, mainly the Danish, came directly across the North Sea; others came round the top of Scotland via the Shetlands and the Orkneys to go down the west coast and were mainly from Norway. As we have already noted, Lindisfarne on the east coast was attacked in 793 and Iona on the west coast in 795. Since the Anglo-Saxons had not settled in the west and north of Britain, the attacks on the north-west coasts were largely conducted at the expense of the Celts who still occupied those regions. There is little evidence that the English had maintained fleets of any size after settling in Britain, for they were an agricultural people, and so were defenceless against raiders who came by sea. Although the West Saxon kingdom did suffer some attacks – one of the very earliest attacks recorded in the *Chronicle* for 787 records the death of a West Saxon reeve by a raiding party in Dorset – its location in the south-west of the country spared it at first from the worst incursions. The first major attack on the south of England occurred in 835 and was directed against Kent, and only gradually did these attacks spread further along the south coast. Most of these attacks took place in the summer and the Danes returned home each winter. Invasion with the purpose of conquest and settlement started with the landing of the Great Army (*micel here*) in East Anglia in 865. In the first years after this invasion the Danes ravaged East Anglia, Northumbria and East Mercia, occupying York and many other eastern settlements. They killed King Edmund of East Anglia, who was subsequently canonised, and then in 870 they turned their attention to Wessex. There were many engagements with first one side and then the other having the advantage. In 871 Æthelred, king of Wessex, was killed and was succeeded by his brother Alfred, who continued the struggle against the Vikings. Somewhat later the Danish army, which had been operating as a single force, split into two units, with one completing the conquest of Northumbria and settling there with its seat of government at York, and the other continuing the campaign in the south. Despite some initial reverses Alfred was able to hold his own against the Danes and ultimately in 878 the Danes agreed to leave Wessex alone; the southern army under its leader, Guthrum, settled in East Anglia. Alfred and Guthrum reached an agreement known as the Treaty of Wedmore, by which the Danes agreed to become Christian and the country was divided into two. Essentially the country was divided along a line drawn roughly from London to Chester. Anything south and west of that line belonged to Wessex; anything north and east to the Danes. That part of the country became known as the Danelaw. What is significant about this division is that the West Midlands, which had been part of the Mercian kingdom, now fell to the West Saxon monarchy.

The Danes, for it is simpler to refer to the Scandinavian settlers in the Danelaw as Danes since they undoubtedly formed the major element, spoke a variety of Germanic which belongs to the eastern group of North Germanic languages. There are a number of important phonological differences between the varieties of Old English and those of Old Norse which help us to understand how the latter may have influenced the former. However, it must be remembered that earlier varieties of the Old English dialects are not well attested in the extant records and so it is not always possible to tell whether a word reflects Old Norse influence or what had existed in some variety of Old English. The initial velars /k, g and sk/ were palatalised to /tʃ, j and ʃ/ in most varieties of Old English and these palatals then caused diphthongisation of following vowels in accordance with the conditions outlined in the last chapter. This diphthongisation is not found in all dialects and thus it remains possible that the palatalisation of these initial consonants did not take place in all Old English dialects. This palalisation is not a feature of North Germanic and so we normally expect a contrast between OE /tʃ, j, ʃ/ and ON /k, g, sk/. We saw in the previous chapter that ON *garðr* is cognate with OE *ʒeard*; other contrasts include OE *cyrice* and ON *kirkja* (cf. ModE *church* and Scots *kirk*), and OE *scyrte* and ON *skyrtr* (cf. ModE *shirt* and *skirt*). Although I have mentioned the differences between these palatals and velars in initial position only, the distinction applies to these sounds in any position, so that OE *dæʒ* (ModE *day*) corresponds to ON *dagr*. If a word starts with or contains <sk> in Modern English such as *skerry*, it is likely to come from Old Norse, though it may also come from Latin or even some other language like Dutch. If the present occurrence of the word is mainly northern, then it is more likely to be of Old Norse origin than anything else. Modern English /k/ may well be of Norse origin if it occurs in the neighbourhood of front vowels, but it is likely to be West Germanic in the neighbourhood of back vowels; thus *kirk* is of Norse, but *come* of West Germanic, origin.

Other consonant changes which were characteristic of Old Norse include the fall of initial /w/ when it occurs before the back vowels /u(:), o(:)/ or their mutated front vowels /y(:), ø(:)/, and before the liquids /r, l/. This can be seen in many place-names; the name of the Lancashire town *Ormskirk* consists of two Old Norse elements: the personal name *ormr* (equivalent to OE *worm, wyrm*) in the genitive case and *kirkja* (cf. OE *cyrice*). The personal name *Óþinn* in Old Norse corresponds to Old English *Woden*, and ON *Úlfr* as an element in a personal name corresponds to OE *Wulf*. Metathesis, whereby two sounds change their order, may have different outputs in Old English and Old Norse, though it is not always possible to ascertain whether a suspected Old Norse form could not have been generated spontaneously in English. ME *brennen* probably comes from ON *brenna* rather than from OE *biernan*, and the same applies to *brest*, which in Old English generally had the form *byrst*. As for vowels and diphthongs, there were a number of important phonological differences between North and West Germanic that help to distinguish Norse loans in Middle English. The Germanic diphthong *ai* was monophthongised in Old English to long *a*. In North Germanic this diphthong was retained and appeared in Old Norse as *ei* so that there is a distinction between ON *steinn* and OE *stān*. The Danish king who preceded Canute is often known in England as Sweyn, whose name comes from ON *sveinn* and has given us the now archaic word *swain*, though we still have *boatswain*. In Old English the equivalent word was *swān*. ModE *bait*, which dialectally can mean 'food', but generally means 'the food used to trap fish', comes from the ON *beitr*, which was cognate with OE *bāt*. It is related to *bītan* 'to bite'. The other Germanic diphthong *au*, which became OE *ēa*, was retained in Old Norse as *au*. Thus there is a correspondence between ON *lauss* and OE *lēas*. The former has given us *loose* and the latter *less*. Similarly what had originally been ON **þouh*, cognate with Old English *þēah*, was probably borrowed into English in the form **þouh*. This has

TABLE 4.1

	Old English	Old Norse
Singular		
nom	stān	steinn
acc	stān	stein
gen	stānes	steins
dat	stāne	steini
Plural		
nom	stānas	steinar
acc	stānas	steina
gen	stāna	steina
dat	stānum	steinum

given us ModE *though*, although after the Old Norse word was taken into English it developed further to *þó*. There are other differences in the phonological developments of the two languages, but sufficient examples have been listed to underline that although the two languages were similar, each may have sounded rather strange to the speakers of the other.

There were also differences in morphology and syntax. The plural of the third person of the personal pronoun had initial <þ> in all cases where Old English had <h>. The endings of many of the noun paradigms were different so that it may have been difficult for speakers in England exposed to the inflections of Old English and Old Norse to grasp precisely what inflection was intended. Thus the declension of the *a*-stem nouns in Old English and Old Norse showed the forms given in Table 4.1. The gap between the two is not great, but it may well have encouraged speakers to replace inflections with a different system. There were similar differences with the verbs. When all of these differing pronunciations are taken into account, communication may have at times been difficult. There were, of course, variations in lexis as well. The West Germanic word for 'take' appeared in Old English as *niman* and survives in ModG *nehmen*. In Modern English we have taken over the Scandinavian word, which occurs in Old Norse as *taka*. There are many other cases where we have adopted the Scandinavian word or even where we still use both the Old English and the

Scandinavian word. The important point to realise is that a group of speakers using a language which was close to, but not identical with, the varieties of English then spoken occupied almost half of what was the English-speaking part of Britain. It is difficult to work out how numerous the Scandinavian settlers were, though it is clear from place-name studies that many of the original Anglo-Saxon inhabitants continued to live and farm their lands. In any case the Scandinavian parts of Britain were gradually reconquered by the West Saxon kings and were thus brought back into the Anglo-Saxon fold. The effects of the Scandinavian settlements did not find expression for some time in written English for reasons which we shall consider in a moment, but one may assume that their influence on the spoken language, at least in areas of the Danelaw, was more immediate, though that is naturally difficult to prove.

Alfred's response to the Scandinavian settlements in the Danelaw took two forms, one political and the other educational. The political response took the form of repairing the defences of his own kingdom by building a succession of forts to protect its boundaries and gradually penetrating into the Danelaw and establishing new forts there to safeguard the West Saxon reconquest of what had originally been Mercian territory. The educational response took the form of initiating a series of translations and other writings which were distributed over those parts of the country that owed allegiance to the West Saxon king. The first of these responses may be considered briefly before the second is reviewed at greater length.

Most of Alfred's reign after 878 was occupied with strengthening the defences of his original kingdom and those parts of West Mercia that had come under his control. The last king of Mercia, Burgred, had fled overseas, so Alfred entrusted the defence of London to a Mercian, the ealdorman Æthelred, to whom he gave his daughter Æthelflæd in marriage. He thus secured the co-operation of those Mercians outside Danish control. He built a series of forts throughout his kingdom for he had to defend it not only against attack from the Danes settled in England but also against those who had not adopted a permanent home and who continued to make attacks by sea anywhere on the coasts of Wessex. Alfred probably died in 899 and was succeeded by his son, Edward the Elder, who was succeeded by three sons in turn, Athelstan, Edmund and Eadred. The West Saxon royal house thus enjoyed a period of sound leadership under the same family which lasted throughout the first half of the tenth century. Edward and his sister Æthelflæd, who was now a widow, gradually advanced against the Danes, incorporating small portions of territory at a time which they then protected by the construction of a fort. Since the Danes had dispersed and appear to have had no effective government, Edward and his sister were able to advance the boundaries of Wessex successfully. By 917 the eastern half of England on a line from Tamworth to the Wash had come under West Saxon control; by 920 the boundary had been pushed northwards to a line from Chester to the Humber; and by 927 Yorkshire and Durham had been incorporated in the West Saxon kingdom. Edward had died in 924, and it was his son Athelstan who made the final extension of the West Saxon kingdom. It was he who in 927 received the submission of the various kings north of Penrith; the boundary between what used to be Cumberland and Westmoreland marked the northern limits of his own kingdom. Lancashire and Westmoreland were effectively ceded to Wessex. Wessex supremacy was confirmed by the Battle of Brunanburh, the precise location of which remains uncertain, in 937. From this time the kings of Wessex could justifiably claim to be kings of England. For the first time since the departure of the Romans, England was once again a single political entity though now it was an Anglo-Saxon one. This new kingdom enjoyed peace for some time, and it was able to enhance its prosperity and to broaden its cultural horizons. In this latter respect it was able to build on the foundations established by Alfred.

The Viking incursions had destroyed many of the monasteries in the north and east of England, and it was in these monasteries in particular that learning had flourished in the eighth and early ninth centuries. That learning was based on a knowledge of Latin. It is, therefore, understandable that Bede should be a famous author who wrote in Latin, not in English. Other learned men of this pre-Viking age – such as Aldhelm, Alcuin and Boniface – all used Latin as their principal medium of written communication. England was one place in Western Europe where the torch of learning was kept alight – but that learning was Latinate. However, not all learning in England was in Latin at that time. 'Cædmon's Hymn' and the runic inscription with parts of *The Dream of the Rood* found on the Ruthwell cross show that poetry in English was composed on religious themes in Northumbria. In Mercia the poet

Cynewulf wrote a number of poems which are still extant in English, and translations such as the *Life of St Chad* are extant. It is possible that more was written in English than survives. Although texts written by English scholars in Latin could be read all over Europe and therefore stood a better chance of survival, texts written in any variety of English were probably for local consumption and so may easily have been lost when the monasteries were destroyed. It would, nevertheless, probably be true to claim that the pre-Viking Age was predominantly one of Latin learning, even if some composition in English occurred. The existence and knowledge of Latin would make it the primary language of written communication throughout the country, and this would in turn inhibit any development towards a standard form of English. Although it remains possible that the varieties of English in Northumbria and Mercia were developing a standardised form, they were not being used as a standard throughout the country.

Alfred's response to the situation created by the Viking settlements was to accept that learning had fallen into decay and had to be revived. He expresses his assessment of the position in his preface to the Alfredian translation of the *Cura Pastoralis*, that work written by Pope Gregory the Great outlining the duties and personal responsibilities of those who undertake the priesthood. The first thing to note is that this book is a translation. Alfred clearly had access to a Latin version, but felt that knowledge of Latin had fallen into such decay that it was better to provide the necessary information in English. This action would naturally increase the respect for English because it could be seen as an alternative to Latin, even if it was recognised that English was a second best. He complains in his preface that he does not think many could understand their service books in English, let alone in Latin, and so he has to start his educational activities at a lower level by producing texts in English rather than in Latin. It represents what we today might regard as a crash programme in education, in that one accepts a lower target of achievement in order that the programme may reach a wider range of people and provide the foundations for later learning at a higher level. It was better to have some education at a lower level than to aim for a higher level immediately and possibly achieve nothing. This book and Alfred's other translations do legitimise translation as an activity and thus help to promote the acceptance that it was possible to have even the most learned books in one's own language. These translations mark the beginning of that continuing influence of translation on the development of English.

In his preface Alfred indicates that he will send a copy of the translation to each bishopric so that it can remain there and be used by those in the diocese in the future. Indeed, it is claimed that one manuscript which is extant, Bodleian Library MS Hatton 20, is the copy that was sent to Bishop Wærferth of Worcester. It appears that, when Alfred or his helpers had finished the translation, a few copies were made in one scriptorium in Wessex and these were then sent to other scriptoria for further copies to be made. When the copies were ready and the prologue had been added, they were despatched to the twelve dioceses under West Saxon control. This is the first time that a programme of sending copies of the same English book to all those parts of England under Anglo-Saxon control was initiated. This naturally raises the question of what variety of English these copies were in. Two early manuscripts of this translation survive and both are written in what is recognisably the same dialect, even if they are not identical. That dialect is nowadays called early West Saxon. What is significant about this is that a form of written English was being disseminated throughout Anglo-Saxon England and thus assumed the status of a standard because it really had no rivals. It is unlikely that the scholars settled down to determine what might be the best variety of English to use; they simply adopted the variety which was current where they were working, and that was Wessex. The people Alfred mentions in his preface as his helpers in his educational reforms are not West Saxons. They included Plegmund, a Mercian who had been made Archbishop of Canterbury by Alfred; Asser, a Welshman who wrote a biography of Alfred in Latin and became Bishop of Sherborne; Grimbold, a Frank from the monastery of St Bertin at St Omer, who was sent to Alfred by the Archbishop of Rheims; and John, a continental Saxon, whom Alfred placed in charge of a monastic community made up largely of Gauls at Athelney. The presence of Plegmund reminds us that Mercia had had a higher level of learning than Wessex before the Viking invasions, and the presence of the others shows how Alfred had to look abroad for men of sufficient learning to help him in his programme. It is hardly surprising in view of these helpers that the language used in the translation of the *Cura Pastoralis* may not have been highly standardised. The importance of the translation is that it creates a feeling that a single variety of English can be used throughout the

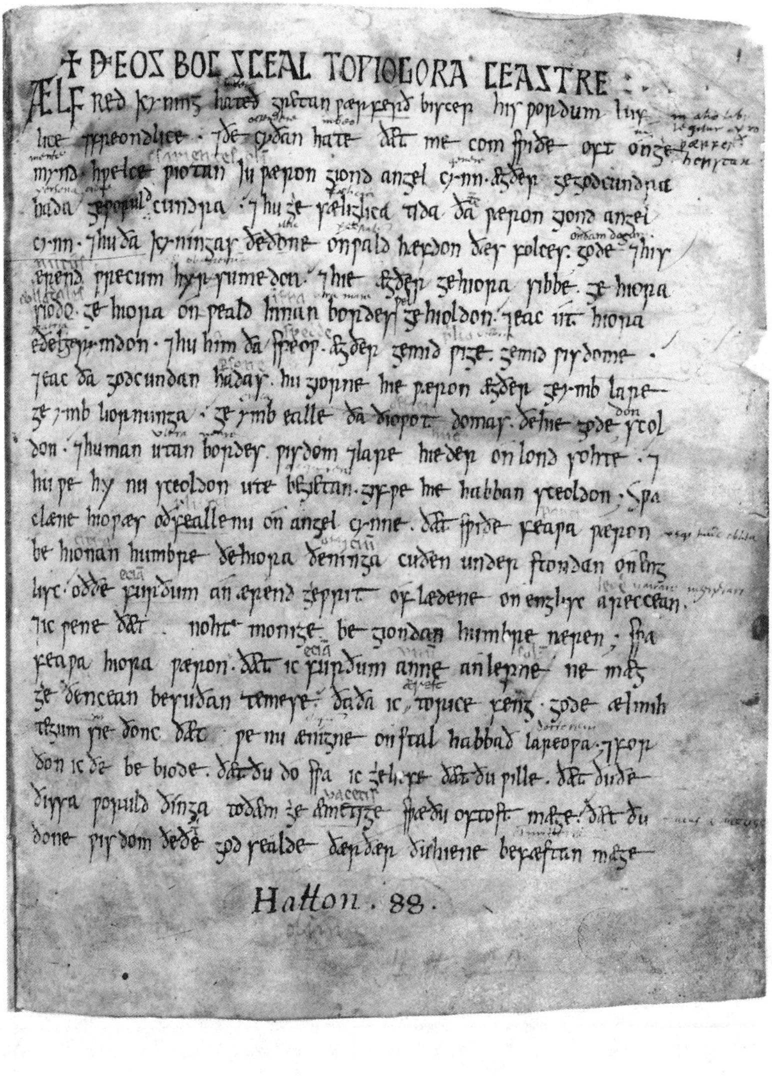
✝ ÐEOS BOC SCEAL TO WIOGORA CEASTRE
ÆLFRED kyning hateð gretan wærferð biscep his wordum luf
lice ⁊ freondlice ⁊ ðe cyðan hate ðæt me com swiðe oft onge
mynd hwelce wiotan iu wæron giond angel cynn ægðer ge godcundra
hada ge woruldcundra ⁊ hu gesæliglica tida ða wæron giond angel
cynn ⁊ hu ða kyningas ðe ðone onwald hæfdon ðæs folces gode ⁊ his
ærendwrecum hyrsumedon ⁊ hie ægðer ge hiora sibbe ge hiora
siodo ge hiora onweald innanbordes gehioldon ⁊ eac ut hiora
eðel gerymdon ⁊ hu him ða speow ægðer ge mid wige ge mid wisdome
⁊ eac ða godcundan hadas hu giorne hie wæron ægðer ge ymb lare
ge ymb liornunga ge ymb ealle ða ðiowotdomas ðe hie gode scol
don ⁊ hu man utanbordes wisdom ⁊ lare hieder on lond sohte ⁊
hu we hy nu sceoldon ute begietan gif we hie habban sceoldon. Swa
clæne hio wæs oðfeallenu on angel cynne ðæt swiðe feawa wæron
be hionan humbre ðe hiora ðeninga cuðen understondan on englisc
oððe furðum an ærendgewrit of lædene on englisc areccean.
⁊ ic wene ðætte noht monige begiondan humbre næren; swa
feawa hiora wæron ðæt ic furðum anne anlepne ne mæg
geðencean besuðan temese ða ða ic to rice feng. gode ælmih
tegum sie ðonc ðæt we nu ænigne onstal habbað lareowa. ⁊ for
ðon ic ðe bebiode. ðæt ðu do swa ic geliefe ðæt ðu wille. ðæt ðu ðe
ðissa woruldðinga to ðæm geæmetige swa ðu oftost mæge. ðæt ðu
ðone wisdom ðe ðe god sealde ðær ðær ðu hiene befæstan mæge
Hatton. 88.

FIGURE 4.1 The start of King Alfred's preface to the *Cura Pastoralis*, MS Hatton 20 fol. 1r (*The Bodleian Library*).

country and that this particular variety has the support of the monarch, for the rise of a standard needs political support if it is to take root. The dissemination of this translation marks the start of a standard English, even if the form it took was not at first highly standardised. This is not something which should surprise us, because clearly to Alfred what was important was to get copies in a similar language out to various bishoprics, not to create a highly standardised English; the time was not opportune for that.

In addition to his translation of the *Cura Pastoralis* Alfred also caused other translations to be made, though not all of these were made in Wessex and many may have been only tangentially connected with the king himself. Even for those translations with which Alfred was personally linked, he must have had considerable help from the band of scholars he had recruited. The next two translations were probably the history of the ancient world by Orosius and the *Historia ecclesiastica* by Bede, though the latter was probably made under Alfred's influence rather under his immediate sponsorship. This translation is in a Mercian-influenced variety of Old English rather than in early West Saxon.[3] This applies also to another translation, that of the *Dialogues* of Gregory the Great, which was made by Bishop Wærferth of Worcester. How far Alfred was involved with this particular translation is difficult to determine. The final books translated were *De consolatione philosophiae* by Boethius and the *Soliloquies* of St Augustine. There are two further texts sponsored by Alfred which were perhaps just as important as these translations. The first is a law code. In a short preface Alfred indicates that he has modelled his code on those that already existed in English, notably those of Ine of Wessex, Offa of Mercia and Æthelberht of Kent. A feature of this code is the retention of certain phrases and words from the Ine code and the establishment of certain formulas which remain in later law codes. The existence of these law codes strengthened the idea of a standard language since they would be used throughout the country and newer versions were based on the codes already in existence.[4] The second text sponsored by Alfred is the *Anglo-Saxon Chronicle*. The *Chronicle* is written as a series of annals and survives today in seven versions, each of which were kept at different institutions. Up to the annal for 891 the annals retain a broad similarity and all seem to have been copied from a version made under Alfred's sponsorship and perhaps at his command. These copies were distributed to various monastic foundations where

TABLE 4.2

Parker	Abingdon	Evesham	Peterborough
wiotan	witan	witan	witan
aldormon	ealdormann	ealdormann	ealdormann
hiene	hine	hine	hine
Bretwalum	Brytwealum (Britwealum)	Brytwealas	Britwealas
was	wæs	wæs	wæs
alle	ealle	ealle	ealle
mægas	magas	magas	magas

they were continued. From this point they diverge in what they relate since the various copies reflect local conditions and what material the writer could acquire. One of the versions, the Peterborough Chronicle, continues its annals into the twelfth century and provides an important record of how Standard English was adapted to meet new political conditions. For our immediate concern the significance of the *Chronicle* is that it is another text which was distributed from the centre to various monasteries, presumably in a series of copies produced at one or more scriptoria. The existence of the *Chronicle* naturally encouraged the use of English for historical purposes, and the English which was used would tend to imitate that found in the original version. It encouraged the use of the standard, even if it did not insist on it.

Some years ago Professor C. L. Wrenn noted that the Parker manuscript (Corpus Christi Cambridge MS 173) differed in many spellings from other early manuscripts of the *Anglo-Saxon Chronicle*.[5] He used manuscripts to represent copies at Abingdon, Evesham and Peterborough and quoted the examples given in Table 4.2. What is significant about these manuscripts is not so much the difference that Parker shows from the others as the standardisation in the other manuscripts. As they were copied in different places it shows that standardisation had progressed considerably so that the same text written by different scribes could be reproduced using many of the same spellings. Even if this process was only begun under Alfred, it was the first step in a move towards even more uniformity.

In the period following the earliest writings in Northumbrian, of which in the last chapter 'Cædmon's Hymn' stood as an example, various further developments in phonology took place. When /j/ or /ɣ/ followed a vowel there was a tendency for it to be vocalised and for the two vowels to coalesce into a diphthong. This happened with /j/ after front vowels and with /ɣ/ after back ones. Words like *dæʒ* and *weʒ* formed diphthongs /ai/ and /ei/, respectively, though the writing was not always altered to reflect this change. But spellings like *sæið* for *sæʒð* are found. The /ɣ/ changed into /u/ to form a new diphthong with back vowels, though this change is also poorly reflected in writing. This *w* was often either retained in writing or reintroduced by analogy. Thus there should not have been any words which ended with a *w* after a back vowel, but they are often found as in *snaw*. Many original diphthongs had -*u* as their second element in Germanic and this was retained at first in English, though gradually that element was lowered to *o*, which becomes the more common spelling after the earliest texts. Gmc *eu/iu* will appear in later Old English texts as *eo/io*, though the *io* itself often appears as *eo*. In West Saxon long and short *ie*, which had arisen from diphthongisation after palatals and front mutation underwent monophthongisation, for the symbol <y> is often used interchangeably with <ie>. Indeed, *ie* occurs in environments where one would expect *i* and this must have been caused by the falling together of *i/y/ie*. In the previous paragraph there was an example of *hiene* for *hine* in the Parker *Chronicle*, where *i* is the historically expected form. In West Saxon there was also a sound change known as palatal umlaut. When either *e* or the diphthongs *eo/io* occurred before /χ/ followed by *t, s* or *þ*, they became *i*. This change occurred when the consonant group causing the palatal umlaut was in the final position, but through analogy the resulting *i* is often found in parts of the paradigm where the group was not final. The place-name *Wight* exhibits this change, for it had originally had the form *Vect-* in Latin. We would expect this /χt/ to cause breaking of *e* to *eo* and this diphthong would be subject to smoothing and palatal umlaut to produce OE *Wiht*. OE *cniht* is cognate with ModG *knecht*. In the Anglian dialects, where smoothing of *eo/io* had occurred, the resulting *e* was still subject to this palatal umlaut, though it seems to have been more characteristic of West Saxon.

Although Alfred had initiated a period of educational and religious reform, it was only in the tenth century that a new spirit of monasticism developed. This was inspired partly by the Benedictine revival associated with the foundation of the monastery at Cluny in Burgundy. The reform movement spread from Cluny north and west and it soon had an impact on England. This development is particularly associated with Dunstan, who became archbishop of Canterbury in 959 when Edgar came to the throne. Dunstan had gone into exile as a result of a quarrel with King Eadwig and had spent his time at the monastery in Ghent, which had recently been reformed on the Cluniac pattern. Edgar, who succeeded in 959, also installed Oswald as bishop of Worcester and Æthelwold as bishop of Winchester. These three worked together with Edgar to reform the church in England, though naturally many others were also involved. New monasteries were established, old ones were reformed and a common observance among English monks was enforced. The variation in practice that had grown up in the older monasteries was abandoned as a result of a synod held at Winchester in 970 which saw the composition of new guidelines known as the *Regularis concordia* put together in an English version by Bishop Æthelwold. Æthelwold was also known for his liveliness in teaching Latin grammar through English. Winchester was thus at the centre of many developments taking place in monastic life. It was also significant for the further standardisation of the language.

Æthelwold's most famous pupil at Winchester was Ælfric. Born perhaps in the 950s, he spent many years at the school at Winchester and then in 987, three years after Æthelwold's death, went as a monk to Cernel, now Cerne Abbas, a new foundation established by a nobleman, Æthelmær. In 1005 Ælfric moved to the new monastery of Eynsham as its abbot. He is the author of many writings including various series of sermons and a Latin grammar in English. The grammar was intended for English people to learn Latin, and is the first known grammar to be written in English. More importantly perhaps, Ælfric had to develop a terminology for grammatical terms in English and he sought to explain Latin grammar through English. He was thus forced to think in contrastive terms, even if this was still rather elementary. He recognised that Latin and English do not have the same linguistic systems and that this made Latin difficult for English people to learn. He saw in grammar the key to understanding the meaning of what was written in books and he stressed its importance. His grammar contains prefaces in English and Latin. These are followed by the explanation of the basic terms in grammar, and the main part of the book is then devoted to a systematic presentation of the eight parts of speech. This discussion includes examples in Latin translated into English and examples in English. Although the grammar is based on the two standard Latin grammars by Donatus and Priscian, it is adapted for use in England and is by no means a slavish copy of those grammars. His grammar and his other works also raise the question of translation, and Ælfric states quite clearly that he will translate sense for sense rather than literally. He includes many translations from the Bible in his writings. His grammar is important for encouraging the study of language, particularly grammatical concepts, at the end of the tenth century. It was a work that was almost certainly, to judge from extant manuscripts, found in all important libraries in the eleventh century, and it was still being used and commented on in the twelfth century. Another work by Ælfric which was popular is his *Colloquy*, which was written in Latin (in one manuscript the Latin is glossed in English, though the gloss was probably not made by Ælfric himself). A dialogue between a teacher and his pupils, it is the only text where conversation about normal subjects is found in Old English, though the language is stylised. The writings of Ælfric and Æthelwold were written in what is now called the late West Saxon dialect, which I have understood to be Standard English, and the forms in their writings are standardised. Some of Ælfric's writings are particularly important in this respect, for he appears to have corrected his earlier writings to bring them into line with what he later accepted was better practice.[6] He came to accept that the correct case after prepositions like *ofer, on, onʒean, oð, þurh, wið* and *ymbe* was the accusative, though earlier he had used both dative and accusative. Equally he accepted in his later writings that in the verb 'to be' the third-person singular should be *bið* and not *is* and the plural should be *beon* and not *sindon*. He corrected previous examples of the no longer acceptable forms wherever he could. It is clear that Ælfric had a clear idea of what he considered 'correct'. We shall examine a passage in late West Saxon later in this chapter.

What is significant about the school at Winchester is its development of a standardised vocabulary which formed part of the standard language taught in establishments outside Winchester. A group of texts from the Winchester school dating from the end of the tenth and beginning of the eleventh century exhibit a remarkable degree of consistency in their choice of vocabulary within the framework of certain themes.[7] These words represent only a small number of the total Old English vocabulary, but what they reveal is a controlling hand dictating preferred options for texts coming from the school. These words are not technical words connected solely with religion; they embrace a wide range of subjects. There seems to be little doubt that the words represent a planned vocabulary. These are some of the words adopted through the school. A distinction between ʒelaðung 'congregation' and *cyrice* 'church, referring specifically to the buildings' is made. It prefers OE *leorningcniht* to translate Lat. *discipulus*, and *weofod* to translate Lat. *altar*. Indeed, it often prefers an Old English word to a Latin loan. It uses *cyðere* rather than OE *þrowere* or Lat. *martyr*. Even among more common words it often expresses a preference for one among several synonyms. *Sunu* is used instead of *bearn* and *cniht* instead of *cnapa*. Lat. *superbia* or *superbus* is translated by *modiʒ* or *modiʒness* rather than by *ofermod* or *oferhyʒd*, which had been found in earlier West Saxon and Anglian prose texts; even less is the new French loan *pryte* employed to translate this word.[8] There are other words which are found in the Winchester texts and which occur also in other texts from this period, but it is not always possible to tell whether their wider adoption was caused by the influence of the Winchester school. What we can see at Winchester is an interest in language, expressed in the teaching of grammar through English and in the construction of a standardised vocabulary and other forms of standardisation. This process may have had the general blessing of Edgar, but its impetus was mainly from the educational and religious instruction provided through the monasteries and dioceses. The reformers must have enjoyed the passive support of the king, even if he had little involvement in the details of the process of standardisation.

The make-up of this standardised vocabulary in this standardised language raises the question of the position of other languages within English in this period. Latin was the language of the church and hence of much educational attainment. The Scandinavian languages had been introduced into England with the Vikings and there were many Scandinavian settlers in England so that the native Anglo-Saxons must have been familiar with many words and concepts these settlers introduced. It is perhaps surprising that more words from both Latin and Old Norse are not found in Standard Old English, and one reason for this must be the existence of the standard itself which, as is often true of standards, tends to be inhospitable towards foreign words. Let us consider the position with regard to potential loans from Old Norse.

It is a feature of the history of the English language that there are a considerable number of Old Norse loans in the language, but the appearance of these loans in writing occurs mainly from the thirteenth century onwards and not from the pre-Conquest period which is when the Viking invasions and settlements occurred. The usual explanation for this is as follows.[9] Most Old English literature which has survived is written in the West Saxon dialect, and that dialect represents those areas of England which were least affected by the Scandinavian invasions and settlements. Hence Scandinavian influence in these areas cannot have been very significant. Even in those areas where the Danes had settled, they continued to live in their own communities and would only gradually have become absorbed among the Anglo-Saxon population. This implies that the new settlers were for a long time regarded as foreigners and no attempt was made to assimilate them. Consequently the introduction of Old Norse words into English was delayed in the Anglian dialects, and their southward drift would be even later than that. It is hardly surprising in this view that words of Scandinavian origin are not found in English in any numbers until the thirteenth century. However, it is far from certain that this explanation is the correct one.

The fact that there are few loan-words from Old Norse in Standard Old English, which is based on late West Saxon, has been taken to mean that no Old Norse words had penetrated the spoken language in the Wessex area, for if they had been found in the spoken language it is assumed that they would have been incorporated into the written language. In other words, since written late Old English contains few Old Norse words, it follows that few of these words were used by the Anglo-Saxons at this time. This cannot be proved and seems on the face of it unlikely. Naturally we cannot tell what spoken Old English was like, but we do know from modern examples that the written language, particularly when it is standardised, is rather intolerant of developments in the spoken language. Modern Standard English is in no way a true reflection of the spoken language, even though we have become much more tolerant in admitting speech into writing than was true of the past.[10] The history of English reflects a southward drift of northern dialect forms, and this is apparent even in the Old English period. The history of Anglo-Saxon England would indicate that this was likely to happen. The West Saxon monarchy gradually incorporated the Danelaw, and so the West Saxons came into contact with Norse words through these conquests. The uniting of the north and south of the country would promote the southward drift of northern forms.

The study of Old Norse loan-words and their English synonyms on an individual basis reveals that there was a greater concentration of these loans in the north and east of the country, but that does not mean that even in that part of the country all Anglo-Saxon words were replaced, or that in the south and west there were no Old Norse words.[11] Rynell has indicated that some Old Norse words 'were accepted down there [i.e. the south] at a surprisingly early stage, in some cases even at the expense of their native equivalents' (p. 63). It is 'surprising' only if we assume that such words should not occur in the South at that time. Among the words found at an early date are *lah* 'low', *la(h)e/lawe* 'law' and *Þur(e)sday/ Þor(e)sday* 'Thursday', which replaced their Anglo-Saxon equivalents throughout the country. Other Old Norse words which were very common, though not to the total exclusion of their Anglo-Saxon synonyms, were *wing* (OE *feðere*), *þrel(l)/þral(l)* (OE *þe(o)w(e)*) and *bað/boðe* (OE *beien/ba/bo*). What is significant about these words is that they are words of common everyday occurrence; they do not belong to a technical or specialised vocabulary. If such words are found throughout the country in the post-Conquest period and have ousted their Anglo-Saxon equivalents, it suggests that they were already present in the spoken language in the pre-Conquest period, even if they do not appear in written texts. An explanation for this is that the southern drift of these Old Norse words took place much earlier than we have previously supposed and that the written standard Old English is not a good guide to the penetration that these words achieved in speech. Standard languages are conservative and do not readily adopt new words which have entered the spoken variety. Words felt to be foreign, as the Old Norse words presumably were, would be even less likely to be adopted than other new words. Although late Old English develops its own restrictive practices as regards lexis, the general concept of a Standard Old English is one that the tenth-century reformers modelled on the West Saxon standard, which had existed in a less standardised form from the time of Alfred. The continuity of West Saxon as Standard Old English would have discouraged the adoption of new words from other varieties and even from other languages. The tenth-century reforms were a continuation of the policies introduced by Alfred, and it is not surprising that the attitude towards standardisation and conservatism should have become more rigid as the standard grew in importance.

It is interesting to note that English in the pre-Conquest period was not very hospitable to foreign loans in general. It has been estimated that the total number of foreign loan-words within the corpus of Old English amounts to no more than about 3 per cent of the total.[12] We have already noted in the previous chapter that there are very few loans from Celtic, even though the Anglo-Saxons and the Celts lived side by side for many years and the amount of cultural interchange was much greater than the level of Celtic words in English implies. Even Latin, which was the language of education and religion, provided fewer loans than might have been expected in view of its status and future attitudes towards it. The Germanic peoples had been in contact with the Romans as soon as the Roman conquest of Gaul led to a common boundary between the two people. Some Latin words were adopted by the Germanic people before the Anglo-Saxons arrived in England. Mostly these are military terms such as OE *burȝ* (Lat. *burgus*). In the period following the arrival of Christianity in England, most words from Latin are found in glossaries and almost certainly never got beyond the glosses into the written or, even less, the spoken language. From then onwards other Latin loans are found in English, but only a few became very common. Since Latin was a learned language and was known to most through religious and historical writings, it is hardly surprising that many words should have found their way into English written texts. In many cases a word is known only from one or two occurrences and was clearly a technical word of restricted use. Some became more common because they reflect aspects of religion which impinged on many people, and a number were made to seem English through their adoption of a native ending. Thus we find *sacerdhad* 'priesthood' and *sealmscop* 'psalmist', where the Lat. *psalma* has formed a compound with OE *scop* 'poet'. There are, nevertheless, a number of words which were probably common among a greater variety of people and they include words like *mæsse* 'mass', *non* 'the canonical hour, midday', *offrian* 'to offer' and *scol* 'school'. Most Latin loan-words were restricted in range and can have been known only to a limited number of people. It is natural that more words from Latin than from Old Norse are found in Old English because the former was a written and the latter only a spoken language in England, and there was considerable translation from Latin texts into English. But the general nature of Old English as a language made the assimilation of foreign words less acceptable, and the development of a standard merely reinforced that tendency.

Another feature of Old English that may have acted as a brake on the adoption of foreign words in written texts that have come down to us was alliteration, which was the primary feature of poetic composition and was common in various prose texts as well. This is because for many Old English poets and for some prose writers the basic linguistic unit was not the word, but the phrase. In Anglo-Saxon alliterative metre, at least two and preferably three words per line had to alliterate. In order to satisfy this demand various phrases and formulas were common. The modern expression *time and tide* in the proverb 'Time and tide wait for no man' is an illustration of what happened in Old English. In *time and tide* the two nouns mean the same thing, because redundancy, or perhaps it may be called variation, was another feature of alliterative composition. In this phrase *tide* in the meaning 'time' has survived in the language, though it is not otherwise used in this sense. Alliterative metre similarly encouraged the retention of many words which were almost certainly archaic and had dropped out of the spoken language. There is considerable dispute as to when the extant Old English poetry was composed, but it is generally believed that some poetry was composed orally even if the poetry which survives is largely later and was composed in writing. A poet like Cynewulf used some Latin sources for his poems and must have composed, as it were, in his study rather than in the market-place. But the metre and vocabulary that poets like him used are traditional and must have been handed down in some way from earlier poets. Because of this, archaic words and traditional phrases are found in that poetry, which made it less receptive to new words and to words of foreign origin, which were likely to be new. Inevitably some Latin words do occur in this poetry, but they are not numerous. Even where a poet has used a Latin source or has modelled how he expresses his ideas on classical precedent, as the *Beowulf* poet is said to have copied the Virgilian extended simile, the resulting expression in Old English is based on native words and elements.

English as a Germanic language inherited the features of lexical enlargement characteristic of its cognate languages and so did not have any urgent requirement to borrow words from other languages, and in this it resembles Modern German. The Proto-Indo-European language had a system of vowel alternation known as ablaut, and this had left many words with the same root which had undergone some form of variation. The difference between the forms of some verbs and nouns, such as *ceosan* 'to choose' and *cyre* 'choice' or *brecan* 'to break' and *bryce* 'a break, fragment', is explicable in part by this variation of vowels in Indo-European, though the vowels have also undergone further changes. In the case of these two pairs that further change is front mutation, which was also an important feature in the formation of words in English. Naturally the use of suffixes and prefixes was also significant. Additional verbs were frequently created by the addition of a prefix to an existing root. A prefix like *for-* could have the sense of 'loss, destruction' so that *forweorþan* meant 'to perish', while the root form *weorþan* meant 'to be, become'. The prefix *ʒe-* implied completion so that the verb *winnan* meant 'to fight', whereas *ʒewinnan* meant 'to be victorious (that is, complete by fighting)'. It was because of this sense that this prefix was often added to past participles and to many adjectives, often originally past participles in form. The past participle of *winnan* was *ʒewunnen*, and had the sense 'having completed the fighting' which was easily understood to mean 'having won'. The past participle *ʒecladod* can be used as an adjective meaning 'clothed'. There were a large number of these prefixes available for lexical enlargement, but many were beginning to lose their transparency by the eleventh century and there is some reason to believe that many prefixes were ceasing to be productive because of this. There were a large number of suffixes, some of which were used to form different parts of speech and others to form different genders. The ending *-ere* is an agent-noun suffix and can be attached to the stem of both strong and weak nouns. The verb *leornian*, formed from stem *leorn* and infinitive ending *-ian*, can form the agent-noun *leornere*, literally 'a learner' but used to mean 'a disciple'. This suffix is still operative today. The female agent-noun suffix was *-estre* and was found in words like *tæppestre* 'a barmaid, female innkeeper' (cf. ModE *tapster*). This ending survived through to the end of the fifteenth century. There were many other suffixes and these have survived rather better than the prefixes, though some are now fossilised. The Old English suffix *-hād* survives as ModE *-hood*, but is found only in certain forms like *priesthood*; it is no longer a living form.

The most important aspect of verbal creativity in Old English was compounding, within which one might also include possessive phrases consisting of genitive + noun. Compounding was encouraged by the alliterative metre and it probably occurred less in ordinary language. However, some compounds were calques of Latin, particularly of religious words. OE ʒōdspell is a calque of Latin (from Greek) *euvangelium* 'good story'. The common principle for forming compounds was that the modifying element should come before the main element or head. Thus *werʒild* means 'man payment' and the word is still used as a technical expression in Modern English discussions of Old English law. In this compound the head is 'payment' and the modifying element, which tells what kind of payment it is, is 'man'; it is 'a man's payment, payment for a man'. Other compounds follow the same pattern so that we find *morʒenleoht* 'dawn', literally 'morning light' and *sæʒenʒa* 'ship', literally 'a sea-traveller, something that travels on the sea'. It is easy to see from this that compound phrases consisting of a genitive with head-noun were easily formed, because in many instances there would be little to choose between such a phrase and a compound. For example, *ȳþlād* (formed of noun+noun, literally 'wave-path') is a compound, and *ȳða ʒewealc* (formed of genitive noun+noun, literally 'rolling of the waves') is a phrasal group with genitive, and both have the sense 'sea' in *Beowulf*. The variation and parallelism found in Old English alliterative poetry encouraged both types of lexical enlargement.

In syntactic matters Old English had already begun to show differences from its Germanic roots. In Germanic the order of sentence elements was usually SOV, but this was no longer the rule in Old English. It would perhaps be fair to say that the word order of sentence elements in Old English is mixed, though there was a tendency to put the verb in second position. This often led to a SVO order, except that when an adverbial came at the beginning of a sentence, this provided an AVSO order to give a clause like *þa cwæð sum oðer deofol* 'then said another devil'. Whereas in Germanic the object had tended to precede the verb, in Old English this was no longer the case, and more often than not the object followed the verb either directly or after the subject. This is by no means invariable, and there were two clausal arrangements where it was infrequent. The first is where the verb consisted of an auxiliary element and infinitive or participle. In this situation it was frequent to have the order S-aux-OV as in *we sceolon eac cristes acenned-*

nysse . . . wurðian 'we must also honour Christ's birth'. The second is in subordinate clauses where the verb was commonly placed at the end of the clause, as in *þæt hi heora lare ʒymon* 'that they attend to their instruction'. Because of these variations there is a dispute among scholars what the precise word-order patterns were in Old English. It was not a verb-second language and it did not retain the SOV order. It was in a transitional stage moving from SOV to SVO, though with a preference for AVSO. This applies to another feature of Germanic. In a noun group, Germanic preferred to place a noun-modifying element after the head, and this can still be found in Old English: the opening of Alfred's *Cura pastoralis* reads *Ælfred kyninʒ hateð gretan Wærferð biscep* 'King Alfred commands to send greetings to Bishop Wærferth'. But as we saw in a previous paragraph, compounds and genitival phrases put the modifying element before the head, and this pattern was found in most noun groups where the modifier was an adjective, as in *to soðre dædbote* 'to true repentance'. It is only with titles and other words which might be considered to stand in apposition that a postposed modifier is found regularly.

In Old English there were no articles as such, though during the period the demonstrative adjective *se, þæt, seo* and the numeral *an* 'one' began to develop some aspects of the definite and indefinite articles respectively. Typically nouns were without articles so that the poem *The Wanderer* opens *Oft him anhaʒa*, which can be translated as either 'Often a solitary man' or 'Often the solitary man'. When a part of the demonstrative *se* is used, it has a more emphatic sense of 'the one just mentioned', though that can readily pass over into the sense of a definite article, since the two are not far apart. Towards the end of the period many endings became blurred in pronunciation and this encouraged the development of prepositions to make the sense clear. This development had not progressed very far by the eleventh century.

In verbs Old English inherited three moods: indicative, subjunctive and imperative. The subjunctive differed from the indicative in having only one singular and one plural form. In the preterite the plural of the subjunctive in *-en* could easily become confused with the indicative form in *-on*. Gradually the weakening of unstressed vowels would make the subjunctive even less distinctive and there was a trend to blur the distinction between these two moods. The subjunctive is used to express hypothetical concepts and wishes as distinct from statements of fact. Already in this period there was a growth in the use of auxiliary forms to help to express various meanings that had been the preserve of the subjunctive. In part this was caused by translation from Latin, which also encouraged the use of auxiliary forms to express compound tenses such as the progressive, the perfect and the pluperfect. The future was expressed in Old English through the use of adverbs, but even here auxiliaries began to be employed. There are a number of verbs which can be described as 'pre-modals' in so far as they are the verbs that will become modal in Modern English. Most were preterite-present verbs, that is verbs which had formed a new present tense from an old preterite and had formed new preterites. These verbs had a limited range of inflectional forms and were always followed by an infinitive without *to*. They differ from their descendants in Modern English in that they could be used as lexical verbs as well as have an auxiliary function. The pre-modal verb *willan*, for example, had the sense 'to wish, to intend', but this sense passes easily into an expression of futurity as well as covering some of the meaning that was otherwise the province of the subjunctive. An expression like *Hi willað cuman* can mean 'They intend to come, they want to come', but it can easily pass over into the future 'They will come'. These verbs were not yet auxiliaries, but they had some of the force of auxiliaries.

The pre-modals were followed by an infinitive without *to*, for in this period there were two forms of the infinitive, one the base form and another with *to* and an inflectional ending *-ne*. The inflected infinitive was used to express purpose and necessity, and thus had some functions which would today more often be expressed through a clause with an initial conjunction like *that*. Indeed, in Old English there were far fewer subordinate clauses than in Modern English, because the style was much more paratactic than it is today. This means that there was more often a series of main clauses linked together by *and* than a mixture of main clauses with subordinate clauses dependent upon them. There were several pairs of conjunctions linking two main clauses together, rather like ModE *both . . . and*, and there were many adverbs which had a sentence-linking function, such as *þeah* and *hwæþere*. It may on occasions be difficult to tell whether a form like *þeah* is a sentence adverb or a conjunction, though often the word order will help, for as we have already seen a sentence adverb may have the verb immediately after it, whereas a conjunction will tend to have the verb at the end of the clause. Those authors who modelled their style on Latin, often because they were translating from that language, will often have more subordinate clauses than those works which were composed without such a model.

The verbs like *weorþan, wesan* and *habban* were increasingly used to form tenses with a progressive or completive aspect. Although *ic cyme* could mean both 'I come' and 'I am coming', the use of an auxiliary like *weorþan* with the present participle could create a more apparent progressive sense. Thus a clause like *þæt scip wæs ealne weʒ yrnende under seʒle* uses this progressive form with the verb *wæs* as an auxiliary and the present participle of *yrnan* to emphasise the continuous nature of the journey. The use of such auxiliary verbs with the past participle could create the perfect or even a pluperfect form of a verb. Thus *he hæfþ onfunden* has the sense 'he has found, discovered', and with the addition of *ær* the sense of the pluperfect 'he had discovered' could be formed. With the verb *cuman* the use of the present participle of a following verb, rather on the pattern of these auxiliaries, came to be more common than the more usual infinitive. Thus one might find both *com ʒanʒan* literally 'came to go, i.e. travelled' and *com fleoʒende* 'came flying, i.e. flew, travelled through the air.'

Other features which may be briefly mentioned are the relative frequency in Old English of impersonal and reflexive verbs. Impersonal verbs need no subject, which can be understood from the verb form, which is in the third person. An expression like *me þyncþ*, literally '(it) seems to me', meaning 'I think, imagine', needs no dummy subject like *hit*. As the period progressed, there was a trend towards introducing *hit* as subject, presumably because there was a growing sense that the subject should be expressed. The number of these verbs was significant in Old English, but they gradually declined as time went on. Reflexive verbs were formed by having the personal pronoun as the object of the verb, unlike some other Germanic languages which had a special pronoun to act as the reflexive. The reflexive form of a verb often had a different meaning from the simple form. Negative sentences were formed by adding negative particles not only to the verb, but also to other parts of speech in the sentence. There was no concept that to have two or more negatives within a clause created a positive. The use of auxiliary *do* was not found in forming negative sentences or even interrogatives at this time. This was something which lay in the future of the language.

It is time now to consider a passage from the Winchester school output since that is the closest we can come to the standard language of the time. I have chosen a passage from Ælfric's *Catholic Homilies, second series* found in Cambridge University Library (MS Gg.3.28).

We sædon eop & ȝyt secȝað. þæt þe ne maȝon ealle ðas race eop be endebyrdnysse secȝan. for ðan ðe seo boc is swiðe micel. & hire diȝele andȝyt is ofer ure mæðe to smeaȝenne; Ða ðry cyninȝas þa hæfdon lanȝsume spræce wið þone ȝedrehtan iob. & ȝewendan him ham syþþan; Ac god hí ȝespræc þa & cwæð þæt he him eallum ðrim gram wære. for ðan ðe hí swa rihtlice ætforan him ne spræcon. swa swa Iob his ðeȝen; Ȝod cwæð him to; Nimað eop nu seofon fearras. & seofon rammas. & farað eft onȝean to minum ðeowan Iobe. & ȝeoffriað þas lac for eop; Iob soðlice min ðeowa ȝebit for eop. & ic his ansyne underfo. þæt eop ne beo to dysiȝe ȝeteald. þæt ȝe swa rihtlice to me ne spræcon. swa swa min ðeowa Iob; Hit wæs ȝewunelic on ealdum daȝum. þæt man ȝode ðyllice lac offreode on cucan orfe. & ða acwealde. ac seo offrunȝ is nu unalyfedlic æfter cristes ðroþunge; Elifaz ða & baldað & sofár. ferdon onȝean to heora mæȝe iobe. & didon swa swa him ȝod bebead. & drihten underfenȝ IOBES ansyne. & heora synne ðurh his ðinȝrædene forȝeaf. (fol. 225v)

This passage represents the manuscript's punctuation and spelling system within the restraints of modern type; the various letter forms for a single character are not retained. The punctuation appears to be somewhat erratic, for there is little to indicate why particular marks occur where they do. The full stop and the semicolon appear to be used interchangeably. The marks also occur at regular intervals and thus appear to indicate pauses for breathing or for rhetorical effects rather than for clarification of the grammatical arrangement of the text. Capitals do seem to be used at the beginning of what could be sentences or an important clause, for *Nimað* starts the clause which reports what God said to the kings. However, capitals are used arbitrarily for names of people, and the descriptive names for God do not have capitals. There are some abbreviations and these are indicated by the ampersand and by italics as in 'þæt', where the last two letters are indicated through an abbreviation. The letter forms <ȝ> and <þ> are still used. The use of

<þ> is rather more restricted than <ð>, for it occurs in the abbreviated form for *þæt* and only infrequently elsewhere. Whereas it was usual in many texts to have *þ* initially and *ð* medially and finally, this does not apply to this text, where *ð* is both common and found in all positions. Even *þ* is found medially in such words as *syþþan*.

Syntactically the passage does not use many conjunctions; the most frequent are *for ðan ðe* and *þæt*. The latter is found particularly after verbs of saying. However, most sentences are relatively short and some exhibit parataxis as in 'Nimað . . . farað . . . ʒeoffriað'. But the sentence following these three clauses has no connecting link with what precedes, and so it is impossible to decide whether it is a statement of fact, 'Job is waiting for you', or whether it should have a causal relation with what precedes, 'because Job is waiting for you'. The word order is mainly SVO and where adverbs occur they are not usually placed in the first position so that we find SAVO rather than AVSO, as in 'Ða ðry cyninʒas þa hæfdon lanʒsume spræce'. There are examples of a different order in the main clause as in 'Ac god hí ʒespræc þa', where *Ac* is a co-ordinating conjunction and so does not need the verb immediately after it. So the order after the conjunction is SOVA. In the subordinate clause 'þæt ʒe swa rihtlice to me ne spræcon' the main verb has been put at the end so that it is separated from the subject by all the intervening matter. In another subordinate clause, 'swa swa him ʒod bebead', there is after the conjunction the order OSV, though in this case the object is in the dative case as an indirect object. Where an auxiliary occurs it is common for the infinitive or the past participle to go to the end of the clause, and this is common in subordinate clauses: 'maʒon . . . secʒan' and 'beo . . . ʒeteald'. There is an impersonal verb in the subjunctive in the subordinate clause 'þæt eop ne beo to dysiʒe ʒeteald'. The subjunctive expresses the hypothetical nature of the clause 'that it should not be accounted a folly in you'. There is no dummy subject used in this clause which has the literal sense 'that to you not [it] be as a foolishness counted'.

A feature of the vocabulary is its simplicity. There are no foreign loan-words apart from the personal names, which in this passage include, apart from the word *crist*, the names of Job and the three kings. In view of the nature of the passage, which retells the story of Job, the absence of Latin loans is particularly striking. There are no compounds composed of two nouns. There are a number of words which are constructed out of normal Old English morphological elements such as *endebyrdnysse* and *lanʒsume*. There are noun groups consisting of a modifier plus head or a noun in the genitive plus head, *ðyllice lac* and *cristes ðropunge*. There is little stylistic repetition or variation. This is a piece of plain Old English which was presumably meant to be readily understood by hearers and readers.

The phonology and morphology in the passage are fairly regular. The endings show little variation except that what are two preterites, *hæfdon* and *ʒewendan*, have different endings: the first has the standard *-on*, but the second has *-an* which was normally only the infinitive ending. This suggests that the vowels of unstressed syllables were becoming unclear in pronunciation so that they could be confused in writing. Even in a text which shows a high degree of standardisation, this blurring is given written expression. This is the only example of blurring in the passage, for otherwise the inflectional endings reflect a high degree of regularity. The form *cucan* must be the weak form of the adjective, where one would have expected the strong form. The weak form usually occurred after various demonstrative and personal adjectives. A feature of the text, as it was of late West Saxon, is the use of <y> where earlier texts might have had <ie> or <i>. Thus we find *ʒyt* and *unalyfedlic*. Generally this *y* occurs where an *ie* had arisen through diphthongisation or front mutation. Where the *i* is of West Germanic origin, it is usually spelt with <i> as in *his* or *-lic*. The *i* which arose through palatal umlaut from *e* or *eo/io* is <i> as in *riht*. When palatal /j/ from WGmc *g* follows a vowel, it is vocalised to /i/ and then forms a diphthong with the preceding vowel. This explains the preterite plural form *sædon*, where the long *æ* has developed in this way: *æʒ* → *æi* → *æ*. But where this palatal /j/ occurs within a paradigm it may be retained, as in *mæʒe*. The occurrence of *æ* is regular and there is no evidence of it moving to *e*, thus *-rædene*, *spræc* and *spræcon*. Before a nasal, *a* appears regularly as <a>, and there is no indication of <o>, thus *lanʒsume* and *ansyne*. The operation of breaking, diphthongisation after initial palatals and back mutation appears to have taken place normally so that we find *ealdum*, *-teald*, *-ʒeaf*, *onʒean* and *seofon*. The form *cucan* from an original *cwicu* shows a type of back mutation of *i* to *u*, followed by the loss of *w* in the group *wu*. The Modern English *quick* in the archaic phrase 'the quick and the dead' comes from a form where this back mutation did not take place and hence loss of *w* could not occur. All in all this text is remarkable for the high degree of regularity it exhibits, which is the result of the standardisation achieved by Æthelwold and his helpers. The passage is thus a good example of the standard language at the end of the tenth and beginning of the eleventh century. This standard was gradually to be undermined largely as a result of the Norman Conquest, and it is that development which will form the basis of the next chapter.

5

The Aftermath of the First Standard

This chapter deals with the gradual decline of the first English standard which led to its abandonment, a development that was completed at the latest by the middle of the thirteenth century. The standard associated with late West Saxon was strongest at the end of the tenth and beginning of the eleventh century. A new series of Danish invasions started at the end of the tenth century, the first of two major conquests that England was to suffer over the next hundred years. One of these incursions resulted in the defeat of the English levies under the ealdorman Byrhtnoth at Maldon in 991, which had in its turn motivated the composition of the poem *The Battle of Maldon*, an example of the late literary flowering of the heroic code. Æthelred the Unready, then King of England, followed a policy of appeasement and paid tribute to the Danish invaders. This took place while many important works by such people as Ælfric were being written and while other important cultural artefacts were being constructed. England was rich and self-confident enough to absorb these attacks. In the early eleventh century renewed Danish invasions began with the aim of incorporating England within a Scandinavian empire stretching across the North Sea; this was accomplished under the Danish king Canute in 1016. Although for Canute England was the prized part of that empire, he nevertheless had to spend time in its other parts, and in order to maintain control over England he divided the country up into four major areas, each governed by an earl. In effect Canute and his successors ruled as English kings and made every effort to continue the policies of the previous Anglo-Saxon monarchy. Canute, married to Emma of Normandy, was – on account of his political contacts and martial exploits – regarded by the English as a bulwark against other invaders. His rule was relatively peaceful and a recognition of the benefits which his reign brought to England can be seen in the drawing of Canute and Emma presenting a cross to the New Minster at Winchester. The church saw in Canute a protector and benefactor, who would strengthen its position and support its policies. Consequently there would have been no need to change the support for the standard which had grown up within the church's embrace and which was now firmly established. Danish as a language posed no threat to this standard because the number of those who spoke Danish in England was limited, and there is every reason to believe that the Danes assimilated quickly to Anglo-Saxon culture, including its language. When the Danish royal line in England came to an end, the throne reverted to the Anglo-Saxon royal house in the person of Edward the Confessor, who had spent twenty-five years in exile in France. Edward did not have the same authority or personal reputation as a warrior which Canute had enjoyed, and this allowed the governors of the four regions in England to assume greater personal power in the kingdom. Meanwhile the other parts of Canute's empire were being fought over by his relatives; in England the outcome of this struggle was watched with some trepidation since whoever emerged as the successful contender in Scandinavia could then turn his attention to regaining control of England. Nevertheless, Edward disbanded the fleet which had been held in readiness to prevent the landing of any invasion force from Denmark or Norway.

When Edward the Confessor died in 1066, Harold Godwinson was elected to the throne. He was the son of Earl Godwine of Wessex, one of the four major divisions instituted by Canute. This election was perfectly legal since the crown was elective in Anglo-Saxon England, although Harold was not a member of the royal family and had no royal blood. His qualities as leader and warrior made him an obvious candidate for the throne, and these qualities were quickly put to the test. Harold Hardrada, having established himself on the throne of Norway, considered himself the heir to Canute's empire and watched developments in England. The death of Edward and the succession of Harold prompted a rebellion in Northumbria against Tostig, who was both Harold Godwinson's brother and the earl there. Tostig was deposed as earl and went into exile. This provided a motive for Harold Hardrada to assert his claim to the English throne. He led an expeditionary force to England and when he arrived in the Humber he joined forces with Tostig; together they had some 300 ships. Harold Godwinson rushed north to defend his kingdom and on 25 September he attacked the combined Norwegian and rebel English force at Stamford Bridge on the River Derwent. Exploiting the surprise which his rapid journey provided, he succeeded in crushing the invading army. He then learned that William of Normandy had sailed with an invading force. William claimed that when Harold Godwinson had visited Normandy he had sworn an oath of allegiance to him and offered to support his claim to the English throne; this is the story depicted on the Bayeux Tapestry. Whatever the merits of this account, William used it as his reason for invading England. Harold hurried back south to defend his kingdom once again and engaged William near Hastings on 14 October. William was victorious and Harold himself was killed. William became King of England, though to assert his authority he had to engage in some ruthless suppression of revolts by the Anglo-Saxons. The Anglo-Saxon monarchy thus came to an end, but the effect of the Norman Conquest on England and its language is a matter of considerable debate.

To many people the Norman Conquest symbolises the submersion of the English language under the influx of French. This is partly because a large number of French loan-words entered English in the period 1066–1500. In fact the majority of these loans date from the latter half of that period and most of them are of a more technical and literary nature than contact between languages at a spoken level would promote. The view that French completely changed the nature of English after the Conquest is not sustainable, and we may now consider what non-linguistic factors may have affected the development of English. The number of people who accompanied William was relatively small and the Conquest did not lead to mass immigration of French speakers into England. It is not possible to give accurate figures for the population of England before the Conquest or for the number of French-speaking immigrants after it. It would be reasonable to suggest that the number of native French speakers can never have been greater than 10 per cent of the total population of England, and a more realistic estimate is probably less than 5 per cent. The greatest part of the population in England at this time consisted of the peasants who tilled the land. They probably formed anything between 85 and 90 per cent of all people here, and it is generally agreed that they would not have been affected by the introduction of French and would certainly have never learned that language. There must have been numerous villages which contained no French speakers or even anyone who could understand French. Some of the soldiers who fought with William may have been given some land to cultivate, though no doubt these would have quickly become assimilated with the local people through marriage. In the towns the situation would not have been too different, though here one might expect that there were more people with some exposure to French, even if they were not themselves French speakers. Naturally some of the larger towns had French garrisons attached to them, and the number of French speakers there would have been greater. The greatest concentration of French speakers was in the south and east of the country, as well as in sensitive border areas. There is no doubt that William followed a policy of bringing in French clergy to fill the important positions in the church. Thus archbishops, bishops and heads of important monastic foundations were likely to be Frenchmen, though the west of the country was the last to be affected by this development. Worcester, for example, retained its Anglo-Saxon bishop until the beginning of the twelfth century. The clergy who worked in the parishes were probably recruited locally from among the native population, though the influence of the bishops and other higher clergy introduced them to French ideas and attitudes, and thus to some extent they became subject to influences from France even if they did not become French speakers. Some at least would be able to read French, if they could read at all. Many monasteries had the numbers of their monks supplemented by French speakers, and many new foundations were not only attached to mother houses in France, but were also provided with recruits from abroad. Exposure to French among the clergy was thus considerable, though the number of native French speakers in the clergy at any one time cannot have been very large. Perhaps it amounted to no more than 2 per cent of the total clergy. As new foundations became established, they would recruit new members from the local population who would be English.

It is among the members of the ruling class that one finds the greatest number of native French speakers, but even here one may distinguish between the greatest nobles and members of the lesser gentry. Many of the Anglo-Saxon smaller landowners retained their lands, though they now owed allegiance to different noblemen. Undoubtedly the Norman conquerors gave land to their friends and family members, but there cannot have been large numbers of these who were provided with lands at the expense of the

Anglo-Saxons. The death of many warriors at Hastings and from subsequent revolts by the Anglo-Saxons created opportunities for the redistribution of lands from Anglo-Saxons to Normans without the need for any large-scale expropriation of lands from those who had not resisted William. Among the lesser gentry, many Anglo-Saxons must have retained their lands, though this was less true of the greater landowners. By the time of the Domesday survey (1086) the majority of the great landowners were native Frenchmen, though there were some Anglo-Saxons among them. Normans were installed in the most important positions in the state and provided the commanders of castles and other strategically important location. These noblemen had many estates in England as well as retaining those that they already possessed in France. Although he became King of England, William was still Duke of Normandy. There was no reason for these noblemen to relinquish their possessions there. It was only in 1204, when Normandy was lost to the kings of England, that it became difficult for them to retain their possessions on both sides of the Channel; they had to decide where their allegiance lay. Until then it was common enough for the nobility to marry into noble French families on the Continent, though members of the lesser gentry no doubt frequently married Anglo-Saxon women. It is thus possible to accept that the number of French speakers in England cannot have been very large as a total percentage of the whole population. The likelihood that England would become a French-speaking country was never very high. As the most important positions in church and state were filled by French speakers, the prestige attached to French was great. After the direct link between England and Normandy was broken in 1204, the French nobles in England would increasingly think of themselves as English, even if their command of the English language may not have been proficient. Certainly by the end of the twelfth century many nobles no longer knew French and had to learn it as a foreign language.[1] The court itself was almost certainly French speaking and there is no evidence that any king knew English before the middle of the thirteenth century, although it is said that William the Conqueror tried to learn it. The monarchy regularly looked for their wives abroad, and of all families in the country, theirs was the least English.

Although two languages, English and French, were spoken in England, it is doubtful whether it ever became a truly bilingual country. The majority of the population was monolingual and only used English. There were some among the clergy and the nobility who may have used only French, though they can never have been numerous and their numbers would have decreased fairly quickly. The nobles had to interact with their dependants who were predominately English speakers, and although at first this might have been accomplished through intermediaries, as nobles intermarried with English women and as their children were increasingly brought up in England, their familiarity with and command of English would have increased. The clergy needed to preach to the native population, and a knowledge of English was therefore imperative. In the monasteries this may not have been so pressing, although there can have been few houses where all the monks were French speakers; and the lay brothers would almost certainly have been recruited from the native English. Where French was important was in writing. French writing systems were introduced; French books were imported and reproduced; and the law and other documents were written in French or Latin. In so far as bilingualism existed it was only in writing, for to be educated involved not only learning Latin but also becoming familiar with French. To many, French was simply a written language in which manorial records, legal precedents and current law cases were composed. Many texts written in French were also imported into England, but at this time most of these were religious. Some literary texts in French were also brought to England, though what circulation they achieved is impossible to decide. The only extant manuscript of the poem, the *Chanson de Roland*, was copied in England.

Apart from Celtic, which was spoken by those on the periphery of the country, three languages were used in England: English and French in both speech and writing, and Latin as essentially only a written language. At the spoken level English consisted of numerous dialects, some of which were probably difficult for speakers of other dialects to understand. At the written level there was the surviving Old English standard, which was gradually becoming outdated because it no longer reflected the speech of most English people. It was also no longer the prestige written language, because French and Latin were now supported by the monarchy. It soon became antiquated and was not the primary language for official business. This, however, would take time to become evident. In many ways England was a more sophisticated and educated country than Normandy, and in matters like law it may well have been much more advanced. It would be a gradual development to replace English with French in legal business. English would eventually stop being used in the law and gradually would be abandoned for religious purposes. Where one might expect it to survive was in historical writings because of the continuations of the *Anglo-Saxon Chronicle*. Even here, writers soon turned to Latin even if they were sufficiently familiar with Old English to be able to read the *Chronicle* to use as a source. The two status languages were French and Latin – French because of its social prestige as the language of the upper classes, and Latin because it was the language of religion and education. By French one must understand Anglo-Norman. As a written language this had advantages over English and Latin. Over English it had the advantage that it was relatively uniform over the country as a whole, though it differed from the French which was used abroad. Over Latin it had the advantage that it was for some people a spoken language, and it had the benefit that it already contained a vocabulary which was used in everday life so that it could refer in charters and other legal documents to features of the countryside or of tenements without difficulty. In Latin words often had to be borrowed from Anglo-Norman or English to express these concepts. French was descended from Latin so that those who knew Latin would find French an easier language to get to grips with than English. It is hardly surprising that under these circumstances French gradually replaced English as the language of bureaucracy and officialdom. We should remember that Latin was widely known among educated people before the Conquest and yet English had been used as the language of the law and of many official documents, such as charters. It is understandable that the change in language should be from English to French rather than from English to Latin. It was only later that Latin would be employed increasingly for such documents.

It is also important to understand that the men who accompanied William included not only Normans, but also Frenchmen from other parts of France. They all spoke their own local variety of French, for at this time the standardisation of French based round the Île de France, which is today known as *francien*, had hardly begun. The French spoken in England was not the French that ultimately became accepted as the standard in the north of France and spread from there to the rest of the country; it is that variety which we know as Anglo-Norman. Many texts were written in this variety, and for most of this period it is Anglo-Norman which is the predominant form of French to be found in England. Inevitably texts written in other varieties of French would have reached England as well, but in both speech and writing most would use Anglo-Norman. At a later date there are occasional comments by various authors which suggest that the Continental French came to look down on the French spoken and written in England; it was a situation which resembles the amusement and contempt which some in France express for the French used today in Quebec. Chaucer, in his description of the Prioress in *The Canterbury Tales*, mentions that she spoke the French of Stratford-atte-Bowe rather than that of Paris. He was not necessarily poking fun at her, but merely signifying that her French was of the sort found in England. Because of the use of Anglo-Norman in England, French loan-words borrowed before the thirteenth century often show the phonological characteristics of Anglo-Norman rather than those of Central French. Two examples can illustrate this distinction, for in many cases English borrowed a word in both its Anglo-Norman and its Central French form, with the second being the later loan. Latin initial /k/ remained in Anglo-Norman as /k/, but in Central French it developed the palatal form /tʃ/. This difference led to the English pair *cattle* from Anglo-Norman and *chattel* from Central French. Similarly the initial /w/ of Old French was retained in Anglo-Norman, whereas in Central French it progressed through /gw/ to /g/. This has led to the following pairs in English from each of these respective dialects: *wage/gage*, *warrant/guarantee* and *wardrobe/garderobe* (where the latter is now used in descriptions of castles and suchlike buildings).

How quickly Anglo-Norman ceased to be a spoken language and to what extent its speakers wanted to speak with the Continental French pronunciation are not easy to decide. Certainly at the beginning of the thirteenth century Gerald of Wales (Giraldus Cambrensis) complains that a nephew of his had not bothered to learn Latin or French. Here Gerald explicitly links French with Latin as a language to be learned, and thus also as a language which a young man ought to learn if he is to get on in the world. French was clearly becoming a language of writing and culture, and was ceasing to be a language used only in its spoken form. Gerald also mentions that another young man, John Blund, had learned to speak excellent French even though he had never been out of England. He had apparently learned the language from his uncles who had been in France for many years, and he presumably spoke it with the approved Continental pronunciation. This is something which Gerald thinks worthy of note, presumably because this was not a general attainment. It showed what could be done. One might assume from this that Anglo-Norman as a spoken language had largely ceased to be common by the beginning of the thirteenth century except in special households like that of the royal family. About the middle of the thirteenth century various manuals for instruction in French start to appear, and these are designed to teach Englishmen how to speak and read French. For example, Walter of Bibbesworth wrote his *Tretiz de Langage* about 1250 for a noble lady, Dyonise de Mountechensi, so that she could teach her children French to enable them to run their estates competently when they were grown up. Dyonise did not know French herself and Walter provides English translations wherever necessary. His treatise covers the necessary vocabulary for estate management by arranging in different groups the words for such things as clothing, food, plants and agricultural implements. French was clearly the necessary language in this kind of management, and it was imperative for noblemen to have some understanding of the language if they were not to be cheated by their employees.

Because works written after the Conquest increasingly used French or Latin, there are few original writings in English. We shall consider some of them in a minute. What is characteristic of this period is the copying of many texts written before the Conquest so that the Old English standard was kept alive. When it became increasingly difficult for contemporaries to understand what the Old English meant, then glosses to difficult words were inserted in these copies. Sometimes translations were provided. Old English charters were often copied into later cartularies because they embodied the claims to lands which monasteries owned. The *Liber abbatiae* of Hyde Abbey from the fourteenth century contains several Old English charters, and each of these has both a Middle English and a Latin translation.[2] Although these translations are not always accurate, they show a generally competent understanding of the earlier language. We have seen in the previous chapter that manuscripts of texts like *The Life of St Chad* were copied in the twelfth century. Malcolm Godden in his edition of Ælfric's *Catholic Homilies, Second Series* includes a list of the manuscripts of these homilies; of those containing the second recension, many were written from the third quarter of the eleventh century onwards.[3] These are Cambridge University Library MS Ii.1.33 (second half twelfth century); Corpus Christi College MSS 302 (end eleventh/beginning twelfth century), 303 (beginning twelfth century) and 367 (twelfth century); Bodleian Library MS Bodley 343 (second half twelfth century); MS Hatton 113 and 114 (third quarter eleventh century); and British Library Cotton MSS Cleopatra B xiii (third quarter eleventh century); Faustina A ix (first half twelfth century), Faustina A x (twelfth century) and Vespasian D xiv (mid twelfth century). Although those from the third quarter of the eleventh century may have been written before the Conquest, overall this is an impressive number of copies of homilies from a single text which were copied in the century following the Conquest. The post-Conquest glosses which are often to be found in Old English manuscripts have been tabulated by Angus Cameron.[4] The thirteenth century alone provides examples of five manuscripts with glosses in English, seventeen with glosses in English and Latin, and six with glosses in Latin. One of the most famous of these glossators was the scribe of the cathedral monastery at Worcester known as the scribe with the 'tremulous hand'. During the first half of the thirteenth century he not only glossed many Old English manuscripts in English and Latin, but he also made a copy of Ælfric's *Grammar*. The copying and understanding of tenth-century texts formed an important activity in certain establishments and was probably a factor in keeping knowledge of Old English, especially the standard, alive.

The continuation of the writing system is attested to in various texts written during this early post-Conquest period. The most significant is probably the *Peterborough Chronicle*, the copy of the *Anglo-Saxon Chronicle* maintained at Peterborough until 1154. The first thing to recognise is that this historical document was continued in English until almost a century after the Conquest in a monastery which was important enough to have many French abbots and in a bishopric which had French bishops. It is also noteworthy that this English continuation, or a closely related text, was known to and used by historical authors writing in Latin. The so-called *Waverley Annals* are a Latin translation of a closely related text until the annal for 1121, and Henry of Huntingdon clearly used this or a similar text as a source for his *Historia Anglorum*. The existence of this text in English is therefore something which needs to be remarked; the *Chronicle* could have been, but was not, continued in Latin or abandoned altogether. The *Peterborough Chronicle* consists of three distinct parts. The first which contains entries up to 1121 are in the same hand and ink, and so they must have been copied from another text after 1121. The second consists of the entries from 1122 to 1131 and are written in the same hand that wrote the first part, but at different times. It is probable that these annals were written in six blocks and were presumably written at Peterborough shortly after the events they describe. The third part contains the rest of the *Chronicle* until 1154 written in a separate hand. From the local references and the identity of the scribal hands with other texts which come from Peterborough, there can be little doubt about its localisation.

Peterborough lies in the East Midlands in what was the Danelaw, and so it lies outside the original West Saxon dialect area. Those annals in the *Chronicle* from 1122 onwards were certainly composed and written down at Peterborough by a scribe resident there; it would be natural to expect them to represent the local variety of English unless the scribe had a different writing system he wished to emulate. The annals up to 1121 were copied from another text and these may be a faithful copy of the original which may have been written in a quite different locality. As the scribe of the annals from 1122 to 1131 had already copied the previous annals, he could naturally have been influenced by the writing system found in these early annals. This would not apply to the scribe who wrote the final part of the *Chronicle*. The language of the annals up to 1121 is essentially Standard Old English, though there are one or two interesting forms which suggest the influence of the standard on those for whom it did not represent their spoken language. In several words the scribe uses <y> where one might have expected <e>: *forðfyrde* 'died' for *forðferde*, and *wyrre* 'war' for the Anglo-Norman loan *werre*. In these examples we can assume that the scribe recognised that <y> was a characteristic feature of the standard written language, though his own variety of English may have had a different sound which did not reflect this spelling, possibly /e/ or /i/. Consequently when he came across a word with the vowel sound /e/, he may have been tempted to reproduce that sound as <y> through hypercorrection. This habit is one which can be found in texts before the Conquest with different spellings. In the Old English poem *The Phoenix*, found in the tenth-century poetic codex known as the Exeter Book, we find the spelling *weordum* for the dative plural of *word* with /o/ written as <eo>.

Since in the group *weor* as in a word like *weorþan* the *eo* is often reduced to *o*, the occurrence of <eo> in *weordum* is probably an example of hypercorrection. Similarly in Farman's Mercian glosses to certain parts of the *Rushworth Psalter*, which were made in the late tenth century, Kuhn has suggested that, although he was a Mercian writing in his own dialect, 'Farman's fluctuation between *e*- and *æ*- spellings probably resulted, like his use of both *e* and *æ* for the West Germanic short *a*, from imitation of West Saxon.'[5] In other words, the scribe Farman may have been influenced by the dominant West Saxon writing system to introduce spellings into his own writing which were a form of hypercorrection influenced by that standard, even though he was himself not supposedly using that system. To return to the copy of the early annals, we may also note that they contain no words which would be out of place in Standard Old English; rather the vocabulary is notable for the many archaic or obsolescent words they contain. These include several words with the prefix *un-* such as *unrad* 'hostile attack', *untid* 'unfortunate time' and *unræd* 'without counsel, advice'. There are far fewer words of this type in the continuations from 1122. Both the early and the later annals show many foreign loan-words, but they are more numerous in the later annals where we may assume the stranglehold of the standard was less dominant and so the language was more receptive to including new words. This applies to loans from Latin and French as well as to those from Old Norse. The later continuations show many Old Norse loans, which must have been in the spoken language for some time, but which only now were beginning to find their way into the written language. These include *brynige* 'mailshirts', *gersum* 'treasure', *huscarl* 'retainer', *tacan* 'to take' and *utlaga* 'outlaw'. As compared with the rest of the *Chronicle*, the text of the early annals is generally conservative and the copy may be accepted as faithful to the original text, which may well have been from a more southern scriptorium.

The annals from 1122 onwards more adequately represent the dialect of the East Midlands, though they are strongly influenced by the Old English Standard. Various forms indicate the East Midlands nature of the language. The front mutation of OE *ēa* is represented by <e> and not by West Saxon <y>, as in *aflemde* 'put to flight'. The same applies to the front mutation of the diphthong *ea* which arose through breaking. The unrounding of /y:/ to /i:/ is a feature of the east and north, whereas in the south and west the rounding is retained. In the *Chronicle* spellings like *dide* and *fir* for OE *dyde* and *fyr* represent this unrounding. In morphology the later annals exhibit in the third-person singular of the present indicative the absence of front mutation and syncope which were found in West Saxon. Thus the *Chronicle* has a form like *ofercumeð* (1123) where Standard Old English might have *ofercymð*. The plural of the present indicative often ends in *-en* and thus contrasts with the singular in *-eð*, whereas in West Saxon the plural form was still *-að*. In the nouns the later annals show a tendency to form the plural in *-s*, whereas in the south *-n* was becoming more regular. Several morphological endings show uncertainty as to what spelling to employ and this must reflect the gradual blurring of unstressed syllables; this blurring found expression in writing as the hold of the standard became less pronounced.

A short passage from the penultimate annal of the *Chronicle* (now MS Bodley Laud Misc. 636) follows to illustrate some of the changes in the writing system and language exhibited by this text. The passage describes events in 1153 just before the death of Stephen and the accession of Henry II, son of the Earl of Anjou.

te eorl of angæu pærd ded. & his sune henri toc to þe rice. & te cuen of france to dælde fra þa king. & scæ com to þe iunge eorl henri. & he toc hire to piue. & al peitou mid hire. Þa ferde he mid micel færd into engleland. & pan castles. & te king ferde agenes him mid micel mare ferd. & þoþþæthere fuhhten hi noht. oc ferden þe ærcebiscop & te pise men betpyx heom. & makede ðat sahte ðat te king sculde ben lauerd & king pile he liuede. & æfter his dæi pare henri king. & he helde him for fader. & he him for sune. & sib & sæhte sculde ben betpyx heom. & on al engleland. Þis & te othre foruuardes þet hi makeden. suoren to halden þe king & te eorl & te biscopes & te eorles & rice men alle. Þa pas þe eorl under fangen æt Wincestre & æt Lundene mid micel purtscipe. & alle diden him manred & suoren þe pais to halden. & hit pard sone suythe god pais. sua ðat neure pas herere.

(fol. 91r–v)

The punctuation uses a full stop, though sometimes it is possible that the manuscript has a punctus elevatus, which is difficult to read. This punctuation is based on clause units and is presumably rhetorical rather than grammatical. As for spelling the text still preserves the Old English wynn <ƿ>, although it also uses <uu>

and <u>. Where Old English had used <c> both for /k/ and /tʃ/, this text has introduced <k> as the symbol for /k/ before front vowels. This is because in French <c> represented /s/ and this symbol was to be adopted in English as in *mice* (OE *mys*). The use of <k> can be seen in *king*, but in other words, particularly medially, <c> is retained: *micel, rice*. OE <cu> has not yet been replaced by French <qu> so that *cuen* 'queen' still retains its Old English form. Equally <sc> as in *sculde* has not developed a spelling in <sh> or some variant of this spelling. In Old English <ʒ> was used for both /g/ and /j/. In this text these sounds are distinguished. A new letter, the Caroline *g*, was introduced from French to represent /g/, whereas palatal /j/ was represented usually by <i> as in *iunge* initially and *dæi* finally. <ʒ> was still used in other texts and did not die out for at least two hundred years or more. Later the symbol <y> which was used only as a vowel in Old English would be used to represent /j/. <þ> and <ð> are still found and are used indiscriminately for the voiced and voiceless sounds, but <th> is also found in such words as *othre, suythe*. The use of <th> is more common medially than initially, where <þ> and <ð> are used as well as <t> in the article. In this passage <ð> is used in abbreviations only. In some words <þ/ð> was replaced by <d> or <t>: *wærd, wurtscipe*. Old English had not distinguished between the voiced and voiceless fricatives which had been written <f, s, þ/ð>. The introduction of many voiced forms from French led to the discrimination between voiced and voiceless forms of /s/ and /z/ and of /f/ and /v/. The voiced /v/ which occurs between vowels medially and initially in some words was usually represented as <u> medially and <v> initially. No distinction continued to be made between the voiced and voiceless forms written indiscriminately as <þ/ð>. <ρ> (wynn) is no longer used regularly, for <u> or <uu> are employed. This letter was to fall out of the language in the thirteenth century. <æ> is still found, but it seems to be used interchangeably with *e* in such pairs as *færd/ferd* or with *a* in such pairs as *sahte/sæhte*. In some words like *æt* it seems to be the regular form, though the symbol was also to be lost from English shortly. There are no examples of <ea> in this passage, because most words which would have had this diphthong in the Old English Standard did not have it in this dialect at this time. Within this passage it is possible that the spelling *fuhhten*, with its double *h*, may be a kind of hypercorrection, for the double consonants of Old English were simplified to single consonants. Hence the use of double consonants in the standard spelling where a scribe heard only a single one may have encouraged him from time to time to insert two consonants where only one was required. Even with these changes in the spellings used by the scribe, the text still looks like Old English and considering it is written 150 years after the passage from Ælfric given in the previous chapter, it shows the power of the standard in maintaining a writing system. Where it differs from the Ælfric passage is in its greater variety of usage so that the uniformity in spelling found there is not replicated here.

The vocabulary of this passage is rather traditional, and although new words were introduced into the *Chronicle* from other languages, the basic vocabulary was unchanged. The older word *Angelcynn* has given way to the newer form *Engleland*, though this was also found in earlier texts. The meaning of *eorl* is that found in late Old English with the sense of 'a member of the noble aristocracy holding land from the king', rather than 'man, warrior' which it had had in earlier English. Typical Old English words like *sib* and *sahte*, which may be retained here because they constitute an alliterative phrase, exist with the new French word *pais*, although their precise meanings are not identical. The new word *castles* from French had been used once or twice before the Conquest, but was now becoming a regular replacement for OE *burh*, which was restricted to the sense 'town'. But OE *ferd* has not been replaced by the French loan *armee* yet. ON *taka* appears in the phrase *toc to wiue* 'married', which suggests that certain Old Norse words were well entrenched in the language. ON *taka* has replaced OE *niman* even in such everyday usages as this. There are compound words like *manred* 'allegiance' formed in the traditional Old English manner. The use of prefixes with verbs is still found in *todælde* 'separated', though it is followed by the preposition *fra* 'from', which may in this text be a borrowing from Old Norse.

The weakening of unstressed syllables has caused the falling together of many unstressed vowels under <e>. OE *sunu* is written here as *sune*. The nouns *eorles* and *foruuardes* represent OE -*as* as -*es*. This development may have been assisted by the borrowing from French of such words as *castles* which already had the plural in -*es*. In *Engleland* the old genitive plural in -*a* has given way to a spelling in -*e*. The ending of the plural of the preterite indicative is now -*en* rather than earlier -*on* and there is thus no difference between the indicative and the subjunctive. But the preterite-present verb has the form *sculde* rather than *sculden*, even though the subject *sib &*

sæhte is plural; as this subject is co-ordinate it might have been thought that a singular form of the verb was sufficient. The infinitive also has the ending -*en* as both the base and the inflected form, though the difference between these two is becoming blurred. In the singular of the preterite the occurrence of -*e* indicates the subjunctive, and therefore *ware* and *helde* have to be understood as implying 'should become' and 'should hold', for these were promises made by each side as to their future actions. But in *helde* the final <e> was added later, as though the scribe was becoming less certain as to the use of the subjunctive. This is hardly surprising since the subjunctive was gradually falling out of use to be replaced by quasi-modals. The subjunctives *ware* and *helde* are paralleled by *sculde ben*, where the *sculde* expresses the same hypothetical promise for the future.

The use of *þe/te* as the definite article is now well developed. Most nouns are introduced by this article where appropriate. However, there is no use of the indefinite article so that with *micel mare ferd* 'an even bigger army' and *suythe god pais* 'an excellent peace' the sense of the indefinite article must be understood. The pronouns show some interesting developments. The most important change among the personal pronouns is the use of *scæ* 'she' instead of *heo*, its earlier form. Probably the monophthongisation of the diphthong *eo* to *e* led to a confusion between the masculine and the feminine singular nominative. The original feminine accusative singular *hi/hy* could also be easily mistaken for the plural nominative and accusative *hi/hy*. The masculine singular *he* and the plural nominative *hi* are retained in this text, though the plural was shortly to undergo its own transformation. The origin of *she* is uncertain, but it is thought that it may be a phonological development of the initial consonant in OE *heo* through the stages [h] → [hj] → [ç] → [ʃ], but the matter is still a subject of dispute. In the other pronouns it looks as though the accusative and dative are being levelled so that there is now a common form for the two. In the clause *he helde him for fader* one might have expected the accusative *hine*. The dative singular and plural are distinguished, for the former is *him* and the latter *heom*, but as these were to grow more alike the plural was ultimately replaced by the Old Norse form.

The use of the genitive of nouns is less frequent, for it tends to be replaced by *of*. Thus in titles we find such forms as *eorl of angæu* and *cuen of france*. The older arrangement of putting the name first and the title second has given way to the modern order in *þe iunge eorl henri*. This phrase suggests that the distinction between weak and strong adjectives, with the former used after demonstratives and possessive adjectives, is still retained, though it was to become less easily maintained as final unstressed syllables disappeared. The original *-a* of the weak masculine nominative has given way to *-e*. The general decline of the inflections in the nouns has encouraged a SVO order as in *he toc hire to wiue*, though this is by no means regular yet. The sentence *Þis . . . suoren to halden þe king . . .* has the order OVS, and the verb is in the plural, whereas in earlier texts it might have been in the singular since the subject follows and is co-ordinate. After an initial adverbial the order is more often AVS(O) as in *Þa ferde he*. In subordinate finite and non-finite clauses the object can be placed before the verb form, as in *suoren þe pais to halden*. But where earlier texts might have put the infinitive after a quasi-modal at the end of a clause, this is not done in *sculde ben betwyx heom*; one might have anticipated *sculde betwyx heom ben*. The use of a verb without a subject is still found in *ðat neure was herere*; the use of a dummy subject was not yet required, though it will increasingly be found.

Changes were taking place in English phonology in this period, though naturally not all of them are attested in this brief passage. It is appropriate to review all these changes now whether they occur in this passage or not. At or before the time of the Conquest a series of changes to vowel and diphthong length occurred, though these changes are not found in the writing system till much later. Consonant groups consisting of a liquid or nasal, *r, l, n, m*, followed by a voiced sound of a similar nature, lengthened the preceding vowel or diphthong. The change did not take place if there were three consonants of which the first two constituted a lengthening group. Thus we would expect words like *land* and *helpan* to have long vowels, and *cild* would have a long vowel, but the plural *cildru* would not because of the group of three consonants (cf. ModE *child/children*). This change was not introduced in all dialects and the variation between different parts of the noun and verb paradigms led to many variations. Long vowels and diphthongs were shortened if they occurred before two consonants or in the antepenultimate syllable of a word. Thus a verb which in Old English had an infinitive *mētan* and a preterite *mētte* has given ModE *meet/met* even though our modern spelling no longer has the two consonants in the preterite. Similarly OE *hāliʒ* has given ModE

TABLE 5.1

	Short				Long			
	Front	Rounded	Back		Front	Rounded	Back	
High	i	y	u		i:	y:	u:	
High–mid	e		o	eo	e:		o:	ēo
Low–mid								
Low	æ		ɑ	æɑ	æ:		ɑ:	ǣɑ

holy and *holiday,* for the shortening of the long *o* in this case must have happened after the raising of /ɑ:/ to /ɔ:/.

At the time of the Conquest one may assume that the Old English vowel and diphthong system, at least as found in the standard variety, was something like that shown in Table 5.1. There were certain dialectal differences in that /æ:/ appeared in some dialects as /e:/. This difference depends on the varying origins of OE ǣ. If it arose through fronting of WGmc *ā*, it is known today as $æ^1$ and appears in the West Saxon and Anglian dialects as <æ>, but in Kentish as <e>. If it came from front mutation of *ā*, it is known as $æ^2$ and appears in West Saxon as <æ>, but in all non-West Saxon dialects as <e>. The first change in the vowel/diphthong system is the monophthongisation of the Old English diphthongs so that *æɑ(:)* became *æ(:)* and fell together with existing *æ(:)*. The diphthong *eo(:)* was monophthongised to a rounded *e* sound, which may sometimes be represented as <e/ee> or as <o/oo>. Forms of a verb like OE *cēosan* in Middle English may appear as *chose* or *chese*. The spellings <ea> and <eo> continued to be used in this period because of the influence of the standard, even though words such as OE *clǣne* and *beam* now had the same vowel sound. These diphthongal spellings were to be dropped in the thirteenth century, only to be reintroduced later in English. But even in a text like the *Peterborough Chronicle* a variety of different spellings can be found particularly in the later annals because of the confusion between the standard writing system and the pronunciation. Thus <ea> can be used in words like *Henri* to give *Heanri* (1131) and <æ> can be used in the French place name *Angæu* in the passage quoted above. The development was further complicated by the merger of short *æ* and *a* in a sound that was written as <a> and this led to the eventual disappearance of <æ> from English writing This meant that the two short low vowels and the diphthong had fallen together.

In the meantime some changes also affected the long low vowels. The front long vowel /æː/ was raised to /ɛː/ and the back vowel /ɑː/ was raised to /ɔː/ in the southern half of England. Although the *Chronicle* does have an occasional example of *mor* for OE *māra*, the passage quoted above has *mare* and *halden*, though in the latter case the /ɑ/ might not yet have been lengthened under changes discussed above. An important split between the north and south of the country was brought about through this raising of /ɑː/, since the north did not have this raising. The boundary for this raising is generally thought to be a line running roughly from the Wash to Chester in the Middle English period.

A series of changes – today the subject of considerable controversy and known under the overall label 'Open Syllable Lengthening' – altered the length and height of short vowels. Short vowels in open syllables, that is when final in a word or when the initial syllable of a bisyllabic word ends with a single consonant, for example ME *maken* (OE *macian*), were lengthened so that *maken* developed a long *a*. Vowels were also lowered by one level in height so that a high vowel became high mid and so on; naturally a low vowel could not be lowered further. Although many unstressed syllables had become levelled as schwa, usually written <e>, they were still pronounced and could cause this lengthening process to operate. The effects of this change are various throughout the different dialects, for it seems to have been more influential in the south than the north, and the results are far from uniform. It is obvious that in many noun and verb paradigms there would be variation between forms with a vowel in an open syllable and those without. The nominative of many nouns had no inflection, so a word like OE *stæf* had a genitive *stæfes*. The former is not in an open syllable, but the latter is and was subject to open syllable lengthening. The result was a difference in the paradigm between short and long vowels in the nominative and genitive respectively. In many cases analogy affected the result, but this example has produced two separate words in Modern English, *staff* and *stave*. If the results had been regular we would expect the following changes to have occurred: /i/ → /eː/, /e/ → /ɛː/, /ɑ/ → /æː/, /u/ → /oː/ and /o/ → /ɔː/. The development of /ɑ/ to a long front vowel meant that there was no replacement for the long vowel which had been lost by the raising of OE /ɑː/ to /ɔː/. The result was that

English now had four heights for long and short vowels, though with gaps where there was no short low-mid or long low-back vowel. There were also some centred vowels, which were usually the rounded forms of front vowels. These underwent developments in different dialects, but it may be simpler to postpone this change until the next chapter.

The discussion of vowels and consonants so far has not taken into account the development of the new diphthongs referred to in the last chapter formed when /j/ followed a front vowel and /ɣ/ a back one. This process appears to have been an ongoing one. With the front vowels the new diphthongs *ai* and *ei* were created, though during the course of this period they fell together under /ai/. With the back vowels and diphthongs, which all had a back vowel as the final element, a variety of different diphthongs were created. Words like *dragan* and *clawu* ended up with the diphthong /au/, usually written <aw>, as in *drawen* and *clawe*. The diphthong *ēo* and the vowel /iː/ formed the diphthongs *eu* and *iu* respectively, which then merged under *iu*. These were written *ew* or *iw*, as in *sniwen* 'to snow'. Words with either long *a* or long or short *o* formed the diphthong /ɔu/, though the resulting spelling takes a variety of forms in Middle and Modern English, though most show *ou* or *ow*. Thus we find ModE *plough, owe, sow, dough* from OE *ploʒa, āʒan, sāwan* and *dāh*. Where /j/ followed an /i/, and /ɣ/ followed a /u/, the resulting vocalisation of the consonants led to the formation of a long vowel as the two identical elements merged. OE *fuʒol* becomes ME *foul/fowl*, but the <ou/ow> spelling represents /uː/. Similarly OE *driʒe* gives ME *drige, drie*, which represents /iː/.

The major developments in the consonants took place with the fricatives, liquids and nasals. In Old English there was no distinction, as we have seen, between the voiced and voiceless fricatives, and the symbols <v> and <z> were rarely found in Old English texts. Although in voiced environments these consonants in Old English may well have been voiced, the voiced forms were in complementary distribution with the voiceless, and so there was no need to distinguish voice with a separate symbol in writing. Although there were the two symbols <þ> and <ð>, they were not used to distinguish voice. Generally voiceless consonants occurred initially and voiced ones medially in voiced environments. The introduction of many loan-words which had voiced forms initially and voiceless ones medially meant that the voiced and voiceless fricatives ceased to be in complementary distribution and became phonemicised. The letters <v> and <z> were introduced to assist the differentiation of what had become phonemes. In Modern English we now distinguish between *fan* and *van* and between *mace* and *maze*. This distinction arose in this post-Conquest period and the symbols to make this explicit were introduced at the same time. Generally, the symbols <u, v> did not have the distribution characteristic of today, since <v> was used at the beginning of words and <u> medially, giving such spellings as *vp* 'up' and *haue* 'have'. With the nasals we notice their blurring and then their loss when final, particularly in unstressed syllables. Many inflections had ended in *-n* or *-m* and these were lost, leaving either a schwa written as <e> or nothing at all. This helped to destroy the weak class of nouns and made the dative plural of many nouns endingless so that gradually they adopted the nominative ending *-es*. Nouns that ended in *-n* in Old English usually lost the ending and the nouns often turned from a bisyllable to a monosyllable; hence ModE *maid* as well as *maiden* from OE *mæȝden* (cf. ModG *mädchen*). Some nouns did retain their ending as ModE *heaven*. The liquids also show a tendency to loss, particularly in a final position or group. Old English words like *ælc* and *hwylc* lose their *l* and give ModE *each, which*.

Two works in this early post-Conquest period are notable for their attempts to create a regular writing system: the *Ormulum* and the *Ancrene Wisse*. I shall deal with the former first because it comes from the east of the country, whereas the latter may be treated as part of the general western dependence on Standard Old English. The opening of the preface of the *Ormulum* reads:

Þiss boc is nemmnedd Orrmulum Forrþi þatt Orrm itt wrohhte.

The name of the author, which he spells *Orrm*, from ON *ormr*, is cognate with OE *wyrm*. This name illustrates the penetration of Old Norse into English in that a man who was writing a homiletic sermon and who was probably a member of a religious house had a name of Old Norse form. More important is the spelling <rr>, for Orm chose to double all consonants after short vowels. This tells us that the system of long consonants, which were written as double consonants, found in Old English had disappeared, and hence there was no longer a distinction between short and long consonants. All consonants were short except where two consonants came together through the formation of a compound with two separate words as in ModE *penknife*. This must be so if Orm can use double consonants for purely orthographic purposes to indicate the length of vowels. In the line quoted above we can see that words like *þiss* and *itt* must have short *i*, whereas *boc* (ModE *book*) has long *o*. The important feature of Orm's poem is that he tried to devise a new, regular system of writing, and in this activity he may well have been influenced by his knowledge of the earlier standard. He also uses three different forms of *g* to indicate the different sounds that might otherwise be represented by this symbol. He invented a new symbol with a flat top to represent /g/, and used the Caroline <g> for /dʒ/ which in Old English writing systems had been written as <cʒ> as in a word like *ecʒ* (ModE *edge*). Old English <ʒ> he used for the palatal sound /j/. Throughout his poem he shows his concern for accuracy. For example, he starts representing OE *eo* as a diphthong, but gradually turns to representing it as a monophthong *e*. He then turned back to earlier parts of his poem and erased the *o* in as many of the previous examples of the diphthong as he could find. However, as his language is probably from the north-east Midlands and as his system seems to have had no followers, there is no need to examine it in detail here. Some aspects of his phonology and lexis are significant. He uses *ʒho* as the feminine nominative singular of the third person of the personal pronoun which had been *heo* in Old English. It is often thought that this might represent a stage on the transformation of OE *heo* to ModE *she*. The plural of the personal pronoun shows the penetration of the Old Norse forms which were later to be adopted in the language as a whole. The nominative is always *þeʒʒ*, the genitive is mostly *þeʒʒre* but sometimes it has a form with initial *h-*, and the oblique form, which includes the old accusative and dative cases, is usually *hemm*, though there are sporadic examples of *þeʒʒm*. The penetration of these Old Norse forms is advanced, but not yet complete. In lexis it is hardly surprising that the *Ormulum* should contain many Old Norse words, for it is one of the earliest texts in which such words make a strong showing. Some of the words are common like those we have seen in the *Peterborough Chronicle*, but others are less usual, such as *naþe* (ON *náþ* 'grace') and *usell* (ON *úsæll* 'wretched'). The *Ormulum* also contains many alliterative phrases which are modelled on Old Norse as well as phrasal verbs, consisting of the lexical verb and an adverbial preposition. The alliterative phrases include *flitenn & farenn* 'to travel, go', *sammtale & sahhte* 'agreement' and *unnbedenn & unnbonedd* 'without being requested'; and among the phrasal verbs there occur such forms as *farenn forþ* and *ȝedenn forþ* 'to travel, go'.

In the west of the country the standard survived longer and the continuity in the literature composed there provides some evidence of its hold on what was written in English. This can be seen in the material written in prose as well as in the occasional poem that still survives. Generally there was less poetry written in English, presumably because those who might be interested in poems, members of the higher classes, were not familiar with English or with the poetic tradition coming down from the Anglo-Saxon period. A poem like *The Owl and the Nightingale* is written in octosyllabic couplets and is thus a harbinger of things to come, as French style, metre and rhyme became adapted to English. This poem, possibly written by Nicholas of Guildford, was written in the south-east of the country at the start of the thirteenth century. More significant for our discussion of the language and the retention of older forms is a different poem, Laȝamon's *Brut*.[6] As its name implies, this is a story about the history of Britain starting with the eponymous founder Brutus and continuing through to the stories about Arthur. It was written by Laȝamon, a priest at Areley Kings on the banks of the Severn in Worcestershire, probably at the end of the twelfth century. This poem survives in two manuscripts from the thirteenth century, though their status remains disputed. Their relationship is important because one contains a language which is rather more archaic than the other, and it is not certain whether the author revised his text or some scribe who was interested in older stories and language deliberately made it more old-fashioned.[7] The poem itself is written in a modernised version of the alliterative metre used in Old English poetry. The changes in the language, especially the fall of inflections and the growth in the number of prepositions, had subtly altered the metrical framework in which the alliterative line was written. However, Laȝamon does try to imitate many features of the older poetry, particularly its vocabulary. The poem contains many 'epic formulas' which may consist of an alliterative pair filling a half-line or of a noun group. Examples include *mid sæhte and mid sibbe* 'in friendship and peace' and *aðelest alre kinge* 'noblest of all kings'. Even though some of these formulas may have no exact parallel in Old English poetry, they certainly maintain its style. Although this poem is based on the French text by a French poet Wace, who in turn based his poem on Geoffrey of Monmouth's *Historia regum Britanniae*, it is notable for the few

French loans it contains. Mostly such loans refer to religious life or to the social life of the upper classes. What is striking is the number of old words which otherwise appear to have been archaic or obsolescent at the time he was writing. These include words like *drihten* 'God', *fæie* 'doomed' and *ofslean* 'to kill', words that had been common in Old English. How Laȝamon got access to these words is uncertain. Some scholars have suggested that a popular poetry of the Old English type survived at an oral level, though this seems unlikely since the older poetry was both aristocratic and religious. It is more likely that knowledge of the poetry and the metre survived through manuscripts which were copied, and that there may have been a deliberate attempt on the part of some to foster its retention. The archaising tendencies apparent in one of the manuscripts suggests that something like this happened. As Areley Kings is right in the west of the country, and as the standard language and many aspects of Anglo-Saxon culture are known to have survived longest there, this would seem not unreasonable. What is significant and needs stressing is the archaising tendency found among certain scribes since this may be explained by the pull and prestige attached to the former Old English standard. Certainly as we shall now see, prose written in the Old English manner and preserving many features of the standard was composed in that part of the country long after the Conquest.

Reference was made earlier in this chapter to the scribe of the 'tremulous hand' who was working in the cathedral at Worcester at the end of the twelfth century. One of the works which survives in his hand is a dialogue between the body and soul in the so-called *Worcester Fragments*, a work that is often thought of as a poem but may be a prose text. It is not certain that the scribe composed this work, but he may have done. It is significant that its status as poem or prose text is uncertain, because in the alliterative style the differences between the two genres was not always clear-cut. Alliterative poetry did not have a set number of syllables per line, and one line was not linked to the preceding or following line by rhyme or similar devices. Prose writers like Ælfric could write sermons which can, with equal conviction, be printed as poetry or as prose. This relationship may have allowed many features of Old English poetry, such as elements of poetic vocabulary and elaborate formulas, to survive in prose so that from time to time writers could later use the prose as a springboard for the composition of alliterative poetry. This may help to explain why poets like Laȝamon could suddenly emerge from a background where alliterative poetry had not been written for some time. If this is so, it would suggest a continuation of some aspects of the Old English standard and of works written in it. Certainly in the *Worcester Fragments* dialogue between the body and soul we find archaic words like *balewen* 'griefs' and compounds like *feorþsiþ* 'death' and *ʒoldfæt* 'treasure chest'. This type of style was also to be found in the works which are associated with the *Ancrene Wisse*. These are prose writings which come from the West Midlands and are notable both for their style and for the writing system in which some of the texts were copied.

The *Ancrene Wisse* and its related prose texts are found in several manuscripts, of which two are particularly significant: Corpus Christi College Cambridge MS 402 [A] and Bodleian Library Oxford MS Bodley 34 [B]. The A and B are the modern abbreviations used to refer to these manuscripts which are important only in that their language is today known as the AB language.[8] Although these two manuscripts are written by different scribes, both are written in an English that maintains a relatively consistent phonology, grammar and orthography. The orthography is traditional and by this date somewhat old-fashioned. Although neither manuscript is a holograph, for both are copies, the traditional orthography is retained. The inconsistencies in language and spelling between the two manuscripts are minimal despite the fact that they are copies and include different texts – A contains *Ancrene Wisse*, and B several related texts such as *Hali Meiðhad*, a treatise on virginity. The representation of the phonology is relatively uniform, an occurrence that was unusual in Middle English and may reflect the influence of the former standard on the originator of this spelling system. It follows that the author or authors of these texts must have used the same dialect and spelling system as the two scribes, and that in turn means that in the West Midlands, for the texts have been associated with Wigmore Abbey in north Herefordshire near the Shropshire boundary, there was a group of people who had developed their own orthographic system to represent their dialect in a traditional manner using as a model the standard form of Old English which survived longest in this part of England. The two manuscripts date from the early thirteenth century, and the texts themselves were probably written towards the end of the twelfth century.

There was then a centre of literary culture centred on Wigmore which presumably included a school in which various scribes were trained to reproduce the spelling system devised by a master or director of the scriptorium. The dialect is certainly that of the West Midlands and has certain affinities with the language found in Laȝamon's *Brut*. The scriptorium must have been attached to a monastic house, which in turn had access to or itself contained a good library with texts in Latin and English. Some of the English texts must have been in the standard Old English associated with the Winchester school and frequently copied, as we have seen, in various centres such as Worcester in the post-Conquest period. Although Wigmore is in a remote spot, it was in contact with the literary developments occurring in the West Midlands; it was by no means an isolated outpost. Certain features of the spelling system in the AB language are notable. It has three symbols <e, ea, a> to represent the short vowels which had by this time ceased to exist as three separate phonemes in all dialects in English Since <ea> was used in this dialect to represent French /ɛ/ as in *deattes* 'debts' (usually spelt *dettes* in most dialects), it is likely that *ea* was a separate phoneme or had been when the spelling system was devised. In other words the spelling system had been devised when the dialect had three separate phonemes /e, ɑ, a/. This suggests that /a/ developed from OE /æ/ and that /e/ was still a separate phoneme and had not fallen together with it. This separation of phonemes was unusual in this period and the spelling system must reflect a state of the language which is considerably earlier than the dates of the surviving manuscripts. The spelling system did not, therefore, reflect the scribes' current pronunciation, but was an artifical orthography that had been learned in their school and had been imposed upon them. This is no different in principle from any standardised spelling which soon fails to represent contemporary pronunciation, but it is unusual at this time and reveals the influence of the older standard as the model which allowed this system to be developed and to survive as long as it did. Other older features of this orthographic system include the use of <h> to represent the palatal spirant /ɣ/ which, as we have seen, had in all dialects become vocalised by the thirteenth century. It also retains the symbols <c, sc, ȝ> which had been replaced in most writings by this time by the French-inspired spellings <ch, sch, g>. When these symbols represent palatals, they are followed in the AB language by *e* so that they are distinguished from the same symbols representing velar sounds. This was the system found in the Old English standard. It is likely that this spelling system was established in the third quarter of the twelfth century and survived at least fifty years in the area around Wigmore.[9] This spelling system was probably influenced by memories of the Old English standard although the system itself is considerably modified from that found in the pre-Conquest period. It has been updated, but its genesis appears to depend upon the earlier standard and is in many respects a development of it. But the influence of this orthographic system was limited; it hardly reached beyond an area stretching at the most into north Herefordshire and south Shropshire. From now on there were no further attempts to create a standard English writing system which could be said to look back to that found earlier, and Old English manuscripts ceased to be living texts which were copied and recopied. A period of uncertainty as to writing in English succeeded, and when a new standard started to arise it would be based on different premises and a different dialect area. This period of transition is what forms the subject of the next chapter.

6

Interregnum: Fragmentation and Regrouping

This chapter deals with the period from the demise of the influence of standard Old English, which occurred in the middle of the thirteenth century, until a new standard began to emerge under the influence of the Lancastrian monarchy at the beginning of the fifteenth. After 1066 three languages were available in England – French, Latin and English – and it is with the position of French and relations with France that we must first begin. Although the kings of England lost their Norman possessions in 1204, they did not cease to have any involvement in French affairs. In the last chapter we saw in the passage from *The Peterborough Chronicle* that in 1152 the French queen divorced the king and married Henry of Anjou, who became King of England in 1154. This French queen was Eleanor of Aquitaine who brought with her as dowry Aquitaine, made up of the two provinces Guyenne and Gascony. But the English presence in Aquitaine was quite different from that in Normandy. The conquerors of England had held lands in Normandy and thus had possessions on both sides of the Channel. Although the kings of England became dukes of Aquitaine, the number of English people who held lands there was small. If anything the tendency was the opposite: Gascons came to England and acquired lands here. Often this caused resentment and anti-French feeling among the English nobles. In 1328 Charles IV of France died without immediate heirs, and as Edward III of England was the son of Isabella of France, Charles's sister, he claimed the throne of France through her, though this claim was dismissed in France since the Salic law did not allow inheritance through the female line. Edward was not strong enough in 1328 to take steps to pursue his claim. The French for their part elected Philip of Valois king. When in 1338 Philip started to support the Scottish king against the English, Edward pressed his claim more strongly and decided to follow up his claim with force. This was the beginning of the Hundred Years War, which lasted until the middle of the fifteenth century when England lost all its possessions in France except Calais. The war fluctuated with now one and now the other side gaining the advantage. To start with England enjoyed some spectacular success, with victories at Crécy in 1346 and at Poitiers in 1356 and the capture of Calais in 1347. At the treaty of Bretigny in 1360 many of the gains in northern France were lost, though Aquitaine remained in English hands. English fortunes remained low until the fifteenth century when Henry V's victory in 1415 at Agincourt swung the war England's way. Since the fifteenth century saw the beginnings of a new standard language in England, the progress of the final stages of the Hundred Years War belongs to our next chapter. In addition to the dynastic quarrels that existed between France and England, the two countries were often involved in trade disputes involving wool. English wool was a major export commodity and was greatly prized on the Continent, particularly in the Low Countries where it was turned into finished fabrics. The export of wool provided the kings of England with an important part of their revenue and they wanted to control the trade. It was important for them to retain access to the markets in the Low Countries and this need often clashed with French interests. In addition the wine trade with Gascony was considerable at this time.

It was impossible, therefore, for France and England not to have conflicts over a variety of issues. France during this period was rapidly achieving some linguistic cohesion in the north where *francien* was assuming the status of the standard variety. In England Anglo-Norman remained the language of bureaucracy and estate management. In literary matters it was *francien* that was becoming more important not only in France, but also in England. Material written in England might well use Anglo-Norman, but texts imported from France, particularly literary and religious ones, were likely to be written in *francien*. French, therefore, had a twofold hold in England at this time: in one form as a language of bureaucracy, and in its other form as a language of literary excellence. With the increasing influence of French literature during the fourteenth century, the latter variety of French may seem the more important because it is so visible. One need only think of the introduction and translation of romances and fabliaux in England to understand this influence, for it is especially significant in the work of Geoffrey

Chaucer at the end of the fourteenth century. But one should not underestimate the influence of Anglo-Norman, even though its effects appear less obvious. All those involved in estate management or legal affairs would need to be familiar with it. Literary and cultured people like Chaucer may have been exposed to a high level of French literary influence, but the average person would be more familiar with Anglo-Norman, because that was a more pervasive factor in the daily lives of those who were outside the sphere of the court and the major nobles. The kings of England may still have been largely French-speaking and this would have affected the linguistic situation at court, but elsewhere English was the language of daily communication, and Anglo-Norman the language of administration.[1]

The influence of Latin should not be underestimated, but it was the language of learning and scholarship. At that level it was predominant. University education was dedicated to understanding the Latin language and its exploitation so that the various authors available in Latin texts, even if they had originally written in a different language, could be studied in depth. The twelfth-century renaissance led to the renewal of the study of Latin, and the foundation of many universities in the thirteenth century provided the culmination of that renewed interest. The advent of new religious and monastic orders such as the Cistercians and the Carthusians might seem to have added weight to the renewed use of Latin, but the affective theology of St Bernard of Clairvaux was transmitted more widely through translations made of his works and the impetus they gave to the composition of similar affective treatises in the vernacular languages. As a language of administration Latin had the disadvantage that it was not a spoken language, and consequently had to borrow many words from Anglo-Norman in England. Many documents in Latin appear to be often little more than Anglo-Norman texts in a Latin dress because so many of the words and formulas used in them have been taken over from the vernacular language. Often indeed the words used in Latin texts are simply carried over from Anglo-Norman or even English in the form in which they exist in the vernacular and are not even given a pseudo-Latin form through the addition of Latin inflections. The Latin of intellectual texts used at university was not the Latin of documents or records. The Latin of these texts is often what is referred to as Vulgar Latin, a version which has few of the forms and inflections of classical Latin. Furthermore, this Latin is often written in these texts in an abbreviated form because so much of what is found in these documents occurs in formulaic phrases and constructions which are repeated from one document to the next. The use of such abbreviations, usually involving the suppression of inflections, and the borrowing of so many words from the vernacular languages meant that these texts, although written officially in Latin, seemed to be much closer to the vernaculars than a difference in language would suggest to us today. When these texts are edited in modern versions, the abbreviations are often expanded to conform to standard Latin usage and thus they assume a different form from that which they have in the original document. Even at the spoken level, those who used Vulgar Latin with few inflections and a word order which resembled that found in Anglo-Norman and English could have made themselves understood. It may be that this Vulgar Latin acted as a kind of lingua franca for many travellers such as merchants and pilgrims and there are reports of some using it at this time.[2] The composite nature of the Latin in daily use is something which has been largely overlooked hitherto. It was only later that the Latin of Cicero was demanded of all users of the language, but when that happened Latin ceased to have any pretensions to be a spoken language. Even Anglo-Norman gradually lost its status as a spoken language during the fourteenth century. It remained an important language in documents and legal writings, but once it ceased to be used at the spoken level, its place would be taken by the French of France for those who wanted to speak French.

English begins to emerge once again as a possible language for documents in the thirteenth century.[3] In 1258 Henry III was obliged to accept the Provisions of Oxford, which were issued in both English and French. The English of this proclamation is essentially south-western and shows some influence of the former standard including, for example, the use of <æ>, which here makes its final appearance in English. That English was needed at the spoken level was clear enough and there are various references to the need for a document to be conveyed to some of the interested parties in spoken English and to preachers to use English in order to make their message clear to their audience. Yet written documents using English in writing are still rare. Gradually new literary writings in English become more frequent, though they occur in different parts of the country and in various dialects. Although literature in English becomes more common, it is often translated from French and the translators or adaptors, as they might more accurately be called, often feel called upon to justify their use of English. The author of *Cursor Mundi*, a northern poem on various biblical topics written about 1300, notes that he translated the work into English because that is the common language of England and that, although texts in French are freely available in England, few English people can read them.

> Þes ilk bok is es translate
> In to Inglis tong to rede
> For the loue of Inglis lede,
> Inglis lede of Ingland,
> For the commun at understand.
> Frankis rimes here I redd,
> Comunlik in ilk[a] sted,
> Mast es it wroght for frankis man:
> Quat is for him na frankis can?[4]

Hence the need to provide texts in English. Such justifications simply reflect the status that French had in relation to English; because French had the higher status, some reason for writing in English at all had to be offered. The increasing recognition that English was the language used in daily communication leads to further calls to make sure that French was used. We saw in the last chapter that Walter of Bibbesworth wrote a treatise for instruction in French, including an extensive glossary, and his example was followed in this period. In addition, we find regulations in monastic institutions and universities proscribing the use of English as the language of conversation, and in 1332 Parliament issued a decree instructing the gentry and important merchants in towns to teach their children French. For its part English had the great disdvantage that there was no longer a standard variety which all could use in writing, for any idea that all should use the same pronunciation was no more realisable then than it is now. This period, which I have called the interregnum – that time when one standard had disappeared and a new standard had not yet arisen – is characterised by the use of the written forms of different dialects because there was no standard written language. Many of the texts which survive from this time may have reflected local pronunciation when they were first written, but they often survive in copies in which the forms of one dialect have been overlaid by those from one or more other dialects. This variety of language in which many texts are written is often referred to today as a *Mischsprache*, a mixed language containing elements from different dialects which have come together through copying. Each *Mischsprache* is different from all others since the elements will never be identical. Consequently interpreting what the original language may have been like and how it was gradually changed through copying is a delicate matter calling for patience and expertise.[5]

In this period the growth in the number of texts in English and the absence of an English standard enable us to record a far greater number of dialects than was possible for the pre-Conquest period. The extant Anglo-Saxon documents allow us to outline only four major dialect areas: West Saxon, Kentish, Mercian and Northumbrian. After the Conquest this remains the basic division, but the individual dialects can often be broken down into subdivisions. The dialects in this period are now referred to by their geographical position in England rather than by the tribal or shire names used for the Old English varieties. The south-eastern dialect corresponds to Kentish in Old English and retains a distinctive character from the one to the other. As a dialect it is notable for one text, the *Ayenbite of Inwyt* (that is, the prick of conscience) written by Dan Michael of Northgate, which survives in what is probably the author's holograph. This text is extant in British Library MS Arundel 57 and was written at St Augustine's, Canterbury, where it was finished on 27 October 1340. The south-eastern dialect includes more than what is the modern county of Kent, for it embraces parts of Sussex and Surrey and had some influence on the speech of London. The south-western variety corresponds to the West Saxon dialect and stretches from Surrey westwards through the counties bordering the Channel, northwards towards a line from the Thames to the Severn. The number of texts in this dialect is limited, for the south-west Midlands variety is much more productive. The Midlands variety corresponds to the Mercian dialect, but in Middle English there is a crucial division between the eastern and western halves of this area. The former is, of course, an area of great Scandinavian settlement and contains many features of language that are significantly different from the latter, which is in its turn one of the most conservative dialects of Middle English. The division between the eastern and western areas follows the line of the Danelaw. These two halves of the Midlands dialect area can each be further subdivided into a northern and southern form to give four Midlands varieties: south-west, north-west, south-east and north-east. Many texts come from the Midlands area and the eastern variety increases in importance as this period continues. The northern variety corresponds to the Northumbrian dialect in Old English, though the number of texts from this area is relatively small and most are more from the east than the west. This area, which stretches northwards from Yorkshire and Lancashire, was ravaged by William the Conqueror to punish it for rebellion and was subject to frequent incursions from the Scots. A region that can hardly be traced dialectally in the Old English period is East Anglia, which with the growth of the wool trade became both populous and wealthy. There are many texts from this area, particularly from the end of the period, and it is of course the home of that famous family, the Pastons, whose letters survive in such abundance from the fifteenth century. In addition to these regional dialects we have also to take into account the position of London. Although kings in the medieval period were peripatetic, Westminster and London gradually took over from Winchester as the principal seat of the court. Henry II transferred the Exchequer to Westminster, and it was there that the Chancery was established and became one of the important parts of the administrative process. One branch of the Chancery was established in London at what is now Chancery Lane. Westminster became the permanent home of the bureaucracy which needed a settled residence instead of following the monarch on his perambulations through the country. At first the scribes imitated the standard they had used at Winchester and this is why the Provisions of Oxford still echo forms found in standard Old English. However, the documents in English issued from the Chancery remained relatively few until the end of the fourteenth century. London itself grew quickly in this period and drew in a large number of immigrants from counties to the north and east. At first immigration was strongest from East Anglia, but during the fourteenth century it appears that it was the East Midlands which became the major source of new settlers in London.[6] As a result of this immigration the dominant dialect in London changed from a more southern variety to become a Midlands type. This is a matter of some importance since it is from the London area that the next standard emerges.

There are, as might be expected, a number of dialect distinctions in this period and it is appropriate to highlight the most important of these, though it should be borne in mind that this is only a selection. As we saw in the last chapter in the south of the country, and that means the south-eastern, south-western and all Midlands varieties, OE *ā* was raised to /ɔ:/, whereas in the north it remained and tended to be fronted and raised. In the south this sound was written as <o> or <oo>, with the result that OE *ān* is the ancestor of ModE *one*, whereas in the north <a> continued, at least at first, to be the written representation. When short *a* occurs before a nasal it is written as <o> in some texts. This change is difficult to interpret because when this *a* occurs before a lengthening group such as *nd*, the sound should be lengthened and then it was available for the change of /ɑ: → ɔ:/. Consequently in some words the *o* may reflect lengthening. But even a word like OE *man* appears as *mon* in texts coming from the west Midlands dialects. In some texts the picture is very confused and we can find examples of the same words with both spellings <a> and <o>. In Old English short *æ* was written as <e> in the west Midlands and south-eastern dialects, and this <e> spelling was retained in these areas during this period in many texts so that *þæt* appeared as *þet*. In the rest of England it was represented as <a> as noted in the last chapter. OE /y(:)/, which was formed from the front mutation of /u(:)/, had already in the pre-Conqest period appeared as <e> in Kentish, where it had been lowered and unrounded, and that spelling continued to be used in the Middle English south-eastern dialect. In the rest of the country there is a division between east and west. Western dialects, which includes the south-western variety, maintained the rounding of this sound and wrote <u> after the French fashion, though it could also appear as <ui, uy>. In the east of the country /y(:)/ lost its rounding and fell together with /i(:)/ and was written <i>. The result was that <y> was in these areas treated as the same symbol as <i> and both could be used interchangeably so that OE *swiðe* could appear as ME *suithe* or *suythe*. A word like OE *hyll* could thus appear in Middle English as *hull*, *hill* or *hell* depending on where the text was written. The proximity of the south-eastern dialect to London has meant that some words with OE *y* such as *myriȝ* have <e> in Modern English, hence *merry*; whereas others may have the <u> spelling even if they have a south-eastern pronunciation, for example ModE *bury* from OE *byriȝean*. The Old English diphthongs <ea, eo> had become monophthongs as we saw in the last chapter. In the west they tended to keep some rounding, but in the east the rounding was lost. In the west OE *eo* was often written <o> to indicate the rounding, whereas in the east <e> was the more usual spelling, and we saw how Orm had changed the forms he had originally spelt with <eo> to <e>. In some western texts the diphthongal spellings are still found as an alternative way of indicating the retention of rounding. Some dialects, principally the south-eastern one but also to some extent the west Midlands types, replace the voiceless fricatives /s, f/ found initially in OE words with their voiced equivalents /z, v/. This gives forms like *zei* and *vox* as compared with *sai/say* and *fox*. Initial /v/ could in fact be represented by different symbols such as <w, u>. In northern and some eastern dialects, possibly under the influence of Old Norse, the velar consonants /g, k/ are retained, where southern and western dialects have palatals or affricates. We may thus find as contrast between *gyue* and *yeue* and between *kirk* and *chirche*. OE initial *hw-* is mostly represented as <wh> in Middle English, but in the north by <qu, q>, and in parts of East Anglia and the east Midlands by <w>.

Some changes in the language were more general rather than confined to one or two dialects. New diphthongs had already been formed in the immediate post-Conquest period, leading to the loss of /j, ɣ/ after vowels. These new diphthongs were supplemented by diphthongs introduced from Anglo-Norman. Some of the words borrowed from French merely reinforced the new diphthongs developed from internal English changes. Thus *faut* and *peutre* had diphthongs which fell in with the newly formed English *au* and *eu*. Foreign diphthongs were /oi, ui/ in such words as *destroie* 'destroy' and *puint* 'point'. Although English borrowed both diphthongs, they tended to merge under /ɔi/ and words with Anglo-Norman <ui> are often written <oi> in Middle English. The example above, *puint*, is usually written *point* in Middle English. This diphthong is unusual in English, coming as it does from a non-Germanic source, and has remained relatively unchanged in the restricted number of words in which it occurs. It seems to have been considered sufficiently outside the normal range of English diphthongs to have maintained its pronunciation. Among the consonants *w* often fell in the initial group *wl* and when it cam before *u* or *o*. OE *swā* and *sweord* now appear as *so* and *sword*, though the latter has dropped the /w/ in pronunciation. An alternative pronunciation of *quote* was /koːt/, as some spellings and puns show. The final [χ] in words like *dough, cough* disappears or in some dialects takes on the pronunciation /f/ as can still be heard in certain of these words in Modern English.

TABLE 6.1

		Vowels		
	Short		Long	
	Front	Back	Front	Back
High	i	u	i:	u:
Mid–high	e	o	e:	o:
Mid–low			ɛ:	ɔ:
Low	æ		æ:	

Diphthongs			
iu	ɛu	au	ɔu
ai	ɔi	ui	

The result of the changes outlined here and in the preceding chapter produced the vowel system shown in Table 6.1 towards the end of the current period in the east of the country; this is the type which was to produce the new standard. The consonants had shown much less change, as is true of the history of English in general.

The system of vowels and diphthongs listed in Table 6.1 refers to a single variety of English in this period, even if it was to become the dominant variety. There was, as already indicated, great variety in pronunciation throughout the country. This variation was recognised and increasingly commented on. A few examples may help to show typical reactions. In a trial held at York in 1364 the judge dismissed the evidence provided by a witness because his pronunciation varied during the evidence he gave among three varieties: Scots, northern English and southern English. The precise variants are not given in the Latin record of the trial, which involved a case of bigamy. What is significant is that, firstly, people recognised differences in pronunciation and, secondly, they assumed that anyone who varied his speech by using different pronunciations must be unreliable. It is not the fact of his using a pronunciation different from that of his listeners which caused this reaction; it is because he changed from one to another.[7] In another example from the late fourteenth century John Trevisa expanded Higden's comments on language when translating his *Poly-chronicon*. Higden, writing in 1327, had commented on the diversity of pronunciation in English compared with French, a lack of diversity which probably applied to Anglo-Norman, but not to mainland French. Trevisa, who made his translation in 1387, underlined that French in France was as diverse as English in England. He explained some of the diversity in England through the 'comyxtioun and mellynge firste wiþ Danes and afterward wiþ Normans, in meny þe contray longage is apayred, and som vseþ straunge wlafferynge, chiterynge, harrynge, and garrynge grisbayting'.[8] In a subsequent passage where Higden had noted that the language of the Northumbrians, especially in York, was difficult for Southerners to understand,[9] Trevisa elaborated on this by writing 'Al þe longage of þe Norþhumbres, and specialliche at 3ork, is so scharp, slitting, and frotynge and vnschape, þat we souþerne men may þat longage vnneþe vnderstonde' (p. 163). The important feature of what Trevisa added to Higden is the tone of condemnation through his use of words like *wlafferynge, harrynge, garrynge grisbayting, scharp* and *slitting* – all words which have a negative connotation, for they imply sounds which grate on the ear of the hearer. Where Higden had been reasonably objective, Trevisa is rather critical. Both Higden and Trevisa accept that the speech of the Midlands is the easiest for all English speakers to understand, partly because of its geographical position in the middle of the country which means that its pronunciation is not too different from all other varieties. Trevisa came from Cornwall, but in later life he spent time at Oxford and at Berkeley (Gloucestershire), and so he was a southerner with exposure to the Midlands dialects. The difference between north and south which has remained one of the dominant differences in speech till this day was evidently accepted then. There is also an implicit judgement by Trevisa that because northern speech is ugly, it is not something to be imitated.

This attitude towards northern speech may also be reflected in Chaucer's Reeve's Tale in his *Canterbury Tales*, probably written in the last decade of the fourteenth century. This example does not refer to differences in dialect; it contains examples of what are purported to be northern speech. The story concerns two Cambridge undergraduates who come from 'fer in the north', as the tale reports. They go on their college's behalf to a miller who has been cheating the college, and the story relates their experiences there. The following is an example of how they speak:

> 'Allas,' quod Iohn, 'Aleyn, for Cristes peyne
> Lay doun thy swerd and I wol myn alswa.

I is ful wight, god waat, as is a ra.
By god hert he sal nat scape vs bathe.
Why ne had thow pit the capil in the lathe?
Il-hail, by god. Alayn, thow is a fonne.'

$(1:4076–81)^{10}$

In this passage one can see differences in several levels of the language. Phonologically, OE *ā* is written with <a> or <aa>, for doubling of vowels was one of the methods increasingly adopted to indicate length: *alswa, waat, ra* 'also, wot (i.e. know), roe (deer)'. In *Il-hail* the second element is probably from the ON *heill* rather a northern form of OE *hal.* The spelling with initial <s> instead of <sc, sh> in *sal* 'shall' is typical of northern texts. The spelling *pit* for 'put' is a northernism, representing the unrounding of /y/ in some parts of the verb which were then extended analogically to others. Morphologically one can note different forms of the verb 'to be'. *I is* and *thow is* are used instead of *I be/am* and *thou art/beest.* The verb *had thow* does not have the inflectional ending *hadst thow* of southern texts. The genitive form of *god* in the phrase 'By god hert' has no *-es* inflection. Lexically there are certain forms borrowed from Old Norse. ON *bathe* was becoming widespread by this time, but had not completely ousted OE *beien.* *Il-hail* 'misfortune' is a compound, both of whose elements are from Old Norse, and both of which have since been adopted into the standard language. Another word probably from Old Norse, though its etymology is uncertain, is *fonne* 'a fool', for elsewhere in Middle English it occurs in texts which contain many Old Norse loans. The interesting features of the representation are that some later copyists of this poem increased the northern features of the students' language, whereas others often abandoned the northernisms altogether. This latter can happen when the poem as a whole is copied in a northern dialect area so that the whole poem assumes northern features. Scribes could clearly understand the differences in writing systems representing different dialects because they often had to 'translate' one dialect into another when they were copying a text. As soon as they realised what Chaucer was attempting they joined in by 'improving' his work. It is difficult to decide whether Chaucer intended the northern dialect to be regarded as a marker of low esteem. On the face of it this seems unlikely since the under-graduates are members of the student population which is likely to be of higher status than that represented by the miller and his family. But the tendency to look down on northern speech found already in Trevisa may indicate that the language is satirical rather than part of the general comedy. At all events, that Chaucer should represent a different dialect rather than simply refer to differences in speech indicates that he felt his own language and northern speech were sufficiently distinctive in their written forms for readers to understand the joke. Even if Chaucer himself did not look down on the northern forms of the language, his use of it here would help to create the climate in which southern language was considered acceptable and other linguistic usages such as represented by the forms of northern speech were both difficult and lacking in status. We may in this passage get the first intimations of the growth of the urban language associated with London and the consequent feeling that all provincial dialects were lacking in sophistication simply because they were not metropolitan. The growth of London and the prestige which the court brought to the variety used there would help to drive a wedge between it and other varieties, which would increasingly be described as *uplandish*, that is provincial. The growth of commerce led to the increasing difference between the very rich and the very poor, and this would in turn promote a lower-class speech which would be markedly different from the approved forms of language. The importance of London at this time is highlighted by the destruction exacted on it by the rebels in the Peasants' Revolt of 1381 and by the consternation it provoked that is referred to by chroniclers in the immediate future.

The difference in attitude represented by the dialects of north and south is worth pursuing because a feature of English, and particularly of English around this time, is that northern lexical and morphological items have been adopted in southern varieties and thus found their way into the standard language. In the passage quoted we have already noted that the Modern English words *both*, *ill* and *hail* are there offered as northernisms. The fall of final *-n* in the infinitive, as in *sal scape*, happened much earlier in the north than the south. Variation in verbal morphological endings also occurs earlier in the north and these forms then make their way southwards. In the students' language Chaucer represents the third person of the present indicative as ending in *-es*, whereas in his own dialect it ends in *-eth*. In the northern dialect the third-person plural of the personal pronouns adopts forms with initial *th-* much earlier than southern ones. The southern varieties have constantly adopted northern features into their speech, but that has not impeded the general disapproval of northern speech.

The absence of a standard dialect at this time and the growth in the number of records available in English have meant that the period has become the one most subject to study of the dialects and their differences. Two recent projects have tried to examine these differences in detail. The first, undertaken by Professor Kristensson and his colleagues in Lund University, was designed to match the survey of modern English dialects by Harold Orton and Eugen Dieth and published as the *Survey of English Dialects*. The modern project covered the whole country by conducting surveys of speakers in rural areas throughout England. The Lund project tries to match this completeness from the fourteenth century by using the material in the Lay Subsidy Rolls. These rolls contain the names of taxpayers listed under their village where they are assessed for tax. The names can be plotted exactly and with confidence on the map and complete coverage of the country is assured. The survey will provide details of the pronunciation throughout the country which can then be matched against the *Survey of English Dialects*. What it cannot do is provide details of morphology or syntax, since the information available is restricted to the names of the taxpayers, their bynames, if any, and the place-names where they lived. The material available covers the whole country but it is of a restricted nature. So far three volumes of this project covering the northern, and east and west Midlands counties have been published.[11]

A more ambitious project, initiated by Professor Angus McIntosh of Edinburgh University in the 1950s, soon involved many other researchers. McIntosh studied linguistic forms throughout the country by dividing it into blocks of about 50 square miles and identifying manuscripts which came from every single block. He realised that it would be difficult to achieve complete coverage of the country for any period prior to 1350 simply because so few manuscripts in English were written in Middle English before then. He therefore focused on the period 1350–1450. He then had microfilms made of as many manuscripts as possible, relying on documents and other administrative material as well as literary manuscripts, because the former can often be localised more easily than the latter. McIntosh recognised that manuscripts are often copies, one or more times removed, of an original. In the past these copies had been disregarded because they were considered corrupt, for they mixed the original dialect with the variety or varieties used by later scribes. But if one could peel back the layers of these various *Mischsprachen*, one could use these copies not only for information about the original language, but also for insights into the varieties which were later superimposed upon the original. The difficulty was trying to sort out where the manuscripts came from and how the different levels in each manuscript could be revealed. It was McIntosh's insight to realise that it was the writing system rather than the phonology as such which provided the key. Every scribe has his own writing system, so that, for example, in the representation of *th* one will only use <þ>, another will use both <þ> and <ð> , whereas a third may use <þ> and <th>, and so on. By judicious analysis of a number of features and spellings, it is possible to achieve individual scribal profiles based on their writing system. These systems are not arbitrary, for they show local influence and cultures. Starting with those manuscripts which can be localised from external factors, one can gradually build up a pattern across the country so that unlocalised manuscripts can be accommodated into the grid through a fit system. By examining the different aspects of the profile of the manuscript, one can deduce where it was most likely to come from. Once one had achieved coverage of the country as a whole, one could then analyse the manuscripts to provide details on the differences in dialect both regionally and chronologically. The results of this project have now been published in atlas form and have been the spur for further dialect study. Some of the details of the history of this period outlined in this chapter and the next spring from the work of this survey.[12]

The SVO word order which had developed in the immediate post-Conquest period was by now fully established as the regular, but not the only, word order. This word order is not necessarily followed when an adverbial is at the head of a sentence, for in these cases inversion of subject and verb is found, to give the order AVSO. When that happens concord between subject and verb is not rigidly adhered to, no matter whether the subject is co-ordinate or not. The presence of a co-ordinate subject in the order SVO may also allow the verb to have a singular rather than a plural form, a variation that is still found today. Otherwise, concord between subject and verb was becoming regular. The gradual disintegration of the inflectional system in nouns and adjectives meant that increasingly the only part of speech which distinguished between subject and object forms was the pronouns so that, for example, the subject form *I* contrasted with the oblique (that is object and pre-positional case) *me*. This meant that with impersonal verbs which had the oblique case of the noun or pronoun as the first element of the clause this initial element appears to conflict with the trend to have the subject first. A clause like *Him is lever* 'he prefers' (literally 'to him is preferable') no longer observes the preferred pattern of English order. Where a noun rather than a pronoun is used, *þe kinge is lever*, the fall in inflections allows the noun to be interpreted as a subject rather than as the oblique case. This put pressure on clauses with pronouns to conform to the new order and to change the oblique case to a subject or else to rewrite the clause by inserting the dummy subject *it*.

In the organisation of the noun group, grammatical gender has now largely disappeared, though it is still found in some texts such as the *Ayenbite of Inwyt* as late as 1340. Even in Old English, grammatical gender had not been consistent, especially where a pronoun had been separated from the noun it referred to. By now the case of pronouns referring backwards or forwards to a noun was dictated by natural gender. Within the noun group itself, the order was similar to that found in Modern English, though there were still many small differences. The basic order of pre-determiner, determiner, pre-modifier, head and post-modifier was well established. The use of adjectives in the post-modifier position, as is still possible in some poetic and fossilised expressions, still occurs; often examples of this order were based on French models as Chaucer's *places delitables* (*Canterbury Tales* 6:191) where agreement of the adjective with the noun is an indication of French influence. Adjectival groups do occur in the post-modifier position, particularly those introduced by *al* or *so*. Naturally heavy adjectival phrases, then as now, occupy the post-modifier slot. It is possible when the adjectival phrase consists of an adjective and a prepositional phrase, such as *acceptable to God*, to put the adjective before the noun and the prepositional phrase after it to give *acceptable offering to God*. During this period the adjectives lost all inflections except for final *-e* other than in the comparative and superlative. This final *-e* could indicate two features: firstly, definiteness which was a hangover from the old weak form of the adjective and was usually found after the definite article or a demonstrative adjective, and, secondly, the plural. These distinctions were less observed in prose than in poetry, where metre may have been a factor in its retention. Adjectives which were used as nouns could in the plural assume the plural form in *-es*, an indication of the analogical process which was extending the range of this plural.

The distinction between determiners and pre-determiners is less rigid than in Modern English, for at this time it is possible to have more than one of what today would be considered a determiner in front of a noun. Expressions like *each a, many a* as well as *some the* and *any the* are frequent before nouns so that the precise definition of what is a determiner and what a pre-determiner is uncertain. Certainly the concept that determiners formed a mutually exclusive group was not operative. As we have seen adjectives generally occupy the pre-modifier slot. We notice in this period the growth in the number of intensifiers which refer to these adjectives. Chaucer has a large number of examples such as *ful, well, faire, ferly* and *al.* Intensifiers are a feature of a more colloquial style and the growth in certain genres, such as the fabliau, and the development of satire and irony may have encouraged the use of these words in written texts. When several adjectives occur together, it is possible to put them all before the noun or to separate them by having one before and a second after the noun, as in *a good man and wise.* The development of *one* as a propword is still a matter of debate, but it was in this period that it developed. This term refers to the use of *one* after an adjective in phrases like *the bravest one, the best one.* The earliest examples date from the thirteenth century. They seem to have developed first with reference to humans and may have been influenced by the use of *one* as an indefinite pronoun.

The occurrence of the inflected genitive in the pre-modifier position is reduced in this period. Examples of the uninflected genitive continue to be found, though they come increasingly to seem like the first element of a compound or the functional shift of a noun to an adjective. Modern English *mother tongue* goes back to an uninflected genitive, but would be understood by speakers today as a compound. The fall of morphological endings encouraged the growth of functional shift whereby one part of speech could be used as a different part of speech, though this phenomenon will be discussed further under the development of the vocabulary. The genitive with *of* increases in frequency. When it occurs in a group which is used as a genitive, the group may be split, with one element before the head and the genitive phrase after it. What in Modern English would be *The Wife of Bath's Tale* with the *Wife of Bath's* as a group genitive is often found at this time in the form *The Wives Tale of Bath.* The development of the genitive without a head, which is so characteristic of Modern English, also dates from this period. The earliest examples involve the omission of the word *church*, and such examples are still common today: *I am going to St Paul's*, where *church* is understood. It was also at this time that examples of double genitive arose to give phrases like *that book of his* where *his* follows the genitive marker *of* although it is already a genitive form. Chaucer has *an old felawe of youres* in The Pardoner's Tale (672).

In morphology the nouns lost most of their endings. In the south the plural was often in *-en*, but the northern form in *-es* gradually became more common. In London English at the end of the fourteenth century *-(e)s* (*-is/ys*) was the regular plural form, though some survivals of older plurals were still found. Although most plurals in *-e* had disappeared, plurals in *-en*, with mutation or without ending survived in greater numbers than today. Chaucer has *-en* forms like *been* 'bees', *shoon* 'shoes' and *foon* 'foes', plurals with front mutation like *keen* 'cows', and uninflected plurals like *hors*, *yeer*, *thing* and *winter*. The genitive singular was *-es* in most nouns whatever their declension in Old English, and the dative had largely disappeared, apart from the use in verse of a final *e* especially at line ends. In the definite article *þe* from OE *se* was now regular and it was matched with *þat/that*, which was the old neuter singular. In the plural the descendant of OE *þā* was *þo/thoo*, which gradually gave way to a new form *thos(e)* with the new plural *-s* added to the old form. But this form itself made way for *the* in the plural so that the article remained uninflected. The new form *those* became the plural of *that*, and new forms *this* and *these* were developed from the old demonstrative adjective. This left *the* as the definite article and *this/that/these/those* as the demonstrative adjective and pronoun. This development was only finally achieved in the fifteenth century, though it was already under way by the time of Chaucer. The indefinite article was also becoming more common, though its use had still to be regulated.

In the personal pronouns the demise of the dual, which had already largely occurred in the earlier period, was now confirmed. In the other personal pronouns the original four forms in Old English were reduced to three with the amalgamation of the old accusative and dative cases. This left for the first person the forms *I*, *me* and *min(e)*. In the south the form *ich* for *I* was found until the fifteenth century. The old genitive forms were detached from the paradigm and began to function as adjectives rather than as pronouns, and new forms without final *n* were created. This led to a distinction between *my/mi* and *min(e)*. At first both forms could be used as pronouns, but gradually this role was taken over by the former and the latter was used predicatively, though this had not been achieved by the end of this period. The predicative form of the pronouns *mine/thine* then encouraged the growth of similar forms in other persons to give new forms like *hers, ours, yours* and *theirs*. This development is well established by the time of Chaucer. The second person of the personal pronoun still existed in both singular and plural forms, and there was a growing use of the singular for specific pragmatic purposes, probably influenced by *tu/vous* in French. The singular had become the marked form used to express familiarity, anger or contempt. This was a change that was still under way and was by no means regular as yet. Each case has to be decided on its merits, though the plural could be used as the polite form with singular reference. With the third person of the personal pronoun the new form *she* was now well established and *(h)it* remained the neuter form of all cases except for the genitive where *his* still remained. In the plural the gradual southern drift of the *th* forms continued. By the end of the fourteenth century the use of *they* as the subject was fairly regular, and *their* was the dominant, but the not the exclusive, form of the genitive, whereas in the oblique case *(h)em* was as common as *them*. In fact *hem* in the form *'em* survives to the eighteenth century.

In the verb, changes in the inflectional system, often caused by phonological developments, continue to simplify the paradigms. In the weak verbs the three Old English types are reduced to two through the weakening of vowels in unstressed syllables to /ə/. The Old English classes I and III formed the preterite and past particple in *-d(e)* and class II in *-ed(e)*, but with the further reduction of *-ed* to *-d* all the verbs tended to fall together into a single group with a few anomalous forms. In the strong verbs a similar simplification was taking place, though it assumed a rather different form. Three trends can be detected. The first is to eliminate variety in the paradigms so that either the preterite singular and plural had the same vowel, as in class I with the preterite <o> in both singular and plural, ModE *ride/rode*, or else the verb of the past participle is extended to the preterite, as happened with verbs in class IV so that the preterite singular and plural OE *bær, bǽron* becomes ModE *bore* (from the OE past participle *boren*). This simplification appears to have commenced earlier in the north and moved south. The second is to transfer strong verbs from one class to another so that the dominant classes survive and less usual patterns collapse. This happens with verbs of class V, which adopt the patterns of class IV so vowels of the preterite and past participle have *o*. The third is for the continued transfer of many verbs from the strong to the weak category. Although some verbs have for a time both weak and strong forms, they go over finally into the weak class in this period or the following one. Verbs like *help, weep* and *sleep* start to transfer to the weak category during this period.

At the same time the inflectional system of the verbs continues to become reduced. With the weakening of vowels in unstressed syllables and then the loss of final *e*, the inflections are reduced to *-(e)st, -(e)þ, -en* or no inflection at all. Many forms of the verb became indistinguishable. The only distinctive forms were second- and third-person singular and the plural of the present indicative, the subjunctive plural in present and preterite, and the preterite indicative plural. Weak verbs had *-(e)st* in the second-person singular of the preterite. The contrast between the present and preterite indicative tenses remains stable because of the vowel changes in strong verbs or the inflections in *-d/t* in weak verbs. Distinctions in inflectional endings which had existed in Old English were gradually obliterated so that finer distinctions were lost. However, the remaining inflections showed dialectal variation. The south had present-tense third singular and all plurals in *-eþ*, whereas the north had *-es* for all these endings, and the Midlands had either *-es* or *-eþ* in the third singular, and either *-es* or *-en* in the plural. There was a southern drift of *-es* in the third singular, though it hardly reached southern varieties at this time, but became predominant in the Midlands. The Midlands also tended to retain *-en* as the dominant form in the plural. As London adopts a more Midlands dialect form, these endings will become characteristic of the capital. But the ending *-en* is liable to blurring and loss, though that is something which will happen later. In the subjunctive the collapse of endings continues to make the subjunctive indistinguishable from the indicative and thus encourages the growth of the modals. The imperative likewise becomes indistinguishable from the indicative, though this process is not completed in this period. The present participle shows distinctive dialectal variation with *-ande* in the north, *-inde* in the Midlands and *-ing/yng* in the south.

The reduction of verb inflections means that there is no longer a close link between case form and semantic function. The expression of the semantic function which had previously been expressed through case now has to be assumed by prepositions. With verbs that means that where previously they may have had nouns in a given case dependent upon them, these nouns now have to be governed by a preposition which depends upon the verb. At first in this period *of* is the usual preposition, but soon other prepositions like *at* and *about* appear; 'I wonder of his appearance' becomes 'I wonder at his appearance'. Many verbs also develop a reflexive form, particularly verbs which had been impersonal or intransitive. Hence a verb like *remember*, which could still operate impersonally, also developed a reflexive form so that *Him remembreth* could also be expressed as *he remembreth him*. Intransitive verbs also have a similar form, and in both these cases the development may be the result of the influence of French. Verbs like *ride* when intransitive and *go* could appear both with and without a reflexive pronoun. Chaucer in the Miller's Tale has 'This knaue gooth hym vp ful sturdily' (1:3428).

Verbs undergo other important developments in this period, though these changes are not grammaticalised yet. These include the progressive, compound tenses and the use of certain auxiliaries such as *do* and *gin*. In the previous periods the inflectional endings of the verbal noun, the present participle and the inflected infinitive became confused. This leads to their roles and functions becoming blurred and each can adopt some of the syntactic features of the others. The verbal noun could now take an object and be modified by an adverb – features that had previously been restricted to verbs. It is also possible that as the prepositional group with verbal noun, such as *on huntinge*, became reduced to *ahunting* it became identified with the present participle and *He was ahunting* seemed no different from *He was hunting*; this would allow for clauses like 'He was ahunting animals' to develop. This in turn would lead to the abandonment of the *ahunting* form. These forms could develop a progressive aspect in this period, though that aspect has often to be emphasised by an adverbial, as in Chaucer's 'Syngynge he was or floytynge al the day' (General Prologue 1:91) where *al the day* provides the progressive sense. The form was an alternative to the simple tenses which were clearly useful for poets grappling with the problems of metre. Similarly the verbs develop perfect and pluperfect forms at this time with the present or preterite tense of the verb 'to have' and the past participle of another verb. The opening of the *Canterbury Tales* has many of these forms, as we shall see shortly. These tenses are not grammaticalised yet and appear to be used interchangeably with the simple verb tenses. There is some evidence to suggest that they may have had a more colloquial feel to them, but this is certainly not true of the opening of the *Canterbury Tales*. It is, however, difficult in the absence of much colloquial material in Middle English to be certain of this. The verbs *gin* and *do* are often used as auxiliaries at this time, particularly in the preterite form. The use of *do* in this function may have been the result of its use as a causative supplemented by the occurrence of *faire* in French in similar syntactic positions. While *do* in this periphrastic function occurs in both poetry and prose, *gin* is much more common in poetry and may have been used as a metrical expedient.

The modal auxiliaries, which had been found from Old English times, were subject to increasing grammaticalisation. It is possible that *shal* adopts future reference as its primary function and loses its other senses rather more quickly than other modals. Certainly it is the only modal which could be used with other modals and this was found even before the beginning of this period. Even so, complete grammaticalisation of *shal* does not occur in this time and so it is still necessary to think of it as a modal rather than as a tense marker. *Shal* is more common than *wil* to express futurity, though this may be because it is considered more formal and so is appropriate in much of the prose of this time. *Wil* may have been more colloquial. The use of modals in place of the subjunctive continued to grow as a result of mutual influence: the growth of modals made the subjunctive less necessary, and the lack of transparency in the subjunctive forms through loss of inflections encouraged the development of the modals. The general changes affecting the modals, though they are not completed in this period, are the loss of their non-finite forms, their growing inability to take an object, the lack of temporal meaning between their present and preterite forms, and their close link with the base form of the infinitive. These changes are in progress, but the modal verbs when used without an infinitive retain the function of a main verb. Chaucer says of the Wife of Bath 'She koude muchel of wandrynge by the weye' (1:469).

An interesting, probably stylistic, development in the verb is the rise of the so-called 'historic present', that is the use of the present tense in a past context. It is often assumed that this use of the present is intended to create immediacy in descriptive passages.

With authors like Chaucer, who was one of the first writers to exploit its potential, its use is restricted to poetry and so it may have been developed partly for metrical purposes, because the third person of the present tense has two syllables compared with the preterite's one. But its occurrence in Chaucer's poetry may be rather the result of its less formal style than that of his prose. It is used extensively in the description of the fight in the lists in the Knight's Tale (1:2602–16). The standard form of negation in the earlier Middle English period was to use *ne* before the verb and *nawiht* or a similar form after it, though other words in the clause could be negated. Two changes affected this pattern The form *nawiht* became reduced to *nat* or *not* and, as happens so often with negation, the negative after the verb became dominant so that *ne* was omitted. This meant that in the verbal group the main negative became *not/nat*, which was usually placed after the verb, but could also be placed in front of it. Particularly when *nat* moved to the pre-verb position, it could be strengthened by some phrase at the end of the clause, though it happens also when it occurs after the verb. Chaucer in the Nun's Priest's Tale has 'Foryet nat this for goddes owene loue' (10:2926) without *ne*, but 'for goddes owene loue' strengthens the negation. It is this development which will lead to the modern negative structure. In this period it can also happen that *ne* is retained and there is no *nat/not*. In many of these cases where *ne* is unsupported, there is already a negative sense present and the *ne* is acting in a type of agreement with that negation.

In this period the development of the relative pronouns, which had begun in the post-Conquest period, continues. The system found in standard Old English had collapsed in the early Middle English period when *þe* and *þat* were both used. But the former was more common in the south and south-east Midlands, whereas the latter was normal elsewhere. The southward drift of *þat* meant that by the thirteenth century it had become the only pronoun available as a relative marker. The situation in the rest of the Middle English period is one of transition. *That* comes gradually to be confined to restrictive clauses and *wh-* relatives are introduced from the interrogative pronouns. *Who(m)* and *whose*, usually in conjunction with a preposition, begin to grow in importance, though *which* is rather slower to develop. The former are mainly used for animate antecedents, but the latter can be used for both animate and inanimate antecedents. These pronouns had been used as interrogatives, but in that function they could also introduce an indirect question as in Modern English 'He asked *who* was there'. Since *that* could also introduce subordinate clauses, it was not surprising that the two functions should overlap in relatives as well. Indeed, *what* was used to introduce subordinate clauses with the sense 'that which' for it could operate as the object of the verb in a sentence like 'He demanded to know what he was making'. As such it could readily have much the same meaning as *that* and be understood as having a relative function. Chaucer in the Friar's Tale has 'Taak thow thy part what that men wol thee yeue' (2:1505), where *what* could easily be understood to have a relative function. It was also possible to have a zero relative. Whereas in Modern English this relative is restricted to the object of the verb in the relative clause 'The house Ø he built was destroyed in the war', in Middle English it could be used both as the subject and the object of the relative clause. An example in subject function occurs in the Miller's Tale 'With hym ther was dwellynge a poure scoler Ø Hadde lerned art' (1:3184–5).

Adverbs were formed in the Old English period from adjectives through the use of an ending, usually *-a*, and from nouns by deploying either the genitive or dative case. One adjectival suffix, that in *-lic*, when it had the dative ending in *-e* added grew in importance as a possible adverbial form. In Middle English the final *e* fell and the suffix developed into *-ly*. This meant that apart from the adverbs formed through genitives and other possible suffixes, most adverbs either had the same form as the adjective or ended in *-ly*. Chaucer has forms like *freely* and *frendly*. Adverbs have not changed much in their formation since then, though individual examples which were previously without ending may have adopted the suffix ending in *-ly*.

The influence of French and Latin encouraged the growth in hypotaxis and this meant cultivating longer sentences with considerable subordination. Much of this subordination came through the expansion in the number and type of adverbial clauses. This in turn promoted the development of new conjunctions to carry this new load. Many potential conjunctions in Old English could be adverbs, and it is sometimes difficult to tell whether we are dealing with a single sentence with a subordinate clause or with two sentences, one of which is introduced by an adverb. Such forms as *for þæm (þe)* could be either adverbs or conjunctions. This may be one reason why new conjunctions were formed, which would seem less ambiguous. *For þæm (þe)*, for example, gradually gave way to *because* as a conjunction, and this word never acts as an adverb. In its adverbial function it was replaced by words such as *therefore*. In order to emphasise that a given word was functioning as a conjunction, it was often followed by *that* so that we find *by (the) cause that* and *because that*. The use of *that* for this purpose meant that it could also be used by itself, particularly as a repeat conjunction, when one adverbial clause was being paralleled by another. This use of *that* is found with all different types of adverbial clause. Examples of *by cause* as a causal adverbial and of *that* acting as a repeat adverbial are common enough in Chaucer, as a couple of examples may illustrate:

> But, sires, *by cause* I am a burel man . . .
> Haue me excused of my rude speche
> (*Canterbury Tales* 6:8–10)

and

> Men sholde hym brennen in a fyr so reed
> If he were founde or *that* men myghte hym spye
> (*Canterbury Tales* 7:313–14)

In temporal adverbial clauses *þa* and *þonne*, which were so frequent in Old English, disappear as conjunctions, though they are still found in Middle English as adverbs. They are replaced by *when/ whan (that)* when reference is to a single occurrence, but overlap in time is indicated through *while (that)* and related conjunctions.

As far as lexis is concerned this period sees an enormous growth in the use of both Old Norse and French words, though for different reasons. The Old Norse words had been in the language since pre-Conquest times, but only surfaced in any numbers in the written language from the thirteenth century. As we have seen, they were not common before then partly because standard Old English was hostile to foreign borrowings, and partly because in the immediate post-Conquest period not many works were written in English and those that were still contained many of the features of the earlier standard. The explosion in French borrowings, on the other hand, arose from the flood of French literature that was imported or translated during the fourteenth century. This meant that many of the new French words were literary and technical, and it is doubtful how many of them ever entered the colloquial level of English. The Old Norse words introduced into English were generally ordinary, though many of them may have been confined to regional dialects. The southward drift of northern features of the language brought many Old Norse words and phrases into the orbit of London English. A good example of this is the adoption in the south of the words *they* and *though*. In standard Old English the equivalent forms had been *hie* and *þeah*. These would have produced in southern Middle English *hi* and *þeih/theigh*. In the north ON *þeir* had already produced in Orm *þeiȝ* and the early ON **þouh* (ON *þó*) had resulted in northern English *though*. In the south the confusion in the subject form of the third-person personal pronouns would have promoted the adoption of the northern *thei(h)* 'they' form, were it not that this would then have created a homophonic clash with southern *theigh* 'though'. In order to avoid this clash, the adoption of *thei(h)* had to be accompanied by the adoption of *though* at the same time. Other words which have survived into Modern English from Old Norse include such common ones as *anger, both, call, neck* and *window*. Old Norse elements are common in place names in the north of the country and such elements include *-by, -fell* and *-thwaite*. It is also to Old Norse that we owe the growth in the number of phrasal verbs which ousted the prefixed verbs so common in Old English and the introduction of the verbal operator *get* (ON *geta*) for its equivalent in Old English is used only as the second element of a compound, as in ModE *forget*. In addition to the extensive use of *get* with particles to form a phrasal verb, we find the simple form used in contexts like the following: 'To gete thee freendes ay do thy trauaile' (*Canterbury Tales* 8:1210).

The French words borrowed at this time are not often so much part of our everyday vocabulary as those from Old Norse. In particular they are likely to fall within the fields of administration, the law, literature and other cultural affairs. In his *Treatise on the Astrolabe* Chaucer naturally used a high number of astronomical terms, and some of these are repeated in his tales in the *Canterbury Tales*. Words like *ascensioun, ascendant, equynoxial, operaciouns* and *mansiouns* are found in the ordinary narrative of his tales. Less technical words, but ones which were nevertheless restricted in register at this time, include *daliaunce, oynement, galauntyne* and *jocounde*, to quote some that are found in Chaucer's lyric *To Rosemounde*. However, French did provide English with a large number of prepositions, among which *by cause* was noted above, of phrases including many modelled on French *faire* plus a verb such as *make (good/bad) chiere*, and of affixes including *-ant/ent, -ity, -ment, con-, en-* and *pre-*. The prefix *en-* became popular in the fourteenth century, and such forms as *engendre, enhaunce* and *entune* encouraged the extension of the prefix often as no more than a stylistic marker of fashion in the fifteenth century. Many French loans were refashioned in a Latin dress after they had been borrowed, but this is a feature more characteristic of the fifteenth and sixteenth centuries. Even in Chaucer one may find both *egal* from French and *equal* from Latin, though the latter examples may be simply French words written as Latin. What in Chaucer appears as *parfait* will become ModE *perfect*. Latin loans are most often at this time from the fields of administration and the law, though religion, education and learning were also significant. Words from Latin include *client, collect, contradiction, diocese, executor, neuter, psalm* and *simile*.

In addition to the increase in foreign borrowings, one must recognise that many words dropped out of the language. The alliterative revival of the fourteenth century produced many new poems in the alliterative metre, but many of the old words associated with this metre failed to survive. Compounding was no longer exploited as a poetic feature by the poets of the Revival and many of the traditional phrases ceased to find expression. Words which were still common in Laȝamon such as *æðeling* and *halwe* are replaced by *prince* and *saint*. Literary style was provided with words borrowed from French and Latin rather than through the retention of an archaic vocabulary found in the old alliterative compositions. However, an important addition to the vocabulary was the ability to exploit functional shift, that process whereby one part of speech could be used as another. This possibility exists mainly for lexical words. With the fall of inflections it was impossible to tell from its form alone whether a word was a noun, adjective, verb or adverb. It was the word order that indicated the function of a word, and so it became possible to exploit this possibility by using words from one part of speech in a different function. It was particularly common to use nouns as verbs. In the fourteenth century such nouns as *chill, fellow, hammer, hawk, spire, sleet, throng* and *wright* occur for the first time as verbs. These are words of Germanic origin, but the same applied to words from French, as *avaunt, forfeit, gest* [story], *issue, outrage* and *trespass*. The reverse change of verb to noun was less common, but was found in *fart, hunt, shake* and *yell* among Germanic words, and *assure, daunt, profess* and *support* among French words. This freedom to change the function of words has continued to be exploited in English.

The fourteenth century is the first in which differences in register begin to be significant in literary works, and here Chaucer is the pre-eminent example. In The Manciple's Tale, for example, Chaucer wrote about the word *lemman*, which he uses in the sense of 'lover':

> And so bifel whan Phebus was absent
> His wyf anon hath for hire lemman sent –
> Hir lemman, certes this is a knauyssh speche!
> Foryeueth it me and that I yow biseche.
> The wise Plato seith as ye may rede:
> The word moot nede acorde with the dede.
>
> (11:203–8)

Chaucer implies that *lemman* belongs to a low register, though elsewhere in Middle English this status is far from evident. He goes on to suggest that *wenche* has the same status as *lemman*, and both need to be distinguished from *lady*. On another occasion one scribe of this poem did not write the word *swyue* 'to copulate' in full at the end of a line: he merely copied the first two letters and then added *&c.* One may assume this represents a delicacy on his part as he is unwilling to spell out a word of such doubtful import, although he did write it in full when it occurs within the line. However, the interpretation of the different levels which words have at this time is difficult. Few writers make explicit comments on register. Yet the import of so many words of French and Latin origin would necessarily create a difference between a high style which used the resources of this foreign vocabulary, and a low style which relied on more common words. This difference is still with us today. As we have already seen, the growth of London and the sense that what was metropolitan was more sophisticated is a trend that one can detect, even if it is difficult to highlight the words which might have carried either favourable or unfavourable overtones. At first the introduction of foreign words may have been principally stylistic when they simply replaced words which already existed in English. A word like *swink* was replaced by *labour*; the Old English word may well have sunk lower in register to indicate various kinds of unpleasant work including sexual labour, and this could well have prompted its demise. The evidence to confirm this development is lacking, though the loss of a word like *lemman* may indicate that this process was not uncommon. In some cases the English and the French or Latin words would develop differences in meaning which were in part the result of a difference in register. Words like *clean* and *pure* may have overlapped in meaning at first, but then the former would increasingly be restricted to physical and concrete features, whereas the latter would retain moral and religious connotations.

It was becoming more common for particular groups of writers to develop their own vocabulary, and at the end of this period this can be traced particularly in the writings of the Wycliffites or Lollards, though one need not assume that it was a trait restricted to them. Expressions which occur in their works, and which therefore help to identify such works as Lollard, are *trewe men, pore men* and *pore prest*. Whole phrases may also indicate Wycliffite writings, such as 'it semeþ to many men' and the verb *to ground*. Presumably such words evoked an emotional reaction among readers as they recognised familiar arguments and a traditional style.[13] The introduction of technical vocabulary would also help to identify certain works as technical and learned. The use of a Latinate vocabulary for such writings rather than using an Anglo-Saxon vocabulary would set them apart from normal writing, and the use of individual 'terms' from the register was no doubt intended to create stylistic echoes and connotations which the receptive reader should pick up.[14] It was becoming much more possible in English to create different levels of language in writing; informal style and different levels of formal writing were now available to be exploited by the thoughtful writer. Naturally, this was not something that all writers could yet manage.

In word formation the changes which we noted in the last chapter continue. Prefixes continue to fall out of the language, though some survive and others, as we have noted, are borrowed from French. Those that were productive include *un-* from Old English, though its range of meanings was now more limited. Those which are either in retreat or obsolete include *a-, ge-, to-,* and *ymb-*. New prefixes include *in-* and *mis-*. With suffixes the same is true, but there are fewer losses among the English ones. Both *-ful(l)* and *-ish* remain productive, and a new ending in *-ling* found in such words as *darling* makes its appearance. French and Latinate suffixes become common as a result of the many borrowings from those languages. These changes are particularly evident in literary works, especially poetry, where borrowing was encouraged to give the style of the work a higher tone. It is not possible to say how far this tendency percolated through to the spoken language, but it seems improbable that it was very significant at this stage.

Many of the points raised so far in this chapter can be exemplified through the opening lines of the *Canterbury Tales* written towards the end of this period.

> Whan that Aueryll *with* his shoures soote
> The droghte of March/ hath perced to the roote
> And bathed euery veyne in swich lycour
> Of which v*er*tu engendred is the flour
> Whan zephirus eek/ *with* his sweete breeth
> Inspired hath in euery holt and heeth
> The tendre croppes/ and the yonge sonne
> Hath in the Ram/ his half cours yronne
> And smal foweles/ maken melodye
> That slepen al the nyght with open iye
> So priketh hem nature/ in hir corages
> Thanne longen folk to goon on pilgrymages
> And Palmeres for to seeken straunge strondes
> To ferne halwes/ kouthe in sondry londes
> And specially/ from euery shyres ende
> Of Engelond/ to Caunterbury they wende
> The holy blisful martir/ for to seke
> That hem hath holpen whan þ*at* they weere seeke
>
> (1:1–18)

This passage is quoted from the Hengwrt manuscript, which may have been written within a couple of years of Chaucer's death; no manuscript dates from his own lifetime. The punctuation is still minimal. The virgule or slash is used, but its function is not altogether clear. It usually comes at the end of a phrasal unit, but it does not seem to have specific metrical purposes. Elsewhere in the manuscript we find, in addition to the slash, an occasional full stop, inverted semicolons, possible question marks, a grouping of dots, and in the prose texts a kind of wedge-shaped mark. In so far as we can tell, the punctuation fulfils a rhetorical rather than a grammatical function; it may have been intended to indicate where a pause in reading should occur. Inevitably, pauses are most likely to occur at the end of phrases or clauses. There are a few abbreviations (and in the passage above they are represented by italics), and mostly they are used for short, common words like *with* and *that*. Their use is not regular and it is difficult to suggest why they are used in some passages and not in others. The use of capitals is erratic; it is found with some proper nouns but not with all. As there is only a single sentence here, it is not possible to show whether it is used to start a sentence. Its use at the beginning of line is more formal.

Spelling shows various developments. The variation between <i> and <y> as a vowel continues from earlier periods, though <y> is now also used to represent /j/ as in *yonge*. The distinction between <v> initially and <u> medially is retained. The letter <h> is found in association with other letters, especially in the groups <gh> and <sh>. The latter has now replaced OE <sc> and was to become the standard spelling through its use in the London area. The digraph <gh> may represent former <h> in Old English so that OE *niht* is now *nyght*. It is not certain whether this <gh> still represented a sound in words like *nyght* or whether palatal *h* had fallen. The word *droghte* comes from a different origin, since the equivalent form in Old English was *drūȝuð*. The /ɣ/ was vocalised and fell together with the long vowel [u:], but its former presence was indicated through <gh> in some words like this. But a similar development in OE *fuȝol* has resulted in the spelling *foweles*, where the <ow> represents [u:]. In words of French origin this sound is written <ou> as in *lycour, flour*. This is some indication that writing was traditional and did not even at this time always represent the sound system of the day. Other symbols used in this manuscript include <ch> for Old English <c> in the neighbourhood of front vowels. The symbol <c> is used for [k] when followed by a back vowel both in Old English words like *Caunterbury* and in French words like *lycour*, but it is replaced with <k> in the neighbourhood of front vowels as in *priketh, eek* and *seeken*. In some dialects, particularly southern ones, this consonant found in *seeken* was often pronounced [tʃ] and written *seche(n)*. The [k] sound was the result of the southward drift of a northern pronunciation. However, <k> was sometimes used where <c> might be expected because the sound existed in Old English in the neighbourhood of back vowels.

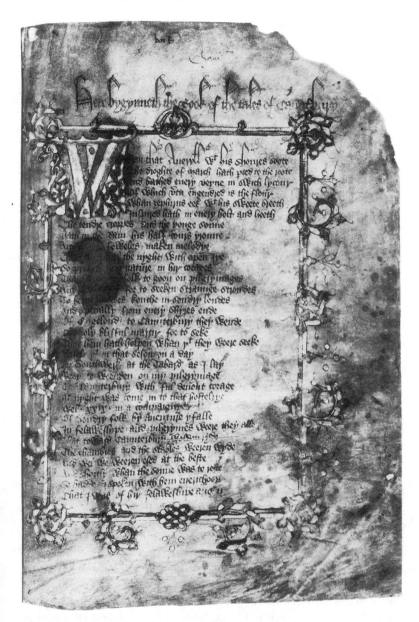

FIGURE 6.1 The opening page of the *Canterbury Tales*, MS Peniarth 392D (the Hengwrt Chaucer manuscript, *c.*1405) fol. 2r (*The National Library of Wales, Aberystwyth*).

In this passage it occurs in *kouthe* where the <ou> indicates Old English [uː]. This word survives in Modern English only in the form *uncouth*, and it illustrates that at an earlier period the use of <c> and <k> had not been regulated. <þ> is used only in abbreviations in this passage, and was infrequent otherwise in the manuscript; <ð> is not used at all. The common form is now <th> except in special circumstances, and the other two symbols were obsolescent. The symbol <a> has replaced <æ> which is not found, and even the older diphthongal spellings in <ea, eo> are rare. Latin <z> is used for proper nouns as in *Zephirus*, though elsewhere in the manuscript it does occasionally replace <s> in the inflectional ending *-es* of the plural. Some consonants are doubled after a short vowel and this may reflect the influence of lengthening in open syllables which created the feeling that the vowel in the first syllable of a bisyllabic word when followed by a single consonant was long. Old English *crop* is represented as *croppes*, but *priketh* has only a single <k> though the <i> is short. Doubling of vowels was an alternative system to indicate length, and in the rhyme *seeke/seke* the first example has a double vowel, but the second may indicate length through the open syllable. The <ee> represents both OE *æ* in *breeth/heeth* and OE *ēa* in *eek*, which had fallen together in a sound which was now probably [ɛː]. However, doubling of vowels and consonants was still erratic, for we find <ll> in *Aueryll* and only <l> in *blisful*, even if some trends can be detected. Whenever what had been <u> as a vowel in Old English came next to a nasal, there was always the possibility of confusion because the minims which formed *u*, *n* and *m* could easily lead to misinterpretation. This difficulty was solved by writing the vowel as <o>, and this is found in *sonne* 'sun' (OE *sunne*) and *yronne* 'run' (OE *urnen, run(n)en*).

The introduction of French words had created variation in the traditional Germanic stress pattern which preferred the stress on the first vowel, unless it was a prefix. In French stress was variable and often fell on the final or penultimate syllable. In English poems the metre indicates that this stress pattern was transferred into English at least for words of French origin. Thus the rhyme makes it clear that stress falls on *a* in *corages/pilgrymages*, *ou* in *lycour/flour*, and *y* in *melodye/iye*, though in the last word <iy> together represent the single sound [iː]. This created a new system of stress in English which became regulated in later centuries. We may assume that the stress patterns found in poetry were also found in prose and the spoken language. The metre also indicates that final *e* was still available as a syllable at least in poetry, though other evidence suggests that it may by now have largely fallen out of the spoken language. It is used to indicate the oblique case of singular nouns and the plural and the weak form of adjectives. The weak form now indicated definiteness and was found after the definite article and possessive adjectives. The parallel position of the two groups *swich lycour* and *sweete breeth* suggests that in the latter group final *e* was sounded to give the required pattern stress–unstress–stress. Other expedients may have been used to keep this stress pattern. The old past participle prefix OE *ge-* had been reduced to *y-*, but had fallen out of most dialects except the southern varieties. This allowed London poets like Chaucer to use it if they needed it for an extra syllable; hence its appearance in *yronne* the past participle of 'ran'. In the opening couplet it is reasonable to assume that *soote* represents the plural of the adjective 'sweet' and *roote* the oblique (old dative) case after a preposition, and that in both words final *e* was sounded.

Some, but not all, changes in phonology can be detected through the writing system. OE *swēte* had an alternative form *swōte*. The former produced Chaucer's *sweete*; the latter lost its [w] sound because it came before /o/ and appears as his *soote*. Both forms are found in this passage, because Chaucer could exploit variants which were found in his own dialect or in the language around him both for stress and for rhyme. The group *ic* in Old English which was found both as the first person personal pronoun and as an ending in certain adjectives and pronouns, and in the adjectival suffix *-lic*, was reduced to [i] in unstressed positions. The personal pronoun was in southern dialects *Ich*, but in northern ones *I*, a form which had developed through weak sentence stress. In adjectives and adverbs with the ending *-lic* the development to *-ly* was now regular. It was added to French words, e.g. *specially*, as much as to Germanic ones. What in Old English had been *a* before a nasal plus consonant is represented here as <o>, though this was less common in London English at this time and is found only in some words today. Hence *lond*, *strond* and *longen*; today it is the words with *ng* which tend to have <o>. The final word of the passage *seeke* exhibits the lengthening of vowels in open syllables together with the lowering of that vowel by one level. Thus /i/ was lengthened to /i:/ but at the same time that /i:/ was lowered to /e:/ to give the form *seeke*. In the paradigm, lengthening did not always take place because the vowel was not always in an open syllable (with final *-k* in the singular and -ke in the plural) which explains why /i/ has been retained in Modern English. Old English ā is represented regularly as <o(o)> as in *goon* (OE *gān*) and *holy* (OE *hāliȝ*). The final -n may be retained or lost. In the past participle it is found in *holpen*, but not in *yronne*. In the infinitive it is retained in *goon* and *seeken*. Elsewhere the -n is lost, though there are no examples in this passage. The ending of the present indicative plural is in -en rather than in -eth, which was the old southern plural. This -en is retained in *maken* and *slepen*, but not *wende*. The plural of the preterite *they weere* has no -n, though in Old English the form was *wǣron*.

In the adjectives there is still retention of the plural and the old weak declension in -e, and in the verbs the ending of the present indicative plural is -en. In the third-person singular of the present indicative the ending is -th rather than -s as in *hath* and *priketh*. The verb *help* retains its strong past participle *holpen*, though in Modern English this verb has become weak. *Run* is a strong verb with past participle *yronne*. Verbs which have come from French almost always adopt the past participle of the weak declension, and that is true of *perced*, *inspired* and *engendred*. The plural of the noun is regularly in -es and the possessive in *of* is found more than the old genitive in -es. A group genitive seems to be the appropriate intepretation of the phrase *euery shyres ende Of Engelond* meaning 'the limit of every shire of England'. The absence of what would be the definite article in Modern English in this phrase may be noted.

Syntactically the word order is rather more mixed than one might expect in a prose text of the time, and this is hardly surprising because Chaucer has tried to compose an elaborate opening for his poem. These eighteen lines constitute a single sentence. This has been achieved through the use of subordination and parallelism. The structure is as follows:

> *Whan that* (adverbial clause 1–4 with co-ordinate
>   main clause 1–3 and a relative clause at 4)
> *Whan* (adverbial clause 5–7a)
> *and* (parallel adverbial clause 7b–8)
> *And* (parallel adverbial clause 9–11 with relative clause 10 and
>   adverbial clause 11)
> *Thanne* (main clause 12–14)
> *And* (parallel main clause 15–18 with relative clause 18).

The structure is relatively simple in that it is based on adverbial clauses of time preceding the main clauses. Within the clauses the word order is more complicated than normal. The opening adverbial clause has the order SAOVA, which puts the object before the verb – the order characteristic of subordinate clauses in earlier English. In the noun group *shoures soote* the adjective has been placed in the post-modifier position for the sake of rhyme, an expedient exploited by later poets as well. The relative clause at line 4 has the subject *flour* after the verb, which is here a passive. The past tense form *inspired hath* has the auxiliary after the past participle as compared with *hath perced* in line 2. In line 8 *hath* and *yronne* are separated with the main verb coming after the object. The perfect is used here where we might today use the pluperfect. At line 9 there is a change of tense and a slight ambiguity in time sequence. This clause is still part of the adverbial clause of time but it refers to a different time, for we move from 'when April has watered the drought of March' to 'when birds sing'. It is uncertain whether we should understand this as a historic present or as a reference to what is customary and perennial, that birds always sing in the Spring. In line 11 there is inversion of subject and verb partly because the subject is co-ordinate. The argument dependent on the verb *longen* consists of two non-finite clauses, the first of which has the form *to goon* and the second *for to goon*. The distance of a second infinitive from the main verb often caused it to adopt the longer form, though in this case metre may be a factor. In line 14 there is a modifier before the noun and one after it, though the latter *kouthe* may have *in sondry londes* dependent on it, though that prepositional group could equally refer back to *strondes*. In line 17 the two modifiers are placed before the noun. In line 18 the order in the relative clause is SOV, which was characteristic of earlier English.

The conjunction *whan* has its status as a conjunction emphasised through the addition of *that* in most examples; it is only when it is repeated in the parallel structure that the *that* is omitted. Prepositional groups characteristic of Modern English are now regular and this gives the passage a much more modern feel than that found in the passage from the *Peterborough Chronicle* analysed in the last chapter. The relative marker for relative clauses is *that*, as in lines 10 and 18, except at line 4 where *which* is used; in this example the relative marker is used in conjunction with a preposition and in those cases *which* was the more usual marker. In line 1 we can note the use of *his* which almost certainly has the sense of 'its' – a form that had not yet been developed. I say 'almost certainly' because with proper nouns like April it is possible, though in this case unlikely, that the poet may have intended to convey a sense of anthropomorphism as the use of Zephirus does. The forms of the plural third person of the personal pronoun have *h*- in this passage in *hir* (possessive) and *hem* (oblique).

The noticeable feature of the vocabulary is the large number of words of French origin. There are few words from Latin or Old Norse, though *Zephirus* comes from Latin rather than French and *roote* probably has an Old Norse form. The two words for months, *Aueryll* and *March*, have a French form, though the former was to be Latinised later to *April*. There is on average at least one French word per line and they include *perced, veyne, lycour, vertu, engendred, flour, inspired* among others. They often have a meaning which has since been lost from the language. *Lycour* means 'moisture' rather than a strong alcoholic drink; *vertu* means 'power, efficacy' rather than 'moral behaviour'; *corage* means 'heart' rather than 'bravery'; and *straunge* means 'foreign, distant' rather than 'bizarre, unusual'. There are, however, many lines which contain only words of English origin, as is true of line 18. There are examples of alliterative phrases such as are found in older poetry, *holt and heeth*, and there are words which were becoming obsolete, *ferne halwes kouthe*. The first adjective was replaced by *far* or *distant*, the noun by *saint*, and the final adjective by *famous* or *well-known*. The word *shire* has survived, but it is much less commonly used than it used to be and its place has been taken by *county*. The word *folk* was also giving way to the French *people*, though it too has not been entirely lost from the language.

Towards the end of the fourteenth century there were many indications that attitudes to English were changing and it was being recognised as the main language for the country. There was an explosion in literary composition. Although much of this was concentrated in the London area where Chaucer and Gower worked, there was alliterative poetry in the north-west, of which the most famous work was *Sir Gawain and the Green Knight*, and Langland started his *Piers Plowman* near the Malvern Hills, though he later moved to London. The works which come from the north-west survive in few copies. This may be the result of the growing importance of London in cultural matters. There were a large number of manuscripts of the works by Chaucer and Gower compared with those from other parts of the country; this is a matter to which we will return in the next chapter. In other spheres Trevisa noted that teaching in English in schools, which he claimed had been introduced by John of Cornwall in the middle of the fourteenth century, was by the time he was writing in 1385 regular in all grammar schools in England. In 1362 the Statute of Pleading confirmed that English should be the language of the law courts, and in that same year Parliament was opened in English for the first time. Two references in Chaucer's works are also significant. In his *Troilus and Criseyde* he refers to the changing nature of language:

> Ye knowe ek that in forme of speche is chaunge
> Withinne a thousand yeer, and wordes tho
> That hadden pris, now wonder nyce and straunge
> Us thinketh hem . . .
>
> (II.22–5)

He does not refer specifically to English here and his words may imply differences in discourse rather than in phonology or morphology. Whatever the precise meaning of the passage, he expresses concern at the fleeting nature of language – a concern that would influence his and others' attitudes towards English. In a short lyric known today as *Chaucer's Words to Adam* Chaucer complains that his scribe Adam miscopies his works and he urges him to be more attentive to his copying in future. Chaucer indicates that he has had to correct the copies to make sure they were accurate. The author shows his interest in preserving his own language or metre, suggesting that the freedom copyists had exercised in their work was becoming less acceptable to writers. However, in this Chaucer was certainly ahead of his time. Once his attitude became more common it would encourage greater standardisation and faithful reproduction of the language.

What could be achieved in this matter is illustrated by the numerous manuscripts which were copied by the Wycliffites or Lollards. They show the development of standardised varieties in the fourteenth century in a manner that prepared the way for that variety which was to become the eventual basis of the new standard. Professor Samuels has studied this development in the greatest detail and he suggests that the Lollard standardised variety of English has the best claim to be the first literary standard after the period of French and Latin domination.[15] This standardised variety was not invented by the Lollards though they had most influence in spreading it. It was based on the spoken dialects of the Central Midlands, especially the counties of Northampton-shire, Huntingdonshire and Bedfordshire, though it was also adopted in several surrounding counties such as Leicestershire, where St Mary's Abbey at Leicester was an important centre for its dissemination. It may be recognised through certain spellings such as *sich* 'such', *mych* 'much', *ony* 'any', *silf* 'self', *stide* 'stede', *ʒouun* 'given' and *siʒ* 'saw'. It survived in some areas until well into the fifteenth century and was used by Reginald Pecock and his copyists in the last quarter of the fifteenth century, even though Pecock, a Welshman by birth, was Bishop of Chichester. It is suggested by Samuels that this standardised variety may have been copied as far away as Devon, and that makes its use by Pecock less surprising. Its dissemination by the Lollards was accompanied by their own special vocabulary which has been noted earlier, though it may be that the link of this variety with heresy was one reason which led to its demise. This variety was labelled by Professor Samuels as Type I and that is how it is referred to today.

Type I is distinguished from his Types II and III which were other standardised varieties which overlap with it, but which did not have the same geographical distribution. Type II is found in a group of fourteenth-century manuscripts which are probably all from the Greater London area. The prototypical manuscript of this type is the Auchinleck manuscript (National Library of Scotland MS 19.2.1). Written about 1330, it is a miscellany of religious and didactic material together with fifteen romances. Much of the material, particularly the romances, was translated from French and it is testimony to the growing importance of English in literature in London at the beginning of the fourteenth century. The manuscript is probably the product of a commercial scriptorium which prepared books for sale to London merchants and other members of the growing middle classes. Seven other manuscripts have so far been identified as having language which belongs to this type. Type III is also a London-based standard. It is particularly associated with the best manuscripts of Chaucer and the slightly later poet Hoccleve who worked as a scribe in the Chancery. Some London documents and one manuscript of *Piers Plowman* have been allocated to this type. Although it is associated with Chaucer, it did not become the basis of the later standard. Features of the two types given by Samuels are shown in Table 6.2.

TABLE 6.2

Type II	Type III (Chaucer)
þat ilch(e), ich(e)	thilke, that ilk(e)
nouȝt, no	nat
eld(e)	old(e)
werld, warld	world
þai, hij	they
þei(ȝ)	though
þerwhile(s), (þat)	whil
-ande, -ende, -inde	-yng [present participle ending]
noiþer, noþer	neither
schuld	sholde
oȝain(s), aȝen	ageyns, ayeyns
wil	wol(e), wil(e)

Although the amount of writing found in Type III and its association with Chaucer and Hoccleve make it the variety most familiar to modern readers, there is nothing to suggest that it became a literary standard. The various manuscripts of Chaucer and Gower exhibit considerable differences, and although Chaucer himself may have written in Type III his influence was not apparently very deep. It was Type IV which was to produce the standard language and that type is the Chancery Standard that is closely associated with the flood of documents issuing from the Chancery from about 1430 onwards. A consideration of this type belongs to our next chapter, which deals with the establishment of the new standard in English.

7

Political, Social and Pedagogical Background to the New Standard

As the period from 1400 to 1660 is central to the development of Modern English and the formation of the standard, it needs much longer treatment than can be included in a single chapter. I have, therefore, divided it into two chapters, the first of which will deal with many of the concepts and attitudes which were in the air as the standard was being constructed and the second with linguistic features of English. This may lead to some overlap between the two chapters.

At the end of the last chapter we saw how different standardised varieties were formed during the fourteenth century. We should remember what a standardised language at this time implies. Different writing systems available to individual scribes, based originally on spoken dialects, gradually became mixed through the amalgamation of different dialect forms. This produced writing systems which did not reflect the sound system of a single dialect with accuracy, and such systems soon developed an existence of their own so that speech and writing drew further apart. The writing systems of the fourteenth century were constructs which reflected nobody's spoken language. The systems were taught to scribes and copyists no matter what their own dialect was. The same applies to the new standardised variety which was con-structed in the fifteenth century and which is now called Chancery Standard or Samuels' Type IV. A standard language is a taught language and we should not expect it to reflect the pronunciation of any group of people. Earlier scholars tried to relate the changes in the written system to the changes in the make-up of the population of London. While it may be true that the population of London showed a change from an East Anglian to a Central Midlands

172

pattern of immigration in the fifteenth century, this did not in itself mean that this was a determining factor in the formation of the Chancery Standard. Where we can identify scribes, as has been done for some scribes of Chaucer and Gower manuscripts, they often come from other parts of the country than either East Anglia or the Central Midlands. While such scribes may occasionally reveal their origins from some forms which they include in what they write, for the most part they follow the system which they had been taught. There was in fact no standard language in London before Chancery standard, although as we have seen there were various standardised varieties.

A standard language is a taught language which each individual has to learn whatever his or her own pronunciation. The presence of the standard in a given document cannot be detected through the assumed pronunciation of an individual's speech, which is not in most cases recoverable with any accuracy from the writing system, but through the spellings and to some extent through the vocabulary chosen by the writer. Where a choice exists, a scribe will in most cases choose those spellings which form part of the standard. Naturally consistency in spelling is not achieved immediately, and has not even been accomplished today. Considerable variety continues to exist, but a pattern of conformity will emerge and this will get stronger as time passes. This conformity will be more marked in official writings like documents than in personal writings, which exhibit greater variety. This is because writings such as official documents are written by trained officials or scribes, whereas personal documents are written by those who might not otherwise write much at all. In addition, people often want to create a less formal feel in their personal correspondence and thus will not insist on using the preferred forms of the standard.

Questions that naturally arise are why did Chancery Standard become the accepted English standard at the beginning of the fifteenth century and how was it formed. Answers to these questions are beginning to become clearer through the work of scholars like John Fisher.[1] The acceptance of Chancery English may be the result of the influence and support of the Lancastrian monarchy, particularly Henry V. During the fourteenth century French was replaced by English in many official documents and in other writings. For example, Chaucer produced an enormous amount of writing of different kinds in English, and a translation of the Bible into English was initiated by the Wycliffites. Although this translation was proscribed by the Church it circulated quite widely through the Lollard network. Most oral communication would take place in English, though often in the fourteenth century the official record might be in French or Latin. When Parliament was addressed for the first time in English in 1362, the records of that meeting were written in French. Towards the end of the fourteenth century, we can see the expansion of composition in English and in the use of English in official meetings, but this use of English is obscured for us today because so many of the records continue to use French. This is perhaps why the standardised varieties which emerged never managed to extend their influence to become standards because the time for the use of English as the official written language had not yet arrived. Although the use of English as the spoken medium was widespread, it was not the official medium of writing. This is a situation which is not uncommon in more modern times, where a prestige variety is used in writing, but most ordinary people use the local variety in speech. In India at the time of the Raj official writing was in English even if the people used their own languages in their daily communication. This situation broke down when India achieved its independence, for this political event created new conditions which allowed for a change in that Hindi joined English as an official language, though there was an attempt to downgrade the role of English. A similar state of affairs can be imagined for England at the end of the fourteenth century. More and more people used English in public and official gatherings; all that was needed was a push from someone to make English the official written language as well. That push came from the Lancastrian monarchy.

Henry IV removed Richard II from the throne in 1399 and although Richard was murdered shortly afterwards, Henry suffered a number of rebellions from his magnates during his reign. While Henry was forced to rely on the support of the Commons against his barons, he did not do anything specific to promote the use of English. The important change comes with Henry V who came to the throne in 1413. In 1415 he renewed the war against France and enjoyed great success. His victory at Agincourt in 1415 was followed by a second invasion of France in 1417, which culminated in his marriage to Princess Katherine of France and the agreement that he or his heirs should succeed to the throne of France after the death of King Charles. Naturally the war against France promoted

English nationalism and brought a huge wave of support and sympathy for Henry V. Perhaps the most important decision for the English language made by Henry V was his use of English for all the letters which he sent from France after he arrived there for the second time in 1417. 'The most interesting feature of this period is, however, the series of signet letters describing the progress of the war, which were addressed to the mayor and aldermen of London, and which seem to have been intended as propaganda.'[2] From 1417 until his death in 1422 Henry used English in almost all his private correspondence, which was produced for him by the Signet Office. The wave of anti-French feeling generated by the war and its successes were exploited by the king to confirm the position of the Lancastrian monarchy. It was an astute move.

The Signet Office was separate from the great offices of state which were under the control of the Council and were more regulated by statute. The Signet Office had grown up to write the letters of the king in an individual capacity rather than in any of his official functions. The Secretary who led the office was in daily touch with the king and fulfilled the function of a personal private secretary today. The Secretary was a highly educated official, usually with a degree, and the office itself was staffed with trained clerks. Letters issuing from this office were sealed with the king's private seal, and on some occasions were written in the king's own hand. Consequently we may accept that the decision to write the letters in English was one taken personally by the king. In this respect Henry V gave the necessary impetus to establish English as the official written language in much the same way as Alfred in the ninth century had made the English of Wessex the standard language of his kingdom. In both cases what was important is that a king should give the necessary impetus to establish a certain form of English as the standard. Once that step had been undertaken, the political backing of the monarch was less significant because the standard developed its own momentum and its promotion and refinement passed into the hands of scribes and scholars. The importance of Henry's lead can be understood from the entry of 1422 in the Abstract Book of the Brewers Guild. In 1422 the Brewers decided to keep their records in English, though this decision is given in Latin. A translation of this minute, presumably made by the clerk William Porson, is given in the Abstract Book as follows in a modernised spelling:

Whereas our mother-tongue, to wit the English tongue, hath in modern days begun to be honourably enlarged and adorned, for that our most excellent lord, King Henry V, hath in his letters missive and divers affairs touching his own person, more willingly chosen to declare the secrets of his will, and for the better understanding of his people, hath with a diligent mind procured the common idiom (setting aside others) to be commended by the exercise of writing: and there are many of our craft of Brewers who have the knowledge of writing and reading in the said English idiom, but in others, to wit, the Latin and French, before these times used, they do not in any wise understand.[3]

This example of the Brewers was followed by other guilds which adopted most of the conventions of the standardised form used by the Signet Office.

An interesting feature of the early fifteenth century is the flood of literary writing in English which is produced in manuscript. There is, for example, no manuscript of the *Canterbury Tales* which can be dated before 1400, the date of Chaucer's death. From 1400 the manuscripts of this poem are produced in great numbers so that there are still over eighty fifteenth-century manuscripts extant. It has been suggested that this expansion in the number of manuscripts may reflect a political attempt by the Lancastrians to establish a national literature in English as part of their drive to promote English nationalism against the French and to bolster the position of the monarchy against the barons by cultivating the support of those for whom English was their natural medium, the merchants and lesser gentry who formed the backbone of the Commons. The development of a canon of English literature would help to establish the credentials of English as a *written* language, even if the works of an author like Chaucer had been disseminated orally during his lifetime.

Although the position of Henry V was crucial in providing the impetus for the use of English, the standardised spelling itself came out of the Signet Office and was extended from there to the Chancery itself. How the Signet Office arrived at its own preferred forms is not known, and it may have been a matter of the influence of one or two of the Secretaries who were able to impose their preferred options on the clerks in the office. The Signet Office was closely related to the Chancery and had taken over some of the duties of the Chancery Office. Close contact was maintained between the two offices. The Chancery was the secretariat of the state in all departments of late medieval government. It was the largest and most important of the national administrative offices, and was responsible for administering writs, summonses, pleas and various customs dues and taxes. It was organised in a hierarchical manner. The twelve senior clerks were the masters of Chancery and constituted the first form. The second form had another twelve clerks. Below them were the twenty-four cursitors. The various clerks had sub-clerks who were able to copy documents but did not have authority to initiate documents or to sign them. The Chancery had a training system whereby new clerks were instructed in the systems used in the office, and gradually the clerks could rise through the hierarchy. It was not unlike a hierarchically controlled scriptorium where the juniors were forced into the mould determined by their seniors. The clerks lived in buildings assigned to the Chancery and were not only kept isolated from other influences, but also formed an élite in the profession. It appears that clerks from outside were also trained in the Chancery, but the Chancery clerks were instructed to keep themselves aloof from these other clerks. As the Chancery acted as a training school not only for its own clerks, but for those in other situations, the influence of Chancery English would soon spread throughout London and Westminster. As documents from Chancery were sent throughout the kingdom and as the English used in its documents carried with it the prestige attached to the court and royal usage, the influence of Chancery English was naturally disseminated throughout the country as well. Several features thus made the Chancery and its English influential. The Chancery occupied the central role nationally in administrative matters, and the documents it issued would find their way to all parts of the country at some time or another. Many of the documents issued from the Chancery had legal status and so had to be written in an English which was precise and not liable to misunderstanding. The organisation of the office with its strict hierarchy was such that it encouraged uniformity in usage among all the clerks. The training programme in the Chancery for the new clerks would lead them to use these forms almost as if they were second nature to them.

An outline of some of the features characteristic of this new standard will give readers an idea of its make-up. Strict uniformity did not arise immediately; certain forms were preferred. These preferences are more marked in words of Germanic origin, because the diversity was greatest in these words since they tended to have different representations in various dialects as compared with words of French origin. Some variant spellings in French words are evident, but these are less common. The variations involve inflectional endings and the form of the pronouns as well as spellings. There was not much insistence on the use of specific characters in spelling. Thus <i> freely interchanged with <y>, and the same applies to <þ> and <th>. Similarly the use of <ʒ> only gradually gave way to <gh> in words like *right*. The preferred spellings include some which have become the norm in Modern English: *any, but, many, much, not, such* and *which(e)/whych(e)*. The modals have the forms *can, coude, shal(l), shulde, wol, wold(e)* and *ought*. Words which could have *-and* or *-ond* regularly have *-ond* spellings at first, though *-and* forms begin to emerge about 1440. Thus early documents have *lond(es)* almost exlusively, though about the middle of the century *land(es)* begins to appear. *And* is always spelt with <a> and never with <t>. The standard form of *if* is *if/yf* after 1430, though before then variants like *yif/yef/ʒef* occur sporadically. In the verb 'to give' the documents have *gave* as the preterite, but *yeuen* as the past participle, and words like *gift* and *again* show a preference for <y> rather than modern <g>. In words of French origin <e> rather than <ea> is found in words like *appear* and <au> rather than <a> in words like *grant*. <gh> spellings in words like *night* are preferred in the later documents. But many words of French or Germanic origin remain unstable in their spelling.[4] What is surprising is that so few dialectal spellings occur in the texts issued from the Chancery since many of the masters came from the north of England, particularly Yorkshire and Lincolnshire.

Most nouns have plural inflections similar to those found in Modern English and the use of articles is very similar. The joining of the <þ> of the article *þe* to words beginning with a vowel, *þabbot* 'the abbot', is common in all documents. Adjectives are not normally inflected except in those cases where a phrase or formula is borrowed from French. With the personal pronoun the first-person singular is always *I*, never *ich*, and the possessive is *my/myn(e)*; the plural is *we* and *our(e)/owr(e)*. The second person uses *ye/you/yow* almost regularly in both singular and plural with *your(e)/yowr(e)* as the possessive. The third-person forms are as their modern equivalents in the singular except for *hit*, though *it* also occurs. The normal plural is *they*, though an occasional form with *h-* is found. In the possessive *thair* or a similar form is used twice as often as *her(e)*, but in the oblique form *hem* is just more frequent than *them* and its related forms. The relative pronoun is usually *that* with an occasional *which*; and *that* is also found in association with other conjunctions like *because* and as a simple conjunction. *Who* occurs very rarely as a relative.

In the verbs the significant difference between Chancery and Modern English is the inflection of the third person of the present indicative, where Henry V himself never used the modern -*s* ending, and other writers use it infrequently. The recognised ending was -*eth*. The subjunctive, when it occurs, has no inflection in the third-person singular. The present indicative plural shows some -*en* forms, but they are not common yet, though they increase as time goes on. Otherwise the plural has a zero inflection. Infinitives and past participles are usually without an ending, though some examples with -*en* occur, particularly if the infinitive is separated from a modal and might need its function emphasising. Weak verbs form the preterite and past participle in -*ed*, though an occasional -*t* is found. The use of initial *y-* with past participles was not part of Chancery practice, though it occurs in some documents copied there which originated elsewhere. The usual ending of the present participle is -*yng/-ing*. In the verb 'to be' the usual present plural form is *be(e)(n)*, but *are* does appear. The verb *do* is used as an auxiliary in a causative sense and *wol* is used as a marker of volition with the force of a command. It is most often used to express the king's 'will'.

The regular ending of adverbs is -*ly* rather than the older -*lich*. *Than(ne)* is used as an adverb and a conjunction, though the former is commoner. The regular negator is *not*, and the normal pattern in the Chancery documents is auxiliary+*not*+infinitive, though the pattern verb+*not* is also used. The prepositions are not employed in the same environments as in Modern English, and this applies particularly to *at*, *in* and *on*. Both *betwix* and *betwene* occur. The occurrence of *for* with *to* attached to an infinitive is common, particularly when the infinitive is separated from the verb on which it depends.

It may help to exhibit some of these features if a letter from Henry's Signet Office is reproduced here. What is most noticeable is how similar the system is to that found in Modern English, if one allows for the permitted variation in spelling which existed then. The example given is dated 1418.

By þe kyng
W[or]shipful fadre yn god / riȝt trusty and welbeloued / We grete
yow wel / And we sende yow closed wyþinne þees oure lettres a
supplicacion [pu]t vn to vs yn the name of oure welbeloued yn
god þe Prieur and Couent of our Cathedrale chirche of Bathe the
whiche supplicacion vs semeþ resonable / So we wol þat þe same
supplicacion seen / and the matere þerinne contened pleinly
vnderstanden by yow / ye do ful execucion of right vpon þe same
supplicacion / aftre youre discrecion / And god haue yow yn his
keping yeuen vnder oure signet yn oure hoost afore Roan þe xxx
day of Aougst.[5]

The Chancery Standard is gradually adopted by other writers,
who at first take over some of the spellings and then come to accept
more and more. This happens during the fifteenth century so that
the distinctive written features of the more distant dialects are
gradually lost. How quickly this happens depends upon the
exposure that individuals may have had to this standard and how
strong the local spelling system was. Two examples can serve as
examples of the spread of the standard. London Bridge was run by
Bridge Wardens who employed special clerks to keep their records.
Documents in French, English or Latin are extant from the early
fifteenth century, but in 1480 it was decided to use only English.
From documents written containing English before 1480 and from
those written after that date one can see that the standard was
increasingly influential in the writing produced by the clerks. The
first extended document in English dates from 1467–8 and already
by then the English reflects the standard quite closely. The clerk
responsible was one William Bourchier and the features outlined
above as characteristic of the Chancery Standard are found in his
document. Unfortunately the absence of earlier documents makes
it impossible to tell when these features were adopted.[6] More
detailed work has been done on the writing system of the Pastons.
The letters written for Margaret Paston are in a variety of hands,
one of which belongs to her son Edmond. From the letters he wrote
for her we can see in the period 1469-79 the replacement of initial
<x> by <sch>, followed shortly after by its replacement through
<sh> so that *xal* becomes *schal* and then *shal(l)*. <sch> is abandoned
for <sh> at roughly the same time as the ending <th(e)> for <ght>
in words like *right*. William, Edmond's brother, uses <ght> forms in
the 'right' words and uses the <th> forms exclusively in the plural

of the third person of the personal pronoun. He adds final *n* to the past participle in the verbs. The changes in the writing system of the Paston letters were far-reaching in the third quarter of the fifteenth century. At that time further changes include the use of *-s* rather than *-th* in the third-person singular of the present indicative and the extension of *yow* to the nominative singular of the second-person pronoun.[7] Further studies like those of Professor Davis need to be undertaken to chart the spread of the standard in detail. It is noteworthy that the spread of the standard in Scotland has been the subject of a full study, but that this has not yet been accomplished for the standard in England.[8] The development and spread of spellings are matters discussed further in the next chapter.

The formation of standardised varieties was something that had started already in the fourteenth century; the adoption of one of these as the standard was a new development which was attributable in part to the political support of the monarchy. That support might have been less effective unless conditions generally had favoured the rise of a standard in England. In the fourteenth century three languages were still used in England: English, French and Latin, with English acting as the primary spoken language and Latin and French as the languages of writing. But the situation was not quite so cut and dried as that. Writing in English was becoming more common, and this was what allowed for the formation of standardised varieties. French and Latin were still used at a spoken level, with French being the language of the court and Latin the language of the Church. Richard II had a French wife and was familiar with French. He was happy to receive French books from visitors like the French poet and chronicler Froissart, who records in his chronicle how warmly Richard received the present he had brought and had it sent to his private room. Although Henry IV had spent some time in exile during the reign of Richard II and so may be understood to have spoken French competently, his court appears to have been English speaking. This may have been part of the Lancastrian policy of encouraging the use of English nationally and promoting the popularity and composition of English poetry. This would mean that French was increasingly restricted to technical purposes such as recording law cases. French ceased to be a spoken language in England and those who wanted to speak it learned it as a foreign language in the form spoken in France. As a written language it remained important in the law and statutes were printed in French until well into the sixteenth century. For most people, however, it ceased to play any significant part in their lives, for locally the law was conducted in English. As for Latin, the rise of humanism meant the reassessment of its nature and function. Humanists were intent on re-establishing the Latin of the classics. They disapproved of the spoken variety known as Vulgar Latin and wanted Latin to be taught and pronounced in its classical state. This effectively made Latin a dead language. To become expert in classical Latin demanded much more study than to be able to use some form of Vulgar Latin. Command of Latin became restricted gradually to scholars. Scholars like Erasmus could write and speak in classical Latin, for Latin remained the language of international scholarship, and authors like John Milton and Francis Bacon could write Latin as well as English and issued some of their works in that language. As fluency and excellence in Latin became more difficult to attain, so fewer people used it. Latin ceased to be a possible competitor with English at the spoken level, and even at the written level its use became restricted to scholarship and to certain formulaic documents and memorials.

Although English could now develop as both the national written and spoken language of the country, the existence of Latin as a dead language and of French as a fashionable literary language cultivated outside England had important implications. A living language like English could never appear as perfect as a dead language like Latin, which was also the language which provided the model for all grammatical systems. Equally a language that had only recently formed standardised varieties and in which approved literary works of merit, such as those by Chaucer, had only just started to be composed could hardly be compared with a language like French, which not only had its origins in Latin, but which could also trace its literary history back several centuries. Not surprisingly the English suffered from an inferiority complex about their language and attempts were made to do something about its perceived shortcomings. The changes that English as a living language was subject to had already started to receive unfavourable mention in the fourteenth century and this criticism soon increased enormously. This problem was exacerbated with the invention of printing for the early printers needed to provide texts in an English that was acceptable to everyone in the country and also up to date. The problems which critics complained of in English centred around its barbarous nature because it lacked the refinement of Latin and French. This meant that it was not

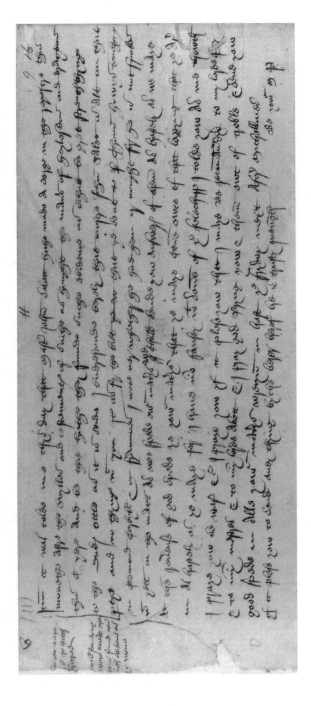

FIGURE 7.1 A letter from Margaret Paston to John Paston, dated 27 September 1465. An example of how the standard was gradually influencing writing in the provinces. MS Additional 27445, fol. 9 (*The British Library Department of Manuscripts*).

expressive enough because it lacked the necessary vocabulary, and what vocabulary it did have was unsophisticated. One could not express oneself elegantly in English. The growth of science and technology, the exploration of the New World, and the changes in religion and philosophy – often as a result of the discovery of hitherto unknown classical texts – highlighted the insufficiency of the language. To many at this time English seemed like a new and upstart language which lacked the antiquity and resources that came with age. It was only towards the end of the sixteenth century that recognition of its merits and its literature began to be accepted so that the litany of complaint changed into a celebration of greatness. A few of the comments made over this period must stand as examples for the large number of writings on the subject. What is significant is the enormous number of comments on the position and status of English; it was a topic which commanded interest. This situation has continued to modern times: nothing arouses so much controversy as the nature of and changes in the language.

The concept that English is a rude, by which he means un-sophisticated, language is a constant refrain in the prologues and epilogues which Caxton, the first English printer, included in his printed editions at the end of the fifteenth century. He carried on the tradition of translating works from French and Latin, but his need to sell his printed books encouraged him to add such prologues to highlight the benefits which his translations brought to the language. Previous translators whose work was issued in manuscript did not find this such a pressing necessity and so it is hardly surprising that Caxton is one of the first to give frequent expression to misgivings about the language. The words he uses to describe English include *broad, common, imperfect, rude* and *simple*. He commends Chaucer for having *embellished* and *made fair* the language and he implies that he will try to emulate this good work done by Chaucer. Some of these expressions may have been little more than formulas used for advertising purposes, but their use must imply that others would respond to what he wrote. Caxton comments on the way English has changed and is changing in his prologue to *Eneydos*:

> And also my lorde Abbot of Westmynster ded do shewe to me late certayn evydences wryton in olde Englysshe for to reduce it into our Englysshe now usid. And certaynly it was wreton in suche wyse that it was more lyke to Dutche than Englysshe: I

coude not reduce ne brynge it to be understonden. And certaynly our langage now used varyeth ferre from that whiche was used and spoken whan I was borne, for we Englysshemen ben borne under the domynacyon of the mone whiche is never stedfaste but ever waverynge: wexynge one season, and waneth and dyscreaseth another season.[9]

A similar complaint is made by John Skelton in his *Phyllyp Sparowe* a few years later:

> Our naturall tong is rude
> And hard to be enneude
> With pullysshed tearmes lusty
> Our language is so rusty
> So cankered and so full
> Of frowardes and so dull
> That if I wolde apply
> To wryte ornatly
> I wot not where to fynd
> Termes to serue my mynde.
>   (1550 edn, Ciiv–iiir)

The complaints are often of a stylistic nature because they naturally refer to the ability to write elegantly in English. These complaints continue throughout our period, and even later than that though for rather different reasons.

In due course praise of English started to emerge, even if it is qualified. Caxton had recognised the stature of Chaucer and praised the way he had improved English. Chaucer, Lydgate and Gower were often held up as the triumvirate who had raised English to new heights. While the latter two were less approved with time, praise of Chaucer continues unabated culminating in Spenser's description of him as the 'well of English vndefyled' (*Faerie Queene* IV.s.32). Praise of English is most marked at the end of the sixteenth century and is motivated by the output of outstanding literary work and also by the sheer volume of what was then available in English. The benchmark against which English is judged is classical literature, and most authors who praise English accept that what Chaucer had started, others brought to perfection so that the status of English is comparable with that of Latin. Barnabe Googe is a good example of the praise uttered at that time, for in the second edition of his translation *Zodiake of Life* (1565) he wrote:

> I know a number to be that can not abyde to reade anye thing written in Englishe verse, which nowe is so plenteously enriched wyth a numbre of eloquent writers, that in my fansy it is lyttle inferiour to the pleasaunt verses of the auncient Romaines. For since the time of our excellente countreyman sir Geffray Chaucer who liueth in like estimation with vs as did olde *Ennius* wyth the Latines. There hath flourished in England so fine and filed phrases, and so good and pleasant Poets as may counteruayle the doings of *Virgill, Ouid, Horace, Iuuenall, Martiall, Lucan, Perseus, Tibullus, Catullus, Seneca,* and *Propertius.* (p. 3v)

The work of Sidney and Spenser confirms the approval of English which was then a commonplace. A language that produced such elegant authors must be acceptable. Further confirmation of the elegance and acceptability of English was found in the translations of the Bible which were made in the sixteenth and seventeenth centuries. Although a Wycliffite Bible had been available from the end of the fourteenth century, the Church had proscribed translations. The suppression of the Catholic Church and monasteries in England introduced a new situation, for the Puritans accepted the Bible rather than the Pope as their guide to Christian belief. Hence the need for translations so that all could be familiar with the Bible became imperative. The culmination of this process was the 1611 Bible which became one of the great totems of the power and elegance of the English language. Since the word of God could find such complete expression in English, it was no longer possible to believe that English was not a fit language for literary composition.

However, the praise of writers like Sidney and Spenser is sometimes tempered by that comparison with Latin which demands that English should imitate Latin in everything. English poetry did not use the hexameters of Latin poetry and therefore it could not be as good as the Latin. This suggested to some that the inability of the language to be used successfully for hexameters was a sign that English must in some respects be deficient. Generally the success or failure of the language was determined by its ability to be used for elegant writing, particularly poetry. Language was for most commentators the handmaid of literature, and it was only good literature which confirmed the excellence of the language. In many respects such writers were attacking the failure of English authors to extend the precepts of classical rhetoric to English composition, but it is not uncommon for apparent failures in writing to be blamed more generally as a shortcoming in the language. After a time some began to react against the excessive introduction of foreign words and elaboration of rhetoric found in some literary works. This reaction was associated especially with the Puritans who preferred a plain English to the flamboyance of much contemporary writing. Their voice was to become much more audible in the seventeenth century and paved the way for calls to purify and regulate the language which we find in the latter part of the seventeenth century.

In the last chapter we saw that differences in spoken dialects were recognised and Chaucer could use the northern dialect for comic effect in the Reeve's Tale. Attitudes towards regional varieties of speech and their lack of prestige began to crystallise in the fifteenth and sixteenth centuries in which comparisons of their forms with those in the approved variety indicate that value judgements were being applied to these differences. One of the varieties that came in for early opprobrium was Kentish. In *Peter Idley's Instructions to his Son*, composed about 1445–50, Idley writes:

> And thoughe myn Englysshe be symple to your entente,
> Haue me excused – I was born in Kent.

The clear inference is that someone who is born in Kent cannot speak as elegantly as those born in or near London. Somewhat later Stephen Hawes in his *Pastime of Pleasure* not only made Kent the home of his foolish dwarf, Godfrey Gobylyve, but he also represented the dialect of his speech:

> 'Sotheych,' quod he, 'whan I cham in Kent
> At home I cham though I be hyther sent.
> I cham a gentylman of moche noble kynne
> Though Iche be cladde in a knaues skynne.'
> (ch. 29)

The tell-tale features are *Iche* for *I* and *sotheych* for *soothly*, and as noted earlier in this chapter neither of these forms was included in Chancery Standard. Caxton exploited this sentiment when he apologised for his indifferent English by claiming in the prologue to *History of Troy* (1474) that he was born in Kent. This attitude towards the Kentish dialect was transformed into the use of a southern variety as a stage dialect to indicate rusticity and foolishness. Examples of *ich, chill* and *cham* are found in *Ralph Roister Doister* (*c*.1550), and similar forms as well as examples of initial voiced fricatives like *zorte* (for *sort*) and *zedge* (for *say*) occur in *Respublica* from about 1553. The best-known example of this stage dialect is in *King Lear* where it is adopted by Edgar when he is leading his father to Dover and meets Oswald. In this scene (IV, vi) Oswald addresses him as *bold peasant* and *slave* and one reason for this acceptance of Edgar's status must be his language which the audience would understand as well.

All of this indicates a recognition that there was an approved variety against which departures were judged socially. In the Second Shepherd's Wakefield play of the Towneley Cycle Mak, a shepherd who has stolen a sheep, tries to disguise himself as a royal official and uses southern forms. This could suggest that in the north at this time royal officials were likely to be southerners and that there the southern dialect carried with it certain overtones of officialdom and the law. Sir Thomas Elyot in his *Governor* (1531) advises that the nurses who look after the children of noblemen in their infancy should speak only that English which is 'cleane/ polite/perfectly/and articulately pronounced/omittinge no lettre or syllable' (L3v).

The *locus classicus* for the proof that London English had become accepted as the standard for pronunciation in the country as a whole is found in George Puttenham's *The Arte of English Poesie* (1589), and the passage needs to be quoted at length. He is referring to the language a poet should use.

Our maker [i.e. poet] therfore at these dayes shall not follow *Piers plowman* nor *Gower* nor *Lydgate* nor yet *Chaucer*, for their language is now out of vse with vs: neither shall he take the termes of Northern-men, such as they vse in dayly talke, whether they be noble men or gentlemen, or of their best clarkes all is a matter: nor in effect any speach vsed beyond the riuer of Trent, though no man can deny but that theirs is the purer English Saxon at this day, yet it is not so Courtly nor so currant as our Southerne English is, no more is the far Westerne mans speach: ye shall therefore take the vsuall speach of the Court, and that of London and the shires lying about London within lx. myles, and not much aboue. I say not this but that in euery shyre of England there be gentlemen and others that speake but specially write as good Southerne as we of Middlesex or Surrey do, but not the common people of euery shire, to whom the gentlemen, and also their learned clarkes do for the most part condescend, but herein we are already ruled by th'English Dictionaries and other bookes written by learned men, and therefore it needeth none other direction in that behalfe. (Bk III, ch. 4)

This passage is of great interest for it highlights that the language which is approved is that of London and the Home Counties. Puttenham also introduces three other features: the problem of change in language, differences in register, and the relationship between speech and writing. While he recognises that old authors like Chaucer were excellent poets, their language is now old-fashioned and cannot be used as a model by contemporary poets. He accepts that language has changed, but he does not elaborate on what these changes consist of. He draws a distinction between the language of gentlemen and the language of common people. They speak differently and one should always take the language of the court as a guide to good pronunciation, and by implication that was the basis of the appropriate written form. Even noblemen who live outside London may use their local dialect and so cannot be taken as a guide to how one should speak. From other sources we know that Sir Walter Ralegh kept his Devon accent till his death, and presumably this is the kind of situation to which Puttenham refers. He may of course also refer to differences in register between noblemen and commoners, for this was a feature which gets much greater attention at this time and is exploited by the dramatists. Finally he distinguishes between speech and writing. He appears to accept two things. Firstly, he recognises that people who spoke with a different accent could still write in accordance with what he understood to be the standard; speech and writing are now separated in his evaluation of an individual's command of language. In order to communicate with their own local people, noblemen from the provinces could use their own dialect in their speech, but when writing letters or documents they might use the standard. This is what happened with the Pastons; although they gradually learned to adjust their spelling to the standard, they did not necessarily (we may assume) adjust their speech as well. Unless individual members of the family spent a considerable time outside Norfolk, one would imagine them continuing to speak with a Norfolk accent. Secondly, he suggests that writing was now very much in the hands of the learned, who apparently set the trend in what is the correct spelling system. Because of the learned books and dictionaries written by scholars, he does not feel it necessary to make any further comment on writing systems because they provided the guidance. Few after Puttenham's time questioned that the best speech was that of London and its environs, but the questions of register and spelling demand further consideration.

It may be noted that several writers, particularly in the sixteenth century, devised new spelling systems for English. Among the most prominent of these are John Hart and William Bullokar. What is significant about new systems such as these is not so much that they were never adopted, but that they were based on the spoken language. They represented a complete break with traditional spelling and used pronunciation as their guide for their recommended spellings. This in turn meant that they had to choose one form of pronunciation as the basis for their spelling system, and not unnaturally they chose what they considered the best and purest pronunciation. What they tell us about pronunciation is something we shall leave to the next chapter. For the present chapter it is sufficient to record that writers like Hart accepted that there was one pronunciation which was both recognised as the best and sufficiently stable to form the basis of spelling. John Hart, both in his manuscript works and in his published *Orthographie* (1569) and *Methode* (1570), states that the speech of London is the best and most perfect. He qualifies that by suggesting that the speech found at the Court and in London represents the 'flower of the English tongue'. It is this speech which everyone ought to aspire to, though he recognises that people who live in the north and west have a different pronunciation and might therefore need a different spelling system. This was a view accepted in part by Edmund Coote in his *The English Schoolemaister* (1596) who suggests that northern speakers may use their own spelling to reflect their pronunciation only in their private correspondence, but that otherwise they should not use this variety publicly.

Differences of register are to be found in the drama and in some of the collections of words and expressions made in the sixteenth and seventeenth centuries. Latin was the language of learning and many Latin words were taken into the language. This meant that there was now a sharper division between learned language and ordinary language – the former being heavily Latinate. Inevitably this led to satire of the language of the learned and the affected pedantry which they could exhibit. In the play *Mankind* from about 1465–70 there is the following:

'Corn seruit bredibus, chaffe horsibus, straw fyrybusque.'
Thys ys as moche to say, to yowr leude wnderstondynge.[10]

The first line is a mixture of Latin and English to suggest that some speakers mangled their English by adulterating it with Latin inflectional endings in order to impress their hearers. This is why it is necessary for the speaker to explain what it means for the benefit of their 'leude wnderstondynge', that is ignorance, lack of education. Shakespeare frequently puts malapropisms in the mouths of his less educated speakers, and these usually involve prefixes or suffixes of Latinate words which would naturally be the words that such speakers misused. Dogberry in *Much Ado About Nothing* uses *suspect* for *respect* and *senseless* for *sensible*. Mistress Quickly in *Henry V* confuses incarnate and carnation. Shakespeare also pokes fun at the pedants in the form of Holofernes in *Love's Labour's Lost*. He is an example of that growing trend not only to use a very Latinate vocabulary, but also to use the spelling as a guide to pronunciation.

I abhor such fanatical phastasims, such insociable and point-device companions, such rackers of orthography, as to speak 'dout' *sine* 'b', when he should say 'doubt', 'det', when he should pronounce 'debt' – 'd, e, b, t', not 'd, e, t'. (V.i.17–21)

We can detect in this passage that sense of unease which would affect those who wanted to speak properly, for that meant they would need to have some guidance as to what was correct. In the absence of any other guide, they would use spelling and so spelling-pronunciations would develop. As pronunciation became a matter of social acceptability, so the importance of not pronouncing words inelegantly would increase.

To judge from certain comments found in plays at this time, another marker of social class was the oaths that individuals used. Shakespeare once again provides us with some clues. In *Henry IV*

Part I when Lady Hotspur exclaims 'Not mine, in good sooth' (III.i.242), her husband exclaims 'you swear like a comfit-maker's wife. . . . Swear me, Kate, like a lady as thou art, A good mouth-filling oath' (243–9). Evidently some speakers recognised distinctions in oaths. Elsewhere in the same play, Prince Hal indicates that the tapsters at the inn use expressions which are confined to their profession. When he assumes the role of a tapster, he notes 'They [i.e. tapsters] call drinking deep "dyeing scarlet", and when you breathe in your watering they cry "Hem!" and bid you "Play it off"' (II.v.14–17). Each trade and profession was developing its own language, just as each class has its own vocabulary. Oaths and obscenities are now found in writing, something which had not happened previously, but this is simply because there had been little drama in earlier periods and what was written tended to be courtly and elevated. Lower-class characters now appear regularly in the literature and they are given a language which increasingly marks them off from their social superiors. Differences in register no doubt always existed in the language, but now they were not only given expression but they also became associated with the prejudices which attached to those not familiar with the standard writing system and correct pronunciation.

This interest in different varieties led to the recording of the vocabulary of certain types like tramps and vagabonds, who appear frequently in the literature at the end of the sixteenth and beginning of the seventeenth century. This interest is a side-effect of the acceptance of polite metropolitan pronunciation and vocabulary as the norm. Those who use a different language become an obvious subject for investigation. Some authors wrote about this underclass in London, which as a large city naturally acted as a magnet for the criminal behaviour commonly associated with vagabonds. Writers like Greene and Nash described the activities which this underclass engaged in to fleece unsuspecting visitors and naïve citizens. A number of glossaries of the language of vagabonds were published. The first of these may have been John Awdeley's *The Fraternitie of Vacabondes*, first printed in 1565. A more substantial collection was Thomas Harman's *A Caueat for Commen Cursetors* (1567). Harman was a magistrate who had frequent dealings with vagabonds in Kent, and he provides accounts of their methods of trickery as well as a glossary of their language, which was probably devised to prevent those in authority from understanding what

122

Loues Labour's loft.

Actus primus.

Enter Ferdinand King of Nauarre, Berowne, Longauill, and Dumane.

Ferdinand.

Et *Fame*, that all hunt after in their liues,
Liue regiftred vpon our brazen Tombes,
And then grace vs in the difgrace of death:
when fpight of cormorant deuouringTime,
Th'endeuour of this prefent breath may buy:
That honour which fhall bate his fythes keene edge,
And make vs heyres of all eternitie.
Therefore braue Conquerours, for fo you are,
That warre againft your owne affections,
And the huge Armie of the worlds defires.
Our late edict fhall ftrongly ftand in force,
Nauar fhall be the wonder of the world.
Our Court fhall be a little Achademe,
Still and contemplatiue in liuing Art.
You three, *Berowne, Dumaine,* and *Longauill,*
Haue fworne for three yeeres terme, to liue with me:
My fellow Schollers, and to keepe thofe ftatutes
That are recorded in this fcedule heere.
Your oathes are paft, and now fubfcribe your names:
That his owne hand may ftrike his honour downe,
That violates the fmalleft branch heerein:
If you are arm'd to doe, as fworne to do,
Subfcribe to your deepe oathes, and keepe it to.
Longauill. I am refolu'd, 'tis but a three yeeres faft:
The minde fhall banquet, though the body pine,
Fat paunches haue leane pates: and dainty bits,
Make rich the ribs, but bankerout the wits.
Dumane. My louing Lord, *Dumane* is mortified,
The groffer manner of thefe worlds delights,
He throwes vpon the groffe worlds bafer flaues:
To loue, to wealth, to pompe, I pine and die,
With all thefe liuing in Philofophie.
Berowne. I can but fay their proteftation ouer,
So much, deare Liege, I haue already fworne,
That is, to liue and ftudy heere three yeeres.
But there are other ftrict obferuances:
As not to fee a woman in that terme,
Which I hope well is not enrolled there.
And one day in a weeke to touch no foode:
And but one meale on euery day befide:
The which I hope is not enrolled there.
And then to fleepe but three houres in the night,
And not be feene to winke of all the day.
When I was wont to thinke no harme all night,
And make a darke night too of halfe the day:

Which I hope well is not enrolled there.
O, thefe are barren taskes, too hard to keepe,
Not to fee Ladies, ftudy, faft, not fleepe.
Ferd. Your oath is paft, to paffe away from thefe.
Berow. Let me fay no my Liedge, and if you pleafe,
I onely fwore to ftudy with your grace,
And ftay heere in your Court for three yeeres fpace.
Longa. You fwore to that *Berowne,* and to the reft.
Berow. By yea and nay fir, than I fwore in ieft.
What is the end of ftudy, let me know?
Fer. Why that to know which elfe wee fhould not know.
Ber. Things hid & bard (you meane) fro common fenfe.
Ferd. I, that is ftudies god-like recompence.
Bero. Come on then, I will fweare to ftudie fo,
To know the thing I am forbid to know:
As thus, to ftudy where I well may dine,
When I to faft expreffely am forbid.
Or ftudie where to meet fome Miftreffe fine,
When Miftreffes from common fenfe are hid.
Or hauing fworne too hard a keeping oath,
Studie to breake it, and not breake my troth.
If ftudies gaine be thus, and this be fo,
Studie knowes that which yet it doth not know,
Sweare me to this, and I will nere fay no.
Ferd. Thefe be the ftops that hinder ftudie quite,
And traine our intellects to vaine delight.
Ber. Why? all delights are vaine, and that moft vaine
Which with paine purchas'd, doth inherit paine,
As painefully to pore vpon a Booke,
To feeke the light of truth, while truth the while
Doth falfely blinde the eye-fight of his looke:
Light feeeking light, doth light of light beguile:
So ere you finde where light in darkeneffe lies,
Your light growes darke by lofing of your eyes.
Studie me how to pleafe the eye indeede,
By fixing it vpon a fairer eye,
Who dazling fo, that eye fhall be his heed,
And giue him light that it was blinded by.
Studie is like the heauens glorious Sunne,
That will not be deepe fearch'd with fawcy lookes:
Small haue continuall plodders euer wonne,
Saue bafe authoritie from others Bookes.
Thefe earthly Godfathers of heauens lights,
That giue a name to euery fixed Starre,
Haue no more profit of their fhining nights,
Then thofe that walke and wot not what they are.
Too much to know, is to know nought but fame:
And euery Godfather can giue a name.
Fer. How well hee's read, to reafon againft reading.
Dum.

FIGURE 7.2 Shakespeare's First Folio, 1623. *Mr William Shakespeare's Comedies*, p. 122, *Love's Labour's Lost*. c39i12 (*British Library*).

they were saying. Among the words listed are *cove* 'man', *fambles* 'hands', *gan* 'mouth', *to nygle* 'to have intercourse', *pannam* 'bread' and *skypper* 'barn'. A few of these words like *cove* have been accepted into informal speech more generally, and the origin of others like *pannam* are not too difficult to deduce, since it is probably related to French *pain*, Latin *panis* (acc *panem*). This language differed from ordinary English only in its vocabulary; the syntax, at least in the examples given by Harman, did not deviate from that of the standard.

In view of the belief that English was an impoverished language, it is hardly surprising that there was considerable debate about how this poverty should be amended. Although the fifteenth century complained about the poverty of English, there was not much discussion then about how to put it right. Writers like Lydgate simply borrowed words from Latin because they felt this was the way to follow Chaucer's lead. In the sixteenth century the debate consisted of two main strands. The first was the provision of manuals of rhetoric to provide rules and examples for English poets to create a high style. Apart from Puttenham's book already mentioned, the best known are Thomas Wilson's *Arte of Rhetorique* (1553) and Abraham Fraunce's *Arcadian Rhetorike* (1588). The primary period for production of these manuals was the second half of the sixteenth century. Usually they provided lists of the various rhetorical figures of speech with examples from Latin, and sometimes also from Greek and modern English authors. By using these manuals a writer could compose his poems with elaborate types of word arrangements and sound effects. The second element was more contentious and involved dispute about how the vocabulary should be enlarged. The possibilities which were canvassed were using the resources of English to create new compound words in English, borrowing words from the classical languages, and exploiting the writings of old poets like Chaucer to reintroduce words which were then archaic. Each method had its own supporters. The way which had become customary of enlarging the wordstock was through borrowing from other, especially classical, languages, and this was the system which was adopted by most writers at this time. However, there were some who borrowed words just for the sake of borrowing because they felt that the more words of classical origin they had in their writing, the better it would be. Many words were borrowed unnecessarily and there were many who objected to this headlong pursuit of classical borrowing in what became known as the 'inkhorn controversy'. Many classical words borrowed at this time have remained in the language, but others are found only once or twice because they served no useful function. Some of the more careful importers of Latin words often used them in conjunction with an English word so that those ignorant of Latin would have some idea of its meaning. This method was promoted and used by Richard Mulcaster in *The First Part of the Elementarie* (1582).

Those who objected to the wholesale importation of learned words urged that English should use its own resources, rather in the way that German still does. The prominent supporter of this position was the Greek scholar, Sir John Cheke, who recommended using English morphemes to construct new English words. He put his proposal to the test by offering a translation of the Gospel of St Matthew which used English lexical resources for new words. There we find such words as *gainrising* 'resurrection', *ground-wrought* 'founded' and *hunderder* 'centurion'. Some of these words were archaic, but most were new formations. Because Latin borrowing became our dominant system of lexical enlargement, these words seem strange to us today, but they were less so in the sixteenth century. Cheke was not generally successful in his aims, but there was a strong trend towards purism in vocabulary which developed from the end of the sixteenth century and with which the Puritans were particularly associated. Such critics often demanded a simpler style as well as a simpler vocabulary, and some regarded Latin as tainted because of its association with the Catholic Church. A different, if related, approach was taken by those who wanted to revive some of the archaic vocabulary found in earlier poets. This found clearest expression in Spenser's *The Shepheardes Calender* (1579) where many words used by Chaucer and his contemporaries were used. This poem had an introduction and notes explaining both the method of borrowing and an explanation of some of the words. These were written by a certain 'E.K.' who accepted that the words were difficult to understand and could appear 'ragged and rustical' because the 'olde and obsolete wordes are most vsed of country folke'. E.K. thus offers the main reasons why archaic words were not adopted by most writers. They are difficult to understand, but more importantly they do not have the necessary stylistic elevation because of their association with rustic language to make them appropriate for works of high literature. Furthermore, archaic words were insufficient in number to satisfy the needs for new vocabulary. In the end borrowing from Latin and Greek became the dominant method of lexical expansion, for as scholarly and learned works were in Latin it was easy to borrow the appropriate words from Latin to express technical concepts in English. In literature the best writers like Shakespeare are often able to mix words of Latin etymology with the shorter words of Germanic origin so that they can provide a contrast in tone and weight.

What we can notice in this debate is that both writers and scholars took part, for it was a subject of national debate. English was a topic of sufficient importance to arouse the concern of people in the highest reaches of society. The debate about English was also an educational debate because it involved how to spell and write, which meant how to study and learn about language more generally. One field of scholarship which unites these two areas is that of dictionaries. In the previous periods occasional glossaries had been constructed, usually to assist the learning of Latin. Glossaries continue to be made in this period for the same reason, but they now show certain developments. Most previous glossaries had been Latin–English ones, in which Latin words were provided with an English gloss. The first glossary in the fifteenth century was the _Promptorium Parvulorum_, compiled in 1440 by a certain Geoffrey the grammarian in Norfolk, which contains about 12,000 English entries arranged alphabetically together with a Latin gloss. It is likely that this glossary was made from turning around a Latin glossary so that instead of being a Latin–English glossary it became an English–Latin one. This is suggested by the occurrence of English phrases and doublets which are glossed by single Latin words and not the reverse. Such entries as '**Daggar**, to steke with men: _Pugio, -onis_; fem.gen., 3 decl.' or '**Dawynce** in cerkyl: _Chorea_; fem., prime' are understandable only if they come from an original Latin–English glossary.[11] Similar glossaries were compiled in the fifteenth and sixteenth centuries.

These glossaries were expanded to become dictionaries. The first of these to be printed was the _Hortus Vocabulorum_, which was published by Wynkyn de Worde in 1500. The sixteenth century witnessed a growth in the publication of bilingual dictionaries, usually only of a foreign language into English. They were mainly Latin–English dictionaries such as that compiled by Sir Thomas Elyot in 1538. Sometimes dictionaries were linked with a grammar of the foreign language, as is true of Jehan Palsgrave's _Lesclarcisse-_

A
Table Alphabeticall, con-
teyning and teaching the true
vvriting, and vnderſtanding of hard
vſuall Engliſh wordes, borrowed from
the Hebrew, Greeke, Latine,
or French. &c.

With the interpretation thereof by
plaine Engliſh words, gathered for the benefit &
helpe of Ladies, Gentlewomen, or any other
vnskilfull perſons.

Whereby they may the more eaſilie
and better vnderſtand many hard Engliſh
wordes, vvhich they ſhall heare or read in
Scriptures, Sermons, or elſwhere, and alſo
be made able to vſe the ſame aptly
themſelues.

Legere, et non intelligere , neglegere eſt.
As good not read, as not to vnderſtand.

AT LONDON,
Printed by I. R. for Edmund Wea-
uer, & are to be ſold at his ſhop at the great
North doore of Paules Church.
1 6 0 4.

FIGURE 7.3 Robert Cawdrey, *A Table Alphabeticall*, 1604. The title-
page of the first English dictionary (*The Bodleian Library*).

ment de la langue francoyse of 1530, though better French–English dictionaries were published by Holliband in 1593 and Cotgrave in 1611. Italian–English and Spanish–English dictionaries were also published. These bilingual dictionaries are important because they compared English implicitly with a foreign language, they provided sources for new words in English, and they promoted the development of English dictionaries.

The first dictionary of English appeared in 1604. Already in 1582 Mulcaster in his *Elementarie* had provided a list of 8000 English words without definitions which should be included in a dictionary. He also wrote that

> It were a thing verie praiseworthie in my opinion, and no less profitable than praise worthie, if som learned and as laborious a man, wold gather all the words which we vse in our *English* tung, whether naturall or incorporate, out of all profesions, as well learned as not, into one dictionarie.

So when in 1604 Robert Cawdrey issued his *A Table Alphabeticall* the ground had been well prepared. This is a list of the hard words in English, usually those of Latin origin, with a gloss normally of a single word, as '*Maladie*, disease'. No further information was given. In fact Cawdrey borrowed most of his material from Latin–English glossaries and schoolbooks, particularly Thomas Thomas's *Dictionarium Linguae Latinae et Anglicanae* (*c.*1588) and Edmund Coote's *The English Schoolemaister* (1596). But Cawdrey had twice as many words as Coote and Thomas, and at least he established the idea of a monolingual dictionary as a separate publication, even if it contained a limited number of words with basic glosses. There was no attempt to be inclusive and Cawdrey simply took over the words he could find in sources like Thomas and Coote, supplemented in a haphazard fashion. Cawdrey's example was followed by John Bullokar's *English Expositor* (1616) and others up to Edward Phillips' *The New World of English Words* (1658). These dictionaries grow in size, but they all concentrate on hard words or those of technical use, and most of them shamelessly plunder the dictionaries of their predecessors so that the effect is cumulative. The wordstock of one dictionary provides a starting point for the next. No attempt is made to exclude words which had no currency or which were included incorrectly. Most, but by no means all, words were of Latin origin and this improved the chances of Latinate words surviving in the language. There was no concept at this time that a dictionary should contain all the words in the language; these dictionaries were useful aids for explaining learned words, and at the same time encouraging the use of such words by writers. The existence of glossaries of the language of vagabonds did not mean that those words found their way into dictionaries.

An important feature of this period was instruction in grammar and the books which were written for teachers and schoolchildren. The teaching of grammar was forced into a straitjacket by the royal diktat that only Lily's Latin grammar was authorised for use in schools from 1540 onwards. This had the effect both of stultifying any advance in grammar teaching in the schools and of encouraging Latin as the universal grammar. The rules found in Lily became a set of prescribed regulations which it was impossible to overlook or get round. As other Latin grammars were prohibited, it meant that all teaching sprang from Lily, and this applied as much to English grammar as to Latin. One means of getting round the restriction was to translate sections of Lily into English, particularly the examples to illustrate constructions found in it which had already been separated off in accompanying volumes called *Vulgaria*. This inevitably produced the result that English was considered to have exactly the same grammatical make-up as Latin. Another means of getting round Lily was to write books in English explaining Lily and the principles behind his grammar. Thus J. Stockwood produced his *A plaine and easie Laying open of the Meaning and Understanding of the Rules of Con- struction in the English Accedence* (1590) which was a commentary on that part of Lily commonly referred to as *Accedence*. Others followed in his footsteps. The existence of such commentaries illustrate that it was impossible to teach Latin through a grammar written in Latin: children had to have some knowledge of English grammar before they embarked on Latin. Inevitably grammar seemed to be no more than a set of rules which had to be learned, and since English could never quite match up to the grammar instituted for Latin, it would seem to be an inferior and corrupted language. But the difficulty of learning Latin through Latin did lead to a widespread acceptance by 1660 that Latin had to be taught through English, and that did provide some spur to investigating the nature of English. One method of instruction which remained popular was that of translation. The system promoted by Roger Ascham in the sixteenth century was that pupils should translate a passage from Latin into English, and then a little later they should translate their English version back into Latin. This encouraged people to recognise the differences between the two languages, without necessarily encouraging them to assume that English though different from Latin was as good as Latin.

William Lily's Latin grammar is a compilation of mixed authorship, which is based upon the traditional grammar teaching going back to the classical grammars by Donatus and Priscian. It was essentially a manual for teaching, and it was not speculative or innovative. It was constructed around the eight parts of speech as follows: noun (including the article), pronoun, verb, participle, adverb, conjunction, preposition and interjection. The adjective was treated as a noun. This system was the dominant one throughout our period, though it was modified by some authors. Nevertheless, the diversity which gradually began to occur in grammars underlined the unsatisfactory nature of this division into word classes, particularly when it was applied to English. Thus the need to establish the article and the adjective as independent classes led to problems for the original classification. The need to adjust the parts of speech to English shows that particularly during the seventeenth century the treatment of grammar was a little more flexible than the dominance of Lily's grammar might lead one to imagine. Although till the end of the seventeenth century every English grammar was either a translation of or closely modelled on Lily, in the following century the system was opened up. At first in this teaching rhetoric and grammar were closely linked and associated with vocabulary through glossaries. This meant that there was a strong link between language and literature. It was also true that any discussion about grammar which referred to English easily passed over into a discussion about language and the position and nature of the English language. It was, however, much easier for writers at this time to consider the position of English rather than its nature, for the stranglehold of Latin made it difficult to see English on its own terms.

Edmund Coote's *The English Schoolemaister* (1596) is a typical example of the kind of schoolbook issued at this time is . Its subtitle is 'Teaching all his scholers, of what age soeuer, the most easie, short, and perfect order of distinct reading, and true writing of our English tongue.' In his preface Coote notes that he will explain hard words and help to instruct those ignorant of Latin. He will include a table containing the true writing and understanding of any hard English word borrowed from English, Latin or French. He also explains the 'true Orthographie of any word truly pronounced', though he qualifies this by saying only for those words whose spelling is settled because there are many words which may be spelt in different ways, such as *malicious/malitious*. He provides an alphabet, which excludes *j* and *v*, because the pairs *i/j*, *u/v* were treated as single letters. He then provides instruction in spelling by using the common system of syllables. One proceeded as a learner to learn all possible two-syllable units, then three-syllable units and so on. Coote provides extensive lists of all syllables which fall into these categories on an alphabetical basis. If one then learned the principles for dividing words of more than one syllable into their constituent syllables, one could spell all words. Indeed, spelling was often defined as dividing words into syllables. As Coote writes 'Thou hast but two principall things to learne, to spell truly any word of one syllable, and to divide truly any word of many.' By providing lists of syllables one had in principle all the building blocks of English, and if a child learned these, he or she could be confident in spelling. It is important to bear this in mind in recognising how words may have been approached when spelling was being regulated. A book of this sort was the means whereby many children learned how to write and read English, which was a stage they went through before learning grammar. The existence of such books naturally led to a greater appreciation and awareness of the English language and would in turn encourage standardisation.

One other aspect of attitudes to English at this time merits attention. One reason why people regarded English as an inferior language was its lack of antiquity. During the sixteenth century studies into previous ages of English became fashionable and many manuscripts from the Anglo-Saxon period were collected. The appreciation that English was a Germanic language led to a re-evaluation of it as a language and a reconsideration of its history and development. This was important at a time when antiquity meant respectability. The very fact that the Germanic people had never been conquered by the Romans could be seen as a cause for pride. The ancient Germans were considered to be the strongest and bravest of nations, and the English had maintained the purity of the Germanic stock by not intermarrying with the Britons who were here when they settled. What came to be emphasised above all else was that the language was derived from Anglo-Saxon and this origin was also regarded as a source of pride. The Norman Conquest was by many regarded as a cause of the dilution and weakening of the language. One result of this growing pride in the Germanic origins of the nation was a reconsideration of the status of monosyllables, because they were regarded as a distinguishing feature of Germanic from Latin. It was also important for the Puritans that Anglo-Saxon was not related to Latin, for this enabled them to press for simple writing in monosyllabic English without the rhetoric and bombast of Latin. It was partly through this sense of antiquity that some, like Cheke, could press for the formation of new words on an Anglo-Saxon base through compounding or the use of English affixes. Whereas at the start of the period covered in this chapter the general attitude to English was one of despair at its lack of elegance, towards its end the growth in the standardisation of English, the frequency of literature of quality in English, and the realisation that English was an ancient language that had had its own church and its own writing for many centuries led people to appreciate its strength and status. This was not a universal view, but it was no longer so easy to dismiss English as unsophisticated. It could be considered a language of comparable stature with Latin, even if in some areas like scholarship it still lagged behind.

8

Language Change from 1400 to 1660

The period from 1400 to 1660 saw some of the most far-reaching changes in the English language, which is hardly surprising as the language was adjusting to the new standard. Once the standard was established, change became more controversial. In this chapter I concentrate on the changes in English within England. I disregard other dialects in Britain such as those in Scotland and Ireland, the former of which developed its own standard. Although America was colonised during this period, it was some time before independent developments in the language there can be detected and for a long period the standard accepted in America was the standard recognised in London. I start with a consideration of some changes in orthography. Since the growth of the standard was outlined in the last chapter, this aspect of English may be dealt with briefly.

In orthography various proposals were canvassed. The main conflict was between those who wanted to standardise spelling around traditional spellings and those who preferred to reform spelling in accordance with pronunciation. The proposals made by the latter group were so far away from the orthography used hitherto that they were not acceptable and this has remained the fate of spelling reformers. The former group contained many who wanted to modify tradition by making the etymology of words in English transparent. Consequently many words borrowed from French were given a Latin dress. It was now that <b> was inserted in *debt* and *doubt*, though without affecting the pronunciation. The same is true of the <c> in *victuals*. Other Latinisations have affected the pronunciation so that we have *admonish* rather than *amonest*, and *adultery* rather than *avoutrie*. Words which were thought to be of Greek origin had their spelling adjusted as well so that *throne* and *theatre* now gained an <h>. The word now spelt *rhyme* had been borrowed as *rime* from French about 1200, a form still used by some, particularly in American English. The spelling with <h>, influenced by *rhythmos* (English *rhythm*), is unetymological. Other changes which do not reflect strict etymology include *parliament* to replace *parlement* and *comptroller* as a variant of *controller* but implying financial control, perhaps because of the French *compte*. At this time <l> was inserted in *fault* (ME *faute*), probably because it was identified with Lat. *falsus*, <s> in *island* (ME *yland*) because it was linked with Latin *insula*, and <h> in *author* (Lat. *auctor*) because of its assumed Greek origin. Through analogy <l> was inserted in *could* because it had become silent in *should* and *would*. When initial *wh* and *w* fell together in some southern dialects and when elsewhere /wh/ retained only the aspirate, it opened up the possibility of spelling words with <wh> which etymologically had initial /h/ or /w/. This has produced modern spellings like *whole* (OE *hāl*) and *whelk* (OE *weoloc*). Spellings common in the sixteenth and seventeenth centuries that have not survived include *phantasy* for *fantasy* and *abhominable* for *abominable*. The former was adopted to show its Greek etymology and the latter because the etymology was understood to be from Latin *ab+homin-* (from Lat. *homo* 'man') rather than from Lat. *omen, omin-* 'omen'. These reformed spellings created uncertainty how the words should be pronounced. Gradually most adopted spelling pronunciations, though both an original and a new pronunciation existed side by side in many cases, and some words never accepted a spelling pronunciation. Etymology was a strong force in the changes in spelling and the examples mentioned here are merely a fraction of those introduced at this time. No doubt the adoption of etymology was partly motivated by the standardised spelling of classical Latin since that allowed English to accept a standard spelling for classical words as a contribution to the overall standardisation of the language.

Another feature of this period was the printing press which had been brought to England by William Caxton in 1476. Before then English became standardised as the Chancery Standard spread through London and beyond. It could spread because most writing was undertaken by scribes taught to use a specific spelling system. The printing press in England was remarkable in two ways: most of the material it produced was in English rather than in Latin, and most of the compositors in the early period were foreigners – few of whom, if any, had any training in the current writing system found in England. Consequently, the compositors were not familiar with the new standard and so produced spellings which were not stand-ardised and did not necessarily reflect the standard in London. In addition, compositors wanted to justify their lines and to do this they often adopted different spellings so that the ends of the lines were even. A word like *top* could be spelt *top, tope* or *toppe* according to the exigencies of justification. However, the printers preferred to avoid using abbreviations, which gradually disappeared from English. The introduction of the press did not at first assist the adoption of the standard, but over time compositors became more familiar with it and helped to ensure its triumph. It was the press which would ultimately be the guardian of the standard. Equally important is the fact that from the fifteenth century onwards writing by private individuals, in the form of letters, diaries, literary works and commonplace books, became more common. Most of these writers were not trained and some, especially those of more fashionable leanings, regarded correct spelling as something fit only for scholars and compositors; many affected a disdain for the humdrum business of regularity. In the development of the standard it is necessary to distinguish the writings of scribes, the printing press and private individuals. It is the scribes who adopted the standard, the press that was later to accept and extend it, and only later still did private individuals fall into line. Many private individuals expected the printers to correct and regularise what they had written, and this applies to literary writers as much as to others.

A consideration for those interested in spelling regularisation was the desire to prevent what had become homophones from also becoming homographs. The loss of many unstressed syllables, particularly final *-e*, and the changes associated with the Great Vowel Shift produced many homophones in English. Some etymo-logical spellings helped to prevent homophones from becoming homographs so that *seen* and *scene*, where the latter was given a Latinate spelling, have the same pronunciation but different spelling. Some differences in pronunciation were reflected in spell-ing, though these differences may be lost today even though the spellings are retained as we shall see. New graphs were introduced into the language. In the fifteenth century <ea> was introduced, probably from Anglo-Norman. Anglo-Norman had borrowed this graph from the first English standard in the early thirteenth century to represent /ɛ:/. In the fifteenth century words with /ɛ:/ from OE /æ:/ were distinguished from words with /e:/ and so it was sensible to spell the former with <ea> and the latter with <ee>. But the workings of the Great Vowel Shift ultimately meant that words with both pronunciations later fell together under /iː/. So *meat* and *meet* have different spellings but the same pronunciation. The introduction of <ea> led to the formation of a new graph <oa>, where the *a* which had been added to *e* to distinguish pronunciations of the two front mid vowels was added to *o* to distinguish the two back mid vowels. Thus <oa> distinguished words with /ɔː/ from those with /oː/ which were spelt <oo>. Another graph which may have been borrowed from Anglo-Norman was <ie> which is usually confined to French words with /iː/ such as *achieve*, but the digraph was also extended to some words of Germanic origin such as *thief*. These spellings were adopted by the printers and gained ready acceptance, though it took some time for the restriction of these spellings to particular words to be regularised.

Increasingly certain considerations were fed into the spelling system. When final *-e* fell in the spoken language, it became available as a free graph. It was adopted as a sign of length. The importance of distinguishing between long and short vowels in writing was recognised, because the difference between them had been accentuated by changes in pronunciation. The following markers were employed, though not consistently. Long vowels could be marked by doubling the vowel, so that <oo> and <o> represented /oː/ and /o/ respectively, or by the use of a final <e> after a single consonant, so that *boke* was an alternative to *book*. A digraph consisting of two vowel symbols, for example <ie, eo, ea>, indicated length. A vowel in a final syllable followed by a single consonant, as in *sun*, was short, but a short vowel in an earlier syllable could be represented by a double consonant or by two consonants, as in *berry* (OE *beriȝe*) or *fellow* (ME *felawe*). A vowel in an open syllable (that is one with a single final consonant followed by another syllable) was long, a reflection of the change brought about by open syllable lengthening. The doubling of the consonant effectively made the syllable closed and thus indicated a short vowel. It hardly needs emphasising that these general principles were not applied consistently, but they do provide some of the motivation to changes introduced in this period.

No distinction between <u> and <v> or between <i> and <j> was made on phonemic grounds at the beginning of the period and this distinction was only gradually introduced. Capitals were used arbitrarily, and in some handwritten documents it is difficult to tell what is a capital because of the irregularity in size of some writing. Capitals tended to be used for nouns and for the beginning of significant clauses. Punctuation was still mainly used for rhetorical purposes, and John Hart in his unpublished *The opening of the unreasonable writing of our Inglish toung* (*c.*1551) compared the full stop, colon and comma to musical notation for they indicated the length of a pause. In Middle English punctuation marks included the virgule (a diagonal stroke of varying length), a full stop (often written as a plus sign or even as a group of dots), an inverted semicolon and a question mark. With printing came in due course the full stop, colon, comma, exclamation mark and brackets. The semicolon and inverted commas were introduced later. The employment of these signs gradually favoured a grammatical over a rhetorical function. Thus a noun group could be marked off with commas even though that meant a comma could separate a subject or object, if extensive, from its verb. This still indicated where a reader might pause and did not necessarily explain the syntactic arrangement of the sentence. The full stop was seen as the marker of a sentence for the sentence as a grammatical concept was better established. Brackets could be used for emphasis or to mark some insertion or aside. The apostrophe was introduced during the sixteenth century to indicate a missing vowel, though its use was somewhat erratic, with *ile* as common as *I'll* for *I will*. In some printed material the apostrophe occurs in quite unexpected places particularly in dramatic texts. The semicolon was introduced by printers at the end of the sixteenth century and quickly became popular, though at first the colon and the semicolon are used indifferently without any separation in their functions. The exclamation mark is also found from the sixteenth century in printing, though isolated examples of it occur in manuscripts before then. The question mark could serve as an exclamation mark in early printed books, and it was only slowly that their functions were regularly distinguished. Inverted commas were introduced in the seventeenth century in the form of double commas usually employed at both the start of the speech and the beginning of each line in it. Finally, it should be noted that printers used a variety of different founts, particularly italic, as well as a range of other symbols, such as asterisks and pointing fingers, for emphasis or other effects. In general the period witnesses expansion in the type and number of punctuation marks which are subject to considerable experimental usage. Consistency was not attained.

As we turn to a consideration of phonology, we should appreciate that the sources for detecting changes in pronunciation are different from those in the past. As spelling became standardised, it becomes a less useful guide to pronunciation. It is true that private correspondence and diaries often give us some indication of how an individual may have pronounced certain words, but interpretation of these unusual spellings is complicated. We have to assess how to interpret the actual graphs used and then decide what social or regional variety may be represented and how far that differs from the pronunciation which might have been the one accepted by speakers in the educated classes in London. Other sources include for the first time writings about pronunciation and grammar. In the last chapter reference was made to the many proposals for reforming English spelling and inevitably that involved a discussion of current pronunciation. Those who produce spelling books or grammars give us some insight into how words were pronounced. Once again it is difficult to interpret this evidence. Is the writer representing his own pronunciation and, if so, where does he come from? Is he influenced by fashion and represents what he thinks people ought to say rather than what they do? Is he old-fashioned and recommending pronunciations already abandoned by educated London speakers? The great advantage of these writers is that some of them are competent phoneticians and they represent the whole system of pronunciation rather than giving an occasional spelling which may be significant. Finally there is the evidence provided by authors, particularly poets. The amount of poetry produced in this period was enormous when compared with the past, and its rhyme and metre can often tell us a great deal about possible pronunciations. Poets naturally rely on many different sources for their language and can often use eye-rhyme or rhymes based on regional or old-fashioned pronunciations to achieve their aims. Their evidence is helpful, but again has to be interpreted with caution.

At the end of the fourteenth century the vowel system in the dialect which produced London English may be represented as shown in Table 8.1. The symbol /ə/ represents a central vowel which had developed from the weakening of the pronunciation of many vowels in unstressed syllables. This pattern of vowels was not reproduced in other dialects, and this is a matter of some significance. In addition there were the diphthongs /ai, ui, oi, iu, ɛu, au, ɔu/, which were all long or at least behaved in the same

TABLE 8.1

	Front		Centre	Back	
High	i	iː		u	uː
High–mid	e	eː		o	oː
Low–mid		ɛː	ə		ɔː
Low	æ	aː			

way as long vowels. Only long vowels and diphthongs could occur as the final element of a stressed monosyllable. Long vowels and diphthongs interchange, but a diphthong will never replace a short vowel or vice versa. By this time there was a qualitative difference between the short vowels on the one hand and the long vowels and diphthongs on the other, and in this period each category underwent changes independently of the other.

The most important development was the operation of that change known as the Great Vowel Shift. Briefly this change meant that front and back long vowels were raised except that /iː, uː/, which could not be raised further were diphthongised and ultimately produced modern /ai/ and /au/ respectively. The nature of /aː/ is disputed since whether it was a front or back vowel is not clear; if it did not have the front quality indicated above, it was fronted before it was raised. The Shift, which was not uniform over the country and embraced several intermediate stages before arriving at the modern configuration, has been interpreted variously. The traditional debate has been whether the change was the result of a pull or push effect. If the diphthongisation of /iː, uː/ occurred first, this would create a gap at the top of the system which would encourage the lower vowels to be raised to fill the gap thus created. This movement of /iː, uː/ would create a pull on the lower vowels. If, on the other hand, it was the lower vowels which were beginning to move upwards, this would squeeze the two top vowels /iː, uː/ and force them to change their nature, and the only reasonable solution to this push effect was for these two vowels to form diphthongs. Recently a different explanation along sociolinguistic premises has been put forward.[1] It is worth considering this explanation in detail as an example of how sociolinguistics may help us to understand developments which took place in English with the emergence of a standard and the conflict of different dialects in larger conurbations like London.

The operation of the Shift was more extensive in southern and Midlands dialects than it was in the north, where it started earlier but was confined to front vowels. In London at least two different vowel systems came into conflict. The traditional London speech, associated with Chaucer and the upper middle classes in the city, distinguished the front and back mid vowels as indicated in the table above. Speakers of this variety distinguished /e:/ from /ɛ:/ and /o:/ from /ɔ:/. At first these two sounds may have been allophones arising often from the lengthening of short vowels in open syllables. As the final -e which was often the residue of the vowel that caused the lengthening disappeared, the phonemicisation of these sounds took place. The pronunciation of /e:/ and /o:/ was tensed and speakers of this variety may have deliberately adopted this tenseness to distinguish their pronunciation from that of incomers to London. If these speakers were, or considered themselves to be, of higher status, they might want to differentiate their speech. Since they could no longer use French as a sign of their status, they had to fall back on pronunciation of English. Tensed /e:/ was also found in French at this time and may have been the model for such speakers. Speakers of other varieties had a different pronunciation. One group consisted of East Anglian speakers who through trade in cloth and for other mercantile reasons were numerous in London in the fourteenth and fifteenth centuries. From the evidence found in Alexander Gil's *Logonomia Anglica* (1619) we know that what he calls Easterners had a different pronunciation of the vowels. Their dialect differed from London speech in having only three heights for long vowels; they did not distinguish between the two mid vowels. When these speakers came into contact with London speech, they would try to adjust their speech to that in London so as not to seem too provincial. In making these adjustments and imitating the London tensed vowels they might have succumbed to overadjustment by modifying the two allophones which constituted their mid vowel range, with the result that their attempt at /ɛ:/ produced /e:/ and at /e:/ produced /i:/. Gil also refers to a group of speakers whom he calls the *Mopsae*. These are not the same as the Easterners, though they may have come from the east of London. Characteristic of these speakers was their attempt to imitate fashionable speech, and in doing so they accentuated certain vowels by raising them – their pronunciation may have formed the ancestor of the more fashionable speech of the later seventeenth century. This is a matter which needs closer analysis and study. At all events it is possible to accept that the trigger for the Great Vowel Shift was sociolinguistic: an attempt by some speakers to imitate the more acceptable pronunciation of London and the potential competition which this provoked. This approach also suggests that although we call this change the Great Vowel Shift, it is not necessarily a unitary change. It involved a number of smaller adjustments to pronunciation spurred on by social considerations which differed in various parts of the country.

The changes which took place in the London area among educated speakers may be described roughly as follows. The two high vowels /i:/ and /u:/ were diphthongised by the development of a front glide vowel which may have started out as [i] and [u] respectively, but was soon [ə], to give /əi/ and /əu/. These, or some developments of them, possibly /ei/ and /au/, remained the pronunciation of these sounds until the end of this period. The new diphthongs developed in the eighteenth century towards their present pronunciation. The two high mid vowels /e:, o:/ were raised to occupy the slots vacated by /i:, u:/ so that words like *meet* (OE *mētan*) and *fool* (ME *fōl*) retain the older spelling but have their modern pronunciation. Some words with /o:/ raised to /u:/ later had this long vowel shortened to /u/, and a few then lowered and centred this short vowel to /ʌ/. Thus *good* has the spelling of the old long vowel /o:/, but it has been raised to /u:/ and then shortened to /u/, whereas *flood* has gone a stage further and exhibits the change of /u/ to /ʌ/. This latter sound was thus added to the inventory of English phonemes for the first time. At the beginning of this period two long low mid vowels /ɛ:, ɔ:/ existed and these were raised to /e:/ and /o:/ respectively. This change may have been somewhat later than the preceding one, though it was certainly operative by the sixteenth century. At least two systems of pronunciation, a conservative and an advanced, may have existed. To complicate matters further some speakers had raised /ɛ:/ through /e:/ to /i:/ so that it fell together with words which had had /e:/ in the previous period. There was a period when two, and possibly three, pronunciations of this vowel existed in London /ɛ:, e: and i:/. The latter two were in particular competition and there may once again have been social and fashionable differences in their use. Some speakers may have retained a distinction between words like *meat* with OE ǣ and *meet* with OE ē̄ to the end of this period. For most speakers the two sounds merged except for certain words which fell together with the new /ɛ:/ which had developed from /a:/ by the same process of raising associated with the Great Vowel Shift. The raising of /a:/ added to the confusion in possible pronunciations which were found in the London area at this time. The conditions for confusion were ideal. Clearly different pronunciations could be heard because we find rhymes which even into the eighteenth century joined *speak* with either *make* or *seek*. Words which today retain a pronunciation reflecting /e:/ at this time, particularly *great, break* and *steak*, are rhymed with words which now have /i:/ like *speak* and *seat*. However, words with Middle English /ɛ:/ followed by /r/ like *pear* retained this pronunciation. A pool of variants existed from which ultimately the language chose single forms as the norm. London speech was a mixed dialect which contained elements from different regions and also probably from different social groups. During this period although many people may have preferred one pronunciation over another, they would be exposed to other pronunciations.

The short vowels were much more stable than the long ones, presumably because the long and short vowels were now qualitatively different, so that movement in one did not necessarily impinge upon the other. The two vowels /a/ and /o/ underwent minor adjustments to their pronunciation. The former became /æ/ which became accepted as the standard form by the end of the sixteenth century, whereas the latter was lowered to /ɒ/ and among some speakers developed further towards /a/. The latter pronunciation became fashionable towards the end of our period and is represented by <a> spellings in Restoration drama in words like *Gad* for *God*. Even before that, occasional spellings with <a> are found and some words have retained those spellings when the expression was accepted into the standard, either from a more technical vocabulary or from slang. Thus *nap* 'surface of cloth' (from Dutch *noppe*) and *drat* (from *God rot* with the latter having the /a/ associated with affected language) exhibit these two tendencies. The vowel /u/ underwent most change in that it split into two phonemes with some words retaining the original /u/ or possibly changing it to /ʊ/ and others changing it to /ʌ/. This change probably took place in the early seventeenth century. Words which had a labial or fricative before the vowel and an /l/ after it often retained /u/, as in *pull*. There were other words with different consonants like *bush* which retained /u/. This change did not happen in the north and the resulting variation is one of the characteristic features distinguishing southern and northern English today, so that a word like *cut* has /u/ in the north, but /ʌ/ in the south. There was also the central unrounded vowel /ə/ which was at first confined to unstressed syllables. There was no symbol to represent this sound and so in private correspondence in particular there was considerable variety in its representation. Many writers, for example, preferred *-ar* for the agent noun ending which in Modern English is usually *-er*, but sometimes *-or*. Where /i/ occurred in unstressed syllables it was retained, and there was a tendency for /e/ often to move towards /i/ rather than to /ə/. In stressed syllables a following /r/ caused the short vowels /e, i, u/ to become the central unrounded vowel /ə/. This happened earlier with /i, e/ than with /u/; with the former it took place around 1600 and with the latter in the following fifty years. However, words with the group *er* in many cases fell together with words with *ar*, and in private correspondence there is considerable variety in the spelling of these two groups. Today this has resulted in some words having one spelling but a different pronunciation so that *clerk* and *Derby* are usually pronounced as though they were spelt *clark* (cf. the proper name *Clark*) and *Darby*. The /ar/ pronunciation in words spelt <er> was heard in affected speech for some time after this period so that *servant* could be pronounced /sɑːvənt/.

Initial /w/ affected a following /a/. Before the sixteenth century speakers pronounced a word like *watch* with /æ/ to rhyme with words like *catch*. But /w/ caused the following vowel to be rounded and ultimately to fall together with /o/, which was developing to /ɒ/. As with many other sounds in London English, the two pronunciations existed side by side for some time. The new sound was only gradually accepted into polite speech, and many speakers continued to use the old sound into the eighteenth century. Certainly poets could rhyme words like *wand* and *hand* in the eighteenth century as Jonathan Swift did with this pair. If a velar followed the vowel, then rounding did not take place so that *wag* still rhymes with *crag*. When the vowel was followed by /r/, lengthening took place when /r/ fell; this is a development which is better treated in the following chapter. We have already noted that after the raising of /oː/ to /uː/ some words which contained this new vowel developed a shortened form of the vowel, either

/u/ or /ʌ/. A similar phenomenon appears to have happened with
/ɛ:/, which sometimes when raised to /e:/ lost its length before it
could be raised further to /i:/. In Modern English a word like *breath*
has the <ea> graph representing OE *æ* which was /ɛ:/ from the
thirteenth century. The word has been shortened, but it has kept
the spelling indicative of long vowels. It is a mark of the
standardisation of the spelling system that once a spelling was
established it was not changed when the sounds within a word
underwent any development. Why certain words developed a
short vowel where a long one had been is not certain. Most cases
involve a monosyllable with a final consonant. Examples of
shortened /u:/ included *flood* and *blood*, and of shortened /e:/
breath and *death*. In most cases two forms of these words, one with
long and one with short vowel, existed side by side for many years.
The move to reduce variation was only gradual.

The diphthongs underwent considerable changes at this time
and some fell together with the long vowels. The two diphthongs
/iu/ and /ɛu/ fell together as /ju:/ so that *new* (OE *nīwe*) with
Middle English /iu/ and *dew* (OE *dēaw*) with Middle English /ɛu/
fell together. Some words with these diphthongs were to undergo further development whereby /ju:/ became /u:/. This was
accepted into polite London English after this period, but may have
started in some speakers long before and been carried over to
North America by them. Words with original /ɛu/ were usually
spelt with <ew> as were many of the words with /iu/, but these
latter words could sometimes be spelt differently. The diphthong
/au/ as in *clause* was monopthongised and became /ɒ:/, though
the spelling <au> was retained in most words except where /au/
had developed from /a/ followed by /l/ as in *all*. Words of French
origin where *a* came before a nasal as in *chance* are often spelt with
<au>, but they developed differently in this period. The reasons for
this difference are almost certainly variant pronunciations among
social classes in London. There probably existed variant class
prounciations of words like *aunt* and *ancient* which have produced
the differences found today. In this period polite speakers probably
pronounced most, if not all, of these words with the same vowel.

The diphthong /ai/ started to change when its first element was
raised through /æ/ to /ɛ/ to give the form /ɛi/, a stage reached
during the sixteenth century if not earlier. This diphthong was then
monophthongised to /ɛ:/. However, many speakers still kept their
diphthongal pronunciation, while others used the monophthong,

and this may have prevented the new monophthong from falling together with the /ɛ:/ which was being raised through the Great Vowel Shift. For some speakers the two did fall together so that *say* (ME *sæȝen*) and *sea* (OE *sǣ*) were pronounced identically. In a different development /a:/ became /ɛ:/ and so fell together with the /ɛ:/ which already existed in this dialect. This meant that *tale* (OE *talu*) and *tail* (OE *tæȝel*) were pronounced alike. In the first word *tale* OE /æ/ became /a/ and was lengthened through open syllable lengthening, after which the final unstressed /ə/ was lost. The result of this change was that there were three sounds which could have the same pronunciation, though most speakers probably pronounced only two of them identically. However, rhymes from this period indicate that words with any of these three different origins could be pronounced alike. In the end London English accepted that /ɛ:/ fell together with /e:/ under /i:/ and that /ai/ and /æ:/ fell together under /ɛ:/. The diphthong /ɔu/ was monophthongised as well and first it became simple /ɔ:/ and was then raised to /o:/. When that happened, it fell together in southern dialects with Old English /ɑ:/ which had been raised to /ɔ:/ in the twelfth century. Thus *soul* (OE *sāwol*) has the same vowel as *so* (OE *swā*) and *sole* (ME *soul*, from Anglo-Norman and ultimately from Lat. *solus*). Once more there was a difference in London English between speakers with conservative and advanced pronunciations, for in the former the diphthong was retained and in the latter the monophthong was regular. The two diphthongs /oi/ and /ui/ fell together as /ɔi/. Some speakers developed a different pronunciation for words which had original <oi>, but the evidence for this is much stronger in the next period and so it is better left for discussion till then.

Already in this chapter reference has been made to the loss of final -*e*. In many varieties this had disappeared before the beginning of our period, though writers like Chaucer had used it in their poetry and there is no doubt that it was available in con- servative pronunciation. In the fifteenth century it appears to have disappeared entirely and so was no longer available. In many other words final unstressed syllables even for words of French origin became blurred so that they could rhyme together. Shakespeare rhymes *departure* with *shorter* as though the former was pronounced as though written *departer* which is implied by the pun involved.

As for the consonants, two new phonemes entered English. In words spelt <ng> and <nk> the first consonant was pronounced

/ŋ/, but this sound was an allophone of /n/. In the former group the final /g/ was lost during the fifteenth century in some varieties of eastern English and this may have included the lower-class variety in London. During the sixteenth century this loss was accepted into mainstream London English. When that happened the /ŋ/ was phonemicised, for it was the only feature which distinguished *sing* from *sin*. This loss occurred only when the group <ng> occurred as the final element of a word; the /g/ was retained medially as in *anger*. The other new phoneme was /ʒ/ which was the voiced form of /ʃ/ and its introduction completed the series of voiced and voiceless fricatives. In words like *vision* the pronunciation of <si> until at least 1600 was /zj/. Early in the seventeenth century the /zj/ changed into the single sound /ʒ/. This new sound also extended to words which had medial /z/ followed by the earlier diphthong /iu/ like *pleasure*. Later it was to be extended to new loans from French like *beige*. At that stage it was possible to use this sound finally; before then it had been restricted to medial positions.

Initial /h/ was always unstable and was frequently dropped in pronunciation. This loss was accentuated by the absence of initial /h/ in many words borrowed from French which in Middle English were often written without <h>. With the introduction of Latin spellings <h> was introduced and this led to the adoption of spelling pronunciations, though even today the pronunciation of /h/ in some words is uncertain as can be seen from the use of *an* rather than *a* as the indefinite article in front of them. In this period <h> spellings encouraged /h/ pronunciations, though this tendency had not developed as far as it has done today. Inevitably it becomes a sociolinguistic marker with the result that different writers recommend its pronunciation in different words. Before /t/ and finally, *h* had had a different colouring after front and back vowels, though the distinction was allophonic, with /ç/ after front vowels and /χ/ after back vowels. The *h* had already begun to fall before /t/ in the previous period and its fall seems to be confirmed not only by spellings like *spight* 'spite' in French words which had never had an *h*, but also by rhymes that link *spite* with *bright*. Although final /χ/ disappeared in most words, it became /f/ in some northern dialects and this sound was accepted in London English in certain words. Thus we have *laugh* with <gh> representing an older *h* but with the /f/ pronunciation. The distribution of this /f/ was different in the sixteenth and seventeenth centuries from that found today. Even more significant, some orthoepists in these centuries have different recommendations about the pronunciation or absence of all types of *h*. There was undoubtedly a sharp divide between the more conservative and the more advanced pronunciations, and each writer made his own proposals as to what was best.

The initial consonant groups /wr/ and /hw/ were simplified in this period and thus followed the path of initial /wl/ and /hl/ which had been simplified earlier. Innovative and conservative tendencies exist side by side so that among some speakers /wr/ became /r/ during the sixteenth century, but others kept it much later. But spellings without <w> for former /wr/ and spellings of words like *whole* from Old English *hal*, noted above, indicate that these clusters were simplified. /w/ was also lost when followed by /h/ and a back vowel as in *who*. It was also lost when it followed another consonant as the pronunciation of *sword* and *two* makes clear. However, the influence of spelling has often led to the reintroduction of this /w/; today *swore* has reinstated /w/; previously it was identical with *sore*. Other consonant groups were simplified, a regular feature throughout the history of English. Groups consisting either of /m/ plus consonant or of /s/ or /f/ plus /t/ lost the final consonant, as in *lamb*, *listen* and *often*. The /t/ has sometimes been reinstated in the second group, but this has not affected the first.

As we saw in chapter 6, the introduction of so many French words created variation in the stress pattern of English. The tendency to push the stress to the front of a word characteristic of Germanic came into conflict with the Romance preference to have the stress further back. The result was uncertainty among speakers of the language as to how to stress particular words, an uncertainty which has persisted to this day as the different pronunciations of a word like *controversy* reveal. Inevitably schoolmasters and other self-appointed advisers on language came forward with their own suggestions. To judge by the recommendations of grammarians many words adopted the Germanic stress pattern, though some have since abandoned it. According to othoepists words like *délectable* and *ácademy* were stressed on the initial syllable. Although some patterns do start to emerge, with stress on the antepenultimate syllable in Romance words, they were by no means regular yet.

The phonology of this period is characterised by the availability of different pronunciations in the variety recognised as the standard. However, pronunciation cannot be regulated as easily as spelling. Whereas spelling was fairly well regulated by the end of this period, the same is not true of pronunciation. There was no uniformity in the recommendations of the grammarians and it is difficult to know what impact their writings may have had on the average speaker. Even today there are variants available in pronunciation, and in this period those variants were far more numerous and regulation far less effective. There were, as there still are, conservatives opposed to innovators, but there was less acceptance that grammarians should tell everyone how they should pronounce their words. But those who wanted to appear fashionable, or at least not too provincial, doubtless tried to discover how they should pronounce their words. Provided one did not use a variety which was too provincial, such as that represented by the southern stage dialect, it is difficult to believe that the desire for respectability was as yet too dominant a force. The mixture of varieties was too profound, the question of what lead to follow too confusing, the stranglehold of Latin on education too powerful, and the availability of reading matter too limited to allow speakers to do much more than begin to make adjustments to their pronunciation.

In morphology the trend towards simplification which charac- terised the earlier stages of the language continues. As the language became more analytic the endings found earlier became less functional and were ripe for disappearance. In the nouns the *-es* of plurals and genitive singular was so well established that the reduction of anomalous forms continues. Plurals in *-n* and zero plurals are reduced virtually to their modern extent by the end of this period. Genitives without ending are more or less eliminated or form virtual compounds with another noun, as in *Lady chapel*. The *-s* genitive was interpreted as *his* by some and this led to forms like *for Christ his sake*. This may have originated through the weak form of the possessive pronoun *his* as *is*. It was also extended to *her* to give expressions like *Venus her shell*. Examples are found sporadically throughout this period.

In the personal pronoun two developments are significant. The genitive of the neuter was *his*, but new forms, *it* and *its*, arose. The form *it* is rare, and *its* is purely an extension of the genitive ending *-s* to *it*. The form *his* survives into the seventeenth century and is replaced by *its* only towards the end of the period. The second singular forms gradually give way to the plural. The use of *ye/you* with a singular meaning was prompted by politeness and the influence of French; it was found already in the fourteenth century. In day-to-day language *you* became the dominant form both for the nominative and the oblique cases in the singular during the seventeenth century or even earlier. The old singular forms *thou/thee* are retained in poetry and formal writing, and so it is difficult to detect how quickly they were replaced in speech. The distinction in usage became similar to that found in French and German today with *you* being the neutral form and *thou/thee* expressing familiarity, contempt or anger. This usage was far from stable, and many writers appear to use the forms indiscriminately. In the possessive pronoun the distinction between forms with or without final -*n* (for example *mine* versus *my*) is increasingly regulated by whether the following word starts with a vowel or consonant, but regularity is not achieved. The development of forms with -*s* in *hers*, *ours*, *yours* and *theirs* formed on analogy with *his* allows such forms to parallel the predicative use of *mine* and *thine*.

With adjectives the use of *more/most* in the comparative and superlative becomes possible, though their use is not regulated. Double comparisons become frequent as *more/most* become commoner. Objections to double comparions arose only at the end of the seventeenth century.

The inflectional system of the verb underwent further simplification. In 1400 the present indicative had inflections as follows:

Singular	First person	-*e* (or *zero*)
	Second person	-*(e)st*
	Third person	-*(e)th* (or -*s*)
Plural	All persons	-*en/eth*

The first person quickly lost its inflection, and the second person would lose its inflection as the plural *ye/you* was extended to the singular. In the third person the -*eth* ending is found in writing until the seventeenth century, but it is increasingly restricted to poetry where its ability to add an extra syllable to the metre made it a valuable resource. It seems likely that the -*s* form was already the usual form in speech by the sixteenth century, but its usefulness in poetry and conservatism kept the -*eth* form alive till much later. In some common verbs like *have* and *do*, the *-th* forms survived longer even in speech. It is possible, however, that forms with *-(e)th* were kept in writing even though they were not used in speech, and this is certainly the opinion expressed by Richard Hodges in his *Special Help to Orthography* of 1643. Even after this date grammarians retain both as possible endings, though this may be the conservatism of teachers. In the plural the inflectional endings drop out in the sixteenth century except in some conservative writings. The inflections in the preterite survive only in weak verbs, where the second singular has *-(e)st* and the plural *-en*. These fall in the same way as the similar endings of the present tense.

With the strong verbs the changes in formation of the preterite and past participle continue the trends noted in the penultimate chapter. Strong verbs develop weak preterites, though for a time individual verbs have both weak and strong forms. The verbs which remain strong are those that either had one of the dominant patterns like class I or are so frequently used that they could survive as anomalous verbs, like *come*. The two major patterns which survived were <i – o – i> of class I and <i – a – u> of class III. Examples are *write* – *wrote* – *written* and *sing* – *sang* – *sung*. Even these patterns take time to settle down and there is considerable variation in different writers. Other patterns which are less strong include <ea – o – o> as in *swear* – *swore* – *sworn*. As can be seen from these examples, the past participle ending in *-n* was frequently retained, but certainly not in all verbs. In weak verbs the preterite was formed by adding *-ed* but the /e/ fell except after /t/ and /d/ where it became /i/. The resulting /d/ remained after voiced consonants, but became /t/ after voiceless ones. This produced *panted* with /id/, *shoved* with /d/ and *talked* with /t/. The main outlines of this system were developed by the middle of the seventeenth century, but variation survived well into the following one.

With irregular verbs like auxiliaries there are a few changes worthy of note. The *be* forms in the verb 'to be' survive and in the plural are still found at the end of this period. It is likely that conservative users preferred *be* forms until the eighteenth century in the present, but in the sixteenth century the singular is more often *am* and *is*, although in the plural the preference of *be* over *are* remains strong. The past participle of 'to go' is both *gone* and *went*, though the former is the commoner. The modal inflections are regularised with loss of the old plural forms. *Shall* was the old singular of the present tense and it had a plural *shull(en)*. This often led to variant forms with a singular *shull*. In these verbs the old singular was extended throughout the present. Writing exhibits contracted forms of these verbs for the first time, though they may have existed in the spoken language much earlier. These contractions are mostly either with the pronoun subject or with the negator, such as *I'll* or *shant*. The examples embraced more forms than we accept today so that we find *hant* (for *haven't*) and *am't* (for *am not*).

In syntax the period sees the continued movement towards an analytic language which increasingly restricts choice in placement of individual parts of the sentence. Equally the influence of Latin grammar encourages more 'logic' in the construction of a sentence and more explicitness in linking together its constituent elements. Thus the idea that each sentence should have a subject and a predicate becomes more dominant. At the same time the growth in literature which seeks to reflect the spoken language means an increase in the number of sentences which are incomplete or imperfectly formed. The insistence on rhetoric and sound effects in language also leads to these taking prominence over the logic of grammar. Thus the effects of standardisation and grammar are undermined by the appearance of language that is highly decorative or extremely colloquial, depending upon the stylistic effect a writer is trying to achieve. This period sees an expansion in the amount of English prose, much of which was more technical and descriptive. But some of the former category, for example Bacon's *Novum Organum*, was still written in Latin.

In the noun group the use of the articles is more regulated but it is still different from modern practice. The demonstrative adjective has three constituents rather than the modern two consisting of *this*, *that* and *yon*. Their meanings might be described broadly as 'close to the speaker', 'close to the hearer' and 'distant from both speaker and hearer'. The use of *yon* may be illustrated from Horatio's 'look, the morn. . . . Walks o'er the dew of yon high eastern hill' (*Hamlet* I.i.147–8). Characteristic of this time was the ability to have a possessive pronoun linked with the demonstrative, a usage that survived in the old Prayer Book in such expressions as 'these our prayers'. The demonstratives and definite article could be intensified by the addition of *ilke*, *same* or *self*. The former dropped out of the language during the fifteenth century, but the other two survived throughout the period. The use of *one* as a non-specific pronoun was found occasionally in the fourteenth century, but it had become very frequent by the sixteenth. Similarly the use of *one* as a propword, where it replaces a noun, is frequent from the sixteenth century in examples like 'I know that one'.

With nouns, the genitive could have both a subjective and an objective sense: *king's assassin* could mean the person who assassinated the king and the assassin employed by the king. While both are still possible today, the former was becoming less common in this period. The distribution of the -*s* and *of* genitives increasingly fits today's pattern, with the former being restricted to animate nouns although it survives in set phrases and proverbs. The group genitive is less often split than formerly, though this is still found, as in 'the Archbishop's grace of York'. Poets found the ability to split a heavy group into two parts a useful tool, but it is less common in other discourse. The double genitive is also very common, as in 'This speed of Caesar's' (*Antony and Cleopatra* III.vii.74). It was possible not only to use a pronoun as the head of a noun group, but also to treat it like a noun and have a determiner and/or pre-modifier and a post-modifier, as in 'the proudest he that holds up Lancaster' (*3 Henry VI* I.i.46).

The verb group in this period is less wordy than it was to become. The occurrence of more than two auxiliaries was rare and even two together was uncommon. The two tenses, present and preterite, continue, but this period is marked by the continued growth of periphrastic forms of the verb group. With *will* and *shall*, there is the beginning of that trend to use the former with the first person and the latter with the second and third persons to express futurity. The use of a part of the verb 'to be' with the present participle grows dramatically in this period and is found with all tenses both active and passive. Although at the beginning of the period the simple tense was often used instead of the progressive, the latter became more regular though it had still not achieved its present extent. The present tense still expresses futurity though forms with *will/shall* increase in number. Variation between the present and the future tense in a single passage is not uncommon. The preterite is used where today we prefer to use the perfect or the pluperfect tenses. Regulation between the perfect and the preterite has yet to divide their functions, for the preterite may be used with an adverbial of present time where today a perfect would be used. Increasingly the subjunctive was replaced by auxiliaries, and doubtless this was caused by the loss of its distinctive morphological endings. The subjunctive remains distinctive principally in the third person of the present indicative and there its use is often retained. The subjunctive when used was not yet formal or learned, for in drama it is used by all types of people in dialogue. The principal use of the subjunctive is in conditional clauses introduced by conjunctions like *if* and in optative clauses to express a wish. However, even in these cases, auxiliaries are frequently found as well. When a conditional clause is expressed through inversion of subject and verb, it is common to find the perfect or pluperfect subjunctive used since that allows the order auxiliary + subject + verb, as in 'Had he been here, we could have . . .'. The modal auxiliaries are still used as full verbs and are occasionally found in non-finite forms and without a following infinitive. This is particularly true of sentences expressing movement and may well have been colloquial. Expressions like 'We must away all night' (*1 Henry IV* IV.ii.56–7) are common in Shakespeare. The use of two modal auxiliaries in the same verb group becomes obsolete in the sixteenth century, as does its use as the second auxiliary after a primary auxiliary, so that expressions like 'may will' and 'had would' cease to be found. A feature of the modals at this time is the development of past tense forms with a modal meaning and these are at first used independently in a modal function though they are increasingly replaced by periphrastic expressions like *have to*.

It is in this period that the periphrastic form with *do* becomes grammaticalised, though variety in its use prompted by sociolinguistic factors continued into the next period, as we shall see. The frequency of *do* use increased dramatically in the period 1550–1600 in questions, both negative and affirmative, and in the period 1650–1700 for negatives. In questions the process started with *yes–no* questions, and the reason for this may be that most of those questions are direct and addressed to another person. This means that they use the second-person singular form which was still operative at this time. As the vowels in weak syllables disappeared, the second singular inflection developed to -*st* and when his ending was attached to verbs ending in consonantal groups, the result was a very long, and probably to many people ugly, consonantal grouping. One way of reducing the heavy consonantal group was to reduce -*st* to -*s*, as we find in Shakespeare, where forms like *affects* replace *affectst*. Another strategy was to use the *do* auxiliary so that *affectst thou?* is changed into *dost thou affect?* As the *thou* forms were gradually lost, the *do* auxiliary forms were extended to the second plural, which was increasingly fulfilling the function of the second singular. No doubt the general growth in the use of auxiliaries at this time encouraged the development of the *do* forms. From *yes–no* questions, the *do* form spread to *wh*-questions. From questions the *do* form spread to negative sentences, though this happened later. In this period many formal documents continue to record *do* forms in simple affirmative statements without necessarily implying emphasis. Because the inclusion of *do* makes the verb group longer, its presence adds weight and emphasis to a statement. This may have made it favoured by style-conscious writers who wanted to point a clause or mark a type of discourse. As the demands for a simpler style emerge towards the end of this period with the Puritans and others, the use of *do* as a stylistic marker decreases and allows it to become restricted to certain grammatical functions. In affirmative statements it became restricted to emphasis. This functional restriction of *do* may be understood as part of the general trend to regulate the use of auxiliaries and to standardise syntactic usage of all categories. This is something which becomes the particular concern of the eighteenth century. In both interrogative and negative clauses there may have been features of word order which helped to promote the adoption of *do* forms. In interrogatives the preference for *do* may have been motivated by the wish to avoid inversion and to keep the subject + verb order intact. In negatives there was a trend to push the negator forward in the sentence and by using the *do* auxiliary the negator could remain before the verb but follow the auxiliary. Such word-order considerations may not have been the primary reasons behind the grammaticalisation of *do*, but they must have helped. In changes of this sort, there was probably not a single cause for the developments which took place.

In the organisation of the sentence elements the preference for the subject + verb + object order was established and influenced the development of certain sentence patterns as we have just seen with *do*. It was this preference which led to the continued disappearance of impersonal verbs and which encouraged the use of object pronouns after parts of the verb 'to be'. It was also this which caused the disappearance of inversion of the subject and verb when an adverb was placed at the head of a sentence. This order remained in poetry for some time yet, but it was less and less common in ordinary affirmative statements. Verbs without an

expressed subject like the old impersonal verbs now either introduced a dummy subject like *it* or created the former dative into a
subject form so that 'Me thinks' became 'I think'. Otherwise some
forms acquire a quasi-adverbial status as happened with *may be*,
which increasingly was represented as a single word. However,
some impersonal verbs such as *happen* survive to the end of this
period. In previous periods the passive was formed by the
conversion of the direct object into the subject. In this period
the range of the passive was extended by the ability to convert
an indirect object into the subject. This could often leave the
preposition governing the object case high and dry at the end of
a clause. Although this usage is now acceptable, most writers
prefer to make the direct object the subject of a passive clause so
that 'The message was given to him' is more usual than 'He was
given the message', but both remain possible. Uncertainty as to the
nature of transitivity is suggested by the use of a direct object
with what might be considered intransitive verbs. Where in
Modern English we would use a preposition with an intransitive
verb, in this period the absence of a preposition made the adverbial into an object. A verb like *wonder* could be used either with *at*
or without a following preposition so that 'I wonder at your
remarks' and 'I wonder your remarks' appear to be inter-
changeable. This variation may be taken together with the variation
that exists between a phrasal verb and its simplex. Many verbs
were developing variants with a preposition, but here usage is not
discriminated and variants occur haphazardly. This is a period
where the meaning of such forms shows considerable expansion
and only gradually were these different meanings restricted in
usage.

Reflexive forms of verbs are commoner in this period than today,
for the tendency has been to convert reflexive verbs into intransitives by omitting the reflexive pronoun. The personal pronoun was
the usual form of the reflexive. The development of forms with -*self*
had not yet taken hold. Some verbs had an ethic dative which
came to seem not dissimilar from the reflexive form. It was used
with verbs of motion and found commonly when those verbs
were imperative. Usually this ethic dative is not co-referential with
the subject, but when it is, it is hard to separate from the reflexive.
This ethic dative was the subject of humour in *The Taming of the
Shrew* where Grumio understands Petruccio's 'knock me here
soundly' (I.ii.8) as an invitation to hit Petruccio. This suggests that

the usage was becoming unfamiliar so that its purpose could be misunderstood.

The adverb has always had a relatively free position within the sentence in English, but that freedom has been reduced over the years. In this period, for example, the ability to place an adverb between the verb and its object was reduced, no doubt because the link between the verb and its object was regarded as so close that if anything else was placed in that position it might mislead the hearer or reader to assume it was the object. Sentences like 'He caught often the train' become less acceptable and the adverbials of this type may be placed after an auxiliary 'He would often catch the train'. In negatives *ne* disappeared except in poetry and was replaced by *not* or other negators. *Neither* could still be used as a simple negator. As we have seen, *not* could be either before or after the verb but, as the use of auxiliary *do* increased, its position after the auxiliary and before the verb became standardised. Double negation was still common. It was only in the eighteenth century that its use was frowned on.

In the formation of complex sentences, one can detect a growing use of conjunctions to make clear the relationship between the various clauses which form a sentence. The growth in the concept of a sentence accelerated this development. In previous periods of English and still today in colloquial English, syndetic co-ordination and subordination are common. Co-ordination could express causality even with no conjunction. *The Merchant of Venice* has 'The Hebrew will turn Christian; he grows kind' (I.iii.177) without expressing the relationship between these two clauses. Examples like this suggest that the distinction between subordination and co-ordination was not so distinct as it is today. The conjunction *and* was itself used not only for co-ordination, but also to introduce conditional clauses. Indeed, it could function as an adverbial, a co-ordinate conjunction and a subordinate conjunction. In the latter function it often took the subjunctive. Examples like 'And it please you' reveal the function of *and* through the subjunctive *please* rather than indicative *pleases*. The increasing regulation of clauses meant that a large number of new conjunctions was needed and the function of those already in the language had to be more clearly distinguished.

The commonest relative pronoun at the beginning of this period was *that*. Soon *which* grew in frequency especially in non-restrictive clauses. This was followed by *whom, whose* and *who*, which may have grown more popular because *that* was not used with a preposition. By the beginning of the sixteenth century *wh*-forms are common in non-restrictive clauses, though *that* seems to have been retained in less formal discourse. *Which* was used for personal antecedents even from the beginning of this period and soon became the preferred form for all animate antecedents. The replacement of *which* by *who* for personal antecedents dates from the beginning of the seventeenth century, but it is not regulated during this period. The growth of the *wh*-forms at the expense of *that* is the result of the latter's heavy functional load. This overload may also have caused its abandonment not only as an addendum to *wh*-forms so that *which that* was simplified to *which*, but also as a feature of conjunctions so that *because that* is reduced to *because*. The zero relative was common in both subject and object functions, though usually only in restrictive clauses. It was particularly frequent after structures with *there is/there are* so that sentences of the form 'There is no beast Ø can hurt me' were common. Within a relative clause the use of a resumptive pronoun which uses a personal pronoun to reinforce the relative pronoun later in the clause or in a co-ordinate clause becomes less frequent, but examples continue beyond this period.

This period in the history of the English language is known as one of great lexical expansion, principally through borrowing from other languages but also through the formation of new words from the language's internal resources. The principal language for borrowing was Latin. This is true even for the fifteenth century where Lydgate is more consciously Latinate than Chaucer, whose borrowings had been more from French. The change to Latin was caused by the new humanism and the pre-eminence which this conferred on Latin, together with the great expansion of technical vocabulary which was almost all Latin-based or at least Greek through Latin. It was in this period that the English vocabulary finally lost its transparency as the large number of words inserted into the lexicon destroyed the cohesion in words belonging to the same semantic field or paradigm. A word like *rural* becomes the adjective for *countryside*, but there is no surface link between them although they relate to the same field of meaning. What is also characteristic of this period is the integration of the loan-words into the lexical structure of the language so that numerous hybrids emerge. Another important aspect is that many words are borrowed for stylistic or prestige reasons, resulting in the creation of an enormous number of doublets that have the same meaning. These doublets can have either different affixes attached to the same base or they can consist of words from several languages all meaning the same thing. What was important for many was the desire to borrow words and to increase the wordstock; regulation of this new vocabulary takes place only in the next period when many of these variant forms are either lost altogether or the words develop different meanings or registers. The relative lack of constraint on borrowing and experimentation and the pressure to write in an approved rhetorical mode served to make borrowing and new formations both acceptable and desirable.

Although many words were being borrowed from 1400 onwards, the period of greatest borrowing was between 1530 and 1660, with the peak in the decades either side of 1600.[2] This period is thus unique in the history of the language. We must also recognise that the period was one of a great efflorescence of literary and technical writing in English and this created the need for a vocabulary which was capable of expressing the new intellectual and other concepts. The desire to improve English was also significant. In the absence of a modern dictionary of the vocabulary of this period it is difficult to know how many new words caught on. A large number of new words were nonce occurrences and others may not have got past the dictionary-makers who had a professional interest in introducing new, difficult words. As we saw in the last chapter, many attacked the inkhorn terms that were created. The literary and other writings of this time probably bear little relation to the language of everyday usage, though inevitably some of the new learned words would enter common use. The way some writers like Shakespeare exploit malapropism reveals that the ordinary people were confused about both the form and the meaning of the loans, and most probably avoided them. Because literary works survive, we can gain a better idea of the vocabulary used by writers than we can of the vocabulary used in daily speech. The common core of the vocabulary probably remained relatively unchanged throughout the period, for it was in certain registers that the new words were congregated. Nevertheless, the creation of the standard must have rubbed off onto the lexis of the language so that certain words were approved and these would have entered the spoken language as well. We may also accept that many words extended their semantic range at this time, though the paucity of our sources makes it difficult to be certain that many of these new meanings that we first meet in this period had not existed earlier. The wealth of sources in English and the amount of scholarship at the time may create a picture of much greater creativity than is warranted.

The Latin loans tend to be bookish in nature because they form elements in a specialised vocabulary. Although some experimented with the use of Germanic words for science, scientists came to accept that it was best to use loans from Latin or Greek. Disciplines like medicine and mathematics used a high proportion of Latin or Greek words. Many of the words were anglicised by the addition of an English affix such as the *-y* in *commentary*. French loans, on the other hand, come from a living language and express the cultural and political contacts between the two countries. They are concerned with such fields as food or warfare. Other languages which contribute to English are Greek, usually through Latin, Italian, usually through French, and Spanish. The words from Spanish reflect the conflicts between the two countries not only in Europe, but also in the New World. Trade was also an important source for all countries with seaports on the Atlantic or North Sea. This is why Dutch added a number of words to the language, for the cross-Channel trade remained of great importance to both parties. Dutch words are also of a maritime nature. Other European languages also contribute to the lexicon, but not extensively. What is significant is the increasing number of words from non-European languages. Words of Arabic origin come through other languages, especially Spanish and Portuguese. A new source of borrowing is the New World with the establishment of English colonies in New England and Virginia. Their number was not large in this period.

The lexicon was expanded by word-formation from within the language. New compounds and derivatives were numerous, and functional shift was very popular with almost all authors. Shakespeare is as noted for these new formations as he is for his loans. The affixes already found in the previous period are enlarged with additional ones mainly from Latin. Negation could be expressed through the prefixes *a-*, *de-*, *dis-*, *in-*, *non-* and *un-*. Noun suffixes included *-eer*, *-er*, *-ess*, *-et*, *-ette*, *-ician*, *-kin*, *-let*, *-ling* and *-y* for concrete nouns, and *-age*, *-ate*, *-cy*, *-dom*, *-ery*, *-ful*, *-hood*, *-ing*, *-ism* and *-ship* for abstract ones, though this division was by no means rigid. Other suffixes existed to convert adjectives into nouns. With adjectives there were numerous Germanic and Latinate suffixes available at the time. The same applies to verbs and, less so, to adverbs. Compounds are sometimes difficult to distinguish because many nouns could be used in the pre-modifier position and some words could be used as intensifiers or as the first element of a compound. It can be difficult to decide whether Shakespearian groups like *soldier servant* and *all powerful* are compounds or not. What is striking is the range of combinations of parts of speech used in compounding; it might be true to say that almost anything was possible. A growing class of noun is the phrasal noun, especially at this time one consisting of a head followed by a prepositional phrase like *man-of-war*. Other parts of speech could lexicalise phrases too. Phrasal verbs continue to grow in number and what is notable is how many of these verbs develop a wide range of meanings. Functional shift increased the number of nouns, especially from verbs and adjectives, though functional shift was important in all word classes. Other processes of lexical enlargement in this period include back formation and clipping. These include *to cobble* from *cobbler* and *spital* from *hospital*. Many of these processes may have been active earlier, but left no trace although the number of words involved was relatively small compared with loans and compounds. They may be more characteristic of the spoken language and so less visible in literary writings of the period.

As a passage to represent the language of this period I have chosen an extract from George Puttenham's *The Arte of English Poesie* (1589). The passage is of interest not only for the language in which it is written, but also for what it tells us about the language of the time. It is a passage from a printed book and as such represents the standard language which printers were trying to reproduce. The extract comes from a chapter dealing with 'single wordes and working by their diuers soundes and audible tunes alteration to the eare onely and not the mynde'.

A Word as he lieth in course of language is many wayes figured and thereby not a little altered in sound, which consequently alters the tune and harmonie of a meeter as to the eare. And this alteration is sometimes by *adding* sometimes by *rabbating* of a sillable or letter to or from a word either in the beginning, middle or ending ioyning or vnioyning of sillables and letters suppressing or confounding their seuerall soundes, or by misplacing of a letter, or by cleare exchaunge of one letter for another, or by wrong ranging of the accent. And your figures of addition or surplus be three, videl. In the beginning, as to say: *I-doen*, for

The Preface to the Reader.

and they which refuse to be directed,I know are such as delight in their sot-
tish ignorance,like *Scoggens* priest, who becaufe he had vfed his old *amnumi-
fir.us* for thefe dozen yeres,would not forfake it,for the others new *affump-
fims*, though it were neuer fo good. Two things generally you muft marke
for the vfe of this booke : firft,the true vnderftanding of it for the matter :
fecondly, the manner of learning it, if thou be onely a fcholer,then the order of teaching it,if thou bee alfo a teacher. And for the firft,where I pro-
fefle to teach with farre more eafe and pleafure to the learner,and therfore
with greater fpeede then other : vnderftand the reafon. Thou haft but two
princ:pall things to learne,to fpell truly any word of one fyllable,and to diuide truly any word of many. For the firft I haue difpofed fyllables fo in the
firft booke (howfoeuer at the firft fight they may feeme common) as that
thou canft meete none but either thou haft it there fet downe,or at leaft fo
many like both for beginning or end,as that none can be propounded vnto
thee,which thou fhalt not be skilful in. And I haue fo begun with the eafieft,
proceeding by degrees vnto harder, that the firft learned,all the other will
follow with very little labour. Thefe fyllables knowne,becaufe al words be
they neuer fo long or hard be made of them, thou haft nothing to learne
but to diuide them : for which I haue layd downe fo eafie & certaine rules,
(beleeue me that haue tried)as that thou fhalt neuer erre in any hard word:
I doubt not, but thine owne experience fhal finde this true, and fo my pro-
mife in that point performed to the full. Maruaile not why in this firft book
I haue differed in writing many fyllables fró the vfuall manner, yea from
my felfe in the reft of the worke : as *templ* without *(e),fun* with one *(n)*and
plums,not *plummes*,&c. my reafon is, I haue there put no moe letters then
are of abfolute neceffitie, when in the reft I haue followed cuftome : yea,
often I write the fame word diuerfly (if it be vfed indifferently) the better
to acquaint thee with any kinde of writing. Touching the fpeeches at the
end of the 1. 2. 4. 7. and 8. chapters,regard not the matter (being vaine)but
my purpofe, which is to bring thee to prefent vfe of reading words of one
fyllable, which thou haft learned to fpell, and fo thou maieft haue nothing
in the fecond booke to learne,but only diuifion of words, and other harder
obferuations. The titles of the chapters and notes in the margent (which I
would alwayes haue thee diligently read and marke)will make thefe things
more plaine vnto thee.

Alfo, where I vndertake to make thee to write the true Orthographie of
any word truly pronounced, I muft meane it of thofe words, whofe writing
is determined : for there are many wherein the beft Englifh men in this
land are not agreed.As fome write *malicious*,deriuing it from *malice*.Other
write *malitious*, as from the Latine *malitiofus*. So fome write *German* from
the Latine,fome *Germain* from the French. Neither do I deale with proper
names,ftrange words of arte in feuerall fciences,nor the vnknowne termes
of peculiar countries, (if they differ from ordinary rules) vnles fometime
vpon fome fpeciall occafion. I know ere this, thou thirfteft that art a teacher,to heare how thou maieft with more eafe and profit teach a hundreth
fcholers then before fortie : follow mine aduife, and I warrant the fucceffe.
                                                                        Let

FIGURE 8.1 Edmund Coote, *The English Schoolemaister*, 1596. Preface
page A3 verso. X989/3900 (*British Library*).

doon, endanger, for *danger, embolden,* for *bolden.*

In the middle, as to say *renuers,* for *reuers, meeterly,* for *meetly, goldylockes,* for *goldlockes.*

In th'end, as to say *remembren* for *remembre, spoken* for *spoke.* And your figures of *rabbate* be as many, videl.

From the beginning, as to say *twixt* for *betwixt, gainsay* for *againesay: ill* for *euill:*

From the middle, as to say *paraunter* for *parauenture, poorety* for *pouertie, souraigne* for *soueraigne, tane* for *taken.*

From the end, as to say *morne* for *morning, bet* for *better,* and such like.

Your swallowing or eating vp one letter by another is when two vowels meete, whereof th'ones sound goeth into other, as to say for *to attaine t'attaine,* for *sorrow* and *smart sor'* and *smart.*

Your displacing of a sillable as to say *desier* for *desire, fier* for *fire . . .*

These many wayes may our maker alter his wordes, and sometimes it is done for pleasure to giue a better sound, sometimes vpon necessitie, and to make vp the rime. But our maker must take heed that he be not to bold specially in exchange of one letter for another, for vnlesse vsuall speach and custome allow it, it is a fault and no figure, and because these be figures of the smallest importaunce, I forbeare to giue them any vulgar name.

(Bk III, ch. 11)

The point of this chapter is to recognise that some words have two forms and that poets can choose either of these forms for their poetry for the exigencies of rhyme or metre. The variants are in both Germanic and French words, and this variation can be achieved by either adding or deleting sounds to or from a word's normal form. Some of the forms are definitely old-fashioned by now, such as *i-doen,* with <i> representing the old prefix of the past participle. The prefixes *en-* and *em-* are seen as purely figurative and not meaningful. The loss of a medial syllable as in *souraigne* represents the norm and the writing with a medial *-e-* may be merely visual. Unfortunately Puttenham does not tell us which variants are pronounced and which are merely orthographic. It is possible that some of the spellings represent pronunciations which were still kept by some speakers from different classes. At the end of the chapter he adds that this figure is so minor that he does not provide an English technical term. This implies that he expects technical terms to be

Latin, though he does convert some of them into English words to assist his readers.

The punctuation is not too far from that found today with full stops, colons and commas. There are no semicolons, but Puttenham does use apostrophes. The use of commas is light, but sometimes they occur where we expect a full stop. The final clauses 'and because . . . vulgar name' deserve to be a separate sentence. Commas might have been expected after 'sometimes by *adding* sometimes by *rabbating*'. In the extract capitals are used only at the beginning of a sentence; elsewhere in the book they are used for some nouns inside a sentence. Italics are used for significant technical words and for examples.

The spelling shows certain expected features: the variation of <i/y>, the use of <ie> rather than <y> as the noun suffix, the employment of <v> initially and <u> medially whatever the sound, the absence of <j>, with <i> acting as both vowel and consonant, the doubling of final <l>, and the arbitrary use of final <e>. Some doubling of consonants to indicate a short vowel is found, but this is not regular and the use of final <e> creates some open syllables where they are not appropriate for length significance as *surpluse*. The <o> of *to* (ModE *too*) is not doubled. His standard plural of nouns is *-es* rather than simple *-s*. In French words /ɑ/ before a nasal is sometimes written <au> and sometimes <a>; we find both *exchange* and *exchaunge*. The sound /i:/ from earlier /e:/ is written <ee> in *meeter* and *meetly*, and <ea> is used in *speach* and *pleasure*. It is not possible to decide whether this <ea> had the same realisation, but it seems unlikely. An <l> is included in *fault* (ME *faute*). Words thought to be from Latin have a Latinate spelling, as *confound*, *suppress*, *alteration*, *sillable*, *figure*, *surpluse*, *custome* and *vulgar*. But *rime* has not been given a spelling with <h>. The Latin abbreviation 'videl.' for *videlicet* (i.e. 'for example') is used. It is impossible to tell from the spelling what the pronunciation of individual words might have been. *Wrong* may or may not have lost its initial /w/ and the diphthong <oi> in *ioyning* may have been /oi/ or /ɔi/ or a development of it. Spelling is no longer a guide to pronunciation; on the contrary it is used for purely literary effects.

The third person of the present indicative is *-eth* in *lieth* and *goeth*, but *-s* in *alters*. The occurrence of *-e* in *forbeare* as first-person singular may not be significant of the retention of *-e* in the present tense. The present participle is always *-ing*. The infinitive is *to say* in cases where it stands by itself, but after a modal as *may heed* it has no *to*. The personal pronoun masculine form *he* is used where we would expect *it*. The personal pronouns have *th* forms regularly in the plural. The generalising *your* is used in 'your figures of addition' and 'Your swallowing', and *our* is found in 'our maker'. The present tense of 'to be' is *is* in the singular in statements, but *be* in subordinate clauses 'that he be not to bold'; the plural is *be* in 'your figures . . . be three'. No preterites occur in this extract.

The use of *and* and *but* to start a sentence is common. Some sentences have no verb, for the sentences with examples simply record the position in the word as though in an abbreviated tabular form. *Which* is used as a relative pronoun, though in 'which consequently alters' it refers to the whole of what precedes rather than to a specific antecedent. *Whereof* is used in the sense 'of which'. The conjunctions used are few, *as, that, vnlesse, because*. The conjunction *and* is inserted where we might leave it out in 'vpon necessitie, and to make vp the rime'. Here its use together with the infinitive suggests the sense 'in order to'. The order of the noun groups is standard. Adjectives precede their nouns. Prepositional genitives are usual for non-human referents and follow their noun, but 'th'ones sound' uses the genitive in -s without an apostrophe. Some nouns and noun substitutes do not have the definite article, 'in course of language' and 'into other'. The use of *any* rather than *a* before 'vulgar name' and of *These many* before 'wayes' may be noted. The two words 'swallowing and eating vp' still retain their verbal character, for they are not followed by *of*, but by an object to the two verbal nouns. Some expressions that would be prepositional groups today have no preposition: 'many wayes' and 'These many wayes'. The sentence elements have slightly more freedom than in modern English. A sentence-initial adverbial causes inversion of subject and verb in 'These many wayes may our maker alter'. But normally the order is SVO. Adverbials have more freedom of position, and particularly noteworthy are 'is many wayes figured' and the embedding of the adverbial clause 'as he lieth in course of language'.

The vocabulary contains many words of Latin extraction, though some had come to English through French. The basic lexis is relatively simple and the sentence structure is not complicated. There are many examples of parts of the verb 'to be', sometimes where one might expect a different verb: 'this alteration is some-times'. There are several phrasal verbs *eat vp, go into, make vp* and possibly *is by*. Some English words are used where one might expect a Latinate one: *maker* and *forbeare* rather than *poet* and *decline*. Doublets are used which may be either of English words 'swallowing and eating vp' or Latinate ones 'tune and harmonie' and 'addition or surpluse', where one word has the same meaning as the other. The phrase 'vsuall speach and custome' is probably best understood as a hendiadys meaning 'customary speech', for *vsuall* and *custome* have much the same meaning. The Latin words are of a somewhat technical nature, but they are mostly words which have survived in the language. The only unusual word is *rabbate* from Old French *rabate* 'diminution', a word which has also given us modern *rebate*. This passage gives a good understanding of how Latin had penetrated English vocabulary, but when used sensibly this lexis played an important and useful role in English. To replace all these words with Germanic ones was no longer an option which writers were prepared to adopt.

9

Establishing the Standard within Social Norms

When Oliver Cromwell, the Protector, died in 1658 the country entered a period of political instability even though his son Richard succeeded him as Protector. This instability led in 1660 to the re-establishment of the monarchy with the recall of Charles II from his exile in France. The Convention Parliament invited Charles to return and he was restored to the throne of England on 29 May 1660. The Restoration had important implications for the language and its development.

The immediate political result was the ending of the Puritan Commonwealth and the reinstatement of the monarchy. But the king had been invited back and did not therefore have the same political power and freedom as monarchs on the continent. He ruled with Parliament and was constrained by the development of a constitutional monarchy. The prevailing situation meant that the royal court had restricted power and influence. Much greater power rested with the governing class which was jealous of its own position, not only against the monarchy but also against the lower classes. The monarchy could lead in many matters of taste and fashion, but it was hedged in by various political constraints. Furthermore, Charles had spent most of his life hitherto in France and so was not as familiar with what had gone on in England as he would have been if he had lived here. His successor, James II, was deposed in 1688 through the Glorious Revolution because of his Catholic leanings and he was replaced by William and Mary. William III, as he became, was a Dutchman who was as unfamiliar with English ways as Charles had been. The death of Queen Anne in 1714 saw the end of the Stuart line and the throne of England passed to the Hanoverians. George I knew little English when he came to the throne; his son George II was better informed; and his grandson George III suffered from periods of mental instability.

Thus throughout this present period the throne was occupied by those who either had little experience of English and the English way of life or who were incapable for one reason or another of exercising great influence on events. This naturally vested more power in the hands of ministers and Parliament generally. This in its turn affected attitudes to language and society. It was John Locke who gave expression to the problem of how to reconcile personal liberty with the needs of society – a problem that also impinges upon language and its regulation. The guardians of the constitution and thus of the language were the 'men of property' for they were those who fashioned what was right and set the standard. The freedom to influence events by those who were without property and without a vote remained small or non-existent.

The restoration of Charles II meant that the period of antipathy towards foreign ideas and attitudes came to an end. Whereas the Puritans had been anti-Latin and had encouraged a plainer style and ordinary English, the Restoration saw the influx of French ideas and social ideals. The centralisation of power and language which had taken place in France naturally exercised a fascination for many English people. The Academie Française was regarded by some in England as the model which should be followed. The antipathy towards anything foreign, particularly if it had a papist tinge, shown by the Puritans was replaced by the wish to emulate all that was sophisticated and modern in France in particular. Latin loanwords became less frequent as French loans proliferated. However, there was an anti-French faction in political life which was able to fall back on the concept of England as a country of free men (at least of those who had property and the vote) and of an unwritten constitution which nevertheless guaranteed the rights of those with property. Hence there was a tendency to praise the 'genius of the language' which was based on custom and usage and was not confined by the petty rules which they associated with the grammars and other writings of the Academie Française. This usage was not the usage of the man in the street or of colloquial language; it was a very restricted usage which was invoked. For this period saw the rise of what came to be known as the English gentleman and one of the most important words in this period was 'polite'. Polite usage was what was aimed at and what was to be taught.

Polite usage was something quite separate from ordinary or colloquial usage. If anything the gap between what was acceptable usage, that is polite, and what was vulgar became more entrenched and pronounced at this time. This can be illustrated through the attitude to pronunciation. It was a common view at this time that pronunciation should be as close as possible to the written form. John Jones in his *Practical Phonography* of 1701 recommends for pronunciation that one should speak 'according to the Sound of the printed Letters, and not as usually sounded' (p. 12). The basis for pronunciation is the spelling and not how the words were actually pronounced in speech. Samuel Johnson in the grammar which was attached to his dictionary of 1755 enunciated the view 'For pronunciation the best general rule is, to consider those as the most elegant speakers who deviate least from the written words' (p. a2v). Any speaker who wished to be polite clearly had to be reasonably educated in order to read and to be familiar with the spelling system of the language. Anyone who merely spoke English in the way they had learned it from their infancy would not thereby be elegant speakers of the language. As Dr Johnson added in his grammar 'PRONUNCIATION is just, when every letter has its proper sound, and every syllable its proper accent' (p. c2v); it follows that one could not speak proper English unless one could spell and knew the rules of orthography. The implication is that there is a polite pronunciation which is taught through education and there is a vulgar pronunciation acquired through listening and speaking as a child but which carried with it no sense of politeness or acceptability. The lower classes were automatically excluded from any consideration of being polite speakers of their own language. One is not naturally a polite speaker; it is an accomplishment that has to be acquired through education. It is equally not an imitation of the pronunciation of the upper classes. Education is important, not birth. Indeed, it is characteristic of this period that there are constant attacks upon the affectation of those who are or want to be members of the nobility and who speak in a strange way. Jonathan Swift could compose a parody of the language of 'polite conversation' in which he attacked the affected language and expressions found among the very fashionable.[1] Partridge thinks that Swift's tract contains 'large chunks of conversation that bears every mark of having been recorded verbatim' (p. 16). Criticism of the affected was something which one finds in the plays of this period which deal with fashionable society and so offer plenty of scope for this type of satire.

Swift's attack on the affected pronunciation of the fashionable was important in that this was a period in which conversation was prized. It was the age of the coffee-house where the educated would gather to discuss important matters. It was an age where the conversation of a man like Dr Johnson could be recorded and regarded as a model of what good talk was. It was also an age in which language was very closely linked to social and moral discipline. A man who talked properly was a man who could be trusted to live a life after a strict moral and social code. His word could be trusted and his behaviour was regarded as exemplary. Hence those who were unable to talk properly were either libertines, as were those who aped fashionable talk, or ignorant and boorish, as were members of the lower classes. Good language should be taught because it inculcated correct attitudes to life. And good language meant a taught language where pronunciation followed writing. Grammars of this period often emphasise the moral purpose of their work for grammar and behaviour go hand in hand. Hence correctness in language was important because it bred correctness in behaviour and social mores. The approved language was one associated with polite society; it was free of fashionable affectations and cant; it was free of provincialisms; and it was free of the vulgarities of the lower classes. At the same time polite language was a language that was abstract rather than concrete. The advances of science were not part of the daily talk of the polite man; the gentleman was an amateur who could talk about everything in abstract terms without relapsing into the vulgarly concrete and detailed. Ordinary language, vulgar language, differed from polite language precisely because it never rose above the merely concrete and everyday things. It was located in the physical world and it could not enter the discourse of ideas and abstractions. The custom and usage which were approved represented what was prescribed by a small circle of people who abrogated the right to pronounce on what others should imitate. They were in a position to do so. Inevitably it bred insecurity among others who did not wish to seem either ignorant or provincial. It also led to an ever-increasing gulf between the written and the spoken language. The written language had its own rules and these were quite separate from the way most people spoke.

It was quite clear at this period that a standard was recognised and accepted. It was centred on London English; it was not regionally based. It was not the language of the royal court as had been claimed for the approved language of the previous period, though even in that period one may wonder how many writers were actually familiar with court usage. What is important is the ideal which is expressed whatever the realisation of that ideal. In the previous period the ideal had centred on the language of the court; in this period it was rather the polite language of gentlemen. The word 'gentlemen' needs to be stressed, since the language spoken by women was often vilified as being either too affected or too coarse. The standard was a taught language, associated with a certain level of education and social position. It was accepted that some who lived outside a certain circle around London might have a different pronunciation, but those who had variant pronunciations tried to lose them. When he came to London James Boswell learned to modify his accent, and when Thomas Sheridan went to Scotland he gave lessons on how to imitate the approved pronunciation. Not all his listeners found his advice helpful or complimentary. Elocution and prosody were regarded as very important and in 1762 Sheridan published his *Lectures on Elocution* which had been attended by large audiences when they were delivered. Elocution was a subject of great interest at this time and numerous books on how to speak well were published.

In the previous period, attention had focused upon two main features: spelling and vocabulary. Although spelling was not completely regulated by 1660, for most writers there was a recognised standard in spelling even if not everyone conformed. *The Writing Scholar's Companion: or, Infallible Rules for Writing True English* was published in 1695. It proclaimed on the title page that it was 'Composed for the Benefit of all such as are industriously Ambitious of so Commendable an Ornament, as Writing True *English* is generally esteemed'. In his preface to the reader the anonymous author notes that

> Here is nothing wanting I presume, to make the meanest Capacity write True *English* Competently well . . . which will soon render the Rules in this Book Easie and Familiar, and consequently the whole *English* Orthography; That your Writing may not Blush to appear before any Impartial Judge. But these Rules must be constantly practised till they come to be habitual.   (p. A2)

The author clearly accepts that there is a 'true writing' of English and that it can be learned through diligent application to the rules of spelling. For him the orthography was now standardised. However, his standard was not ours for, as can be seen from the quotations, he uses capitals for most nouns and adjectives. His book commences with some remarks on the letters of the alphabet; <j> and <v> are recognised as consonants. He claims that these

> are most justly now allowed, to be different Letters; . . . and are accordingly printed in our Bibles of latter impression for above these fifty years last past, yet remain still undistinguish't in several Writings, to the shame of the Writer, following the old unreasonable Custom of Writing always a (v) Consonant at the beginning of a word and a (u) vowel in the middle as they are Printed in our Bibles of former Editions; But reason, (one would think) should at length prevail, against such an absurd custom.
>
> (pp. A2–B)

It is interesting that he should accept the Bible as his standard for spelling and that he should date the adoption of the letters in their present distinctive uses from fifty years before his time, about 1645. He then continues with the general approach adopted by earlier writers by understanding that spelling comes from knowing how to write words of one syllable and how to divide multi-syllable words up into their constituent syllables. He then gives a whole set of rules as to when particular letters are used, which he follows with his rules for punctuation. In this list he includes most of the marks found in earlier writings and adds one or two additional marks such as the caret for omissions and the asterisk for illustration. He includes a list of abbreviations which may be used, but discourages the reader for employing them 'Because it argues disrespect, . . . Because many do not understand them' (p. G2). He then provides a list of words 'vulgarly spoken, and grossly mistaken in Writing' (p. G3) such as the spelling *Chimly* for *Chimney*. This is an indication of the way spoken forms were not to be used as a guide to their written representations. He then adds a list of homophones which have a different spelling or a different meaning. Other tables of various spellings complete his book. There never seems any doubt in this writer's mind that there is a standard spelling system, which has been regulated recently and is now properly taught to children who wish to be accepted as educated.

The other linguistic activity characteristic of the previous age had been lexical enlargement through extensive borrowing from Latin and other languages. This exuberance of borrowing was intended to make English a proper language for literary writing. When this was achieved, borrowing became less important and had towards the end of the previous period been somewhat circumscribed by the Puritans who regarded Latin as almost a heretical language. The distrust of elaborate vocabulary and rhetoric was something that the post-Restoration writers shared with the Puritans, because they were interested in a language which was transparent and allowed the meaning to shine through clearly without the distorting mirror of rhetoric and metaphor. They were also more interested in syntax than they were in vocabulary because syntax lay at the heart of rational discouse and was an important subject of study among those who were interested in the concept of a universal language. It was because of this interest in syntax that they attached importance to punctuation, which now formed a section in every book of grammar. Punctuation helped to clarify the syntax and thus was changing from being purely rhetorical towards a more grammatical function.

By 1660 the choice of educated London English as the basis of the standard had been accepted, but standardisation had progressed no further than achieving a high degree of consistency in spelling. It had not achieved any regulation of usage. The effect of new attitudes towards polite language and a standard was to decrease the choice that had existed previously. Certain forms were now selected as acceptable and hence formed the standard. This naturally created problems. There was no academy which could adjudicate on what was acceptable and so contradictory statements are inevitably found. The choice of what was acceptable was arbitrary. What was important was that a choice was made and that a given usage was elevated in esteem and all competing forms were relegated to the rank of vulgar usage. This in turn created difficulties for those who wanted to acquire the standard: the standard was constantly changing, and only those in the know could feel they were users of correct language. The development of the standard also promoted an increasing gap between spoken and written English. Equally it encouraged a divide between formal and informal English. When one is speaking one may be a little more relaxed about what is said, but writing is more permanent and is open to everyone to scrutinise to see if the language matches up to the required norms. This is particularly true of what one might call public or formal writing. Even someone like Dr Johnson was more careful in his usage in printed material than he was in letters and similar documents. Politeness as such provides no criterion for selection among various alternatives, but once a choice is made as to the approved form, to ignore it could have social consequences. Certain types of language naturally tend to disappear. Regional vocabulary and syntax decrease and generally people were much less interested in the usage associated with the regions. The regional differences were sufficiently pronounced that all could recognise them and avoid them. Much more important were class differences, for these were more difficult to detect and yet they were fundamental to polite society. To use the language linked with a trade or profession was inappropriate in polite society; to use the lexis of lower social groups could be disastrous; and to show an ignorance of current polite usage was damning. Where the previous age had been interested in the language of vagabonds and thieves because that was so different from their own, this age was more interested in the nuances of usage which marked out classes which were not at the periphery of society. The result was that many grammars and dictionaries concentrated as much on what should be avoided as on acceptable usage. Grammars increasingly adopted rules which were illustrated by mistakes drawn from even the best authors, and dictionaries accepted the habit of 'branding' words which were considered to be not acceptable in English.

The Restoration put an end to the circulation of the popular books which had been widely read by the Puritans. There was a distrust of many of the attitudes of the previous age and this can be seen in the change in meaning of a word like *enthusiasm*. In this period it takes on overtones of disapproval because enthusiasm is thought to reflect unrestrained passions or thoughtless hysteria which was in no way subject to the control of rational discussion. The emotions had to be restrained within an appropriate framework of rational control. An indication of this new attitude is provided by Samuel Parker in his *A Discourse of Ecclesiastical Politics* of 1670:

> Superstition and Enthusiasm have out-faced the Laws. Confident men have talked so loudly of the inviolable Sacredness and Authority of their Conscience, that Governours, not thoroughly instructed in the nature and extent of their Power so lately restored to them, have been almost scared from intermedling with any thing, that could upon this score plead its Priviledges and Exemption from their Commands. (p. 58)

Here the linking of *enthusiasm* with *superstition* and the apparent fear of private emotion and conscience as compared with public and social control are significant. It was necessary to rewrite books like Foxe's *Book of Martyrs* to make them less emotional and 'enthusiastic'. To some extent this attitude spilled over into language as well, and even Shakespeare was rewritten at this period. His language and his emotional outbursts were felt to be unacceptable. Dr Johnson could comment unfavourably on Shakespeare's language, for he felt that his use of certain words was inappropriate in the contexts in which they occurred. In *The Rambler* no. 168 (1751) he notes:

> We are all offended by low terms, but are not disgusted alike by the same compositions, because we do not all agree to censure the same terms as low. No word is naturally or intrinsically meaner than another; our opinion therefore of words, as of other things arbitrarily and capriciously established, depends wholly upon accident and custom.[2]

He goes on in this essay to criticise Macbeth (though he means Lady Macbeth) for the use of *dun* and *knife* in the lines:

> Come, thick night,
> And pall thee in the dunnest smoke of hell,
> That my keen knife see not the wound it makes.
> (I.v.49–51)

His objections consisted of the facts that *dun* was an 'epithet now seldom heard but in the stable, and *dun* night may come or go without any other notice than contempt' and that *knife* was 'the name of an instrument used by butchers and cooks in the meanest employments'. Contemporary dictionaries support Johnson's views about the connotations of these words, for *dun* is related to the colour of horses and *knife* is associated with household and slaughterhouse functions. Johnson's point is that the passage in which these two words occur is one of lofty sentiments and dramatic nobility, and words that are related to trades or professions can only detract from the literary style and noble sentiments expressed. In drama, as in life, one's language should fit the subject and the occasion. By failing to fit his words to the individual characters in his play, Shakespeare failed to observe decorum.

Basically the Augustans believed that there were two types of language, genteel and vulgar, and that each type differed in vocabulary, pronunciation and syntax. It was part of the job of a writer to allocate appropriate language to the various characters in his plays. Genteel language was learned, civilised, abstract and classical, whereas vulgar language was ignorant, barbarous, concrete and Germanic. In view of the fact that classical words tended to be long and Anglo-Saxon words short, this distinction was also fed into attitudes about polite language. Many objected to the abbreviated forms of words which were becoming popular. Swift in his *Proposal for Correcting, Improving, and Ascertaining the English Tongue* of 1712 was particularly critical of such words as *mob, phizz* and *pozz*. These were abbreviations of classical words which had proper forms like *(vulgum) mobile, physiognomy* and *possible*. To abbreviate such words not only turned classical words into what looked like Anglo-Saxon words, it also confused their status and gentility.

Another aspect of language which needs to be borne in mind is its close association for most people with politics, and Swift is again a good example of this link. Writers were often identified with one party or the other, and Swift was a strong Tory supporter. In considering the comments he makes about language, it needs to be remembered that they often have a political dimension. He was of his time in assuming that language was closely linked with the wider social, religious and political issues of his day, and he was quite happy to attack the Whigs for their corruption of the language. For Swift good language meant using a stable language which was uncorrupted by the fashionable and the temporary; language should not be adapted to passing whims and new-fangled ideas. High-sounding language can deflect attention away from the true meaning of what is said or written and thus tends towards deception; bad language discourages thought since it uses a vocabulary which conceals rather than clarifies meaning. He often quotes from the Bible or from proverbial and other sources of folk wisdom because they enshrine lasting moral virtues. Bad politics, on the other hand, promotes unacceptable behaviour and general corruption of morals through the political system. Bad language is the start of a slide towards degeneration and social misery.

> When up a dangerous faction starts,
> With wrath and vengeance in their hearts;

> *By solemn Language and Cov'nant bound,*
> To ruin, slaughter, and confound;
> To turn religion to a fable,
> And make the Government a *Babel*:
> Pervert the Law, disgrace the gown,
> Corrupt the senate, rob the crown;
> To sacrifice old England's glory,
> And make her infamous in story.[3]

The corruption of language is clearly linked with other forms of degeneration and political malpractice.

Following the Restoration, Charles II established the Royal Society in 1662. It is characteristic of this time that this Society, which we consider today to be associated purely with science, felt that language was part of its overall remit. In December 1664 it established a committee consisting of 'persons of the Society whose genius was very proper and inclined to improve the English tongue'. The committee contained among its members John Dryden, John Evelyn and Thomas Sprat, the secretary of the Society. The committee hardly met because of illness and other commitments among its members, but John Evelyn, who was unable to attend for one session, wrote a letter in which he outlined the various tasks which it could promote. His proposals included a grammar, a reform of orthography, a general dictionary and collections of special words, such as those connected with trade. Clearly what lay behind these proposals were the concepts which were then very much in the air, the need first to purify the language of all barbarisms, then to regulate its usage, and finally to fix that usage in immutable form. It was a common belief that language could indeed be stabilised and made permanent. This committee achieved very little and was soon associated with calls for the establishment of an academy which could undertake the same sort of tasks. The committee failed and no academy was established for several reasons. Firstly, there was insufficient political support in the higher reaches of the government. Secondly, the proposal also became embroiled in politics, since the Whigs could easily represent calls for an academy as attempts to repress the free spirit of Englishmen. Finally, grammarians and lexicographers started to produce a stream of grammars and dictionaries which in effect took over the functions which an academy would have had. One of those lexicographers was Dr Johnson who made it quite clear that,

although in *The Plan of a Dictionary* of 1747 he had expressed the
hope of fixing the language, his work on making the dictionary led
him to conclude that such a task was impossible. His words put
paid to the idea of an academy, and his works and those of the
grammarians provided the necessary guidance that many were
looking for.

As already suggested, language was closely related to most
intellectual pursuits at this time. In part this was because there
was an attempt to understand the bases upon which a universal
language could be established. Many were interested in the construction of a new language which would incorporate the surface
features of existing languages and so be most conducive to rational
debate and argument. As there were no complete dictionaries of
any language available, this was not a realisable proposition. But
the subject exercised great fascination and many books and
pamphlets were published. The foremost exponent of many of
these ideas was John Wilkins, whose *An Essay towards a Real
Character, and a Philosophical Language* was published in 1668.
Wilkins tried to produce the groundwork for a complete inventory
of all material and abstract ideas so that they could then be given
separate signs or marks. The theory presupposes that there will be
one and only one sign for each material object or abstract concept. It
would not be possible to have different words for the same thing or
to use words in a metaphorical or poetic way. As such, proposals of
this sort were anti-rhetoric, but chimed in with the views of bodies
like the Royal Society which wanted a clear and logical language in
which the findings and concepts of scientific discovery were
unambiguously presented. It thus presupposes that there are no
registers, no dialectal differences and no poetic circumlocutions.
The universal grammars did insist that words had to be rationally
organised, that there was sequence in the system, that the signs
used made visible sense, and that the basic elements of the system
were the most important features around which everything else is
built. Although these proposals emphasised the singleness of
individual things, they were also interested in the process of
relating one sign to another. It was not sufficient to name
everything: communication involves linking different ideas or facts
together. Locke had himself emphasised that language
communicates ideas, not things. But this was something which was
difficult for universal grammars to achieve and in so far as they
tried they tended to imitate Latin as the model for how languages

should organise their parts. Gradually they gave way to more practical grammars.

The more practical grammars tend to follow Locke's view that words are purely arbitrary; there is nothing in a word which reveals what it means and so his views were in opposition to the universal grammars which tried to make their signs transparent of their meanings. The arbitrary quality of words tended to throw more emphasis on the ways in which they were joined together. There was a tendency to downgrade the role of lexical words at the expense of the grammatical ones. It was accepted that the latter provided the framework for meaning in the language since they formed the backbone of the system which allowed lexical words to be understood. Hence there was considerable interest in the role and scope of such classes as the prepositions and conjunctions.

The grammar which became the standard for the latter half of this period was *A Short Introduction to English Grammar: with Critical Notes* published anonymously in 1762. It was the work of Robert Lowth, successively Bishop of St David's, Oxford and London. It was reprinted frequently in England, and editions in America and Ireland were numerous as well. Lowth's name appears only in the editions published abroad. In his preface Lowth notes that English has undergone considerable improvement in recent times, except in the matter of grammar:

> THE English Language hath been much cultivated during the last two hundred years. It hath been considerably polished and refined; it hath been greatly enlarged in extent and compass; its force and energy, its variety, richness, and elegance, have been tried with good success, in verse and in prose, upon all subjects, and in every kind of stile: but whatever other improvements it may have received, it hath made no advances in Grammatical accuracy. (p. i)

He goes on to complain further:

> Does it mean, that the English Language as it is spoken by the politest part of the nation, and as it stands in the writings of our most approved authors, oftentimes offends against every part of Grammar? Thus far, I am afraid, the charge is true. Or does it further imply, that our Language is in its nature irregular and capricious; not subject, or not easily reduceable, to a System of

rules? In this respect, I am persuaded, the charge is wholly without foundation. (pp. ii–iii)

English is a language that needs to be regulated according to grammar and is readily susceptible to such treatment. There is nothing wrong with the language, it is the users who have neglected to submit it to rules. It is partly because the language is a relatively uncomplicated one which has caused this neglect of grammar. We may speak the language from childhood, but we have made no efforts to make it conform to grammatical precepts, for grammar is hardly taught. It is incumbent on anyone who is educated and who wants to address the public 'to express himself with propriety and accuracy' (p. ix). The purpose of a grammar is to enable us to express ourselves with propriety and 'to be able to judge of every phrase and form of construction, whether it be right or not' (p. x). The way to do this is to provide rules which explain the structure of the language and which make clear what is wrong. No one should embark on writing literature unless he has a clear grasp of the grammatical principles of English and anyone who has acquired English grammar can pass on easily to Latin and the modern languages.

Lowth is sufficiently of his time to start his work with the comment that universal grammar 'explains the Principles which are common to all languages' (p. 1) and that a grammar of an individual language applies those common principles to that language. His grammar then follows the established trend of starting with the letters, and going on to syllables and words, which are divided into nine parts of speech: article, noun, pronoun, adjective, verb, adverb, preposition, conjunction and interjection. Each of these is defined briefly and then characterised in their own chapters. In these chapters there are not only examples of usage drawn from good writers, but there are also many footnotes which show the mistakes which some authors have made in what Lowth considers basic grammar. Thus of the indefinite article *a* he notes that it 'can only be joined to Substantives in the singular number' (p. 19) and then adds the following footnote:

'A good character should not be rested in as an end, but employed as *a means* of doing still farther good.' ATTERBURY'S Sermons. Ought it not to be *a mean*?

Although *a means* was and remains a common expression in English, the rigid application of the rule about the indefinite article indicates that it is wrong, despite what people actually say. So Lowth indicates the mistake. His examples are, for the most part, chosen from poets and writers of the seventeenth and eighteenth centuries, and there are examples from the Bible. For example, he objected to '"Crist his sake," in our Liturgy, which is a mistake, either of the Printers, or of the Compilers' (p. 26). This was part of the process which established a canon of good writing, even if in Lowth's case the good writers that he quotes from often illustrated mistakes. This was intended to show that even good writers could err; bad writers were by implication so bad that their writings were almost totally wrong grammatically. A review of some of the points regularly criticised by the grammarians will follow later in the chapter. Lowth then proceeds to punctuation, which is used both to express 'different degrees of connexion between the several parts of sentences' (p. 155) and for accurate pronunciation. He includes all the major punctuation marks and is also forced to offer definitions of the sentence and its parts in order to elucidate how the marks are used. Thus a simple sentence is said to have 'but one Subject and one finite Verb' (p. 160) His book finishes with an example of what he calls *praxis*, but which we would know as 'parsing'. Six verses of the New Testament are analysed word by word so that each part of speech is described. In many ways this is an admirable teaching grammar and it is not surprising that it remained popular for so long. It may set out to be descriptive, though its rules and lists of mistakes make it prescriptive. It was characteristic of its time in choosing examples of usage from literary writers and in focusing attention on smaller aspects of usage. The emphasis on good writers put formal writing in a prominent position, because it was easier perhaps to attack written texts than pronunciation, where examples would be somewhat more problematic. It raised writing to a lofty position in general esteem and focused grammatical attention on good writing. The emphasis on small aspects of usage meant that people could often complain that a writer broke what came to be grammatical taboos, even though his or her overall style was acceptable. Too much attention came to be paid to these smaller details instead of to the whole.

At the same time as grammars were produced in quantity, numerous dictionaries appeared. The developments in dictionaries followed those in grammar, and many of them actually included grammars. This period sees two major developments: in the early part the trend towards universal dictionaries became established, and in the second part an increasing emphasis on pronunciation was the major characteristic. At the same time encyclopaedias appeared and these influenced the development and contents of the dictionaries. The two earliest writers of encyclopaedias, John Harris (1704) and Ephraim Chambers (1728), attempted to describe the terms associated with all branches of human knowledge and expertise. Harris's work had the title *Lexicon Technicum: Or, An* Universal *Dictionary of Arts and Sciences*. The word *universal* became a standard feature of titles of dictionaries at this period, though it could sometimes give way to *general* or *complete*. Completeness of the vocabulary was now the watchword of dictionary-makers and they often claimed that their own dictionaries were more complete than others which had been compiled hitherto. At the same time the dictionary-makers wanted to expel from their work those words which were archaic, regional, foreign or vulgar. J.K.'s dictionary of 1702, for example, complained of previous diction-aries that they had often included Latin words which were not part of English as well as foreign words, including Old English ones, which were obsolete or never used in contemporary English. The ordinary English words were completely hidden by these foreign words which were not really part of the language. J.K. (possibly John Kersey) adds in the preface of his dictionary 'ours is intended only to explain such English Words as are genuine, and used by Persons of clear Judgement and good style'. So the principles established for what words should be included in dictionaries are that the words should be in regular use and that they should be the words which are employed by good writers and stylists. This is not to say that the practice necessarily reflected the principles outlined in the prefaces of the dictionaries. Many Latinate words were still included because dictionary-makers tended to borrow words from other sources. But J.K.'s dictionary is important in introducing common words into dictionaries, although the definitions of such words are often not helpful since they give examples rather than definitions. Thus we can find an entry like '*About*, as about Noon'. The link between dictionaries and spelling books is clear from examples like this and also from J.K.'s interest generally in spelling.

The most popular dictionary before Dr Johnson's was Nathan Bailey's *An Universal Etymological English Dictionary* of 1721. In addition to this dictionary Bailey compiled other dictionaries, a spelling book, a grammar and translated various Latin texts. His dictionary contains common words, hard and technical words, words from old charters, their etymology, interpretations of family and place names, dialect words and a collection of proverbs. Its contents amount to much more than one finds in modern dictionaries and show the influence of encyclopaedias. Its novelty was the inclusion of etymologies, which now became a standard feature of dictionaries. At this stage pronunciation begins to appear in dictionaries and one of those to show this new trend is the *Lingua Britannica Reformata* by Benjamin Martin of 1749. He shows what he considers the true pronunciation of words by using, where necessary, single and double accents to indicate stress and numbers to indicate the number of syllables in individual words. He also provides what he considers the correct spelling of words in accordance with the usage of approved modern writers. He is one of the first dictionary-makers to omit <k> in words like *logic*. He also includes a much wider range of definitions for each word than found previously, though the distinction between these definitions is sometimes less than clear. It was part of Martin's general approach to correctness that he used the process of branding extensively in his dictionary. Branding is the process of marking by some sign any word which was considered unacceptable English for some reason, usually because it was vulgar or obsolete. The principle had been introduced in 1658 in Edward Phillips's *The New World of Words* and was extensively used in the 1727 edition of Bailey's dictionary. Most of this branding was arbitrary and it was abandoned in Johnson's dictionary, where it was replaced by descriptive labels which fulfilled the same function. What is important to note is that the use of branding helps to confirm the view that certain words were not good English, just as certain grammatical constructions were deplored by the grammarians. The dictionaries contributed to standardisation of the language and to the principle of linguistic politeness through their emphasis on proper spelling and pronunciation and on their willingness to judge whether words were appropriate to polite language or not.

Johnson himself was affected by these attitudes. In his plan of 1747 he claimed his dictionary would help to fix the pronunciation of English, preserve the purity of the language, and confirm usage. Johnson undertook a programme of reading to provide the words for his dictionary and that meant reading authors who were accepted as part of good literature. He took the view that he should

A GENERAL

DICTIONARY

OF THE

ENGLISH LANGUAGE.

A

A, The first letter of the European alphabets, has, in the English language, three different sounds, which may be termed the broad, open, and slender.

The broad found resembling that of the German *a* is found, in many of our monosyllables, as *all*, *wall*, *malt*, *falt*; in which *a* is pronounced as *au* in *cause*, or *aw* in *law*. Many of these words were anciently written with *au*, as *fault*, *mault*; which happens to be still retained in *fault*. This was probably the ancient found of the Saxons, since it is almost uniformly preserved in the rustic pronunciation, and the Northern dialects, as *maun* for *man*, *haund* for *hand*.

A open, not unlike the *a* of the Italians, is found in *father*, *rather*, and more obscurely in *fancy*, *fast*, &c.

A slender or close, is the peculiar *a* of the English language, resembling the found of the French *a* masculine, or diphthong *ai* in *pais*, or perhaps a middle found between them, or between the *a* and *e*; to this the Arabic *a* is said nearly to approach. Of this found we have examples in the words, *place*, *face*, *waste*, and all those that terminate in *ation*; as, *relation*, *nation*, *generation*.

A is short, as *glass*, *grass*; or long, as, *glaze*, *graze*: it is marked long, generally, by an *e* final, *plane*, or by an *i* added, as, *plain*.

A, an article set before nouns of the singular number; *a man*, *a tree*; denoting the number *one*, as, *a man* is coming, that is, *no more than one*; or an indefinite indication, as, *a man may come this way*; that is, *any man*. This article has no plural signification. Before a word beginning with a vowel, it is written *an*, as, *an ox*, *an egg*, of which *a* is the contraction.

A is sometimes a noun; as, a great *A*, a little *a*.

A is placed before a participle, or participial noun; and is considered by Wallis as a contraction of *at*, when it is put before a word denoting some action not yet finished; as, I am *a*-walking. It also seems to be anciently contracted from *at*, when placed before local furnames; as, Thomas *a* Becket. In other cases, it seems to signify *to*, like the French *à*.

A hunting Chloe went.   *Prior.*

They go *a* begging to a bankrupt's door.   *Dryd.*

May pure contents for ever pitch their tents
Upon these downs, these meads, these rocks, these mountains,
And peace still slumber by these purling fountains!
Which we may every year
Find when we come *a* fishing here.   *Wotton.*

Now the men fell *a* rubbing of armour, which a great while had lain oiled; the magazines of munition are viewed; the officers of remains called to account.   *Wotton.*

Another falls *a* ringing a Pessennius Niger, and judiciously distinguishes the found of it to be modern.   *Addison on medals.*

A has a peculiar signification, denoting the proportion of one thing to another. Thus we say, The landlord hath *a* hundred *a* year; The ship's crew gained a thousand pounds *a* man.

The river Inn, that had been hitherto shut up among mountains, passes generally through a wide open country, during all its course through Bavaria; which is a voyage of two days, after the rate of twenty leagues a day.   *Addison on Italy.*

A is used in burlesque poetry, to lengthen out a syllable, without adding to the sense.

Vol. I.

A B A

For cloves and nutmegs to the line-*a*,
And even for oranges to China.   *Dryden.*

A is sometimes, in familiar writing, put by a barbarous corruption for *he*.

A, in composition, seems to have sometimes the power of the French *a* in these phrases, *a droit*, *a gauche*, &c. and sometimes to be contracted from *at*; as, *afide*, *aflope*, *afoot*, *afleep*, *athirst*, *aware*.

If this, which it avouches, does appear,
There is no flying hence, nor tarrying here.
I gin to be *a weary* of the sun;
And wish the state of the world were now undone.   *Shakespeare's Macbeth.*

And now a breeze from shore began to blow,
The sailors ship their oars, and cease to row;
Then hoist their yards *a-trip*, and all their sails
Let fall, to court the wind, and catch the gales.   *Dryden's Ceyx and Alcyone.*

A is sometimes redundant; as, *arise*, *arouse*, *awake*; the same with rise, rouse, wake.

A, in abbreviations, stands for *artium*, or arts; as, A.B. bachelor of arts, *artium baccalaureus*; A.M. master of arts, *artium magister*; or, *anno*; as, A.D. *anno domini*.

AB, at the beginning of the names of places, generally shews that they have some relation to an abbey.

ABA'CK. *adv.* obsolete. Backwards.

But when they came whereas thy skill didst shew,
They drew *aback*, as half with shame confound.
Shepherds to see them in their art out-go.   *Spenf. Past.*

ABA'CTOR. *n.f.* [Lat. *abactor*, a driver away.] Those who drive away or steal cattle in herds, or great numbers at once, in distinction from those that steal only a sheep or two.   *Blount.*

A'BACUS. *n.f.* [Lat. *abacus.*]
1. A counting-table, anciently used in calculations.
2. In architecture, is the uppermost member of a column, which serves as a sort of crowning both to the capital and column.   *Dict.*

ABA'FT. *adv.* [of *abaptan*, Sax. Behind.] From the fore-part of the ship, towards the stern.   *Dict.*

ABAI'SANCE. *n.f.* [from the French *abaisser*, to depress, to bring down.] An act of reverence, a bow. Obeysance is considered by Skinner as a corruption of *abaisance*, but is now universally used.

To ABA'LIENATE. *v.a.* [from *abalieno*, Lat.] To make that another's which was our own before.   *Ainsw. Lex. Jur.*

A term of the civil law, not much used in common speech.

ABALIENA'TION. *n.f.* [Lat. *abalienatio.*] A giving up one's right to another person; or a making over an estate, goods, or chattels by sale, or due course of law.   *Dict.*

To ABA'ND. *v.a.* [A word contracted from abandon, but not now in use; See ABANDON.] To forsake.

Those foreigners which came from far
Grew great, and got large portions of land,
That in the realm, ere long, they stronger are
Than they which fought at first their helping hand,
And Vortiger enforced the kingdom to *aband*.   *Spenser's Fairy Queen, b. ii. cant. 10.*

To ABA'NDON. *v.a.* [Fr. *abandonner.* Derived, according to *Menage*, from the Italian *abandonare*, which signifies to forsake his colours; *bandum* [*vexillum*] *deserere.* Pasquier thinks

B   it

not include any words from authors before Sidney and was generally more disposed to include words from writers before the Restoration because they represented 'pure sources of genuine diction' (*Dictionary*, Preface, p. C1r). However, there are many writers from the late seventeenth and eighteenth centuries quoted in the dictionary. Indeed, Johnson is somewhat unusual in sticking to the preference for pre-Restoration writers as the model of pure English. Although this had been a frequently expressed opinion at the start of our period, towards the second half of the eighteenth century it was Addison who was increasingly regarded as the model of polite writing. What is significant is that Johnson saw it as his task to collect the words from written texts; the idea that spoken vocabulary might be included was not considered. This helped to confirm the primacy of the written word and to establish certain authors as the canon of good writing and literature.

Johnson attempted to provide a dictionary for general use which was a compromise between a grammatical dictionary and an encyclopaedia. But he was sufficiently of his time to prefer words which are of a more general and abstract character rather than specific words such as those of trade or the professions. The title page of his dictionary is worth quoting in full:

A DICTIONARY of the ENGLISH LANGUAGE: in which The WORDS are deduced from their ORIGINALS and ILLUSTRATED in their DIFFERENT SIGNIFICATIONS by EXAMPLES from the best WRITERS. To which are prefixed A HISTORY of the LANGUAGE, and AN ENGLISH GRAMMAR.

In his preface he comments on the language 'which has itself been hitherto neglected, suffered to spread, under the direction of chance, into wild exuberance, resigned to the tyranny of time and fashion, and exposed to the corruptions of ignorance, and caprices of innovation'. The language was, to quote his famous phrase, 'copious without order, and energetick without rules'. He then presents an account of how he had attempted to bring order into this confusion. One important feature of this work was his collection of quotations from established writers. Each headword is provided with its part of speech and etymology. The definitions are divided into groups, each of which is numbered. Most definitions are accompanied by a quotation from an approved author. Sometimes some comment about the word is also included. On the first page, for example, we find comments like '*ABACKE* obsolete', '*ABALIENATE* A term of the civil law, not much used in common speech', and '*ABAND* A word contracted from abandon, but not in use'. He has several different headwords for *A* including 'is used in burlesque poetry to lengthen out a syllable, without adding to the sense' and quotes Dryden's 'For cloves and nutmegs to the line-*a*'. Although he mentions which author the quotation is taken from, he gives no exact reference. There is no system to the way his comments on the words are included, but they are more informative than the previous branding. He is fairly comprehensive in what he includes. Thus he includes both *dun* and *knife*, which he had objected to in *Macbeth*. Although he quotes from Newton on optics to illustrate *dun* 'A colour partaking of brown and black', he quotes from *Macbeth*, Crashaw and Dryden to exemplify *knife* 'An instrument edged and pointed, wherewith meat is cut, and animals killed'. For Johnson the lexicon is closely associated with grammar and the language's history, and his dictionary attempts to display the words of the language which constitute usage, particularly good usage.

The latter half of the eighteenth century attached more importance to pronunciation than earlier dictionary-makers. Thomas Sheridan produced a dictionary in 1780 with the title *A General Dictionary of the English Language; one main object of which is, to establish a plain and permanent standard of Pronunciation*. A dictionary along the same lines was produced by John Walker in 1791. What Sheridan and Walker did was to produce a series of signs, consisting mainly of superscript numbers, like an elementary phonetic alphabet to show the pronunciation of the various sounds in all words. Sheridan and Walker recognised that there were many differences in pronunciation, and the former chose what he considered the pronunciation at the court of Queen Anne as the standard he would follow. That was the period, he claimed, when due propriety was paid to pronunciation. It was the period in which the pronunciation of the court was recognised as the best and imitated by others. Inevitably, things always seem to have been better in a previous age.

Dictionaries were clearly produced as part of the drive towards standardisation and improvement of the language. Although several lexicographers like Johnson came to realise that fixing the language was impossible, they nevertheless wanted to set a standard that people should imitate. Dictionaries were both descriptive and prescriptive, but even those which were descriptive like Dr Johnson's were readily understood as prescriptive as we can see from Henry Tilney's comments in *Northanger Abbey*. The later dictionary-makers were also interested in trying to give a lead to the best pronunciation. From their time onwards some indication of pronunciation becomes a standard feature of dictionaries. Whether the less educated actually used dictionaries and consulted them for pronunciation is uncertain; it is doubtful whether many of them could afford to buy them. But dictionaries supported grammars in providing the rules which could guide people as to what was good English. The regulation of the language was now well established although at the cost of driving a permanent wedge between the polite and the rest of society. The remaining chapters in this book will deal in part with the struggle of the disenfranchised to win a place in the sun.

From the various quotations from eighteenth-century writers that have already been included in this chapter, the reader can grasp that the standardisation of spelling had arrived at a stage which is not too different from that prevailing today. The letters <i/j> and <u/v> had been separated out as vowels and consonants respectively. Some spellings still differ from modern English. The use of <k> in the ending -*ick* in words like *music* survive with some writers, including Dr Johnson, until the end of the period. Other words still exhibit uncertainty as to whether they are spelled with <i> or <y>, like *style*. In his dictionary Johnson sometimes comments on variation in spelling. Of the word *chord* he notes 'When it signifies a rope or string in general, it is written *cord:* when its primitive signification is preserved, the *h* is retained'. His first definition of *chord* is 'The string of a musical instrument'. He also has an entry for *cord* in the sense of 'rope'. It is perhaps in the use of capitals that the greatest difference from modern English is found. Capitals increased in frequency from about 1650 to 1750 and there appear to have been two different strategies employed. The first used capitals for all nouns, and the second only for nouns which demanded emphasis. The spelling books of this period often discuss the use of capitals and try to dictate when they should be used. However, in the end it appears as though the practices in the printing houses were more important in regulating usage. After 1750 the use of capitals falls off quickly and by 1800 usage approximates closely to what is found today, though uniformity of practice was not achieved. Occasionally in this period capitals occur with other parts of speech than nouns. The punctuation marks we are accustomed to today are all now present, but their use is different. The use of commas, for example, to mark a long noun phrase even though it breaks up a subject + verb or verb + object sequence is common. Perhaps the most interesting feature of spelling at this time is the existence of two spelling systems, the approved and various private systems. Dr Johnson himself often has one form in his dictionary, but another in his private correspondence. He spells *Friday* with <i> in the dictionary, but <y> privately. He uses three spellings of *does*, including *dos* and *do's*. *Duchess* may in his private correspondence appear as *dutchess*. Johnson is not alone in this more cavalier attitude towards spelling in private material. Dryden and Addison, who are also firm in their pronouncements on language, have two spelling systems. It may well be that we see here the continuation of the policy that printers were responsible for spelling and they imposed their system on whatever they printed. In a spelling manual *Right Spelling very much Improved* published in 1704 it says of the noun and verb forms of *bowl* that they are written similarly but the context should make clear which is intended. However, the author adds of the verb that it 'may very well be distinguished by *ou* when the Printer or Compositor shall think fit' (p. 16). The same book comments of words spelt with <our> like *honour* that 'in these words now-a-days the (u) generally obtains in Manuscript (especially) to be omitted' (p. 109). This difference is also found in the use of capitals. At the beginning of the eighteenth century capitals were frequently added to all nouns in printed prose texts, but after about 1750 they gradually decrease and disappear almost entirely by 1800. In their private correspondence writers tended to be more discriminating in their use of capitals, reserving them for emphasis rather than adding them to every noun. There was a standard printed spelling, but even those who set the standard for others did not always keep this standard when writing privately.

In phonology this period continues and brings to a modern stage some of the changes which were initiated in the previous one. During the eighteenth century /æ/ moved through /a/ towards /ɑ/ and was lengthened to give /ɑ:/ under certain conditions, normally before *r*, before groups like *lm* and *lf/lve*, and before the dental written *th*. This gave the modern standard pronunciation in the south of the country of words like *bar, calm, calf, bath* and *father*. There was some uncertainty among orthoepists about which words had this new pronunciation, but there can be no doubt that the sound was accepted by the end of the century. Some already recognised that this /ɑ:/ also existed in words with final *ss, st* or *n* followed by any consonant; in words, that is, like *pass, past* and *chance*. This change did not pass without a struggle for acceptability and increasingly any changes in pronunciation met a similar hurdle. The onset of standardisation meant that the processes of analogy which reduced many of the anomalies in the language could not operate effectively, because orthoepists and grammarians often tried to freeze the language in its current form. There seems to be evidence that the sounds /e:/ and /ɛ:/ had fallen together by the end of the eighteenth century in polite pronunciation, though differences were still common in dialects. Some orthoepists like John Walker tried to keep them as separate sounds, but gave up the attempt after consulting people like Garrick the actor. There was uncertainty over those words like *great* which retained the old pronunciation. Dr Johnson complained to Boswell that Lord Chesterfield said that words like *great* were pronounced to rhyme with *state*, but Sir William Yonge said that they were pronounced like *meet*. He was puzzled what to do as two such polite speakers had contrary opinions, though the former pronunciation was accepted by 1800..

The diphthongisation of /i:/ had proceeded to a sound like /əi/ by the end of the previous period, but in this one it developed further towards the modern pronunciation /ai/. Before it did so, it fell together with the diphthong which had developed from French /ui/, usually spelt <oi> in English. Words which had had French <oi> were not affected, for it was only those with <ui> which, when it suffered unrounding of the first element, had a pronunciation which was similar to that developed from earlier /i:/. Thus for some, perhaps most, speakers words like *line* and *loin* or *pint* and *point* were homophones. This can be seen from rhymes and puns found throughout the eighteenth century, and in some cases earlier. Pope, for example, rhymes *join* with *line*. Probably because of the spelling <oi> and existence of the other words which were spelt this way and pronounced /ɔi/, this pronunciation was extended to all words spelt <oi> and words like *join* and *line* ceased to rhyme together.

The most important development at this time was the fall of /r/ after certain vowels. This /r/ was vocalised and when it followed short vowels it disappeared with lengthening of the preceding vowel. With /a/ and /o/, the result was the expected long vowels /ɑː/ and /ɔː/ to give us the modern pronunciation of words like *car* and *horse*. However, after /i, e, u/ the result was different. Ultimately they all fell together as the long vowel /əː/. Today words like *fir*, *fern* and *fur* all have the same long vowel. The changes in these vowels occurred at different rates so that they did not all fall together at once. There was a special problem with words in *er* since they had fallen together with words in *ar* in the previous period. There was considerable debate about what pronunciation the *er* words should have and the result was that some ended with /ɑː/ like *sergeant* and others with /əː/ like *merchant*. When /r/ followed a long vowel, it led to the centring diphthongs which we find today in words like *bear* and *more*. When it followed a diphthong, it created triphthongs, which were a new development within the system of English sounds. The diphthongs /ai, au/ when followed by original /r/ produced the triphthongs /aiə, auə/ in words like *fire* and *flour*.

Most vowels in unstressed syllables continued to be weakened to /ə/ and in some cases disappeared altogether. In many cases there appear to have been two pronunciations, a formal and an informal one. When people spoke slowly or formally they might pronounce initial *o* in a word like *obey* as /o/, but informally and in quick speech they would reduce it to /ə/. In the consonants the groups consisting of initial *k* or *g* followed by *n* lost the initial /k, g/ so that words like *knave* and *nave* became homophones. This process may have started in the previous period but was completed probably by 1700. There has been little change since in the received pronunciation of the consonants, though the influence of spelling continues to make itself felt. Even in the eighteenth century the sounding of initial /h/ in certain words like *honest* and of written consonants which had not previously been pronounced continued.

There were only minor developments in morphology during this period. The plural in *-s* had already become established as the regular plural of nouns and the only movement was in the continued drift of anomalous plurals to the dominant pattern. In the eighteenth century many mass-like nouns like *cannon*, which had had an uninflected plural hitherto, adopted the *-s* plural. But in this as in other features of morphology the development of rules, including lists of exceptions, inhibited too many levellings from taking place. In the genitive singular there had been frequent variation in /f – v/ between the base and the genitive in forms like *knife – knives.* The latter form occurred in the plural as well. In the eighteenth century the genitive form with /v/ was recessive, though the plural tended to be more resistant to the power of analogy. In the personal pronoun the two most significant changes are the replacement of *his* by *its* in the neuter and the final loss of the distinction between the second singular and plural forms. The former can be understood only within the wider framework of the existence of four forms in the previous period: *his, thereof, of it* and *of the same.* The gradual loss of the second and fourth of these options made *of it* parallel to *his* which created an anomaly within the system. The result was the adoption of *it* and *its* as alternatives to *his* with the final triumph of the latter as the only form, partly because *its* was distinguished from *it* in its other functions and partly because it harmonised with the genitive singular pattern in *-s* found in the nouns and in *his*. The increasing use of *of it* also played a key role in the emergence and acceptability of *its*. In the second person the number distinction between *you* and *thou* had already been lost and the difference between the two was a matter of pragmatics, but in practice the pragmatic distinction was not always well observed. Its use was probably optional, and this lack of functional clarity may have led to the disappearance of the old singular form in the eighteenth century. The use of *thou* was restricted to special environments like poetry by the middle of the century, if not earlier. The same applies to the difference between *ye* and *you*. The former had been the old subject form and the latter the oblique one. But *you* had gradually taken over from *ye* in the subject form as well and by the middle of the eighteenth century *ye* was restricted to specialised contexts, such as poetic apostrophes.

In adjectives it is only the comparative and superlative forms which require comment. The use of the inflectional endings *-er/-est* varied with the periphrastic forms with *more/most*. During the eighteenth century the rule was increasingly applied that the former should be used with monosyllabic and the latter with polysyllabic adjectives. The practice was not quite so uniform as the recommendations of the grammarians suggest. Indeed, it seems as though more polysyllabic words adopted the inflectional endings for comparison during this period. Dr Johnson in the grammar prefixed to his dictionary gives a list of those adjectival endings like *-some* and *-y* which cannot take *-er/-est*, which seems to imply that other polysyllabic adjectives could, though he gave the rule that polysyllables should use *more/most* for comparison. More attention was paid to the use of double comparisons and most grammarians were generally opposed to forms like *most unkindest* found in Shakespeare's *Julius Caesar* because they are illogical. In his edition of Shakespeare Pope emended such forms out of the text wherever possible, and earlier Dryden had objected to Ben Jonson's use of *more stricter* which he described as a 'gross way of two Comparatives'.

In the inflectional system of the verbs the use of *-th* in the third-person singular survives in words like *hath* and *doth*, but it was a purely written form and is not evidence of what occurred in speech. Examples of *-th* in the plural continue to be found into the eighteenth century, but were becoming rare. In the strong verbs there is continued movement in the forms of the preterite and the past participle as well as in the change from strong to weak. There was a development for strong verbs to have only two forms, the infinitive/present and the preterite/past participle, rather than the three found in many cases. This trend was cut short by the grammarians who made a choice as to what were the preferred forms of the strong forms and thus inhibited analogy influencing the verb paradigms. By the end of the eighteenth century the verbs had mostly reached their modern patterns, though some changes took place after then. Finally, in the adverbs the demand for logic in the language system led to the desire to separate adjectives from adverbs morphologically. Since the adverbial ending *-ly* had increased in frequency in earlier periods, it was seized on as the proper adverbial inflection and attempts were made to reduce the number of inflectionless adverbs. The influence of the grammarians was insufficient to convert many common adverbs like *fast* into *fastly*, but their recommendations had a more significant effect on less common adverbs, except perhaps when they were used as intensifiers of adjectives or other adverbs.

In syntax there were some interesting developments, though it is sometimes difficult to distinguish what were synchronic differences caused by style and what were more permanent changes. In the noun itself the genitive form was a matter of debate. The singular form became well established by the middle of the eighteenth century and was represented by *-'s*. But the plural remained in a state of confusion right through this period with some writers using *-s* with no apostrophe and others using *-s'*. Particular problems were caused by nouns ending in *-s* in both singular and plural. Some grammarians and other writers introduced the apostrophe in other words where it was not justified historically. Instead of *whose*, some preferred the more logical *who's*. Confusion continued to exist in these cases until the end of the period. In the demonstrative adjective *yon* and *yonder* ceased to be used, though the latter survives in poetry and Restoration drama. In the noun group there was a growing trend towards circumscribing the freedom which had existed earlier. The use of two determiners before the head was discouraged and the words which could occur as a pre-determiner decreased in number. Words like *any* and *both* are less often met with in this function. The breaking up of a group of two adjectives so that one is a pre-modifier and the other a post-modifier is increasingly rare. In the relative pronoun the role of *that* decreases. The *Spectator* no. 78 published a piece by Steele on 30 May 1711 called 'The humble petition of WHO and WHICH', in which these two pronouns complain about the recent spread of 'the Jacksprat THAT'. In this he showed his ignorance of the history of the language since *that* was the oldest relative pronoun then in the language. These pronouns complained that they had been slighted by both clergy and lawyers, and added that sometimes they were not used at all and when they were used they could be used wrongly. This was because Steele accepted that *which* should be used for inanimates and *who* for animates. In the *Spectator* no. 80 of 1 June 1711 the following defence of *that* appeared as 'The just Remonstrance of affronted *That*'. *That* suggested that *Who* and *Which* could not compose a sentence as elegantly as he could and referred to the utterance of a great Orator who was accustomed to begin: 'My Lords! (says he) with humble Submission, *That* that I say is this: that, *That* that, that Gentleman has advanced, is not *That*, that he should have proved to your Lordships.' The example shows the overload which *that* could carry, although in speech such apparent ambiguities are disambiguated by intonation. Addison's comments are indicative of the emphasis placed on restricting its role to the advantage of *which* and *who*. There was almost regular condemnation of *that* instead of *who*, which increased in importance. It was also felt that *which* should be restricted to inanimates so that *who* was reserved for animate antecedents. Since *whose* was thought to be the possessive form of *who*, its use as the possessive of *which* was deplored by some, but in the absence of any alternative this recommendation was less influential. The use of the zero relative is restricted in this period to the object function.

In the verbs auxiliaries continued to expand their functions, though grammarians tried to regulate their use. They insisted on a distinction for *shall* and *will*, with the former used in the first person for futurity and in the second and third persons for commands and threats, and the latter in the opposite roles. However, this distinction was probably never followed in speech and only intermittently in writing. In the formation of the past tense *have* had gradually replaced *be* except with intransitive verbs, especially those of motion. In the eighteenth century *have* was increasingly used with these verbs as well, though at its end examples with *be* are still found. The reduction in *be* forms is probably the result of the overload of *be*, particularly with its growing use in progressive and passive verb forms. The progressive form may have developed through the use of a preposition, usually *on*, often reduced to *a*, followed by a verbal noun. Examples of this structure survive until the end of the seventeenth century, but after that the simple progressive predominates. At the end of the eighteenth century the passive form of the progressive is found in sentences like 'The house is being built'. In speech the more usual form may have been 'The house is on [*or* a] building' and the development of the progressive passive may have been adopted because of the recommendations of the grammarians who saw it as being parallel to the active progressive. The passive form was not fully acclimatised until the nineteenth century. Before then the active progressive was employed for the passive, though this usage was criticised by the grammarians.

In the use of the various tenses the differentiation between the preterite on the one hand and the perfect and pluperfect on the other was only achieved during the eighteenth century, though examples of the preterite used for the other tenses can be found after that. The historic present continues to grow in popularity, which may in part be the result of genres which demand a more vivid style. As for the subjunctive, the grammarians tend to encourage its use and this may be a reason why forms with the subjunctive, particularly in conditional clauses, are found in formal writing. The optative still continues to use the subjunctive, and sentences with preterites expressing a wish that something should have happened continue to be found. The subjunctive is otherwise from now on expressed through modals rather than through the old forms of the paradigm. The preterite forms of the modals *would* and *should* develop a polite form to express a wish, though these verbs can also be used in conjunction with *rather*. Forms like 'I would rather he . . .' and 'I should wish . . .' are common.

As we saw in the last chapter, the *do* auxiliary was grammaticalised in questions before the Restoration, but its grammaticalisation in negative sentences occurs only in this period. However, variation in the use of *do* forms continues, because for many its use was subject to stylistic needs. It has been suggested that 'there is a clear correlation between the amount of variation [in the use of *do*] found and the social class the author belongs to'[4] which may to a large extent be related to the educational level of the writer. Although a pattern is hard to detect, there appear to be important differences in usage caused by both social and stylistic parameters. The differences in usage vary from one individual to the next and the variation is not strictly chronological. Upper-class speakers seem to have been least affected by the changes which *do* usage was undergoing. Some authors clearly were influenced by the language of the Bible in their use of *do*-less constructions so that in their more formal writing they aspired to a slightly archaic style. In view of its elevated nature, it is hardly surprising that poetry retains the older constructions. The advance of the *do* forms was promoted through speech and so it is not surprising that plays tend to show the modern stage of *do* more regularly than essays or poetry.

The grammarians tackled a range of other issues in syntax, some of which may be briefly mentioned.[5] They were anxious to distinguish transitive from intransitive verbs. It is hardly surprising that they tried to make people conscious of the distinction between *lie* and *lay*. They were also affected by Latin grammar to encourage the 'proper' use of cases in the pronouns. Thus a preposition should always be followed by the accusative (or oblique) form and the verb 'to be' should always be followed by the nominative (or subject) form. Expressions like 'between you and I' or 'It is me' were deemed incorrect. Equally the use of *whom* for *who* as in the biblical 'whom do men say that I am' was condemned by most of them. Concord between the subject (especially when it was compound) and the verb was insisted upon so that sentences like 'John and I was there' were not acceptable. However, a single noun coupled with another one through a preposition like *with* takes the singular: 'He with his wife is coming tonight'. Abbreviations even of the type *I'll*, *don't* and *haven't* were discouraged. Double negatives were roundly condemned as illogical because it was said, on the model of Latin, that two negatives made a positive. In fact most grammarians used the same type of example 'I cannot eat none', and it seems probable that expressions of this sort had dropped out of educated speech even in the seventeenth century. The impact of the grammarians was limited on the speech of most people, though it did lead to uncertainty with some as to what precisely a double negative was.[6] Another feature which was attacked was the faulty placing of *only*, which should always come before the verb. Many of these points remained as shibboleths of usage until the twentieth century, but their effect was always stronger on formal writing than on speech.

The growth in the number of pamphlets issued and the start of journals and periodicals meant that there was far more comment on the language and issues connected with it than in any previous period.[7] Most of these comments relate to style and are frequently connected with vocabulary and points of grammar. This period set the tone for all future general discussions of language in this type of publication. Many felt able to comment, usually to criticise, usages of which they disapproved, often from no better standpoint than their own prejudice. Vocabulary is the most obvious target for attack since there are so many words which were being introduced into the language and because comments of this sort exposed the critic less than comments on syntax. This period continued to borrow words from many sources, but it is noteworthy for the introduction of words from languages which had hitherto hardly made any impact on English. This was the result of the colonial expansion not only to America and the Caribbean, but also to India and the Pacific. However, languages nearer home continued to supply new words. The Restoration naturally led to the intro-duction of new French words. From now on French words often retain their French spelling, as in *manoeuvre*, and something like their French pronunciation, as in *clique*, because the effects of most English sound changes were no longer operative. The latter word has [i:] rather than [ai], as one might otherwise have expected. The first word has a military association which arises from the wars fought against France in the early eighteenth century. Indeed, Addison was amused by the fact that although the Duke of Marlborough was defeating the French armies on the continent he had to report his successes in language which was full of French words.

The present War has so Adulterated our Tongue with strange

Words, that it would be impossible for one of our Great-Grandfathers to know what his Posterity had been doing, were he to read their Exploits in a Modern News Paper. Our Warriors are very Industrious in Propagating the *French* Language, at the same time that they are so gloriously successful in beating down their Power.[8]

Other words include *bivouac, corps, terrain* and *enfilade*. The end of the century saw more words coming in as a result of the French Revolution, such as *depôt* and *sortie*. The critics were quick to criticise the new French words, though as often in such cases many of the words became well established. The *Critical Review* of 1756 attacked words like *appendage, misanthrope, emanate* and *bilious*. French words occur in most walks of life including society, architecture, dancing, geography, dress, food and behaviour. This is not surprising since French manners and attitudes were those which were copied through most of Europe at this time. Perhaps the prevailing attitude to French borrowing is neatly summed up in the *Critical Review* of 1775: 'We are obliged to the French for a great number of terms and phrases, some of them used by men of taste and learning; others only by *coxcombs* of both sexes, who *affect* to speak à la Mode de Paris.'[9]

Words from Dutch continue to be borrowed, but they are mostly of a maritime nature, reflecting to some extent the Dutch wars at the end of the seventeenth century and the competition with Holland in colonial territories. *Schooner* is typical of the nautical words, but others from trade and colonial expansion include *gin, geneva* and *springbok*, the last being from South Africa through Dutch. Words from Spanish and Portuguese include those for seafaring and words of American origin introduced through these languages. They include *flotilla, maté* and *alpaca*. Words from Italian become more prominent as Italy was the major destination of the Grand Tour which so many young noblemen undertook at this time. Music and the arts generally were among the main areas of borrowing, including words like *soprano, fantasia, terracotta, extravaganza* and *cicerone*. Two new important sources of borrowing were the new colonial territories such as America and words of Eastern origin. In both cases many words from these sources came through other languages. India provided such words as *nawab, wallah, baksheesh, bungalow* and *shampoo*. America provided such words as *totem, hickory, caribou* and *kayak* from the north, and *cashew, pampas, tapioca* and *angostura* from further south. The southern words are most often borrowed through an intermediary language.

The classical languages continue to provide new words, but their number is not as great as in the previous period. The development of all sciences in the eighteenth century naturally meant that many new words for discoveries had to be created. Some of these words may have come through other European languages. Latin words include *stimulus, nucleus, inertia* and *herbarium,* and Greek ones *pharynx, phlox, bathos* and *triptych.* Different suffixes added to the stems of words to form other parts of speech continue to be employed, but this period restricts the profusion of variants which were characteristic of the previous one. Most words are now confined to a single form. This restriction applies to affixes as a whole, no matter from which language it may be derived. The profusion among variants found in Shakespeare which allowed the words *entreat, entreatment* and *entreaty* as nouns was curtailed.

The criticisms of language were levelled both at snobbery and affectation at one end and at cant and vulgarity at the other. Sometimes it is difficult for us today to understand what particularly aroused the animosity of some critics to certain words. Affectation included using Latinate words instead of English ones: some attacked the use of *existence* and *novel* for *life* and *new.* Others objected to the fashion in literature for Arcadian language, by which nothing in the countryside was referred to by its real name. It is hardly surprising that objections were raised against the circumlocution *sons of rusticity* for 'agricultural labourers' in a treatise on agriculture. Equally the language of passion was considered too effete so that instead of saying simply *I love,* a hero or heroine might say *a secret flame consumes me* or *I languish night and day.* Euphemism was also criticised, particularly where it suggested that the decline in moral standards was condoned. To call fast living *sporting* or dissipation *seeing life* appeared to approve of this lifestyle. One critic noted that advertisements, then as now, could recommend things quite inappropriately. Alcoholic concoctions made of gin could be advertised as the *spirit of Adonis* or *Parfait Amour,* whereas the lower classes used more appropriate terms like *Strip me naked.* The language of trade and even of the professions was regarded as a specialised variety which should not be used in polite society. With the former it was the language of business letters which was particularly attacked, including such expressions from the stockmarket like *below par.* While it was recognised that every scholarly discipline needed its own vocabulary, it was not felt that this vocabulary should be used in other circumstances. Naturally the criticism was often satirical, as when a doctor asked a man with a pain in his head about his *cephalick symptoms*. Some words were considered low and impolite, though many we might think of as colloquial. They include *funk, fuss, hands off* and *spick and span*. Quite a number of phrasal verbs, like *set off*, were included in this category, though most are now fully integrated into the language. Since many of them were relatively recent innovations, it is not surprising they should be attacked. Dr Johnson is the first lexicographer to recognise the existence of these verbs. He referred in the preface to this 'class of verbs too frequent in the *English* language, of which the significance is so loose and general, the use so vague and indeterminate, and the sense distorted so widely from the first idea, that it is hard to trace them through the maze of variation'. However, he did try to record them, but often ends his entries with some comment like the following on *make*: 'This is one of the words so frequently occurring, and used with so much latitude, that its whole extent is not easily comprehended, nor are its attenuated and fugitive meanings easily caught and restrained.' Many critics of the time were interested in clarity of thought and expression and therefore recommended that proper distinctions among words should be maintained. Some of these words have continued to exercise the guardians of the language even today. The distinction between *hanged* and *hung* was emphasised. Critics insisted on the need to avoid confusing *ingenious* and *ingenuous*. We have already noted the pair *lie* and *lay*; other pairs included *flee/fly* and *mutual/common*. It can be seen from this paragraph that many of the concerns highlighted in the eighteenth century have continued to haunt discussions about what is acceptable in English. This is hardly surprising because it was this period that laid down rules for polite English and set the tone for all future discussions about language.

The English used in this period is illustrated by a passage from one of Addison's contributions to the *Spectator*, no. 135 dated 4 August 1711, in which he comments on some aspects of the English language.[10]

The same natural Aversion to Loquacity has of late Years made a very considerable Alteration in our Language, by closing in one Syllable the Termination of our Præterperfect Tense, as in the

Words *drown'd*, *walk'd*, *arriv'd* for *drowned*, *walked*, *arrived*, which has very much disfigured the Tongue, and turn'd a tenth part of our smoother Words into so many Clusters of Consonants. This is the more remarkable, because the want of Vowels in our Language has been the general Complaint of our politest Authors, who nevertheless are the Men that have made these Retrenchments, and consequently very much increased our former Scarcity.

This Reflection on the Words that end in *ed*, I have heard in Conversation from one of the greatest Genius's this Age has produced. I think we may add to the foregoing Observation, the Change which has happen'd in our Language, by the Abbreviation of several Words that are terminated in *eth*, by substituting an *s* in the room of the last Syllable, as in *drowns*, *walks*, *arrives*, and innumerable other Words, which in the Pronunciation of our Forefathers were *drowneth*, *walketh*, *arriveth*. This has wonderfully multiplied a Letter which was before too frequent in the the *English* Tongue, and added to that *hissing* in our Language, which is taken so much notice of by Foreigners; but at the same time humours our Taciturnity, and eases us of so many superfluous syllables.

The spelling system of this passage is much the same as that which is found in modern English. Addison uses <æ> which he has taken over from Latin because that is the letter form used in Latin for *Præterperfect*. This <æ> was retained for words of Latin origin in formal writing until the twentieth century. The apostrophe marks the plural in *s* in a word which already ends in *s*, namely *Genius's*. Although Addison appears to be criticising the use of apostrophes for purposes of abbreviation in the preterite of weak verbs, he has examples like *turn'd* and *happen'd*, although all other verbs are spelt with -*ed*. In punctuation almost all nouns are provided with an initial capital, except a few like *part*, *notice* and *room*, though the last may have been considered less significant because it is part of the phrase *in the room of* which may have been considered almost a preposition. The use of full stops is modern, but commas are sometimes found where stylists today would discourage their use. In the expression 'we may add to the foregoing Observation, the Change' Addison has a comma which separates the verb *add* from its object *Change*. Equally in the clause 'Letter which was before too frequent in the *English* Tongue, and added' he has no commas to mark of the relative clause, but he does have one at the end of the first part of the relative clause which separates the subject *which* from its verb *added*. This particular feature of punctuation is found in several other places.

Other differences from modern English occur in the use of words and some points of syntax. The vocabulary is notable for its Latinate words, which may have been chosen for part of the satirical effect. The words which he uses for examples, *drown, walk, arrive*, are simpler and much commoner. The result of the Latinate vocabulary is to create an elevated and periphrastic style: *Aversion, Loquacity, Alteration, Termination* are used for *hatred, talking, change, ending*. Many of these words occur in noun groups consisting of two nouns linked with a preposition: *Aversion to Loquacity, Alteration to our Language, Clusters of Consonants*. However, many of these Latinate words are not unusual in formal language, and the tone of this passage is quite removed from the colloquial. Even though the subject deals with corruptions in the language that might be associated with speech, the language in which it is written is at the other end on the scale of formality. The Latinate nature of the vocabulary gives a slightly abstract feel to the passage, because such words seem to be removed from the day-to-day events of ordinary life. Some words and expressions now strike us as archaic or old-fashioned. We could not use *closing* to mean 'shortening'. We would not use *want* to mean 'shortage'. Expressions like 'of late Years', 'very considerable', 'very much disfigured', 'smoothest Words' and 'politest Authors' are uncommon today, though the words themselves are still used. The connotations of the words have changed. One could, but one does not often today, refer to the *disfiguring* of the language; and one does not refer to a language as a *Tongue*. The phrase *in the room of* would now almost certainly be a simple 'in'. The use of *wonderfully* as an intensifier is now rare and would be regarded as slightly precious.

The syntax is generally straightforward. The second paragraph begins with the object 'This Reflection . . . end in *ed*' placed before the subject and verb. The precise subject of the verb *humours* in the final sentence is not evident. Mostly the sentences have a regular word order, though they often have prepositional or other phrases attached to the main clause so that the sentence seems to be somewhat incremental as though it reflects the organisation of speech. In consideration of the views expressed in the *Spectator* about *that, which* and *who*, it is surprising to find *that* used so frequently. In one example the printed version has *which* although the copy text had *that*. There seems to be little to choose between the two forms used in this passage. For the comparison of adjectives he employs the ending *-est* even in bisyllabic words like *polite*. For most readers today this passage would suggest something rather formal and possibly pompous, but would not cause many problems of comprehension. We have arrived at a stage of the language which seems modern and differs from our own variety more in its nuances and connotations than in its basic structure. The debate about English would from now on concentrate on matters of style and its fitness for purpose.[11]

10

Emancipation, Education and Empire

This chapter starts with the symbolic date of 1798, for that year saw the publication of the *Lyrical Ballads* which contained poems quite different from those that had appeared in English up until then, and included a preface which attacked the assumptions of previous attitudes to language, though it was primarily aimed at poetic diction. In this preface Wordsworth, who was the author, criticised the artificiality of the diction of the poems which had been written in the eighteenth century and suggested that poetry ought to replicate the real language of men. This did not mean that he used colloquial language, but he provided the impetus to make poetic language, particularly dialogue, take account of contemporary speech and to make the speech of its characters less stilted. Equally, the subjects of his poetry were not going to be ideas and abstractions, but lives and emotions of real people. He moved away from the abstract to the concrete. For Wordsworth real people included ordinary people from the country, children and members of classes other than the sophisticated urbanites who had been the principal participants in poetry up till then. In this way Wordsworth signalled the break with the Augustan period and the onset of Romanticism which focused attention on the spirit of the folk in language, particularly as represented in dialect and in earlier poetry, and on the supernatural and the unusual. Old romances and ballads sprang once more into literary prominence. If the poems that Wordsworth included in the *Lyrical Ballads* were not too outrageous for contemporaries in their language, their subject matter was certainly different because they dealt seriously and sympathetically with people who had hitherto not been regarded as proper subjects for poetry, other perhaps than in satire. Clearly if poetry was to deal with people who were rustic and on the fringes of decent society, and to represent their speech in straightforward language, it would call into question some of the assumptions about polite language and its restriction to those who were educated. Or rather it would widen the range of language and what might be considered acceptable usage. It was, however, the poems by Coleridge in the anthology which particularly attracted attention, because a poem like *The Rime of the Ancient Mariner* was written in a language that no one could consider polite. For the impact it made we need to remember that the previous hundred years or so had witnessed attempts to purify the language and to set boundaries around what was permissible in polite speech and formal writing. It was one thing for novelists like Fielding to introduce characters into their novels from lower life or from the distant country who could speak in a way that allowed the readers to enjoy it either with scorn or with condescension. It was quite another matter to read in poetry, which was considered the highest expression of literary art, language that had been banned from polite writing, apparently for ever. It is hardly surprising that this poem should attract considerable antipathy because it seemed to undermine all that had been won in the previous century.

There were many indications before 1798 that the system of polite language which had developed in the eighteenth century was under strain. Four may be highlighted. The first is the freeing up of restrictions on newsprint and copyright. The second is the American Revolution leading to the independence of the former American colonies. The third is the French Revolution and the impetus that provided for democratic movements and the inevitable backlash from those who wanted to preserve conservative values and social standards. The fourth is the discovery by Sir William Jones that Sanskrit was related to Latin and Greek as well as possibly to other languages. These events became associated with other developments which took place during the nineteenth century to put the old system under pressure.

In the eighteenth century copyright law was uncertain, but the fear of prosecution under the law inhibited many printers from publishing material for which they thought they could be put in prison. Those who wanted could interpret the provisions of copyright very widely so that anything which suggested a previous publication could be regarded as a breach of the law and its perpetrators brought to justice. In 1774 the limits of copyright were clarified and it became far easier to publish material that might previously have been considered suspect. This did not immediately stop the prosecution of those who published material to which the government took exception, and during the Napoleonic Wars various acts restricted liberty and freedom of expression. However, the end of copyright and the general availability of newsprint meant that many new cheap editions were issued so that those who could read might have better access to reading matter other than the Bible. During the nineteenth century circulating libraries grew in importance and there was a growth in literacy. Newspapers became more widespread, and in 1835 the repeal of the newspaper stamp duty meant that newspapers came down in price and could therefore reach a wider audience. Writers who supported the development of democracy like Tom Paine could now be published more easily than before. The availability of the written word enabled ideas to spread more quickly. As the audience for writing grew, it became difficult to assume that good writing was restricted to a certain class alone. Dr Johnson had written in the preface to his dictionary: 'illiterate writers will at one time or other, by publick infatuation, rise into renown, who, not knowing the original import of words, will use them with colloquial licentiousness, confound distinction, and forget propriety' (p. C2r).

This was the challenge that William Cobbett took up.[1] For Johnson and his followers in the late eighteenth and nineteenth centuries, education meant learning Latin and Greek. Eighteenth-century writers saw language as an attribute of class. To use correct English one had to be knowledgeable in the classical languages, to move in polite society and to read the ancient authors frequently and fluently. These requirements became the principle for restricting education for other classes to a basic reading knowledge of English: the poor could read the Bible, which was as much learning as they required. If the aim of education was to become acquainted with the language and literature of the classics, the English that needed to be taught was that which would enable a child to pass on to these more sophisticated languages. Hence children of all classes could learn the same amount of English, whereas those to be educated further would go on to the classics. Anyone without that accomplishment was in Dr Johnson's view 'illiterate'. Literacy was not simply knowing how to read, but knowing the language and culture of the classics. This was the aim of grammar schools and because to some extent the knowledge so acquired was without much practical value in later life, it was not taught to those who were to remain in the working and middle classes. They were to be taught just as much as they required to undertake their functions in society. Indeed, when governors of Leeds Grammar School petitioned in 1805 to include arithmetic and modern languages in their curriculum, the request was refused because a grammar school was a school for teaching the learned languages. Therefore, legal opinion was that the endowment of the school prevented it from offering anything other than the classics.[2] The question Cobbett had to face was how to provide the less educated with the means to fight against this type of exclusion.

Cobbett published his grammar in 1818 in New York and its success was immediate. It was reprinted in London the following year and in 1823 an edition containing six letters intended to prevent statesmen from using false grammar was published.[3] Further editions were published in the nineteenth century in England and America, and the grammar was translated into French. Cobbett had had a colourful career and was for parts of it adopted by the Tory government of the day. However, he later came to attack the policies of the government and felt he could do this through his grammar. After all a grammar book could hardly be regarded as seditious since it was simply setting out to do what many other grammarians had done, namely to explain the structure of the English language. However, Cobbett tried to make his grammar, which according to the title page was intended for 'Young Persons in general; but more especially for the Use of Soldiers, Sailors, Apprentices, and Plough-boys', more user-friendly than those published hitherto. It was written to James, who was fourteen, in a style which was intelligible to a fourteen year old, divided into letters (rather than chapters) and numbered sections, and with numerous cross-references and helpful tips. It was seditious in that it used loaded examples to illustrate grammatical points. He attacked the use of Latin in education by including examples like this one on the use of *there*: '*There are* many men, who have been at Latin-Schools for years, and who, at last, cannot write six sentences in English correctly' (§ 61). He also criticised previous grammarians and writers on the language. Letter XXI contains according to its title 'SPECIMENS OF FALSE GRAMMAR, TAKEN FROM THE WRITINGS OF DOCTOR JOHNSON AND FROM THOSE OF DOCTOR WATTS'. In it he writes:

Another object, in the producing of these specimens, is to convince you, that a knowledge of the Latin and Greek Languages does not prevent men from writing bad English. Those languages are, by impostors and their dupes, called 'the *learned* languages;' and those who have paid for having studied them are said to have received 'a *liberal* education.' These appellations are false, and, of course, they lead to false conclusions. *Learning*, as a noun, means *knowledge*, and *learned* means *knowing*, or *possessed of knowledge*. Learning is, then, to be acquired by *conception*; and it is shown in *judgment*, in *reasoning*, and, in the various modes of employing it. What, then, can *learning* have to do with with any particular tongue? Good grammar, for instance, written in Welsh, or in the language of the Chipewaw Savages, is more *learned* than bad grammar written in Greek. The learning is in the *mind*, and not on the *tongue*.

Other examples he provides attack the system of government of the day which he regarded as tyrannical without necessarily naming it. To illustrate a problem of concord his example is 'The Tyrant, with the Spy, *have* brought Peter to the block' (§ 246). As an example of inconsistency with nouns of number he pilloried the House of Commons in this context: '*they*, one year, voted unanimously, that cheap corn was an evil, and the next year, *it* voted unanimously, that dear corn was an evil' (§ 181).

The beauty of this approach was that he exploited the very weapon against those who were using it to keep the lower classes in their place. The examples also make the text enjoyable and stimulating, and help to maintain the interest of the reader. The overall point that Cobbett strove to achieve is that education is a powerful weapon in what later became known as the class struggle. Those who claim that the lower classes are illiterate can be shown to make elementary mistakes themselves. In other words their superiority is based on fraudulent premises since they are no better in their language abilities than those they despised as uneducated. Cobbett underlined the fact that there were many different pronunciations in Britain, but that they were unimportant.

But, while all inquiries into the causes of these differences are useless, and all attempts to remove them are vain, the differences are of very little real consequence. . . . Children will pronounce as their fathers and mothers pronounce; and if, in common conversation, or in speeches, the matter be good and judiciously arranged, . . . hearers, whose approbation is worth having, will pay very little attention to the accent. (§ 7)

In this way he cut the ground from under the feet of those who claimed that there was a polite pronunciation and that all other pronunciations were vulgar. He brought to the discussion common sense instead of prejudice. The members of the poorly educated classes can improve their position and their status through education, particularly grammar, which is the foundation of education. Properly used, this tool could lance the pretensions and snobbery of the educated. While Cobbett's grammar did not necessarily alter attitudes overnight, it helped to create a new climate. Inevitably it also created a reaction from those whose privileges were threatened. The bitter social conflicts of the early nineteenth century often found expression in attitudes to language and grammar, and this coloured the debates on language which followed in the rest of the century

The Declaration of Independence in America in 1776 produced a profound change in the attitudes of the American settlers towards England. Previously they had been accustomed to observe and follow the dictates of England and this had naturally imbued the settlers with the idea that the language which was fashionable in London was the language appropriate for America. Many people, particularly in positions of power and influence, travelled from one side of the Atlantic to the other and thus helped to maintain the sense that all that was sophisticated emanated from London. With independence arose the view that the language found in America was different from that in Britain, and so different usage and hence other rules should obtain. The person who expressed this view most powerfully and effectively was Noah Webster. His consistent motivation was that the American variety was different from the British variety and had its own history and should continue to develop in accordance with its own genius. At the end of the eighteenth and beginning of the nineteenth centuries he produced several works, of which the two most influential were *The American Spelling Book* (1783) and *An American Dictionary of the English Language* (1828). The titles are significant because they include *American* and indicate that this is a different variety from British English.

Politics was not far from Webster's mind, because as a nation which had achieved political independence America could not be subservient to another country in matters of such central importance as language. An independent nation must have its own language. In spelling he accepted the desirability of omitting all superfluous and silent letters, though he came to accept that modifications could not be far-reaching if they were to be accepted. He advocated dropping the final <k> in words like *musick*, reversing <re> to <er> in words like *centre*, omitting <u> in the ending *-our* in words like *honour*, simplifying the double <ll> in words like *traveller*, adopting <ck> instead of <que> in words like *cheque*, and omitting final <e> in words like *machine*. All of these proposals except the last were adopted into American English and are now standard in that variety. As for lexis he recognised that there were many words in American usage which were not found in Britain, and equally there were words in British English which were not used in America. Naturally the resources of American-Indian languages and of the languages brought by other European settlers, especially at first from France and Holland, had produced a whole wealth of vocabulary that was unique to American English. Webster may also have had some impact on pronunciation, especially in his insistence on sounding unstressed syllables and on the placing of stress, but this was less obvious at first in England. What is significant about the development of American English is that there was now another source of standard English than educated London English. It became increasingly difficult to maintain that those who did not conform in their writing and speech to the London standard were ignorant and uneducated. While the impact of American English on British English took time to manifest itself, it was a timebomb waiting to explode and shatter the British view that educated speakers in England were the sole arbiters of the English language. For most of the nineteenth century the English could pretend to ignore the example of American linguistic practice, partly because America had not yet achieved the status of a superpower and partly because English writers could pour scorn on the corrupt English usage emanating from the other side of the Atlantic. Writers like Henry Alford were quite happy to express contempt for American English as much as for regional varieties of British English. The corruption of language at the hands of the Americans was an indication of their corrupt morals. He commented on:

the process of deterioration which our Queen's English has undergone at the hands of the Americans. Look at those phrases which so amuse us in their speech and books; at their reckless exaggeration, and contempt for congruity; and then compare the character and history of the nation – its blunted sense of moral obligation and duty to man; its open disregard of conventional right where aggrandizement is to be obtained.[4]

The book in which this appeared, *The Queen's English*, not only established the British right to the language, but also gave the approved language the authority and status attached to the queen.

The loss of America did not discourage the British from continuing with their imperial expansion in other parts of the world. The rest of what became the Empire was much more compliant linguistically. In colonies with a resident white population, such as Australia and Canada, the number of immigrants was relatively small and was continually reinforced by new settlers from England. The colonisation tended to proceed from one or two major centres, in Australia's case on the coastal fringe, so that linguistic attitudes could be reinforced and made to conform within limits to the approved language. Even in these countries there was an indigenous population who were being 'civilised' and so the need to maintain a common front socially and linguistically against the natives encouraged a greater uniformity in language use. Before these colonies became dominions, there were frequent changes of officials from Britain. In the colonies in Africa and India, the white administrators and soldiers remained a tiny part of the overall population. They might serve in these places only for a few years before being redeployed elsewhere. Often the administrators came themselves from the classes which belonged to polite society or which aspired to do so, and consequently they took with them many of the attitudes to language characteristic of their peers in England. The threat posed by these future dominions and colonies seemed inconsiderable when compared with that posed by the United States. On the contrary, the growth of the Empire led to that sense of the superiority of English as a language and the dominant position of Britain in the world. Self-confidence in England and the role of English grew the wider the Empire extended. Even such a scholar as W. W. Skeat declared that England was 'a modern nation which is fit to lead the world, especially in the very matter of language'.[5]

The political use to which language could be put and to which people like Cobbett objected is illustrated by the refusal of the

House of Commons to accept petitions which were presented to them from members of the lower classes because they were not written in proper English. The decades leading up to the First Reform Bill of 1832 were filled with demands for an extension of the suffrage and for abolition of rotten boroughs. These petitions were presented by various social groups, but they were almost all rejected. Many argued that the language of the petitions was no different from the language used by Members of Parliament. But objection was raised to the 'highly indecent and disrespectful language' of these petitions and Wilberforce claimed on one occasion that 'Liberty of speech and freedom of discussion in that House, formed an essential part of the constitution; but it was necessary that persons coming forward as petitioners, should address the House in decent and respectful language.'[6] The great advantage of this type of rebuttal was that no one other than the Members of Parliament knew what the correct speech to use to the House was. The House could set its own rules and not inform others what they were. It is hardly surprising that many believed that their language was not the real reason for the rejection of such petitions.

In the eighteenth century the study of language fell into two categories: the more intellectual study which saw in language a reflection of the workings of the mind and therefore pursued the matter of universal grammar with enthusiasm, and the more practical study which saw as its task the provision of books on grammar for educational purposes, particularly for those members of society who were born into the less fortunate classes. The successor of the first type is represented by the work of Horne Tooke, whose *Diversions of Purley* was published in two volumes in 1778 and 1805; the third volume never appeared. This book dominated discussions about language in England for the first third of the nineteenth century. The emphasis of language study in the eighteenth century following the lead of Wilkins was to see language in a universal perspective and that meant an intense interest in the origin of language to understand the original relationship of language and mind and to understand how that developed. This led to an interest in etymology. Such studies were impressive in their intellectual sweep even if their linguistic foundations were suspect. The implication of this kind of approach was that language, as its divine origins might suggest, had origin-ally been perfect and had gradually become corrupted through time and use. The desire to improve and fix the language was in part an effort to restore some of the original purity of language. This made language closely related to religion and morals, a link that it maintained through most of the nineteenth century though this association came under considerable strain. It was partly through the close association of language with morals that the intellectual and the practical study of language came together.

Because language and thought were closely related, thinking was in essence an element of language and so it is not surprising that many accepted that those who had an incomplete command of language were unable to think rationally. Tooke held the view that language could be reduced to two categories: nouns (in which category he appeared to include verbs, though their position in his system was ambiguous) and other words. The first category, nouns, originated as direct signs that referred to features in nature and represented them. Thus originally men spoke a language that reflected the material world exactly either through the designation of material objects through individual signs or through inter-jections which expressed emotional reactions and other sensations which were then converted into signs. However, because of the need for communication, which grew ever more rapid, it was necessary to join words together in order to get across a message in detail. The speed of communication meant that speech became abbreviated and thus the original signs were corrupted so that their original meaning could not be seen in present words. It was the aim of any study of language to discover through etymology the way in which current words had been corrupted and what their original roots and meanings were. This made language study appear to be scientific and it was often compared with chemistry. Language consisted of original signs which could be compared with the elements in chemistry; these words were then joined or abbreviated through communication in much the same way as compounds in chemistry are formed from the various elements. This overall approach by Tooke was understood by many to indicate a materialistic view of the world and language, and he was attacked for undermining the moral nature of language. It was for this reason that he was often regarded with respect by the Utilitarians. Quite apart from the Utilitarians, Tooke's book achieved enormous influence in English intellectual life and prevented the pursuit of more historical studies which were now more fashionable in France and especially in Germany.

These views of Tooke rekindled an interest in universal grammar and also sparked off studies in etymology and the origin of language. The origin of language became one of the favourite intellectual pursuits of many at the time. The study of language was thus both philosophical and speculative, and interest in the language of everyday use and how it had developed was left to the grammarians. Of these there was no shortage. The work of Lowth was followed by that of Lindley Murray whose *English Grammar* was first published in 1795 and reissued at least forty-five times in England before 1832. It became the favourite textbook for use in private schools. Other grammars followed Murray later in the century and most were of a highly prescriptive nature because their purpose was the instruction of the young to reform their morals.

The historical study of language was given a tremendous boost by Sir William Jones, who discovered the relationship between Sanskrit and the European languages. He established the Asiatick Society in India and his Anniversary Discourses, which were published in the Society's *Asiatic Researches*, commanded a wide readership and aroused enormous interest among many language scholars on the continent. He proposed that the Society should investigate the history, science and art of all of Asia and parts of Africa. He excluded language, which he considered to be merely an instrument of real learning that had been 'improperly con- founded with learning itself'. This approach was directly opposed to the views characteristic of the eighteenth century and promoted by Tooke, for it presumed a much more pragmatic and empirical study of language. Jones knew many Eastern languages as well as the classical ones and he was able to make many advances in the relationship of the Proto-Indo-European languages and in the establishment of etymology as a more rigorous discipline. He recognised that to establish kinship among languages one had to beware of loan-words, especially among more learned words, and to look for links in the core vocabulary and in morphology. 'By making it strictly historical, comparative and structural, Jones caused a revolution in the study of language.'[7]

Jones's work was taken up by Schlegel and Herder in Germany where the philosophical study of language that had been dominant in England had never taken hold. In Germany the influence of Johann Michaelis of Göttingen University had directed language study towards what became known as philology. Michaelis recog- nised that language was democratic in that usage was decided by the majority of speakers of a language, for the learned formed an infinitesimal part of those speakers. Individual languages are the result of usage from one generation to the next of all speakers of a language, whether illiterate or not. This was a concept which struck at the very heart of proper language as the preserve of an educated élite. Naturally this view tended also to work against the divine origin of language since individual languages were the result of developments within particular societies. These views became commonplace in Germany during the first years of the nineteenth century where the universities had entered into a phase of stimulating intellectual ferment. The prevailing views were translated into the historical development of the Germanic languages by Rasmus Rask in Denmark and Jacob Grimm in Germany. They were able to map out the extent and growth of the Germanic languages through a series of mainly phonological discoveries.

English universities meanwhile languished in a state of intellectual torpor. Here the universities were closely identified with the Church of England. Most academics were clergymen and the Test Acts prevented non-Anglicans from being members of the two universities. The classics were the primary object of study at Oxford and Cambridge, though at the latter mathematics also held a prominent position. The lecturers at the universities were for the most part happy to accept the close relationship between language and mind since that enabled them to maintain the link between language study and religion. This situation began to change with the foundation of University College in London in 1828 since it was outside the ambit of the Anglican Church and could take a fresh approach to academic disciplines. But it was only when English scholars like Thorpe and Kemble went to study in Denmark and Germany that the new philology could begin to make any inroads into English academic life. Gradually attitudes in the universities changed and historical study of languages was followed with increasing attention. However, this development made little impact more generally on English intellectual life because the cult of the gentleman amateur was well entrenched and many dilletantes continued to take an interest in language matters. This is not surprising because the new philology aroused antipathy on two fronts: it was considered a foreign import which could undermine the English way of doing things, and it was seen as fundamentally anti-Christian because it appeared to contravert the divine origin of language. The idea that language might have started from barbarous origins among savages and developed to the levels of sophistication found in contemporary society was not a concept that many found congenial. It took time for this idea to win acceptance in England, and it later became associated with Darwinism which was equally repugnant to many Christians.

The growth of historical studies of language had several effects. It promoted an interest in the English language's history and led to calls for a dictionary to chart the development of each word. It promoted the study of the early stages of the language so that considerable scholarship was devoted principally to Old English and less to Middle English, which prompted Frederick Furnivall to found the Early English Text Society in 1864. However, it tended to draw attention away from the development of the language in the post-medieval period. In the universities it attached too much weight to older varieties of language and discouraged attention being paid to contemporary usage. It aroused considerable antagonism because of its perceived anti-Christian and anti-moral bias, and thus encouraged the separation of the historical study of language from the teaching of English grammar, which continued on the course inaugurated by the previous century. It also discouraged the study of the origins of language which had become discredited through the work of earlier writers like Tooke. Modern scholars wanted to distance themselves from the older language studies, and the Philological Society, which was founded in 1842 to give opportunity for propagating the new philology, turned its back on the whole question of the origin of language. It was both tainted by the past and contentious because of its links with religion.

The emphasis on the historical study of language had several important effects. The main discoveries made in the historical development of Proto-Indo-European, such as Grimm's Law, were in the development of sounds. This produced an emphasis on the laws of historical change which were all related to phonological change: for most people the laws of historical development meant sound rules. This naturally caused a re-evaluation of the primacy of the written word and ultimately of literature. In Victorian life literature occupied a prominent position in its view of culture, and any attack on the pre-eminence of literature was not regarded favourably. The ultimate logic of this view was that literary language was an artificial construct which bore little relation to real language. While the Victorians never came to this position, it was one that many saw as a threat to their beliefs. The growing under-standing of how Proto-Indo-European developed also encouraged the view that all languages were equal. Again this was not a view which was accepted readily at this time and it certainly did not influence the attitudes of ordinary people. In due course it would be possible to study what many considered 'barbarous' languages in the same way as one studied English. Naturally the need to save the souls of the colonial peoples in the Empire meant that trans-lations of the Bible into their own languages needed to be made and hence knowledge of these languages increased. But for the present, the apparent lack of any historical development in these languages and the conviction that they were in some way inferior and primitive prevented most people from considering them in the same league as a language like English.

The historical dimension now bestowed on English led to a heightened regard for it that with some became almost hysterical. Kington Oliphant in his *Standard English* of 1873 linked the history of English to its Teutonic background, which made it strong and noble. For him good English was still very much a class issue and the higher classes knew how to use English properly, whereas the lower classes tended to corrupt English by introducing foreign words or using Latin words incorrectly. He also sees the problem as coming from the invention of cheap newspapers: 'the penny-a-liner is the outcome of the middle class' (p. 325). This class is

day by day pouring more sewage into the well of what can no longer be called 'English undefiled'. From the one quarter [the educated class] comes all that is lofty and noble in the literature of the day; from the other all that is mean and tawdry. (pp. 322–3)

Kington Oliphant objects to such features as the death of the subjunctive, the misuse of Latin words, the employment of tired clichés, incorrect use of grammatical rules such as those for *who* and *which*, the use of abbreviated forms of words like *exam*, the dropping of *h*, and the general abandonment of the models provided by the best authors of the past. This is all presented in a book which shows the rise of standard English leading to its present position. This book embodies many of the older prejudices about language dressed up in a historical guise.

Others adopted a different approach. Prominent among these

was Richard Cheveneux Trench who became Archbishop of Dublin in 1863, but who remained a prominent member of the Philological Society. The close link between the Church and education is still evident. Indeed, Trench saw the English language as fossil history which could be unearthed through diligent study, particularly of the words in the language. For him nationalism and pride in being an Englishman found expression in his love of the English language. As he wrote in *English Past and Present*, first issued in 1855:

> If the noble acts of that nation to which we belong are precious to us, if we feel ourselves made greater by the greatness, summoned to a nobler life by the nobleness of Englishmen, who have already lived and died, and have bequeathed to us a name which must not by us be made less, what exploits of theirs can well be worthier, what can more clearly point out their native land and ours as having fulfilled a glorious past, as being destined for a glorious future, than that they should have acquired for themselves and for us a clear, a strong, an harmonious, a noble language? For all this bears witness to corresponding merits in those that speak it, to clearness of mental vision, to strength, to harmony, to nobleness in them who have gradually shaped and fashioned it to be the utterance of their inmost life and being.[8]

It is hardly surprising in view of this that Trench should have been one of the primary movers in the promotion of what became the *New English Dictionary on Historical Principles* (later the *Oxford English Dictionary*), which was intended to provide the complete history for every word which existed in the English language. He also called for the introduction of English studies in schools and universities. For Trench there was a clear connection between language and morality, and his opinions received wide publicity in the second half of the century because several of his books were constantly reissued. His book *On the Study of Words*, first published in 1851 but constantly reprinted, devoted Lecture II to 'On the Morality in Words'.

The two ancient universities were committed to the learned languages. The nine public schools saw their function as feeder institutions to Oxford and Cambridge. Hence they felt it necessary to provide teaching principally in Latin and Greek, for without them their pupils could not go to university. Grammar schools provided some elementary instruction in English, but otherwise aped the public schools. Instruction in English was left largely to the private schools which were run by individuals, who in previous ages might well have become tutors to the children of the rich and noble. The private schools taught English grammar from Lindley Murray's grammar. A series of investigations into schools and universities during the nineteenth century led to significant changes. The position of Greek and Latin came under serious threat because, although some continued to press the opinion that universities were providing a general rather than a professional education (for which the classics were ideal), it was acknowledged that the education which school and university students needed should fit them more adequately for life. Philology as a discipline was introduced into universities as part of the new historical concerns with language, and teaching in English was often first introduced into universities through external lectures. The first professor of English to be appointed in England was the Reverend Thomas Dale at University College in 1828. He shared Trench's views on the close link between morality and language, as did one of his successors, Henry Morley, who saw English literature as sustaining 'the spiritual side of life . . . as a natural corrective to the materialist tendencies of the age'.[9] As a counterweight to literature, which some regarded as either mere fashion or the superficial reading of a hundred books, philology was incorporated as a steadying influence, though the historical tendencies of the age would have dictated the inclusion of all branches of the language and literature. Indeed, it was contemporary language and literature which were excluded from university study. While universal education was provided for by the 1870 Education Act, it did not significantly alter the type of English taught. Grammar through rules and parsing as laid down in the previous century by Lowth remained the backbone of the teaching of English language. Those who passed through the state schools would accept that there was a correct English, and those who got to university would learn something of the nature of English language and literature within a framework of the excellence of the English language and its proper usage. The tradition of teaching through mistakes was well established and continued unabated in the period. If there was a new development it was simply that they now picked up faults in the work of their fellow grammarians rather than in literary works. By the end of the century the teaching of English had spread quite widely through the country, but it was largely confined to the lower ends of the educational system. However, one development which had given a boost to the teaching of English was the introduction of examinations for admission into the Civil Service following the report of a commission in 1855. Papers on English and the history of English were included in this examination well into the twentieth century.

Naturally, knowledge of other varieties of English became greater as travel increased with the railways and the steamships and as other inventions like the telephone were introduced. But this did not affect the general view of the appropriateness of the standard and its position at the head of the linguistic hierarchy. Novels and poetry responded to the new interests in language. Novels, such as those by Dickens, presented a wide gallery of speakers from other classes and other regions than the educated class in London. But his heroes and heroines usually speak or learn to accept the standard language as their natural medium. However attractive as characters, the speakers of other varieties continue to move on the periphery of society. In the poetry of someone like Kipling the language of the soldier may be lower class, but it creates a comforting sense that all classes are working together for the national good, even if some are not well educated. The link that existed between language and character meant that people who spoke in non-standard varieties could never be accepted as fully developed human beings with a fine sense of morality and proper behaviour. People were judged by the way they spoke. Other poets like Byron and Browning could use a language which was more colloquial and thus extend the range of what was acceptable within the approved language of poetry. Later, a poet like Hopkins would pursue the current interest in historical English further by constructing a poetic language which by relying on certain aspects of Old English poetry created a new, artifical language. Gradually the gap between ordinary language and literature would increase and it became increasingly difficult for people to claim that literature provided the guide for what was correct and appropriate in language. This stage was only reached in the next period, but signs of it already appear in this one.

One of the main tasks the Philological Society set itself was the provision of a new dictionary on historical principles. The interest in etymology and the new advances in historical linguistics made this a natural object to which to direct its energies. Proposals for

A NEW

ENGLISH DICTIONARY

ON A HISTORICAL BASIS.

A (ē¹), the first letter of the Roman Alphabet, and of its various subsequent modifications (as were its prototypes Alpha of the Greek, and Aleph of the Phœnician and old Hebrew); representing originally in English, as in Latin, the 'low-back-wide' vowel, formed with the widest opening of jaws, pharynx, and lips. The plural has been written *aes*, A's, *As*.

c 1340 HAMPOLE *Pr. Consc.* 481 And by þat cry men knaw þan Whether it be man or weman, For when it es born it cryes swa. If it be man it says a! a! That þe first letter is of þe nam Of our forme-fader Adam. *c* 1386 CHAUCER *Prol.* 161 On which was first i-write a crowned A, And after, Amor vincit omnia. 1401 *Pol. Poems* II. 57 I know not an *a* [A] from the wynd-mylne, ne a *b* [B] from a bole-foot. 1678 BUTLER *Hudib.* III. i. 1006 And loue your Loues with *A*'s and *B*'s. 1765 TUCKER *Light of Nat.* II. 89 Tully tells us, a hog has been known to make a perfect letter A with his snout upon the ground; but nobody ever saw, or thought it possible to see, the whole poem of Ennius scratched out in that manner: and I believe he might have added safely, that no man ever saw a single A written by a hog, without a multitude of other irregular scratches round about it. *a* 1842 TENNYSON *The Epic* 50 Mouthing out his hollow oes and aes, Deep-chested music.

Forms of A, and *Sounds* historically represented by it: see INTRODUCTION. The sounds now represented by A are thus symbolized in this work:—

(1) ē¹ in name, nē¹m. (4) ā in father, fā·ðəɹ.
(2) ē ,, bare, bēəɹ. (5) ǭ ,, water, wǭ·təɹ.
(3) æ ,, man, mæn. (6) ǫ ,, want, wǫnt.

The vowel in chant, past, varies with different speakers from 3 to 4, with various intermediate sounds, and is here, with intentional ambiguity, indicated by

(7) ɑ as tʃɑnt, pɑst (without determining the quantity or quality).

In unaccented syllables these vowels are modified, and obscured; thus:—

(8) ė (i) in village, marriage, vi·lėdʒ, mæ·ridʒ.
(9) ē¹ (e) ,, separate, *v.* se·pārē¹t (-ə̄t, -et).
(10) ĕ (ĕ) ,, separate, *adj.* se·pārĕt (-ə̄t).
(11) ǣ ,, antarctic, ǣntā·ɹktik.
(12) ă ,, lunar, amœba, liū·năɹ, ămī·bă.
(13) ǫ̆ ,, authority, ǫ̆þǫ·rīti.

1 and 2 are also commonly represented by the digraphs *ai, ay*, as in pain, pay, pair (pē¹n, pē¹, pēəɹ); and 5 by *au, aw*, as in *laud, law* (lǭd, lǭ). *Ai, ay* rarely represent a diphthong (ai), as in *ay*, Isaiah (ai, əizai·ă, also əi, əizē¹·ă); *au* is a diphthong (au) only in foreign words.

Except in syllabic, or strictly rhetorical utterance, 10, 11, 12 are practically = ə (*e* in water, wǭ·təɹ); and 13 = ŏ (as in collect, kŏle·kt), sinking colloquially to ə (ǫ̆þǫ·rīti, ŏþǫ·rīti, əþǫ·rīti), to which also 9 (but not 8) falls in careless speech. In rapid utterance this ə may become a mere voice glide ('), or entirely disappear, as separate *adj.* se·pārĕt, se·pərət, se·p'rət, se·prət. These phonetic variations in actual speech are reflected in variant spellings like mackarel, mackerel, mackrel; abanet, abnet; caravel, carvel; Catharine, Catherine, Cathrine; dependant, dependent; and common 'mistakes' in spelling, such as seperate.

II. The letters of the alphabet, or some of them, are also used to indicate serial order and distinguish things in a series, as the notes of the musical scale, the 'quires' or sheets of a book, classes of ships, propositions in logic, quantities in algebra, points, and hence lines and figures in geometry. As the order is in some cases fixed, *A* or *a* has some specialized uses:

1. In *Music*: The 6th note of the diatonic scale of C major, or the first note of the relative minor scale of C, corresponding to *la* in the Tonic Sol-fa notation. Also, the scale of a composition with A as its key-note; as 'a symphony in A.'

1609 DOULAND Ornithoparcus *Micrologus* 22 In the first part set *A* Base, in the third *D sol re*, in the fifth *A lamire*. 1806 CALLCOTT *Gramm. of Music* The notes of Music are named from the first seven letters of the alphabet, A, B, C, D, E, F, G. When the Melody, or Tune, exceeds these seven, the same series of letters must be repeated. 1880 GROVE *Dict. Mus.* I. 192 The beautiful and passionate Sonata in A which was inspired by and dedicated to his [Beethoven's] friend Madame Ertmann.

2. In *Nautical language*: see A 1 below.

3. In *Logic*: a universal affirmative.

1866 MANSEL (in Bowen *Logic* 201) *A* is declared by Aristotle to be the most difficult proposition to establish, and the easiest to overthrow.

4. In *Abstract reasoning, hypothetical argumentation, Law*, etc. A means *any one* thing or person, B another, C a third, etc.; as, A becomes surety to B for C; C fails in his engagements, on which B, etc.

1870 BOWEN *Logic* iii. 49 Every conceivable thing is either *A* or *not-A*. Of course *A* and *not-A*, taken together, include the universe.

5. In *Algebra*: *a, b, c*, and other *early* letters of the alphabet are used to express known quantities, as *x, y, z* are to express the unknown.

III. *Abbreviations.* A., a., *a.*, stands for

1. *anno*, in the year, as A.D. *anno domini*, in the year of our Lord; A.M. *anno mundi*, in the year of the world; A.U.C. *anno urbis conditæ*, in the year of the city (Rome) having been founded. 2. *ante*, as 'a.m.' *ante meridiem*, before noon; a. 1600 or *a* 1600, before 1600. 3. *adjective*; *active* (verb). 4. *artium*, as A.B. *artium baccalaureus*; A.M. *artium magister*; which in England are now written B.A., M.A., Bachelor, and Master, of Arts. 5. *alto*. 6. *accepted* (of bills). 7. *Associate*, as A.L.S. Associate of the Linnæan Society. 8. R.A. Royal Artillery, Royal Academy or Academician; F.S.A. Fellow of the Society of Antiquaries; F.R.A.S. Fellow of the Royal Astronomical Society, and many similar titles. 9. A.B. able-bodied seaman. 10. *a* or *aa* in Med. ANA, q.v.

IV. *Phrases*, 1. **A per se**; the letter A when standing by itself, especially when making a word.

The word *a* was formerly spelt 'a-per-se, a,' that is, '*a* by itself makes the word *a*,' whence also the letter itself was sometimes called *A-per-se-A*. So also *I per se, O per se, &-per-se* (*and-per-se, an-per-se, amperse*).

Hence b. *fig.* (also formerly **Apersie, Apersey, A per C**) the first, chief, most excellent, most distinguished, or unique person or thing; one who is *facile princeps*, or in modern phrase, *A* 1.

1475 HENRYSON *Test. of Cresseide* 78 (Speght's Chaucer) The floure and A per se of Troie and Grece. *a* 1500 *MS. Cantab.* Ff. ii. 38 f. 51 Thow schalt be an apersey, my sone, In mylys ij, or thre. 1501 DUNBAR *Poems, Suppl.* (1865) 277 London, thowe arte of townes A per se. 1567 DRANT *Horace Epist.* II. i If they make them A per se Aes that none are like to them. 1578 *Gude and Godlie Ballates* 128 Christ Jesus is ane A per C, And peirlesse Prince of all mercy. 1602 MIDDLETON *Blurt* III. iii Who, that is the a-per-se of all, the very cream of all.

2. **A 1.** Applied in Lloyd's Register to ships in first-class condition, as to hull and stores alike. 'The character A denotes New ships, or Ships Renewed or Restored. The Stores of Vessels are designated by the figures 1 and 2; 1 signifying that the Vessel is well and sufficiently found.'—*Key to the Register*. Added to the names of ships, as 'the fast-sailing ship "Sea-breeze," A 1 at Lloyd's,' or used attributively, 'the splendid A 1 clipper-built ship "Miranda."'

Hence, *fig.* (familiar and savouring of commercial phraseology), *A* 1, or in U.S. *A No.* 1, is used adjectively for 'prime, first-class.'

1837 DICKENS *Pickwick* 341 (1847) 'He must be a first-rater,' said Sam. 'A 1,' replied Mr. Roker. 1851 MRS. STOWE *Dred* I. 313 An A number one cook, and no mistake. 1861 COL. G. WOLSELEY (*Reynolds' Newsp.* Nov. 24) The Chinese police are certainly A 1 at such work.

†**A**, *adj.*¹ definite numeral. *Obs.* or *dial.* Apocopate form of *an, ane*, used only before a consonant. [OE. *ān*, one, of which the *n* began to disappear before a cons. about 1150. In the definite numeral sense, *ān* and *ā*, following the ordinary course of OE. long *ā*, became in the south bef. 1300, *on* (*oon, one*), *o* (*oo*); and eventually *o* became obs., leaving *one* as the form in all positions; while *an* and *a*, pronounced lightly and indistinctly, became the 'indefinite article.' See next word. But in the north *an* (or *ane*) and *a* were written in both senses, the stress or emphasis alone distinguishing the numeral from the article.] See AN(E, O *a.*, and ONE.

c 1200 *Trin. Coll. Hom.* 39 Ure drihten drof fele deules togedere ut of á man, þe was of his wit. *c* 1300 *K. Alis.* 5955 An eighe he had in his vys, And a foot, and no moo Iwys. *c* 1350 HAMPOLE *Prose Tr.* 32 Some ere of a tre and some er of anoþer. 1483 CAXTON, *Geoffroi de la Tour*, lf. iiii b, They satte att dyner in a hall and the quene in another.

A in the various forms *a, ae, eae, eea, yea, yā*, is still the regular form of the numeral *one* when used adjectively, in the northern dialects, the absolute form being *an, ane, ean, yen, yān*, etc.

A (toneless ă, ə; emph. ē¹), *adj.*², called 'indefinite article.' Before a vowel-sound **an** (ăn, emph. æn). [A weakening of OE. *ān*, 'one,' already by 1150 reduced before a cons. to *a*. About the same time the numeral began to be used in a weakened sense (usually unexpressed in OE. as *he wæs gōd man*, 'he was a good man'; cf. Chron. 1137 'he wæs god munec & god man,' and 1140 'he wæs an yuel man'); becoming in this sense proclitic and toneless, *ăn, ă*, while as a numeral it remained long, *ān, ā*, and passed regularly during the next cent. into *ōn, ō*; see the prec. word. Though *an* began to sink to *a* in midl. dial. by 1150, it often remained bef. a cons. to 1300; bef. sounded *h*, *an* was retained after 1600, and somet. after 1700, as *an house, an heifer, an hermitage*. The present rule is to use *an* bef. a vowel-sound (incl. *h* mute, as *an hour*); *a* bef. a consonant-sound (including *h* sounded, and *eu-, u-* with sound of *yū-*, as *a host, a one, a eunuch, a unit*). But in *unaccented* syllables, many, perhaps most, writers still retain *an* bef. sounded *h*, some even bef. *eu, u*, as *an historian, an euphonic vowel, an united appeal*, though this is all but obsolete in speech, and in writing *a* becomes increasingly common in this position. *A, an* has been indeclinable in midl. and north. dial. since 1150, but vestiges of the OE. declension (as nom. f. *ane*, gen. m. *anes*, gen. & dat. f. *are*, acc. m. *anne*) remained much later in southern. In north. *an* was frequently written *ane* (with *e* mute), the use of *a* and *an* (*e* being as elsewhere; but about 1475 Scottish writers began to use *ane* in all positions, a practice which prevailed till the disuse of literary Scotch after 1600. Quotations illustrating the history of the forms:—

c 1131 *O. E. Chron.* (Laud. MS.) anno 1125 Se man ðe hafde an pund he ne mihte cysten ænne peni at anne market. *c* 1150

VOL. I.

1

FIGURE 10.1 J. A. H. Murray, *A New English Dictionary on Historical Principles*, 1888. Page beginning with A. 12987gl (*British Library*).

this were published in 1858 and the Society established a committee consisting of Furnivall, Trench and Herbert Coleridge to carry the proposal forward. In the end it was Oxford University Press which came to sponsor the dictionary under the editorship of J. A. H. Murray. Many readers throughout the country were enlisted to read for the dictionary – an indication of both how much interest in etymology and dictionaries existed and the dominance of the written word in their make-up. The first fascicle of the new dictionary appeared in 1888 and the last only in 1928. In the first fascicle Murray explained the general principles behind the dictionary. It contained all words since about 1250 within the following limits:

> [I]t is the aim of the Dictionary to deal with all the common words of speech and literature, and with words which approach these in character; the limits being extended farther in the domain of science and philosophy, which naturally passes into that of literature, than in that of slang or cant, which touches the colloquial.[10]

Words which were colloquial would not be included. This included slang, dialect words and words considered obscene and not in polite use. This meant that a word which occurred once or twice in a fifteenth-century text and which had probably never entered the spoken language was included, but a word which was used daily on the streets of London in 1888 might not be. Even less polite senses of words in accepted literature like the plays of Shakespeare were overlooked. The distinction between the standard language and non-standard varieties was thus firmly entrenched in what became a work of massive authority. Indeed, the publication of *The English Dialect Dictionary* edited by Joseph Wright at the end of the century merely confirmed that the two areas of language were quite separate. Later, dictionaries of slang and cant would appear and help to confirm the gulf that existed between the standard and colloquial speech. For despite what Murray says about 'speech' in his preface, the readers worked from written texts and predominantly from literary ones, partly because these were more generally available. The dictionary was historical in its principles, but the words it dealt with were restricted in register.

After the headword, the dictionary gives its pronunciation. Murray did not state what pronunciation he represented, but he did indicate that 'A recognized difference of pronunciation is also shown', which suggests that he was recording recognised pronunciations of a word. How these were collected is not stated. Some words have no pronunciation, such as *often*. Murray did not try to force spelling pronunciations on his readers. He recognises that *Wednesday* is bisyllabic, and for *medicine* he gives the bisyllabic pronunciation first and records the trisyllabic pronunciation as a recognised alternative only. For *waistcoat* he gives the pronunciation which reflects that of the two elements separately, though he recognises that the medial [t] is optional. He goes on to characterise the older pronunciation [weskət] as '*colloq[uial]* or *vulgar*'. Clearly guidance as to the acceptable pronunciation was being provided as this reflects for the most part what became known as Received Pronunciation. There followed the 'grammatical designation' or part of speech to which the word belonged. This was followed by the technical area to which the word belonged and its status. Words could be described as obsolete, archaic, colloquial or dialectal, though words in such categories as dialectal were only included if they had been part of the accepted language earlier (what Murray calls 'formerly in general use') and were now dialectal. The morphology and the meanings of the words were then given and these were based upon the many quotations which the readers had collected. These parts were the great achievement of the dictionary, for many of the comments on individual words amounted to small essays on their history and use. In this part Murray freely acknowledged the assistance he had gained from the work of previous lexicographers. The exact reference of each quotation was provided and, as Murray justifiably claimed, this was 'a special feature of this work'.

The effect of the dictionary was to create a storehouse of information about acceptable usage. Words not in the dictionary could only be regarded as not part of polite English, and the history and usage of the words provided guidance as to how they were properly used. The dictionary remains a testimony to nineteenth-century industry, but it also helped to confirm the pride people felt in the English language. But that sense of satisfaction in English was already being put to the test by the time the final fascicle of the dictionary appeared. The failure to tackle the language of its own time comprehensively led to the issue of supplements.

It will be apparent that at this time spelling was more or less regularised. Indeed, Cobbett in his grammar dismisses it as of no great importance and so does not dwell on it (§ 6). Later writers also accept that spelling was now largely standardised and merely comment on certain words and the uncertainty they cause. Indeed, much comment on language is now mostly a matter of discussion of individual points rather than of general principles. Thus Henry Alford in *The Queen's English* (1864) complains that there is doubt as to how the words *ecstasy* and *apostasy* are spelt. Other forms to attract his attention include *to* and *too*, faulty doubling of consonants in words like *benefited*, and *lose* and *loose*. It is interesting that he should be among the first to note 'It is in newspapers, and especially in provincial newspapers, that most frequent faults in spelling are found' (p. 35). As for punctuation, Alford was told as a young man by a publisher that punctuation was always left to the compositor and so he had little to write on it, though he felt there were still illogicalities left in custom. Both Alford and, somewhat later, Trench refer to the proposals which were becoming common to reform spelling to make it conform to pronunciation. Both reject these calls, which may be taken as a sign that the standardisation of spelling was now so well established that people were no longer concerned with minor adjustments, but with wholesale change. In morphology Cobbett recognised the modern position with the possessive form of nouns, and although he regarded the use of the apostrophe unnecessary in some cases, he recommended its use. Almost all writers on language have something to say about the apostrophe, usually to complain that it was not used properly and to issue some guidelines for it. Alford complained that it was used incorrectly with plurals even when they were not in the possessive. The use of the second singular verb form was now rarely found and most writers regarded it as archaic or provincial. Otherwise the morphology was much the same in the last century as it is in this.

Pronunciation continues to attract attention, though the books written on it may be divided into two types. The first contains arbitrary comments on individual points of pronunciation, whereas the latter are descriptive accounts of pronunciation at the time. Among the latter are B. H. Smart at the beginning, Alexander Ellis in the middle, and Henry Sweet at the end of the century. Sweet is particularly associated with putting phonetics on a professional basis, though all three writers were both well informed and conscious of the need to develop an overall system. All recognise that it is the pronunciation of educated people in London which should form the norm, and they use this pronounciation as the basis for their descriptions. They were not affected by spelling to introduce spelling pronunciations, though in certain cases, like unstressed *e*, they were careful to distinguish when it was pronounced and when not. Certainly in the nineteenth century certain words were influenced by spelling in their pronunciation. Thus *fertile* adopted /ai/ in the second syllable, where /ə/ had been regular before then. This example is characteristic of some changes which were now occurring; they are often random and are caused by social pressures, of which clear enunciation was one, for the middle classes wanted to show their status was different from that of other classes. In many cases there may well have been alternative pronunciations and one of these gradually became accepted as the standard one and was enforced through schooling and social propriety. It is likely that the shortening of /ɔ:/ to /o/ before consonant groups like *st*, *ss* and the single consonant *th* occurred through a selection of the short sound in preference to the long one on social grounds. Thus we find the modern pronunciation of words like *cross* and *cloth*. The modern pronunciation of *often* with /o/ rather than with /ɔ:/ dates from this time. With consonants we may notice the same tendency to restore sounds which had previously been lost and this still continues today, especially in place-names. Words like *swollen* and *quote*, and place-names like *Ipswich*, had their pronunciations changed by the inclusion of /w/. Equally /d/ which had become silent at the end of many words was often heard again in pronunciation, as in a word like *husband*.

One sound that became almost a standard item for comment by any writer on the language was initial *h* and the problem of when it was sounded. Correct pronunciation of this feature was regarded as the surest test of class by most commentators. But their advice was not always consistent. Alford is typical when he writes 'let me notice that worst of all faults, the leaving out of the aspirate where it ought to be, and putting it in where it ought not to be' (p. 37). Its wrong pronunciation is characteristic of 'persons of low breeding and inferior education'. Other pronunciations which aroused attention were the affected pronunciation of the final sound in words like *idea*, which some writers describe as adding an *r*, and the use of /u:/ in words like *duty* and *Tuesday*. Writers like Alford make comments on individual words and do not attempt to outline a system of pronunciation. He still recognises many pronunciations which are different from the spelling and criticises those who would ignorantly try to introduce spelling pronunciations.

Examples he gives include *vineyard, cupboard, halfpenny, victual* and *medicine*, in which the last word has only two syllables.

Both descriptive and prescriptive writers comment on the placing of stress in words, but neither can achieve an overall system. They are forced to provide a list of examples. Many words which still cause uncertainty, like *controversy*, figure in these lists. In the lists there is often a noticeable number of words which are said to have stress on the first syllable, where now we prefer to put the stress later in the word. This applies not only to *controversy*, but also to *formidable, lamentable, chastisement, fanatic, despicable* and *compulsory*. The application of Germanic fronting in the placing of stress was counteracted by other tendencies in the language arising either from knowledge of the classical languages or from the preference for stress on the antepenultimate syllable which was characteristic of words ending in *ible/able* or *ory/ary*.

In syntax the standard had more or less reached the position that still prevails today. For example, the word order of sentences was now almost inflexible apart from poetic usage, and the use of prepositions and auxiliaries was approaching the modern position. This did not prevent writers from complaining about individual points of syntax, sometimes from a historical position. For example, Alford tries to instil the proper use of the subjunctive, which he recognises in the verb 'to be' in forms like *I be* and *I were*. For the rule he states that a matter of fact takes the indicative and when doubt is expressed we use the subjunctive, even though this rule was not known to previous writers of English, especially in the Bible. He despairs of usage, for he writes: 'We have a well known logical rule, prevailing in our own and in other languages, and laid down by grammarians as to be followed. But it would seem that it never has been followed universally' (p. 197). He does accept that the subjunctive was now usually formed with an auxiliary which had replaced the former simple subjunctive. This passage is instructive because syntax was now becoming a matter of class usage and that usage was often dictated in some people's opinions by historical considerations. Unfortunately history was not always a helpful guide, and grammarians resorted to logic and Latin. For others, usage was dictated by what the educated classes did, for syntax was used like pronunciation to distinguish the educated from the ignorant. Written English was accepted as different from colloquial English, and although grammarians may have influenced the former, the latter was dictated by usage associated with class. Some accepted that bad usage could gradually percolate through into good written usage. Alford noted that there was 'a use of the word *"but"*, principally to be found in our provincial newspapers, but now and then "leaking upwards" into our more permanent literature' (p. 85).

Certain features of syntax that appear to be characteristic of upper-class usage have been isolated by Ken Phillipps in his *Language & Class in Victorian England* (1984). Among the features he mentions are the following. Transitive verbs used intransitively: 'Playing at being a hero and not doing it does not *answer'*. Expressions like *did not* (or *didn't*) *use to* instead of *used not to*: 'You *did not use to* like cards'. *I didn't ought to* was used instead of *I ought not*. The verb 'to be' was often omitted after auxiliaries, where the meaning can be referred back to the previous verb. The perfect infinitive after a verb was common, though deplored by the grammarians: 'I did mean *to have returned* to Milton'. However, the preterite was often used where we might prefer the perfect as in 'I never *was* at a Royal Academy Exhibition'. Among upper-class speakers the subjunctive was often found in its simple form, thus *had* and *were* occur where we today might use *would have* and *would be*: 'The distaff *were* more fitting for you'. The indefinite use of *one* was common and has remained a feature of this type of speech: 'A few startlingly good characters surprise *one'*.[11]

The last example is interesting because the use of *one* as a propword grew in the nineteenth century. As we have seen earlier, this is when *one* replaces a noun and it was a development that had been started earlier in English than this period. In many cases it is used to avoid repetition, but also to provide a head for the nominal group. In a sentence like 'My wife likes pink roses, but I prefer red ones', *ones* is used to avoid repetition of *roses* and to prevent *red* from becoming isolated syntactically. The usage came to incorporate forms like *this/that one* and plurals *these/those ones*. From there it was not long before *one* could be post-modified by a relative clause: 'the *ones that I miss* are simple forms of the subjunctive'. Other uses of indefinite pronouns indicate that the nineteenth century still saw indefinite pronouns as largely singular and were thus followed by pronouns in the singular. This could be *his* or *its*, for the feminine *her* was less common. It would be usual to have a sentence like 'Everybody must take *his* place' without causing any ambiguity as to the referent of *his*. Usage with the plural was found in the nineteenth century, though it was less common. Among the personal pronouns the question of whether one should use the subject or oblique form after certain prepositions and conjunctions was a constant source of comment by grammarians. Here, usage usually failed to live up to the grammarians' injunctions.

In adverbs the tendency to insist on the *-ly* ending continues, especially when adverbs are used as intensifiers of adjectives or other adverbs. Equally the comparison of adjectives is now more regulated with the endings *-er/-est* restricted increasingly to monosyllables or certain bisyllables.

In the verb the contest between *have* and *be* to form the perfect of verbs was won by the former during the nineteenth century. Statistical analysis of the forms suggests that in the early nineteenth century verbs which had previously taken *be* were reduced by a half and by the end of the century by more than three-quarters.[12] The occurrence of a perfect form using *have* and *be* as auxiliaries with verbs of motion became obsolete except with 'go' from the second half of the century. Examples like 'He *has been advanced* for some time' cease to occur, though this construction can later occur with an adverbial as 'He has been out for hours'. With some features it may be difficult to decide precisely in which direction a development is going. This is perhaps particularly true of auxiliaries. Whether there was and is any regularity in the use of *will* and *shall* and their preterites *would/should* is difficult to decide. In speech this is not so much of a problem since abbreviated forms occur. But in writing it is possible that *will* expanded at the expense of *shall*, though usage is rather haphazard as it is between *would* and *should*. The same applies to *may* and *might* for the roles of these two have tended to overlap so that the latter is no longer the past form of the former. This may be part of a general loss of tense distinction among the modals. Modals like *need* and *dare* are increasingly used in their present tense forms with a past meaning. As for *may*, the distinction between it and *can* was gradually lost, as the complaints of the grammarians reveal.

The development of the passive form of the progressive was anticipated in previous periods by the use of the progressive in some verbs with a passive meaning, as in *the house was building*. Eighteenth-century grammarians were critical of this construction, but it was accepted by nineteenth-century ones. The development of forms like *is being* with the present participle *being* was inhibited by the view of some grammarians that the verb 'to be' could not have a progressive form. So there was antagonism against a progressive passive form altogether. Despite this opposition the progressive passive gradually grew in the nineteenth century, for its adoption made the English verb system symmetrical. It also helped to avoid the ambiguity of *the house was building* as compared with clauses like *the man was working*. The progressive passive involves a verb group of three elements as in *the house is being built*, and its adoption may also have been assisted by the growth in the number of auxiliaries in a single verb group found during the nineteenth century. Before that time one or at most two auxiliaries were the rule, but in this period three or more became more common. In fact, a greater load was placed on the verb group through the auxiliaries so that finer nuances of meaning might be achieved, though often one feels their use has as much to do with style as with meaning.

A characteristic feature of English in this period is the development of the form *have got* which replaced *have* in some of its uses. Expressions like *He has to do it* gave way to *He has got to do it*. *Has* had taken over some of the meanings of *must* and this sense was then strengthened by the addition of *got*. It seems to have become accepted from the end of the nineteenth century, though it may have arisen in speech and then become tolerated in writing. It soon became regular and has ousted simple *has* in this function. Another development with *get* was its use as a passive marker, a development which seems to have been well established by the beginning of this period. Once again it may have been more common in speech and gradually accepted in writing. Sentences like *The boys got caught stealing apples* are found from the early nineteenth century onwards.

With negatives we can still find examples of the older forms of negation at the beginning of the period, but one could say that during the nineteenth century double negatives and other older forms of negation were finally outlawed from the standard. Grammarians had for a long time complained about double negation and contractions of the negator after auxiliaries. As the author of *The Vulgarities of Speech Corrected* (1826) wrote, 'Some of these are much less vulgar than others, but not one of them could be admitted into correct and elegant conversation.'[13] In fact the upper classes used forms like *ain't* and *don't* regularly and saw no reason to give them up. The latter seems to have been acceptable until the end of the nineteenth century in such circles, for it is found in *Tom Brown's Schooldays* and the novels of Trollope. Education and the disapproval of grammarians seem to have finally ousted these forms by the turn of the century.

This period is witness to the increasing gap between writing and speech. In the eighteenth century polite conversation and writing were supposed to go hand in hand; the one set the standard for the other. In the nineteenth century it was recognised that it was difficult to control speech, particularly as more varieties came to be heard and tolerated. The efforts of grammarians and teachers were focused on writing. At a lower social level children who went to Board Schools would have learned one form of English which was quite different from the one they used at home. Even higher in the social scale, it was important to write correctly. Naturally in polite society the way one spoke would also be crucial to how others regarded you, but there was greater tolerance for different usages in speech. Thus the use of *ain't* or of slang words was more readily accepted in upper-class speech than it was in writing. Naturally, the popularity of the novel, which tried to represent speech in dialogue more realistically, reveals that the spoken language had wider limits of tolerance than the written one.

In vocabulary more attention was focused on differences in register because such differences were an important marker of social class. We have already seen that the *New English Dictionary* did not seek to include all words which were related to trades and professions, and this exclusion reflects a general view that the subjects of individual trades and professions were not suitable for social conversation. It is a feature of the nineteenth century that language was regarded as a certain way of placing anyone socially and this for the most part was done through vocabulary and pronunciation. The result is also that many words change their status and connotations in this period. Among the most difficult words to use properly were *gentleman, lady, man* and *woman*. The first two were becoming words used by the lower classes and when they were used to people in higher social positions they could create the sense of flattery or unctiousness. The upper classes tended to use *man* or *woman*, though one could if necessary use *person*. Equally the word *genteel* had gone down in the world, and as the *New English Dictionary* stated of its use 'A few years before the middle of the 19th c[entury] the word was much ridiculed as being characteristic of those who are possessed with a dread of being taken for "common people", or who attach exaggerated importance to supposed marks of social superiority'. This illustrates one of the problems as society became more mobile and as those who had made money as manufacturers or through trade tried to claim a position in high society: as they appropriated words to describe themselves and their aspirations, these words became unusable by others because they were tainted with those associations. The connotations of words could change rapidly.

English absorbed a huge number of foreign words during this period, partly because of the advance of science and teachnology, partly because of the development of new political ideals, and partly because of the colonisation of large parts of the globe. It was French which provided the most loans, and this period saw the greatest number of French loanwords entering the language since the Middle Ages. The French Revolution followed by the Napoleonic Wars and the universal European acceptance of French as a sophisticated language meant that many concepts and words for fashion and eating entered the language. From now on French words often retain their spelling and only a slightly anglicised form of their pronunciation. The Napoleonic Wars led to words like *guillotine, tricolour* and *epaullete*. Food and fashion introduced words like *café, menu, trousseau, lingerie* and *chiffon*. The Romantic movement and its love of the wild countryside produced *avalanche* and *crampon*, and literature and art provided *fin de siècle, rococo, cor anglais* and *cliché*. Italian remained important for art and music, though the number of Italian words was not large. Words like *prima donna, intermezzo* and *pizzicato* come from Italian in this period. German loans have never been extensive in English, though this century sees a greater interest in German music and philosophy. Among words from German we find *leitmotiv, kapellmeister, kindergarten, zeitgeist* and *rucksack*. Latin and Greek continue to supply words for the language, though they are increasingly technical, scientific and medical.

The New World increases its contributions to English, though naturally we need to distinguish between British and American English in this respect. Many words referring to life in America came into British English through Spanish, such as *lasso, stampede* and *pueblo;* others are adapted from native American words such as *mescal, quinine* and *coyote*. Other words come into British English through American such as *chipmunk* and *apache*. Words from the Pacific area become significant in this period, though most belong to specialised lexical fields such as plants and animals. They include *sarong, kiwi, wombat, koala* and *boomerang*. African languages also start to provide more words, though the number is limited. They include *tsetse*, *impi* and *indaba*. More words come from Afrikaans, the South African variety of Dutch, including *meerkat*, *aardvark*, *trek*, *laager* and *commandeer*. The Boer War was responsible for several words. The main colonial country to provide words for English was India because of the close association of India with Britain. Many different types of word were introduced, including those for food like *chutney*, for animals like *gazelle*, for dyes like *purree*, for clothes like *pyjamas*, and for other areas like *loot*, *polo* and *dinghy*.

The recognition that there were differences in register in the English vocabulary and the greater exposure given to non-standard registers meant that there was more openness to accepting words from slang into conversation, if not into writing. As mentioned earlier, the development of greater naturalism in literature meant that novelists came to represent speech with more colloquial features than had been accepted previously. If upper-class speakers were not to seem terribly stilted if they spoke only standard English while lower-class characters used their own local or class varieties, some colloquial colour had to be inserted into their language. Slang allowed speech to be more realistic and also more lively. It also needs to be remembered that the inclusion of lower-class words and expressions in novels made them familiar to a wide range of educated speakers and thus could encourage their use higher up the social scale. One may imagine that younger people, then as now, were not slow to appropriate some of these expressions so that what was at one stage vulgar gradually came to be tolerated. The upper classes had its slang at public schools and universities; the military had its own variety. The growth in publications like *Punch*, which took a more relaxed view of the world than other journals, and the need for newspapers to appeal to an ever wider audience also had an impact on the spread of registers among different classes. Words to describe those of whom one disapproved were a rich source of slang. Thackeray used *cocktail* to describe men who showed a lack of good breeding and *snob* those who pretended to tastes and social attitudes which were not truly theirs. Thackeray was to write *The Book of Snobs* in 1848, and thus the word passed into more general usage, though *cocktail* did not. The word *fellow* clearly had a restricted usage, for many thought of it as a word to be used by men only and deplored its use by women. It seems to have been a word appropriated in particular by young men, and if older men used it they might be thought of as patronising their juniors. There appears to have been a feeling, at least at the start of this period, that it was not appropriate for women to use slang all. To judge by attitudes in some nineteenth-century novels, women who belonged to the higher social classes were not expected to use slang, though as always those in the highest class could easily ignore such petty social restrictions.

The language used in this period is illustrated by a passage from Henry Alford's *The Queen's English*, which dates from roughly midway and which illustrates the manner in which grammarians wrote about the language. We should remember that Alford was a clergyman, being Dean at Canterbury, and like so many writers of the time was a self-appointed guardian of the language.

> I am now going to speak of a combination of words which is so completely naturalised, that it would be vain to protest against it, or even to attempt to disuse it one's self. I mean, the joining together of a present and a past participle, as we do when we say *'The letter was being written,' 'The dinner is being cooked.'* Such combinations were, I believe, not used by our best and most careful writers, until a comparatively recent date. The old and correct way of expressing what is meant by these phrases, was, *'The letter was in writing,'* or *'was writing;' 'The dinner was cooking;'* the verbs being used in a neuter sense. The objection to *'being written'* for *'in the process of writing,'* is this, – that *'written'* is a past participle, indicating a finished act. When I say *'I have written a letter,'* I mean, I have by me, or have as my act accomplished, a letter written. So that *'being written'* properly means, existing in a state of completion. *'My letter being written, I put it in the post.'* And, strictly speaking, we cannot use the combination to signify an *incomplete* action. Still, as I have said, the inaccuracy has crept into the language, and is now found everywhere, in speech and in writing. The only thing we can do in such a case is to avoid it, where it can be avoided without violation of idiom, or giving harshness to the sentence.   (pp. 153-4)

There is very little in this passage which from a grammatical point of view could not be found today. The spelling is regular, though the verbal ending in *ise* often gives way to *ize* today. Also, we might prefer today to use *oneself* rather than *one's self*. The punctuation does not always conform to what we might do today. To separate the subject 'The objection . . . *writing*' from its verb *is* by a comma, which also occurs in the previous sentence, is still found today, but this use is discouraged. Equally the use of a comma followed by a dash would now be considered excessive. The verb form *is naturalised* would have the passive form *has been naturalised*. Equally we might use *in vain* rather than *vain* in the expression *it would be vain*, because *vain* by itself would now suggest vanity. The verb *disuse* is now obsolete, for we often replace verbs of foreign origin of this type with phrasal verbs like *give up*. The rest of the vocabulary is rather formal and books on language would now try to achieve what we would think of as a more user-friendly style. Expressions like 'violation of idiom' sound strange and the precise meaning of this one is uncertain. We would not talk today of a verb being in a 'neuter sense', for this expression too would create problems of comprehension to a modern reader. In the structure of his sentences, we find structures that occur today, but are surprising in a mid-Victorian piece of writing by a stickler for correct English. He begins one sentence with 'So that' which is normally a conjunction introducing a subordinate clause, but is here treated as a main clause as if 'So that' is adverbial. He starts another sentence with 'And', which is a usage criticised by many grammarians because *and* was understood to be only a co-ordinating conjunction which could consequently not open a sentence since that meant it was not being properly used in a co-ordinating function. It is particularly in matters of style and usage that the next period differs from this one, and it is that to which we must now turn our attention.

11

World Domination and Growing Variation

The period that forms the content of this chapter starts in 1914 and continues to the present day. 1914 is a symbolic date in that it witnessed the outbreak of the First World War, for the twentieth century is the first to have experienced world wars and the development of mass methods of destruction. Both world wars saw conscription into the armed forces which meant that many who had had little experience of the world outside their home environment were suddenly forced into proximity with people from other parts of Britain as well as from other parts of the world in situations that forced them to work together. They were exposed to different language varieties from Britain and the rest of the Commonwealth and to varying social habits and lifestyles. Experience of this kind inevitably affected their attitude to their environment and to their language. It encouraged the demand for changes to society and the loosening of the stranglehold of the standard which was often seen as both élitist and inhibiting. Exposure to other accents and types of language broadened the linguistic horizon of those involved in the war effort and led them to believe that the way they spoke had as much right to be heard as more approved varieties. The end of the Second World War left two superpowers, the United States of America and the Soviet Union, to contest supremacy over the rest of the world. The western world was dominated by America and hence English became the dominant language of the western alliance as it faced the eastern bloc countries in the Cold War, which lasted from the end of the Second World War until 1990. The western powers were helped by Marshall Aid to rebuild their economies and joined together in the North Atlantic Treaty Organisation (NATO) to form a joint military force to defend their interests against the eastern powers united militarily under the Warsaw Pact. America dominated NATO and provided many men for the defence of western Europe who were housed in military garrisons throughout the region in case the Eastern bloc broke through the so-called Iron Curtain which divided the two sides. With the ending of the Cold War and the collapse of communism in the east, many of the former members of the Warsaw Pact tried to liberalise their economies by introducing capitalism in place of state planning. Inevitably they looked to America and to western Europe for a lead and economic assistance. One result of this development was that where Russian had been an obligatory school language in countries like Poland, it was replaced by English as soon as Russia withdrew its armies and political control. English extended its influence even further throughout the world.

The twentieth century has seen an increase in rural–urban migration. The countryside has either been depopulated, or – in much of the developed world – has been transforemd into satellite towns, feeding commuters into nearby cities. This transformation has put the older rural dialects under increasing strain. Towns and cities have grown larger, and in the second half of the century industrialisation in developing countries and in those on the Pacific rim has led to the run-down of many traditional industries in the United Kingdom. It is no longer economic to mass-produce certain goods in Britain, since they can be imported more cheaply from abroad. In the 1960s and 1970s many textile mills closed, in the 1980s and 1990s it was the turn of steel, ship-building and coal-mining. Whole communities which were built around a single industry such as a coal mine have been fragmented through the closure of the factory or mine on which the community's economic well-being depended. This has forced many to leave their native areas to look for work elsewhere at the same time as it has fractured the language and society of the area. However, expectations about living standards have continued to rise and many people did indeed become far more affluent than their parents could ever have aspired to. This in turn led to their ability to take foreign holidays, where again they would meet people from different regions in England as well as from different countries. The traditional holiday for industrial workers whereby the factory closed for a week or a fortnight and everyone went to the same British seaside resort has largely disappeared. This has increased social mobility and the exposure to outside influences for all classes. Traditional industries have given way to service industries such as tourism, and this has in its turn encouraged many to use a language that is more appropriate for a wider range of clients than that which they had used to the work-mates they knew in their own industry. This change in working patterns has led to a growth in the number of women and a reduction in the number of men in employment.

These social changes have been prompted by the revolution in travel and communications. Since the Second World War air travel has become cheaper: it is now almost as cheap to fly from Edinburgh to Spain as it is to take the train from Edinburgh to London. The telephone is now found in most houses and, even if it is not, people freely use the many public telephones found on the streets and in businesses. The development of the computer has enabled people to correspond through email immediately across the world. The world has shrunk to what is sometimes referred to as the 'global village'. In order to facilitate this revolution in com-munications it has been necessary to use a language in which communication could take place. This language is English. Much international business is now carried on through the medium of English. A Japanese businessman visiting Spain is likely to com-municate with his hosts in English. All air traffic control is carried on in English. Much of the information available through the international computer networks is transmitted in English. The United States is the dominant player in the development of science and technology, though its position appeared to be threatened by the Soviet Union during the Cold War and is challenged in some areas by countries like Japan and Germany. But the domination of the United States means that the publication of most scientific material is now done through English. Where before the First World War in countries like Sweden scientists might publish their scientific papers in German and diplomats carry on their activities in French, both would now almost always use English. Most countries now teach English as the first foreign language their schoolchildren learn. In many countries the teaching of other languages like German or French has suffered as a result.

English, it could be said, is the language of international education. In part this is due to the use of English for educational purposes in what were the countries in the British Empire. When these countries received their independence, as most did in the period after the end of the Second World War, they needed to retain a language for education which would be common to all their inhabitants because they often had speakers of many different languages within their boundaries. In India, for example, there are many languages spoken and this itself promotes racial tensions as speakers of languages other than Hindi do not want their culture to be submerged by the dominant indigenous language. It defuses tensions and promotes efficiency, flexibility and ability to trade in the world market, if their citizens are fluent in English. So English often maintained its place in education and was accepted as a second official language. For scientists and others, knowledge of English opens the path to education outside their own country, for it has been a striking feature of the post-war period how many students from other countries have gone to the United States or England for further and higher education. Even a country as rich and economically powerful as Japan has sent many of its future professors to study abroad. Inevitably this has meant that local varieties of English have grown up around the world which may differ in pronunciation, vocabulary and syntax from either British or American English. The vast number of people who either speak or try to learn English has created an enormous market for English-language publications, which has in its turn reinforced the dominant position acquired by the English language. There is a mass market for books on teaching English as a foreign language and for dictionaries of English. One might consider, for example, the case of a scholar working in Japan who has to decide whether to publish in English or Japanese. To choose the latter means that the work will be read only within Japan or by a few other scholars who know Japanese, which at best is not likely to amount to a hundred million; to choose the former means that the potential readership could run into hundreds of millions. Naturally work published in English will be better known and thus the reputation of the author that much more widespread.

The development of communication has also involved the growth of radio, television and film. The dominant film industry is that found in Hollywood and its films are seen throughout the world. Although many other countries produce films, their films, even if they are produced in considerable numbers, are usually not as widely distributed as American ones, because distribution networks are dominated by American companies. The radio acquired an important position during the war when broadcasts from the BBC were listened to throughout occupied Europe and beyond. The BBC acquired a reputation for truthful and honest reporting. That reputation was enhanced during the Cold War when many citizens in East European countries felt that they could only find out what was really happening in the world by tuning in to the BBC. Although the BBC broadcasts in many languages, its World Service primarily transmits in English and these transmissions made English well known and respected by those who tuned in. The impact of television has been less marked so far, for although many programmes were seen in other countries, they were in the past usually dubbed. With the onset of satellite and cable television, individuals can now see programmes direct from the country of origin, and this may well mean that more people will watch programmes transmitted directly from England or America.

A significant development in social attitudes, particularly after the Second World War, has been the growth of tolerance and libertarianism. This was accentuated by the student riots of 1968 in which it seemed as though the old order was crumbling. Greater freedom was given to young people, who were both more affluent than and whose culture became increasingly separated from that of adults. The language of the young, which has always been different from that of their parents, was given greater status and recognition. It differed from that of their parents much more than in the past because it was fed by attempts to incorporate linguistic features of other social groups, such as the immigrant communities, the disadvantaged and those involved in the drug culture. Although parents have always complained that they could not understand their children, parents in the post-war world had more reason to do so because of the divergent vocabulary and syntax often deliberately cultivated by adolescents. Many of these young people were more affluent than their predecessors, and were recognised by advertisers and marketing people as a group with plenty of spending money and a separate identity. This development coincided with an enormous increase in the immigrant population in the United Kingdom. Many immigrants arrived in the post-war period to tackle jobs that white Britons no longer wanted to do in an age of full employment. Others came as a result of political events and racial discrimination in former British colonies, such as Uganda. While employment remained relatively easy to come by, racial harmony could prevail; but in the 1980s the increase in unemployment created racial tensions which tended to polarise communities. Naturally the question arose as to whether such immigrants should maintain their own culture or whether they should be integrated into the dominant culture in Britain. In turn, the way the immigrants spoke English and the vocabulary which they introduced spread to other people here, particularly those who wanted to identify with them and help them against discrimination.

This overall attitude interacted with developments in the study of language itself, developments which are today associated with the growth of what is accepted now as the separate discipline of linguistics. The philosophy of language study underwent profound change which the new name emphasises: philology gave way to linguistics. Historical study became less significant as linguists turned their attention to contemporary language. The impetus for this change came from the posthumous publication, under the title *Cours de linguistique général*, of lectures given by Ferdinand de Saussure in Geneva before his death in 1913. His former pupils collected their lecture notes to issue this book in 1916 and it became the seminal work in promoting the study of linguistics and in establishing the intellectual approach which goes under the name of 'structuralism'. Saussure saw language as consisting of two elements: *langue*, which is the underlying structure of a language, and *parole*, which is an external manifestation of that structure usually in the form of speech. Nineteenth-century neogrammarians had concerned themselves with changes in *parole*, and so they had ignored the essentials of language: *langue* is the underlying structure and any historical changes should refer to changes in that structure. All of us may mispronounce something in our speech or make errors in syntax, but such slips are not changes in any real sense for it is only changes in the structure of the language, its *langue*, which are permanent. Hence changes should not be seen in isolation, because any change, which merits that name, will be a change in the structure of the *langue*. Thus a language may have only a single word in its vocabulary to express the concept *see*. When another word with a similar meaning, for example *perceive*, is introduced, this word will cause a readjustment of the meaning of *see* since there are now two items to cover the sense that had previously been expressed by one alone. The implication is that very few changes occur which do not have some impact on the *langue* and thus influence the overall structure of the language.

Saussure was not especially interested in the history of languages, for he accepted that language could be seen from two perspectives: synchronic and diachronic. The former is the way in which a language is examined at a specific moment in time without reference to what has happened in the past and what will happen in the future. The latter is the way in which a language is examined through time and as it changes to meet new circumstances. The diachronic approach was dominant in the previous centuries, and the idea that a language should be studied as a meaningful entity in its own right at a single moment in time was relatively new. The historical study of language was knocked off its pedestal and suddenly made to seem unimportant. More significantly, the development of synchronic linguistics inevitably led to the idea that any language or variety of language was worthy of study and must by its nature be a suitable means of communication. It meant that all 'primitive' languages could be seen as competent means of communication, and equally that dialect varieties of a single language must be regarded as methods of linguistic communication that were as satisfactory for their purposes as the standard was for its. This attitude would pave the way to upgrading the respect paid to dialects within Britain as well as to varieties of English in what had been the British Empire. Varieties of a language are from a linguistic point of view different, not worse. This would strike a blow at the supremacy of the standard written form and at the unquestioned acceptance of Received Pronunciation as the best spoken variety.

The basis of the structure which Saussure accepted in languages was a binary system of oppositions. If a sound, for example, was meaningful because its replacement by another sound in the same word would produce a different word, then those two sounds were phonemes in that language and the phonemes were part of its structure. Varieties of the same language might have different phonemes which would result in a different structure. Hence diachronically the changes which took place in the phonemic structure were the only ones that had any significance. Saussure also undermined the link between words and things which had been so popular in the nineteenth century. For him the linguistic sign consisted of a *signifiant* (which can be thought of as the actual form of a word or image as in a road sign) and a *signifié* (which is the idea or thing to which the *signifiant* refers). But, and this is the crucial point, the relation between the *signifiant* and the *signifié* is arbitrary. There is no reason why in English the word *cat* should refer to the domestic animal rather than to a table. A reason may be offered on diachronic grounds as to why it refers to the animal, but this is irrelevant on synchronic grounds. It is this arbitrariness of the linguistic sign which allows for changes in the structure of the *langue* to take place, for if there was any inherent link between the *signifiant* and the *signifié*, it might be difficult to have two words which referred to the same thing.

This approach by Saussure chimed in with the increasing attention paid to other languages. In North America many of the American Indian languages were being studied before, it was feared, they disappeared for good. Elsewhere anthropologists studied primitive tribes and tried to understand their view of the world in its own terms instead of assuming that it was either a corrupt version of a more sophisticated philosophy or that it was simply naïve and primitive. This would in its turn breed a new respect for different cultures, which were no longer seen as poor relations. In due course this attitude fed back into western society itself, where dialects of the standard languages were given greater attention and even the languages of different age groups were treated as languages in their own right. In particular the language of adolescents in Britain was increasingly accepted as a variety in its own right. Furthermore, as local radio and television grew, they employed announcers and commentators who had a local accent so that local people would identify with them. This gave a tremendous boost to the credibility and exposure of local varieties of language. As new countries in the developing world wanted to assert their own identity, they came to regard their own variety of English as a separate language. Dictionaries and grammars of such varieties as Nigerian English appeared.

Within linguistics the growth of the subdiscipline of socio-linguistics accentuated this trend. Sociolinguistics studies, among other things, variation in use according to the situation in which a speaker finds him or herself. It was realised that we all vary our speech according to differing social situations and purposes. In the pub we might use a more colloquial vocabulary and informal pronunciation than we would in a meeting at work. For example, all of us drop initial /h/ in certain social environments, but many of us prefer to think that we never do so, because its pronunciation is for some a sign of class and education. We do not like to think that we may drop initial /h/ because we feel that those who do so are less well educated than we are. It is just that some speakers drop initial /h/ more frequently than others, and some may even introduce it incorrectly through hypercorrection. It became more difficult for speakers to accept that there was an absolute boundary between those who dropped initial /h/ and those who did not.

Almost everyone pronounced it sometimes and dropped it sometimes; the difference lay in how often initial /h/ fell and not in whether it did so. The concept that some speakers always used proper pronunciation and others never did was no longer tenable.

Changes in the educational system also worked towards breaking down social divisions and perceptions of speech differences. Various education acts increased the number of years of compulsory education for children and the content of what was taught became more regulated throughout this period, particularly towards its end. More children stayed on after the compulsory leaving age, and higher education was expanded in the 1960s and again in the 1980s so that the number of students in higher education increased from about 8 per cent to something approaching 30 per cent. More significantly, the curriculum saw important modifications. As the old grammar schools were replaced by comprehensive schools in the post-Second World War period, Latin ceased to be a major subject in schools. Most universities dropped it as a requirement for admission in the 1950s, if not earlier, just as they dropped the requirement to know a foreign language. In schools in the 1990s the number of school-children who learned Latin had probably dropped below 5 per cent, and even for some of these the amount they learned was relatively small. In the reorganisation of university departments in the 1980s, many classics departments were closed or amalgamated with those in other universities. This was a very significant change because Latin had always been the yardstick which provided the model against which English and its grammar could be measured. As fewer people knew Latin, it became impossible to use it in this way any longer. This state of affairs fitted in with the view in linguistics that each language had its own structure and that each structure may need to be described in its own way. The domination of Latin grammatical terms came to an end as linguistics proposed alternative systems to describe the make-up of individual languages. Many of the new descriptive labels referred to the function or position of sentence elements. In this book, for example, I use the terms pre-modifier instead of adjective or post-modifier instead of relative clause or prepositional phrase where function is a significant feature in the discussion. As Latin grammatical terms have been abandoned and as Latin has become less familiar, the stranglehold that Latin exercised over discussions of what is correct English has been loosened. Because English has become a world language and Latin is for most people an unfamiliar language, there was no longer an external language which could act as the model for English, and this has given greater force to the decision of linguists to look for a descriptive terminology from within the resources of English itself. The idea that a language outside the one which is being described could act as a model for it is now largely discredited.

In education the position of English language was reduced during the middle years of the century. Grammar taught through rules was deemed prescriptive and thus inhibiting for school-children who were expected to express themselves as well as they could. Expression was considered by many teachers to be more important than its correct formulation and packaging. In this period English literature was a more usual subject than English language in schools. Consequently many pupils issued from the schools with no knowledge of Latin and very little understanding of how English as a language worked and what its component parts were. Parsing and other grammatical exercises were abandoned in favour of creative writing. This situation changed to some extent in 1988 with the establishment of the National Curriculum in England, which made English language one of the core subjects which children had to follow throughout their school career and with the setting up of A-level examinations in English language. Even by the end of the century the position of English language remains somewhat uncertain if only because it has not finally been resolved what should be taught as part of that subject and whether the teachers already in the schools will be able to teach it because of their commitment to English literature. The questions of what one means by 'English' and whether teaching should be confined only to a single variety, the standard, have not been fully answered. As the teaching of English language becomes more politicised, so it becomes more difficult to come to decisions in a rational and unemotional way.[1]

For many people, re-establishing some form of standard English as the variety to be taught means putting the clock back in a way that they find unacceptable. At the beginning of this period it was still recognised that there was a form of English which was 'correct' and a pronunciation which was approved. Precisely what that pronunciation was could never be agreed on; it was often easier to define what it was not. H. C.Wyld, in a tract of the Society for Pure English, decided that it was the speech associated with officers in the armed forces.[2] He also claimed that if one were to compare the vowels of Received Pronunciation with those in non-standard dialects no one could possibly deny that the former sounded more pleasing and sonorous than the latter. Certainly experiments which have been carried out testing how English people respond to different accents have revealed that most rate the sounds of Received Pronunciation more highly than other varieties, though this merely reflects the power and status implications of that variety rather than any inherent superiority. It was Daniel Jones who felt that a standard of pronunciation had to be established and devised the concept of Received Pronunciation in the first quarter of the century.[3] In part pedagogical reasons demanded that one variety of speech had to be the model for those who wanted to learn the language. Nevertheless it is clear from his writings that he viewed many non-standard accents with distaste. He accepted that there was such a thing as a correct pronunciation which reflected his own pronunciation and that of educated speakers in southern England, particularly those of men who had been educated at the public schools. The basis of the standard pronunciation, as far as Jones was concerned, was established on geographical, gender and class considerations. In part this need to affirm Received Pronunciation reflected the spread of education not only in England but throughout the Empire. What was to be taught needed to be delineated and codified. Jones's views carried authority because of his position as a Professor of Phonetics in London University and because of the large number of books he produced, which were frequently reprinted. It was also felt that the establishment of a standard in pronunciation was part of that general movement of progress which would lead to the elimination of all regional varieties of the language. Education would produce a more homogeneous linguistic environment in which those who had been less well educated would gradually come to imitate those who were better educated. This view was subscribed to by Wyld, who felt that all speakers aspired to that kind of non-regional English which passed as the standard. This is a view which has remained the goal of many politicians and some educators, but it proved increasingly difficult to attain for reasons which have been outlined.

The question of what is correct and what is good usage has continued unabated throughout this period. Most influential at the start of the period was Henry Fowler's *Dictionary of Modern English Usage* (1926), which has been reprinted many times and revised twice. Fowler was not averse to making his own views clear and made recommendations as to what was the best usage to follow. Many of the items he objected to were well established features of books on usage and have continued to be repeated to the present. For example, the use of a pronoun in the subject form after a preposition, as in 'between you and I', was criticised as false grammar as was *who* for *whom* in sentences like 'Who did you hear that from?' Fowler's dictionary, like traditional grammars, high-lighted typical faults which needed to be corrected, as though good English consisted of little more than the avoidance of particular solecisms. It was only when linguists began to realise that school grammars were never based on present-day English that change set in, not only with school grammars, but with works written for the general public. One factor which became increasingly important was the development of the computer since this allowed for large corpora of linguistic material to be collected and then analysed. It became possible to base a grammar and a dictionary on actual usage as represented by such data collections. This development also had the effect of basing grammars and other books about language on spoken English rather than on writings in English literature, which had in any case become rather more open to non-standard influences during this century. In Eliot's *The Waste Land* (1922) there is not only incomplete syntax, but also many styles from a wide range of registers, including Cockney and pastiche Shakespeare. James Joyce's writings exhibit an extreme case of experimenting with the language so that some find his *Finnegans Wake* difficult, if not impossible, to understand. Dialect has been used much more frequently as a medium of expression in novels in its own right in modern times. Hence the idea that there was an approved English was being undermined by literary authors at the same time as it came under attack from the linguists who could use the new technology to put some of their ideas about usage into practice.

An important feature of the current scene in discussions about English is the prominence attached to new words and to the development of new senses of words. In this respect it is interesting to compare the situation in the seventeenth and eighteenth centuries. In that period dictionaries concentrated on words that were Latinate and learned. Dictionaries vied with one another to see which could include the most exoticly learned words, many of which may never have entered the spoken language or even been used in writing. Today there are many dictionaries of new words and these are often produced every two or three years by different publishers. Their approach is very much to record words which are up to date and which are used frequently, if not exclusively, in speech. The *Oxford Dictionary of New Words* (1991) has as its subtitle *A Popular Guide to Words in the News*. This contrasts vividly even with nineteenth-century attitudes to dictionary making. A word had to be in writing and to occur several times before a compiler of a dictionary would accept that it had entered the language. Words that occurred only in speech or were part of some specialised vocabulary would not so readily be incorporated into the dictionary. This Oxford dictionary, for example, includes words like *fundie* 'a fundamentalist' and *headbanger* 'In young people's slang: a deranged or stupid person'. Such words would never have been accepted into mainline dictionaries in earlier periods and underline how attitudes to the language have changed.

Another important influence on the language has been the rise of feminism and political correctness, though one should not forget the whole matter of charters which the Conservative governments of the 1980s and 1990s promoted. Feminists have claimed that the English language is dominated by men who have imposed their own bias upon it. In particular the use of pronouns like *he* to indicate a human being when either male or female may be implied or of morphemes like *man* to indicate humans in general in such words as *mankind* indicate to them that the world is viewed from a male point of view. It has become common to avoid expressions which might cause offence by suggesting that males are the norm in society. Thus instead of *he* it is now common either to use the plural *they* or some version of *he or she* such as *s/he* or *(s)he*. Words like *humanity* are preferred to *mankind*. The same applies to political correctness which objects to the marginalisation of certain sections of the population on grounds of their age, gender, race or class. This has spawned a whole new vocabulary to avoid those words which might cause offence to such groups. Naturally, as with all euphemisms, they cannot get rid of the social attitudes and conditions which may have caused the words to arise in the first place. It is rare nowadays to find a word like *cripple* in formal discourse; it gave way at first to *handicapped*; this in turn gave way to *disabled* or *disadvantaged*; and to some these alternatives have now been replaced by *physically challenged*. Interestingly some of the words like *cripple* and *spastic*, which have been driven out of formal discourse, have been taken over by the young who use them colloquially as terms of abuse. The euphemisms have become more cumbersome which is one reason why not many of them have been adopted. These circumlocutions are more common in America than in Britain, where some of them are ridiculed as being unnecessarily convoluted. With regard to the citizens' charters, these could cynically be represented as an attempt to make people feel that they are more in charge of their own lives. In practice they often represent the attempt to introduce into different walks of life the ethos of the free market, even in those environments where that was not a feature of particular institutions or professions. Everything in society is in danger of being reduced to a cash basis. In universities, for example, we are encouraged to think of students as *customers* or *clients* and not as *students*. On the railways *passenger* has been replaced by *customer*. There is a change in the relationship between providers of services and those who receive them and this is reflected in the language which has been employed.

All of these changes have produced uncertainty in the minds of many speakers of English as to what precisely constitutes good English, even if something like that could be said to exist any more. One interesting change which took place early in the century was the replacement of the expressions Oxford English or the King's/ Queen's English by Standard English. The period has witnessed the struggle between those who insist on maintaining the proper standard of English and those who prefer to enjoy the richness and variety of English. In the early part of the century the Society for Pure English produced a range of tracts designed to promote the standard, though it was recognised that the standard was under threat as it was used by only a small minority of English people. Numerous government committees have investigated the position of English within the school curriculum. To start with, their reports were more in favour of promoting standard English. Many regretted that English language was not given a higher position in the school curriculum, and the Newbolt Committee indicated that if a child was not learning 'good English' it would be learning 'bad English' and almost certainly 'bad habits of thought'.[4] The committee recommended practice in acquiring good pronunciation and standard English in writing. Although later committees have often noted that all children should have access to standard English, they were more relaxed about the use of other varieties of English. However, at the end of the century the debate over the establishment of the National Curriculum brought the controversy into prominence again. The Cox Report suggested that children should have confidence in their own varieties while becoming familiar with the standard.[5] However, there is a strong movement to make the standard the main subject of the curriculum and this was expressed through the document *English our English* by John Marenbom issued by the Centre for Policy Studies (1987). Marenbom criticised many of the liberal views towards English which had become widely accepted through the Bullock Report and the views of school inspectors and other advisers. For him a new orthodoxy of teaching had developed in the 1960s and this was characterised by a neglect of standard English in favour of other varieties so that anything was permissible. This he saw as partly the result of the growth of modern linguistics and the claim that teachers should become familiar with the writings of linguists. For him the only solution was to reject all teachings of the new orthodoxy and to insist on grammatical English and Received Pronunciation. The views of the Centre for Policy Studies have had some impact on government thinking and have informed the nature of the curriculum, though these views have not found particular favour with many teachers of English. English language is included as a core subject within the National Curriculum, although English literature is not. What effect this will have on the teaching of English remains to be seen, but it is unlikely that in the immediate future what is taught in schools will greatly influence the way people write and speak. So much is now available in both mediums and so many people now use computers where standard English seems to have made little impression that it is difficult to imagine that the position which standard English enjoyed in the nineteenth century will be re-established.

It is not easy to record changes in individual aspects of the language because the standard has become less significant and because so many different varieties are now recorded and accepted as being acceptable methods of communication. Certain trends may be outlined. Sometimes these trends appear to move in contrary directions. The more relaxed attitude towards language found among some sections of the population may be set against the demand for correctness and clarity made by others. This is particularly true of the writing system. It is now common to find that the apostrophe, for example, is either not used at all or is used in the wrong places. Many native speakers of English do not know how to distinguish *its* from *it's*. Others simply leave it out altogether and there is a widespread view that the apostrophe will disappear altogether within the next twenty years. Even certain organisations such as Barclays Bank have dispensed with the apostrophe. The influence of advertising in particular, but of a more relaxed attaitude to language in general, has led to written forms which would have been unthinkable in the nineteenth century. A fish and chip shop may have on its shopfront the sign *FishnChips* or *FishanChips* or some variant of this. The conjunction *and* is constantly abbreviated in commerce. Advertising enjoys employing puns and this can lead to spelling variants being adopted to make the pun clearer. Newspaper headlines, which prefer to use a short word or form of a word, also rely on spellings which reflect pronunciation rather than the accepted orthography.

As we have seen, Received Pronunciation was recorded by Daniel Jones and others, but as it is calculated that not more than 5 per cent of the population in England use it, its influence has varied according to the political and social attitudes of the day. It was the pronunciation which was heard on early radio and so its influence before and during the Second World War was prominent. From the 1950s onwards its influence waned, but in the last few years the government has encouraged the use of what it calls Standard Spoken English, by which no doubt it means Received Pronunciation, though that is not absolutely clear. More important has been the influence of American English and in the last decades of the twentieth century other varieties of English from around the world and from immigrants to Britain. The influence of other varieties of English such as Australian and Caribbean English has come from immigration and from television. Television programmes like *Neighbours* have made Australian English very familiar, and the immigration of large numbers of people from the West Indies and from India, for example, has made these varieties well known. It is true that American English carries more prestige than other varieties because of the political and cultural dominance of the United States, but some other varieties of English, such as that from the West Indies, have had considerable impact on certain sections of the population in the United Kingdom. And the trend to make sure that all varieties are given a proper hearing and are accepted as valid methods of communication has meant that the prejudice which used to attach to certain forms of English has been less marked. Within Britain the domination of south-east England in political and cultural matters has continued and this has reinforced the standing of Received Pronunciation as a variety based on educated speech in the south. But recently some scholars have detected the rise of a variety they call Estuary English, that form of English which is associated with the lower reaches of the Thames on both banks. These scholars have claimed that Estuary English has begun to change the nature of Received Pronunciation, though this view is not accepted by all scholars.

A very important influence on pronunciation is the continued growth of spelling pronunciations. The apparent divorce between spelling and pronunciation in English is well known and makes English a difficult language for foreigners to pronounce. Even with native speakers, this separation between spelling and pronunciation can be a cause of difficulty and embarassment. Writing has led to adjustments in pronunciation throughout the history of English, but its influence has been particularly marked in the recent past because of the immense amount of writing available to a wide range of people and because of the more general movement towards a meritocracy. In some cases spelling pronunciations have been introduced from or at least assisted by pronunciations found in America. A word like *often* was characteristically pronounced as /ofn/ in English and is still pronounced in this way by many people in informal situations. But a pronouncation in which the /t/ has been reintroduced is now heard more frequently, especially in formal environments. American spelling may also influence British pronunciation. There is a difference between British *speciality* and American *specialty*, in both writing and pronunciation. The American form is now met with in British writings and the pronunciation as a three-syllable word is not infrequent in Britain. The same applies to the position of stress in words where American influence has led to the adoption of some American stress patterns. Words like *laboratory* and *lavatory*, for example, have different stress patterns in each variety and the American one has made some inroads into British pronunciation.

Some forms of American pronunciation are much the same as those found in other non-British varieties of English and even in dialects in Britain. Consequently it is difficult to decide whether the change has been introduced from outside or whether it is one that would have occurred in Britain anyway and simply mirrors a change which has a more universal distribution than Britain. In many instances of stress there appear to be two tendencies in addition to following American example. The first is to move the stress towards the front of the word so that *contríbute* becomes *cóntribute*, and the second is to give greater stress to syllables which previously had been unstressed. To go back to an example quoted above, the word *often*, when it regains its medial /t/, may be pronounced with a final vowel rather than a vocalised *n*. This vowel may vary from /e/ to /i/ or even /ə/. The latter is doubtless a further influence of writing and the need which some people feel to keep their pronunciation as close as possible to the written form.

Some aspects of pronunciation which are found in many non-British varieties and which are paralleled by developments in Britain include the following tendencies. Vowel sounds are shortened so that /ɑ:/ is shortened to /æ/. The variation between these two sounds has been a feature of English for centuries, but the tendency to replace /ɑ:/ with /æ/ is now more prominent and may reflect in part a reaction against what is considered an élite pronunciation. The clear demarcation between long and short vowels has been eroded, particularly with /o:/ and /o/. The word *project* may be pronounced with either a long or short first vowel. In this word and in some others the influence of American pronunciation may be detected. The central vowels which are such a characteristic feature of British English may be replaced by front or back vowels. Once again one may regard this as the influence of the writing system and the felt need to pronounce all vowels clearly. A tendency to simplify diphthongs is also apparent in the speech of some speakers, and this is achieved by leaving out the final element of the diphthong and sometimes changing the nature of the first element as well. The diphthong /ei/ found in words like *take* may be simplified to /e:/ or to /ɛ:/, or even among some speakers reduced to a short vowel sound. This pronunciation is one that can be found in various dialects in Britain and may have penetrated from there into more educated speech, particularly as speakers from different regions have risen socially.

With single consonants some of the tendencies that have been found throughout the history of English have become more prominent as the hold of Received Pronunciation has slackened over the utterances of educated speakers. For example, it has been characteristic of English throughout its history not to pronounce the final consonant in a word. In the last example quoted in the preceding paragraph there are many speakers who fail to pronounce the final /k/ in *take*. Equally the loss of aspiration at the beginning of words is much less of a shibboleth than it used to be, and so initial /h/ is less often heard than was the custom with educated people at an earlier period. In consonant groups the tendency to reduce heavy groups by omitting one of the sounds is another feature characteristic of English throughout many centuries and is given greater expression today because of the loosening of the restraints imposed by attitudes towards correctness. This is particularly true of three consonants in a group where the medial one might fall. In a word like *dialects* pronunciation of the /t/ is uncommon so that the word ends in final /ks/. It may be appreciated that some of these changes work in contrary directions. The need which some people feel to be precise in the way they pronounce words is countered by the acceptance that English can be spoken in a more relaxed way than used to be acceptable. In the first case the sounds may approximate to the written form, whereas in the latter case the sound may be omitted altogether.

There are certain vowel changes which are regarded as typical of Estuary English. Some of these may be local forms which have achieved greater prominence in the last twenty-five years with the growing importance of Essex and north Kent. One feature is the loss of /l/ in words like *salt* and *told*. There are more significant changes in the pronunciation of certain vowels, and these can be heard from time to time on the radio and television. These include the use of /a/ where Received Pronunciation has /ɔ/, particularly in words where this sound is preceded by /w/ as *waft, wander* and *quagmire*; the replacement of expected /ʌ/ by /ɔ/ in words like *done, government, some* and *worry*; and the occurrence of /ɔ/ in words where the expected pronunciation would be the diphthong /əʊ/, as in *bolt, gold* and *whole*. How far these sounds will become more generalised in the population as a whole remains uncertain. There are so many competing pronunciations and our ability to record the variations which exist in one individual's speech is so great that it is difficult to outline precisely what trends are dominant and how far specific pronunciations extend. The idea that all speakers should adhere to something referred to as Standard Spoken English as recommended by the government is unlikely to be realised. The competition from other pronunciations both in one's daily life and from radio and television is so great that it is difficult to know what models individuals will follow.

Changes in word-formation and vocabulary are the most

noticeable feature of the way the language has developed in the twentieth century, partly because they are more visible and easier to detect. Various tendencies can be noted. Through radio and television, events from across the world can be reported to the rest of the world almost as soon as they occur. English has always been receptive to borrowings from other languages, but in the modern period many new words come into the language and often fall out again fairly quickly. As different countries become newsworthy and then fall out of public attention, words from their languages may enter English for a short period without becoming permanently established. In the 1980s, for example, words like *perestroika* and *ayatollah* could be seen almost every day in British newspapers, but today they are found infrequently, if at all. In America a Mrs Bobbitt cut off her husband's penis because of his aggressive behaviour towards her and for a time the verb *to bobbitt* entered the language in the sense 'to exact physical retribution on a male partner', but this too seems to have been a temporary phenomenon. Even within England itself words associated with an individual may become prominent for a time before relapsing into obscurity again. The verb *to handbag* in the sense 'to dominate men and impose one's will on them' was associated with the Prime Minister, Margaret Thatcher; this new verb gained some of its force from its word-play on *to sandbag*. When she ceased to occupy this office, the verb fell into disuse. In the early 1980s the Gulf War produced many words which had a short life. The Scud, a missile used by Iraq, was well known at the time, and the weapon used to counter it was known as a *scudbuster*.

The employment of compounds such as this one often for humorous effects has been a feature of English for centuries. A development of this was the form *scudstud* used of journalists who covered the Gulf War. The morpheme *stud* is used to express the concept of a man who is highly sexed, and the humour springs from the belief that in Saudi Arabia, where most journalists were based, opportunities for sexual activity were minimal. Sometimes instead of compounds one finds blends. The word *blaxploitation*, which was more widely used when it was introduced into the language, is based on a blend of *blacks* and *exploitation*. Over the last twenty years it has come to be used in a more technical sense in the film industry where it refers to films which portray the exploitation of black people. Some blends never seem to achieve more than a fleeting presence, often because what they stand for fails to catch on. The word *skuit* was coined in the early 1990s when the fashion industry tried to persuade men to wear suits which consisted on a skirt and a jacket. *Skuit* is a blend of *skirt* and *suit*. As the idea never gained any favour with men, the word disappeared as well. Another word that has arisen recently which may also not survive very long is *broadloid*. This an amalgamation of *broadsheet* 'quality newspaper' and *tabloid* 'popular newpaper' and refers to the deterioration in standards of quality newpapers as they try to emulate the tabloids without sacrificing their own pretensions to quality. It was coined by the editor of the *Guardian*, though it has not achieved much prominence so far.

Another trend has been the continuing exploitation of functional shift. This is a feature which has run riot in more recent times and is often criticised by those who regard themselves as guardians of the language. In football goals can be *gifted* and in cricket batsmen can *top-score*. Matches can be *fixtured*. A businessman can *expense* an investment. Those in a hurry can *concorde* to America, a verb formed from the aeroplane the *Concorde*. Even military slang such as *attrit* for *attrition* can be turned into verbs so that a newspaper can refer to 'targets being attrited', as happened during the Gulf War. Clipping of words such as *attrit* has been common in English for centuries and in an earlier chapter reference was made to Swift's displeasure at the many words formed in this way. Today the distaste which such clippings used to attract is less noticeable. All professions spawn their own examples and in universities it is usual to refer to *undergrads* rather than to *undergraduates*, and student societies will often be known by a form ending in *Soc* such as *FilmSoc* or *DramSoc*. A further feature of the vocabulary has been the widespread use of acronyms. Earlier in this chapter I referred to NATO, and organisations such as this are most often referred to by their initials – many people may not even know what the initials refer to. This may even be true of such a familiar acronym as BBC. Many government *quangos*, which is itself an acronym, are referred to by their initials, such as SCAA. In most cases the creators of acronyms try to provide a form which can be spoken easily and thus the acronym may consist of more than just the initials of the title. *Quango* itself is an acronym for Quasi Autonomous Non-Governmental Organisation, though some claim that the *n* stands for National. *Unprofor* stands for the United Nations Protection Force. During wars military acronyms become more widely used as was true of the Gulf War when a word like *humvee* appeared in the newspapers for a time; it stands for High Mobility Multipurpose Wheeled Vehicle. Its military abbreviated form is HMMWV, but in order to say it this form is changed to *humvee*.

The use of phrasal verbs, which as we saw earlier replaced verbs with prefixes, has grown in this period and a new development has been the transformation of such verbs into nouns or adjectives. Many phrasal verbs appear to have little connection with the simple verb form. A verb like *to kick* can produce phrasal verbs such as *kick off*, *kick up* and *kick in*. Although the first and last of these are clearly related to the simple verb in that one 'kicks off' in a game of football and one 'kicks in' a door, the middle verb is related to *kick* only figuratively since one might 'kick up' a fuss, that is one would make a scene in order to get some recompense for whatever was the matter of annoyance. The first of these phrasal verbs produces the noun *kick-off* 'the start of a match'. The others have not yet produced nouns, but they may well do so. Some of these verbs and their nouns have acquired a variety of meanings which can be somewhat obscure in relation to the meaning of the simple verb. Sometimes noun and verb have a different range of meanings, as in the case of *pick up*. As a verb it is used of the police arresting a suspect, but the noun is not used in this way. As a verb and noun it may be used to pick up a member of the opposite sex in a casual manner and possibly for sexual purposes, but it is used only in the verb form when someone is picked up by prior appointment. The noun is used for a free lift in a car or lorry, but the verb would refer to the driver rather than to the person(s) picked up. The noun without verb equivalent is used for a small truck or van. It is also possible to have the word *pick-me up* to refer to a tonic, though there is no equivalent verb. The verb may refer to picking up radio signals, but the noun is not used in this way.

Nouns formed from phrasal verbs may spawn new nouns on the same pattern which have no verbal equivalent. Thus *to black out* has led to the noun *black-out*, which has in its turn generated *white-out*, *brown-out* and others like it; similarly *to sit in* has produced a *sit-in*, which has in its turn generated such nouns as *love-in*, *pray-in*, *teach-in* and *swim-in*, none of which have a verbal form. This noun pattern is very common at a colloquial level and has led to such words as *balls-up*, *bog-up* and *screw-up*, which all indicate a mistake or calamity. Although most verbal phrases and their nouns are formed from monosyllabic adverbial prepositions, those with longer prepositions occur, as in *walk-about*, *hang-over* and *take-away*, not all of which exist as both verb and noun. If the plural of these nouns is required, the bound morpheme -*s* is added and some words now exist only in the plural, for example *left-overs*. When the preposition ends in a vowel, some prefer to use -'*s* for the plural so that a *lean-to* has the plural *lean-to's* or *lean-tos*. Some of these phrasal verbs also generate pre-modifiers. It is possible to meet a *live-in partner* or to buy food which has a *sell-by date*. *Clip-on lenses* can now be referred to simply as *clip-ons*.

A noun formed from a phrasal verb does not necessarily have the same sense as the same verb with a prefix which is converted into a noun. *Input* and *put-in* are not identical in meaning: the former refers to information fed into some plan or other activity, whereas the latter is the action of putting the ball into the scrum in rugby. A *break-out* refers to an escape from a jail, but an *outbreak* means the spread of a disease.

The most prominent feature of the vocabulary in the twentieth century has been the gradual demise of Latin as a principal source for borrowing except in certain technical fields such as medicine. Because Latin has not been available to most speakers of the language, other sources for new words have been found. This has meant that words from a colloquial or slang register have been taken into the more formal language used by educated speakers. In part this development has been helped by the lifting of social restrictions on this kind of language and in part by the growth of a popular press and broadcasting. Many words which were previously taboo are now commonly used in circles where they would never have been heard previously. On stage and television even the so-called four-letter words are used frequently and without causing much offence. But slang words such as *booze* for alcoholic drink or *lousy* as a general adjective of disapproval would pass unremarked in most social environments. In a newspaper recently I saw a headline stating that one cricket team had *out-tonked* another. This word contains the element *tonk* used in the sense 'to hit out, score runs quickly' and the prefix *out-* implying 'to perform better', so that *out-tonk* means 'to hit runs more quickly than the opponents'. The two world wars and the popularity of the slang associated with them created the feeling that language could be more open. The vacuum caused by the lack of borrowing from the classical languages has been filled by this expropriation of slang and by the general infiltration of words from social groups whose language would in the past have been considered incorrect and offensive. Younger people often deliberately cultivate the language of black people, of the drug scene or of minority groups in order to shock their parents; but often these words are then taken up by the older groups and neutralised. Words like *fix* or *crack* are familiar to most people today. The young also go through an enormous number of vogue words, especially those that indicate approval or enthusiasm. These change rapidly – *great* gives way to *brill*, which in turn is replaced by *cool* or *wicked*. To create an impression of being up to date, the young have to change their vocabulary to be in fashion in much the same way as the fashionable man-about-town did in the eighteenth century. This has led to many words in the language being incomprehensible to a large number of speakers of English, to say nothing of non-native speakers. One of the advantages of English, that it contained a high proportion of Latinate words which were understood by speakers of many languages, has been eroded by this influx of words from colloquial and slang registers into acceptable, if not necessarily approved, usage.

Although phrasal verbs may now be more popular than prefixes, this does not mean that prefixes have become obsolescent in forming new verbs. The example *out-tonk* was mentioned in the previous paragraph. The prefixes *de-* and *dis-* remain popular. Among recent coinages with the former are *de-skill*, used when a job which was previously done by skilled people is controlled by computers which can be supervised by unskilled operators, and *de-air*, which in the Gulf War was used to mean 'to destroy the enemy's air attack capability'. As for the latter I read in an academic article that some evidence did not *disconfirm* a particular hypothesis. I took this to mean that the evidence was not sufficient to disprove the hypothesis. Other affixes also remain productive with other parts of speech. Two common noun suffixes are *-ism* and *-speak*. The former has been used in English for many centuries, but has grown in importance in the twentieth century with the raising of various attitudes into quasi-philosophical concepts. In the political sphere one thinks immediately of *Nazism, Marxism, Fascism* and *Communism*. In the realm of political correctness one finds forms like *feminism, ageism* and *heterosexism*. Many of these words have the noun agent form in *-ist*, though some words formed with *ist* may not have an equivalent in *-ism*. Thus *defeatist* and *pacifist* are more common than *defeatism* and *pacifism*. Other suffixes which have been very productive recently include the noun suffix *-ee* and the verb suffix *-ise/ize*. From the former we have words like *divorcee* 'a divorced person' and *biographee* 'a person who is the subject of a biography'; from the latter *hospitalise* 'to take into hospital' and *urbanise*, which can have several senses including 'to convert rural areas into urban developments' and 'to make a country person adopt manners of the town'. The suffix *-speak*, popularised by Orwell's 'Newspeak', has become very popular, especially in newspapers. It usually means 'the typical language associated with the preceding noun element' so that *football-speak* is 'the language of football or footballers' and *manager-speak* is 'the language characteristically used by managers'. In one instance when a Conservative minister Michael Jackson unfortunately used the word *liberated* to refer to those who became unemployed because they were free to find another job, one newspaper described the impending redundancy of some other workers as their being *liberated (Michael Jackson-speak for unemployed).*

The prefix *un-* is very productive and is now used in a variety of contexts where it has not been used before. The opposites of such words as *rich, funny, freedom* are normally other words like *poor, sad, slavery*, though it has always been possible to use the negative *not* within a sentence like 'He is not rich' rather than 'He is poor'. Words like *rich* and *poor* are at opposite ends of a continuum and sometimes one wants to refer to a position in between these two extremes, and that is what 'He is not poor' has been used for. Nowadays it is becoming common to use the prefix *un-* in the form *unpoor* to indicate that someone is not very poor, but not that rich either. This prefix can also be used in this way with nouns. One linguist has referred to the absence of *unfreedom* in certain syntactic structures. Perhaps the very productivity of this prefix has assisted the resurrection of certain words which had become fossilised with this prefix. Thus the word *uncouth*, which is formed from OE *un+cūþ* (though the latter element ceased to be an independent word hundreds of years ago), is now being treated again as though it consisted of a bound and a free morpheme. So one can say once again that someone is *couth*, though there is an implication that the opposite was expected and its usage is colloquial. Similarly one can hear colloquially that someone is *gruntled* (from *disgruntled*) or *traught* (from *distraught*). Forms like these are not found in formal writing, though they do occur in novels, plays and some newspapers. The prefix *un-* is also used in other contexts, such as *unDutch*, which when used of an *interior* in a television programme meant 'not characteristic of the average Dutch interior'. The prefix *re-* is also extremely popular, even in contexts where it might seem inappropriate such as the word *reinvent*, since one might assume that something could only be invented once, though *reinvent* means 'to invent something for a second time'. Words like *redistribute*, *regroup, retrain* have become common in the latter half of the century.

In syntax a few of the changes which have taken place may be highlighted. In the noun group some uncertainty has developed in the use of articles which may be caused partly by the growing tendency to place descriptive labels before rather than after the head. This is something introduced into British English from America, and originated as a journalistic usage. Thus we can say *Prime Minister Major, bored housewife Mary Jones,* and *Head of English Department Dr Smith* instead of *Mr Major, the Prime Minister, Mary Jones, a bored housewife,* and *Dr Smith, Head of the English Department.* This usage is less frequent in more formal writing. But the articles may now be omitted in ways that remind one of French or German usage. It would not be surprising to see an article with the title 'Tynan as critic' rather than 'Tynan as a critic'. Book titles often omit the article where one might have expected it, one of the best known being Joyce's *Portrait of the Artist as a Young Man* rather than *A Portrait of the Artist as a Young Man.* In phrases like 'all the summer' it is now more common to find this as 'all summer'. It is also possible to use demonstrative adjectives like *this* to introduce someone or something that has not been referred to before. One can imagine a story starting 'There was this fellow . . .'. This was an older usage which disappeared from formal English and may have been reintroduced from speech.

The growth of nouns in the pre-modifier position has been a feature of modern English, and may have been encouraged by its use in newspapers and in bureaucratic language; it is now very common in scientific and technical language. It reduces the amount of post-modification and thus saves space in newspapers. It is sometimes difficult to distinguish whether a noun used as a pre-modifier forms a compound word with the head, and this difficulty is accentuated by the position of any adjective before nouns used as pre-modifiers. One would normally expect the phrase *a long metal wrench* rather than *a metal long wrench* so that the position of *long* encourages the idea of the close association of *metal* and *wrench* as though they should be considered a compound. This is even more so when two nouns pre-modify the head, for the second will seem to have closer links with the head than the first, as in *the missing Volkswagen ignition key*. In a family with more than one car, this use could replace *the missing ignition key for the Volkswagen*. In some instances the use of nouns as pre-modifiers has replaced the equivalent adjective so that one refers to a *sex offender* or a *sexual offender*. In many cases where nouns are used as pre-modifiers there may be ambiguity as to the meaning. We all accept that *child abuse* means 'abuse of children' (and not by children), but *teenage vandalism* means 'vandalism by teenagers' (and not of teenagers), and *teacher guidance* could mean either 'guidance of teachers' (by school inspectors) or 'guidance by teachers' (of their pupils). In most cases the context makes clear which sense is intended, though in certain types of discourse such as advertising both meanings may be implied.

Among auxiliaries the continuing decline of *be* in favour of *have* when followed by a past participle has continued. In speech the reduction of the auxiliary to *'s* makes it difficult to know which one is intended. The phrase *it's gone* could be thought to represent *it is gone* or *it has gone*. The former was the regular usage in the past, but the latter has now largely replaced it. The auxiliary *do* is used much more widely than used to be the case. It has therefore lost some of its emphatic quality, becoming more a way of increasing the stylistic weight of an utterance. In a sentence like 'When on holiday, make sure you water the flowers before you go', the imperative would most probably now be 'do make sure'. This use of *do* is very common in speech and may have entered the written language from there. *Do have* now often replaces *have got* so that one can go to a shop and ask 'Do you have any size 6 slippers?' rather than 'Have you got any size 6 slippers?' Even if one asks the question in the latter form, one may get a reply 'Yes, we do' rather than 'Yes, we have'. In tag questions and clauses added as afterthoughts *do* may well replace *have*. It is now possible to have 'We have nothing else to eat, do we?' or 'She has nothing left to cook – or does she?'

With verbs the subjunctive has made something of a recovery in American English and this has had some impact on the British variety. Even so, it is still unusual to hear a sentence like 'He agreed that he come tomorrow' in British English. But the frequency of the subjunctive in American English has encouraged the use of simple verb forms in subordinate clauses in British English rather than forms with an auxiliary like *should* so that many prefer to say 'He suggested that I come tomorrow' rather than 'He suggested that I should come tomorrow' or even 'He suggested that I came tomorrow'. Even without this possible American influence there are many examples where the form with an auxiliary is rejected in favour of a different structure: 'It is important that buses are banned from the city centre' rather than 'It is important that buses should be banned from the city centre'. The use of a preterite instead of a perfect is growing in popularity, especially in speech. On coming out of a shop a child might say to its mother 'I bought a rocket' instead of 'I have bought a rocket'. This is more characteristic at present of younger people who have been influenced by American usage, but it is growing among all sections of the population. The growth in phrasal verbs continues, though some verbs develop a simple form and can also be used intransitively when that happens. A phrasal verb like *cope with* was originally transitive and was used in sentences like 'I don't know how he is going to cope with the new teacher'. Now it can be used as the simple verb *cope* intransitively: 'I don't know how he is going to cope'. Equally, reflexive verbs continue to lose their reflexive pronouns and are used intransitively, as is true of many other verbs. 'We are going to improve' is now more common than 'We are going to improve our behaviour'.

During the modern period there has been a shift away from using the *to* infinitive in favour of the *ing* form as the object of many verbs. Thus what might in earlier periods have been 'Do you recollect to have seen him in Venice?' would today probably appear as 'Do you recollect seeing him in Venice?' Similarly with a verb like *delay*, one would expect an advertisement today to have 'Don't delay sending your order' rather than 'Don't delay to send your order', though forms with the *to* infinitive remain possible, though obsolescent. When a gerund in *-ing* has a subject expressed, it is now more frequently put into the oblique form rather than the possessive, particularly in speech. Thus 'I don't like you arriving so late' is now to be expected rather than 'I don't like your arriving so late'. The latter form is the older of the two and emphasises the noun function of the gerund.

The influence of spoken forms means that many verbs can be used without a subject or that verbs themselves can be omitted. In speech it would be quite common to greet a neighbour with 'Been a nice week so far' without including 'It's' at the beginning. In newspapers and advertisements this usage is common enough, such as 'Ever thought how you could cope in an accident?' The omission of the verb is particularly common after interrogative pronouns and adverbs like *who, how* and *what*. Sentences like 'Who to ask?', 'What to do?', 'How to tackle this problem?' are found in many types of discourse today. It is regarded by many as an Americanism which first infiltrated the spoken language and is now to be found in many written texts.

The variation between adverbs with or without the ending -*ly* is noteworthy and is again a feature of American usage. 'He did real bad' would sound American to many British speakers, though it is popular among the younger generation. In fact such usage is not unknown in English dialects, and the use of *proper* instead of *properly* in a sentence like 'He did it proper' would probably sound non-standard to many British speakers, but it would not be judged an Americanism. The various cases of personal pronouns are coming increasingly to seem unnecessary because English uses word order, not inflectional endings, to indicate function. For many centuries the question of whether a pronoun must be in the object form after a preposition has exercised grammarians, who have consistently attacked examples like 'between he and me'. However, forms like this are more common than they used to be especially in speech, and the use of *me* in the subject form especially in a co-ordinate structure is increasingly heard. Many speakers would say 'Me and Eric' in answer to a question like 'Who is going to the film tonight?' and some would undoubtedly say 'Me and Eric are'. However, older speakers would still resist saying something like 'Me and Eric are going to the film tonight', though it is used increasingly by younger people. In this the personal pronoun is following the path of the relative pronoun where *whom* has largely given way to *who* even at a formal level. It is also notable that *myself* appears to be used instead of *me* in the modern period and thus re-establishes a usage that was found in early Modern English. In some cases this may result from uncertainty on the part of the user as to whether *I* or *me* would be the correct usage. To say 'between John and myself' avoids the necessity of deciding whether *I* or *me* would be right here. It also occurs where such difficulties do not exist as in 'He invited myself, John and Harry to dinner'. Perhaps under the influence of French *myself* can also be used to emphasise the subject pronoun as in 'Myself, I hate French cooking'. But it is possible that this is simply a formal variant of the colloquial 'Me, I hate French cooking'.

One of the features of the modern period has been the overall fragmentation of the concept of standard English as different varieties have been accepted as not only permissible, but also as worth encouraging. Thus in England there is a marked difference in language between the broadsheets and the tabloids. The former try to maintain a language which is not too far from what an educated readership might tolerate as not too far from the standard, whereas the latter are content to exploit the various resources of the language by using new spellings, employing words which are slang or even invented, and by paying less attention to complete sentences or standard punctuation as recommended in formal grammars. One has only to compare the same story in different newspapers to see how the language differs drastically from one to the other. This difference is not simply a matter of style: the readers of each type of newspaper regard the language of their paper as being an acceptable norm and for some it may be their principal daily reading. Outside the United Kingdom, works in English – literary and journalistic – are published in the local variety. Each English variety has its own grammar, vocabulary, phonology and semantic interpretation of words. It is not possible to provide examples of these different forms here because of space and because this book is mainly concerned with the development of the standard in Britain. It is important to remember not only that these different varieties exist, but also that they have status in their own countries. While most users of British English may not come across these varieties frequently, some of them influence British English either because of their international status, such as the American variety, or because of their use by first- or second-generation immigrants within Britain. The future will probably see attempts resembling those of the eighteenth century to shore up the standard in Britain against the influences of these other varieties, though it will be much more difficult to achieve success now than it was then. Not everyone would accept that this is a necessary, or even a desirable, aim. The differences which have always existed in English have now won greater recognition and exposure because they are more widespread. A corollary of this development has been greater status for these different varieties, both in England and abroad, and those who try to re-establish norms in Britain will find it difficult to control the development of English within Britain, let alone in the rest of the world.

Notes

1. WHAT IS A HISTORY OF ENGLISH?

1. H. Sweet, 'The History of English Sounds', *Transactions of the Philological Society* (1873–4) 620.

2. BACKGROUND SURVEY

1. Quoted as a translation from a work by Wilhelm Scherer in H. Pedersen, *The Discovery of Language* (Cambridge, Mass.,1931; repr. Bloomington, Ind., 1962) p. 292.

3. BEFORE ALFRED

1. Quoted in H. Aarsleff, *The Study of Language in England 1780–1860* (Minneapolis, 1983; originally published in 1966) p.133.
2. In line 1 *herʒan* the <a> replaces an earlier <e> which has been dotted beneath for deletion and <a> is written above it.

4. THE FIRST ENGLISH STANDARD

1. The standard work is K. Sisam, *Studies in the History of Old English Literature* (Oxford, 1953) pp.1–28.
2. These are discussed in R. Vleeskruyer, *The Life of St Chad: An Old English Homily* (Amsterdam, 1953) esp. pp. 38–71.
3. See D. Whitelock, 'The Old English Bede', *Proceedings of the British Academy*, vol. 48 (1962) 57–90.
4. For the influence of the laws on a standard, see Mary P. Richards, 'Elements of a Written Standard in the Old English laws', in *Standardizing English,* ed. Joseph B. Trahern, Jr (Knoxville, Tenn.,1989) pp. 1–22.
5. See C. L. Wrenn, *Word and Symbol: Studies in English Language* (London, 1967) pp. 57–77, esp. pp. 66ff.
6. See M. R. Godden, *Ælfric's Catholic Homilies: The Second Series*, EETS ss 5 (London, 1979) pp. lxxviii ff.
7. See H. Gneuss, 'The Origin of Standard Old English', *Anglo-Saxon England*, vol. 1 (1972) 63–83.
8. See H. Schabram, *Superbia: Studien zum altenglischen Wortschatz* (Munich, 1965).

9. See, for example, Erik Björkman, 'Scandinavian Loan-Words in Middle English', *Studien zu englischen Philologie*, vol. 7 (Halle, 1900) esp. pp. 3–4.

10. For a study of this relationship, see N. F. Blake, 'Speech and Writing: An Historical Overview', *Yearbook of English Studies*, vol. 25 (1995) 6–21.

11. See Alarik Rynell, 'The Rivalry of Scandinavian and Native Synonyms in Middle English especially *Taken* and *Nimen*', *Lund Studies in English*, vol. 13 (Lund, 1948).

12. See D. Kastovsky, 'Semantics and Vocabulary', *Cambridge History of the English Language, vol. I: The Beginnings till 1066*, ed. R. M. Hogg (Cambridge, 1992) pp. 290–408 for further discussion.

5. THE AFTERMATH OF THE FIRST STANDARD

1. M. Richter, *Sprache und Gesellschaft im Mittelalter: Untersuchungen zur mundlichen Kommunikation in England von der Mitte des 11. bis zum Beginn des 14. Jahrhunderts* (Stuttgart, 1979) pp.68, 159.

2. Edward Edwards, *Liber monasterii de Hyda*, Rolls Ser. vol. 45 (London, 1866).

3. M. Godden, *Ælfric's Catholic Homilies, The Second Series: Text* (London, 1979) pp. xxvff.

4. A. Cameron, 'Middle English in Old English Manuscripts', in Beryl Rowland (ed.), *Chaucer and Middle English Studies* (London, 1974) pp. 218-229.

5 S. Kuhn, 'E and Æ in Farman's Mercian Glosses', *PMLA*, vol. 60 (1945) 666–7.

6. The author's name is spelt in a variety of ways in modern times; one of the other common spellings is *Lawman*.

7. For a recent discussion of this problem, see C. Cannon, 'The Style and Authorship of the Otho Revision of Laȝamon's *Brut*', *Medium Ævum*, vol. 62 (1993) 187–209.

8. The seminal article on the language and relationship of these manuscripts is J. R. R. Tolkien, '*Ancrene Wisse* and *Hali Meiðhad*', *Essays and Studies*, vol. 14 (1929) 104–26.

9. For a discussion of the spelling system and its date and localisation, see E. J. Dobson, *The Origins of Ancrene Wisse* (Oxford, 1976) esp. ch. 3.

6. INTERREGNUM: FRAGMENTATION AND REGROUPING

1. For a discussion of the status and use of the various languages in this period, see W. Rothwell, 'The Trilingual England of Geoffrey Chaucer,' *Studies in the Age of Chaucer*, vol. 16 (1994) 45–67.

2. Ibid., p. 53.

3. For a general account of this period leading to the flowering of

Notes 335

English, see Basil Cottle, *The Triumph of English 1350–1400* (London, 1969).

4. R. Morris, *Cursor Mundi*, vol. 1, EETS 57, pp. 20–2 based on British Library MS Cotton Vespasian A.iii in the northern dialect.

5. The best account of this feature of ME copying is M. Benskin and M. Laing, 'Translations and *Mischsprachen* in Middle English Manuscripts', in *So meny people longages and tonges*, ed. M. Benskin and M. L. Samuels (Edinburgh, 1981) pp. 55–106.

6. See E. Ekwall, *Studies on the Population of Medieval London* (Stockholm, 1956).

7. C. Clark, 'Another Late Fourteenth-Century Case of Dialect Awareness', *English Studies*, vol. 62 (1981) 504–5.

8. Churchill Babington, *Polychronicon Ranulphi Higden Monachi Cestrensis*. Rolls Series, vol. 2 (London, 1869) p.159.

9. 'Tota lingua Northimbrorum, maxime in Eboraco, ita stridet incondita, quod nos australes eam vix intelligere possumus' (ibid., p.162).

10. Edited in N. F. Blake, *The Canterbury Tales edited from the Hengwrt Manuscript* (London, 1980) p. 165.

11. For a general account of the project, see G. Kristensson, 'On Middle English Dialectology', in *So meny people longages and tonges*, ed. M. Benskin and M. L. Samuels (Edinburgh, 1981) pp. 3–13. The first volume of the project, which contains more details, is G. Kristensson, *A Survey of Middle English Dialects 1290–1350: the Six Northern Counties and Lincolnshire*, Lund Studies in English, vol. 35 (Lund, 1967); the second volume, covering the West Midlands counties, was published in 1987; the third, covering the East Midlands counties, in 1995.

12. For a brief account of the project, see M. Benskin, 'The Middle English Dialect Atlas', in *So meny people longages and tonges*, ed. M. Benskin and M. L. Samuels (Edinburgh, 1981) pp. xxvii–xli. For the atlas, which has further details, see A. McIntosh, M. L. Samuels, M. Benskin with assistance of M. Laing and K. Williamson, *A Linguistic Atlas of Late Medieval English*, 4 vols (Aberdeen, 1986).

13. This vocabulary is discussed in Anne Hudson, 'A Lollard Sect Vocabulary?', in *So meny people longages and tonges*, ed. M. Benskin and M. L. Samuels (Edinburgh, 1981) pp.15–30.

14. See J. D. Burnley, 'Chaucer's *termes*', *Yearbook of English Studies*, vol. 7 (1977) 53–67.

15. M. L. Samuels, 'Some Applications of Middle English Dialectology', *English Studies*, vol. 44 (1963) 81–94.

7. POLITICAL, SOCIAL AND PEDAGOGICAL BACKGROUND TO THE NEW STANDARD

1. See J. H. Fisher, *The Emergence of Standard English* (Lexington, Ky., 1996), and D. A. Pearsall, 'Hoccleve's *Regement of Princes:* The Poetics of Royal Self-Representation', *Speculum*, vol. 69 (1994) 386–410.

2. J. Otway-Ruthven, *The King's Secretary and the Signet Office in the XV Century* (Cambridge, 1939) p. 46.
3. As given in R. W. Chambers and Marjorie Daunt, *A Book of London English 1384–1425* (Oxford, 1931, repr. 1967) p. 139.
4. Details of spellings in Chancery documents are given in John H. Fisher, Malcolm Richardson and Jane L. Fisher, *An Anthology of Chancery English* (Knoxville, Tenn.,1984).
5. Ibid., no. 37 (p.102). The square brackets represent tears in the manuscript.
6. See C. Paul Christianson, 'Chancery Standard and the Records of Old London Bridge', in Joseph B. Trahern, Jr, *Standardizing English: Essays in the History of Language Change* (Knoxville, Tenn., 1989) pp. 82–112.
7. Norman Davis, 'A Paston Hand', *Review of English Studies*, n.s. 3 (1952) 209–21 and 'The Language of the Pastons', *Proceedings of the British Academy*, vol. 40 (1954) 119–44.
8. See Amy J. Devitt, *Standardizing Written English: Diffusion in the Case of Scotland 1520–1659* (Cambridge, 1989).
9. Dated about 1490 and quoted from N. F. Blake, *Caxton's Own Prose* (London, 1973) p. 79.
10. M. Eccles, *The Macro Plays*, EETS 262 (London, 1969) p.155.
11. See A. L. Mayhew, *The Promptorium Parvulorum: The First English–Latin Dictionary*, EETS e.s. 102 (London, 1908).

8. LANGUAGE CHANGE FROM 1400 TO 1600

1. J. J. Smith, 'Dialectal Variation in Middle English and the Actuation of the Great Vowel Shift', *Neuphilologische Mitteilungen*, vol. 94 (1993) 259–77.
2. See R. Wermser, *Statistische Studien zur Entwicklung des englischen Wortschatzes* (Bern, l976), for statistics relating to this period.

9. ESTABLISHING THE STANDARD WITHIN SOCIAL NORMS

1. See Eric Partridge, *Swift's Polite Conversation* (London, 1963). In fact Swift's attack is here mostly against fashionable words and idioms which are peculiar to the upper classes. He writes 'I HAVE rejected all Provincial, or Country Turns of Wit, and Fancy, because I am acquainted with a very few; but indeed, chiefly, because I found them so very inferior to those at Court, especially among Gentlemen Ushers, the Ladies of the Bed-Chamber, and the Maids of Honour. I must also add the hither end of our noble Metropolis' (p. 36).
2. *Samuel Johnson The Rambler*, ed. W. J. Bate and A. B. Strauss, vol. 3 (New Haven, Conn. and London, 1969) p.126.
3. 'On the Death of Dr Swift', in *Jonathan Swift*, ed. Angus Ross and David Woolley (Oxford, 1984) p. 526.

4. I. Tieken-Boon van Ostade, *The Auxiliary Do in Eighteenth-century English: A Sociohistorical-linguistic Approach* (Dordrecht, 1987) p. 228.
5. They are discussed fully in S. A. Leonard, *The Doctrine of Correctness in English Usage 1700–1800*. University of Wisconsin Studies in Language and Literature 25 (Madison, Wis., 1929; repr. 1962).
6. See I. Tieken-Boon van Ostade, 'Double Negation and Eighteenth-century English Grammars', *Neophilologus*, vol. 66 (1982) 278–85.
7. See Susie I. Tucker, *Protean Shape: A Study in Eighteenth-century Vocabulary and Usage* (London, 1967).
8. *Spectator*, no. 165, 8 September 1711.
9. Quoted in Tucker, *Protean Shape*, p. 109.
10. Edited in the *Spectator*, vol. 2 by Donald F. Bond (Oxford, 1965) pp. 33–4.
11. For this period, see John Barrell, 'The Language Properly So-called: The Authority Of Common Usage', in his *English Literature in History 1730–80: An Equal, Wide Survey* (London, 1983) pp.110–75; and Dieter Stein, *The Semantics of Syntactic Change: Aspects of the Evolution of 'do' in English* (Berlin, 1990).

10. EMANCIPATION, EDUCATION AND EMPIRE

1. On William Cobbett, see F. Aarts, 'William Cobbett's "Grammar of the English Language"', *Neuphilologische Mitteilungen*, vol. 95 (1994) 319–32.
2. J. W. Adamson, *English Education, 1789–1902* (Cambridge, 1930) p. 43.
3. Quotations are based on the 1823 edition in the reprint prepared by R. Burchfield (Oxford, 1984).
4. H. Alford, *The Queen's English: Stray Notes on Speaking and Spelling* (London, 1864) p. 6.
5. W. W. Skeat, 'The Proverbs of Alfred', *Transactions of the Philological Society* (1895–8) 415.
6. Hansard's *Parliamentary Debates* xxx 779, quoted in Olivia Smith, *The Politics of Language 1791–1819* (Oxford, 1984) pp. 30–1.
7. Hans Aarsleff, *The Study of Language in England, 1780–1860* (London, 1983) p. 134.
8. Quoted from the seventh edition (London, 1870) p. 3.
9. H. S. Solly, *The Life of Henry Morley, LL.D.* (London,1898) p. 330.
10. 'General Explanations' in the *Preface* reprinted in W. F. Bolton and D. Crystal, *The English Language*, vol. 2: *Essays by Linguists and Men of Letters 1858–1964* (Cambridge, 1969) pp. 59–79.
11. K. C. Phillipps, *Language & Class in Victorian England* (Oxford, 1984) pp. 70–8.
12. See M. Rydén and S. Brorström, *The Be/Have Variation with Intransitives in English* (Stockholm, 1987).
13. Quoted in Phillipps, *Language & Class*, p. 69.

11. WORLD DOMINATION AND GROWING VARIATION

1. See further Brian Cox, *Cox on the Battle for the English Curriculum* (London, 1995).
2. H. C. Wyld, 'The Best English: A Claim for the Superiority of Received Standard English', *Society for Pure English*, vol. 4, tract no. xxxix (Oxford, 1934).
3. Daniel Jones, *The Pronunciation of English* (Cambridge, 1909); this book was frequently reprinted.
4. Henry Newbolt, *The Teaching of English in England: Being the Report of the Departmental Committee appointed by the President of the Board of Education to enquire into the Position of English in the Educational System of England* (London, 1921).
5. *English for Ages 5 to 16* (London, 1989).

Suggested Further
Reading

For a general study of historical linguistics, see Winfred P. Lehmann, *Historical Linguistics*, 3rd edn (London and New York, 1992). For books on the processes of change in language, see Jean Aitchison, *Language Change: Progress or Decay?*, 2nd edn (Cambridge,1991); William Labov, *Principles of Linguistic Change: Internal Factors* (Oxford, 1994), and April M. S. McMahon, *Understanding Language Change* (Cambridge, 1994).

The standard history of the language is the *Cambridge History of the English Language* (gen. ed. Richard Hogg, Cambridge University Press), of which three volumes have so far [1995] been issued: vol. 1, *The Beginnings to 1066*, ed. R. M. Hogg (1992); vol. 2, *1066–1476*, ed. N. F. Blake (1992); and vol. 5, *English in Britain and Overseas: Origin and Development*, ed. Robert Burchfield (1994). The other three volumes are vol. 3, *Early Modern English*, ed. Roger Lass; vol. 4, *Modern English*, ed. Suzanne Romaine; and vol. 6, *English in North America*, ed. J. Algeo. Each volume contains an extensive bibliography. There are numerous other histories of the language. A wide-ranging approach is adopted in Richard W. Bailey, *Images of English: A Cultural History of the Language* (Cambridge, 1992). A good general account is to be found in Roger Lass, *The Shape of English: Structure and History* (Dent, 1987). Important general issues are raised in M. L. Samuels, *Linguistic Evolution with Special Reference to English* (Cambridge, 1972). Colloquial language is dealt with in H. C. Wyld, *A History of Modern Colloquial English*, 3rd edn (Oxford, 1936).

For texts to illustrate the history of English, see David Burnley, *The History of the English Language: A Source Book* (London, 1992). The Helsinki corpus contains texts in computer form derived from modern printed editions and covering various genres until the seventeenth century; for details see M. Kytö, *Manual to the Diachronic Part of the Helsinki Corpus of English Texts* (Helsinki, 1991). Texts to illustrate the origin and development of Chancery English are given in John H. Fisher, Malcolm Richardson and Jane L. Fisher, *An Anthology of Chancery English* (Knoxville, Tenn., 1984). For readings to illustrate attitudes towards the language see Susie I. Tucker, *English Examined: A Collection of Views on the Nature, Resources and Use of the English Language by Writers of the 17th and 18th Centuries* (Cambridge, 1961); W. F. Bolton and D. Crystal, *The English Language*, vol. 2: *Essays by Linguistis and Men of Letters 1858–1964* (Cambridge,1969); and Tony Crowley, *Proper English? Readings in Language, History and Cultural Identity* (London, 1991).

For the question of authority in language, see James and Lesley Milroy, *Authority in Language: Investigating Language Prescription and Standardisation*, 2nd edn (London, 1991). See also Richard Foster Jones, *The Triumph of the English Language: A Survey of Opinions conerning the Vernacular from the Introduction of Printing to the Restoration* (Stanford, Calif., n.d.); S. A. Leonard, *The Doctrine of Correctness in English Usage 1700–1800* (repr. New York, 1962); Olivia Smith, *The Politics of Language 1791–1819* (Oxford, 1984); K. C. Phillipps, *Language and Class in Victorian England* (Oxford, 1984); Tony Crowley, *The Politics of Discourse: the Standard Language Question in British Cultural Debates* (Basingstoke and London, 1989); Lynda Mugglestone, *'Talking Proper': the Rise of Accent as Social Symbol* (Oxford, 1995); and John Honey, *Does Accent Matter?* (London, 1989).

For books on grammatical teaching and linguistic theory, see Ian Michael, *English Grammatical Categories and the Tradition to 1800* (Cambridge, 1970) and his *The Teaching of English from the Sixteenth Century to 1870* (Cambridge, 1987); G. A. Padley, *Grammatical Theory in Western Europe 1500–1700: Trends in Vernacular Grammar* (Cambridge, 1985); Murray Cohen, *Sensible Words: Linguistic Practice in England 1640–1785* (Baltimore and London, 1977); Hans Aarsleff, *The Study of Language in England 1780–1860* (Minneapolis and London, 1983); and Holger Pedersen, *The Discovery of Language: Linguistic Science in the 19th Century* (Cambridge, Mass., 1931, repr. 1959).

For spelling, see D. G. Scragg, *A History of Spelling in English* (Manchester and New York, 1974). For English phonology, see Charles Jones, *A History of English Phonology* (London, 1989); and E. J. Dobson, *English Pronunciation 1500–1700*, 2 vols, 2nd edn (Oxford, 1957). For syntax, see E. C. Traugott, *A History of English Syntax* (New York, 1972) and F. Visser, *An Historical Syntax of the English Language*, 3 vols (Leiden, 1963–73). For lexis and word formation, see Mary S. Serjeantson, *A History of Foreign Words in English* (London, 1935); Susie I. Tucker, *Protean Shape: A Study in Eighteenth-Century Vocbulary and Usage* (London, 1967); G. Cannon, *Historical Change and English Word-Formation* (New York and Bern, 1987); James B. Greenhough and George L. Kittredge, *Words and their Ways in English Speech* (London, 1900); and Richard W. Bailey, *Dictionaries of English: Prospects for the Record of Our Language* (Cambridge,1989).

For books about individual periods, see J. W. Clark, *Early English* (London, 1957); R. M. Hogg, *A Grammar of Old English*, vol. 1: *Phonology* (Oxford, 1992); A. McIntosh and M. L. Samuels *et al.*, *A Linguistic Atlas of Late Medieval English*, 4 vols (Aberdeen, 1986); M. Görlach, *Introduction to Early Modern English* (Cambridge, 1991); Amy J. Devitt, *Standardizing Written English: Diffusion in the Case of Scotland 1520–1659* (Cambridge, 1989); and Brian Foster, *The Changing English Language* (London, 1968).

For non-British varieties, see H. L. Mencken, *The American Language: An Inquiry into the Development of English in the United States* (London, 1922); David Simpson, *The Politics of American English, 1776–1850* (New York and Oxford, 1986), and J. Platt, H. Weber and M. L. Ho, *The New Englishes* (London, 1984).

Appendix

GLOSSARY OF TECHNICAL TERMS

The following list contains both linguistic and other terms which may be unfamiliar to the reader.

ablative absolute A phrase consisting in Latin of a noun in the ablative case and a participle agreeing with it acting as a non-finite clause; when imitated in English the noun is in the dative (in older branches of the language) or otherwise the base and the participle agrees with it where possible. Cf. OE *siʒe ʒewunnenum* 'the victory having been won' and ModE 'the mission accomplished'.

ablaut Variation in the root vowel of a word to form different parts of a paradigm or different words from the same root. Ablaut is found in PIE and its descendants. Cf. ModE *ride, rode, ridden*.

accusative In traditional grammar the direct object case usually indicated by an inflection.

active A clause in which the subject is the actor of the verb; cf. **passive.**

adjective In traditional grammar a word which describes a noun, thus *lovely* in *a lovely day*; an **adjectival group** is a group of words occupying the same position and function.

adverb, adverbial In traditional grammar an **adverb** describes a verb or some other parts of speech like an adjective, as in 'He drives *slowly*' and '*extremely* unlucky'. An **adverbial** is any word or words which fulfil the function of an adverb.

affix A general term for a bound morpheme embracing **prefix** and **suffix** as well as a morpheme inserted in the middle of a word.

affricate A consonant formed by stopping the air flow and then releasing it to a fricative.

agent-noun A noun which expresses the person who deliberately does an action, so 'a murderer' is someone who murders.

alliteration The repetition of the same sound at the beginning of two or more words in close proximity, as in 'Time and tide wait for no man'.

allophone An individual sound which is one of those which together make up a **phoneme.**

alveolar Sounds formed by the tongue closing the air passage at the alveolar ridge (immediately behind the front top teeth).

analogy The tendency to make all examples of a feature (e.g. plurals) conform to the dominant pattern (in English -*(e)s* to form the plural).

analytic A term referring to languages which express grammatical

341

relationships through arranging words in a specific order rather than through inflections.

archaism A word or phrase which has become obsolete and is reintroduced into the language.

article In traditional grammar the name given to *a, an* (indefinite article) and to *the* (definite article).

aspirate Principally used to refer to /h/ at the beginning of words.

assimilation The process whereby two different adjacent sounds become similar or identical, so that /st/ becomes /ss/.

auxiliary A verb which is part of a verb group, but is never its head; it 'helps' the lexical verb by indicating tense or modality.

back vowel A vowel formed when the tongue constricts the air flow at the back of the mouth.

Black English Vernacular A term given to the language of young black Americans.

bilingualism Referring to the ability to speak two languages fluently.

bisyllabic A word consisting of two syllables.

borrowing The process of taking words from another language and naturalising them.

branding A system used in some dictionaries to mark words which the compiler disapproves of.

breaking (or fracture) A sound change by which a vowel when followed by certain consonants is turned into a diphthong.

calque A compound word which re-creates in one language the components of a word in another, e.g. ModE 'skyskraper' produces ModG 'Wolkenkratzer'.

cartulary A collection of charters and other documents belonging to a (religious) foundation

case In traditional grammar case refers to the different functions of a noun or adjective expressed through inflectional endings, e.g. nominative.

central vowel A vowel made when the tongue constricts the airflow in the centre of the mouth.

clause In traditional grammar a clause consists of a group of words with at least a subject and a verb; the **main clause** makes sense on its own; a **subordinate clause** needs a main clause to form a complete sentence.

closed syllable A syllable that when final ends with a consonant and otherwise is followed by two consonants.

complementary distribution The situation where two linguistic features, e.g. sounds, are found in mutually exclusive environments though they are not phonemic. The voiced and voiceless forms of <th> occur in different environments, e.g. 'thin, then', but are not phonemically distinctive.

completive Words or morphemes which convey a meaning of completion.

complex sentence A sentence consisting of a main and at least one subordinate clause.

compound noun A noun which consists of two free morphemes, e.g. 'war-weary'; the process of forming such words is known as **compounding**.

conjunction A word which joins together words, groups or clauses. A **co-ordinating** conjunction joins together elements of equal weight, e.g. 'and', and a **subordinating conjunction** joins together elements of unequal weight such as a main and a subordinate clause, e.g. 'when'.

connotation The associations attached to a word which are not necessarily reflected in that word's dictionary definition.

consonant A sound produced by blocking the airstream through the mouth either totally or partially.

co-referential A part of speech which refers to the same person or thing as another part of speech is said to be co-referential with it.

dative In traditional grammar the case which denotes the indirect object or follows prepositions with the general sense of motion towards.

declarative A clause which expresses a statement rather than a command or question, and in Modern English usually has the word order SVO.

dental A consonant sound made when the tongue touches the upper teeth.

descriptive Used to describe a grammar or dictionary which is based on features actually found in a language as compared with those which ought to be used, cf. **prescriptive**.

determiner A member of a mutually exclusive group which comes before the head of a noun group. Examples include 'the, those'.

diachronic The study of language historically, i.e. over time.

dialect A variety of a language which is treated as a sub-group of that language rather than as a language in its own right; the boundary between dialectsand languages is blurred and often depends upon political considerations.

digraph Two letters used to express a single sound, e.g. <th>.

diphthong Two vowel sounds in succession which remain as a separate group; to **diphthongise** is to change a vowel into a diphthong.

double negative The use of two negatives in a clause to increase the sense of negation, as in 'I don't want none'. This type of negation was condemned by prescriptive grammarians.

dual see **number**.

dummy subject A subject like 'it' introduced because the grammatical system demands that a subject is included in a clause.

ethic dative A dative which has little sematic input, but which is used with some verbs for emphasis.

etymology The study of the origins of words.

finite A clause which contains a part of a verb which can stand alone so that the clause is a complete entity. 'He lives here' is an acceptable sentence, whereas 'He living here' is not; 'lives' is a finite part of the verb and 'living' is **non-finite**.

formal/informal Used to refer to different levels of language in use with **formal** being close to the written mode and **informal** to the colloquial one.

fossil A linguistic feature which has been preserved in a language without regard to changes in the linguistic system as a whole. Old past participles in -*en* like 'proven' are fossils in English.

fracture see **breaking**

fricative A consonant made when the air passage is constricted rather than closed completely.

fronting The process whereby a back vowel is changed to the corresponding front vowel. In Old English there was a first and a second fronting.

front mutation The sound change caused by an /i/ or /j/ in a following syllable which caused back vowels to be fronted to their corresponding front ones; also known as **i mutation.**

front vowel A vowel made when the tongue constricts the airflow in the front of the mouth.

functional shift The process whereby one part of speech is used in a different function, thus a noun like 'power' can be used in the adjective position in 'power cut'.

gemmination The process whereby a consonant is doubled for some cause.

genitive In traditional grammar the case which expresses possession as in 'the *boy's* book'.

Germanic One of the Proto-Indo-European language groups consisting of East, West and North Germanic. English is a West Germanic language.

gerund A noun derived from a verb participle, e.g. *smoking* from *to smoke.*

grammatical function The employment of lexical items for a grammatical rather than a lexical purpose.

grammaticalise The process whereby a linguistic structure which had been optional is made compulsory, as when *do* which had been optional in negatives is made obligatory to express negation.

graph A written symbol which may or may not have a phonetic realisation in itself.

great vowel shift That process operative in England during the fifteenth and sixteenth centuries whereby long vowels were raised or, if already high vowels, were diphthongised.

head That element of a group, e.g. noun group, upon which the other elements depend, so that in 'this happy band of brothers' *band* is the head.

hypercorrection The introduction through analogy or social pressure of a linguistic feature where it is not etymologically appropriate, so that Amsterdam may be pronounced with initial /h/ because sounding initial /h/ is considered to be a marker of social class.

hypotaxis The employment of complex sentences with subordinate clauses.

imperative A sentence which expresses a command; in Modern English imperatives have no subject. 'Fire' is an imperative sentence.

impersonal A verb with no expressed subject or with a dummy subject like 'it' such as 'It's raining'.

indicative A clause which expresses a statement rather than a command or wish.

infinitive The infinitive is a non-finite part of the verb and usually acts as the headword of a verb in dictionaries. Its forms include the base form (the verb itself 'see'), the *to*-form ('to see'), a perfect ('to have seen') and a passive ('to have been seen'). Earlier English had an inflected form which could express purpose.

inflection A bound morpheme usually attached to the ends of words to express the grammatical function the word has in a clause.

inkhorn controversy The name given to the dispute in the sixteenth and seventeenth centuries about the propriety of borrowing classical words into English.

instrumental In traditional grammar the case which is expressed today by the prepositions 'by' or 'with' and implies the instrument with which something is done.

intensifier An adverbial which 'intensifies' the meaning of an adjective or another adverb, as in '*really* interesting'.

interjection In traditional grammar that part of speech which is outside the boundary of a normal clause and expresses some emotional reaction to what is stated, such as 'Oh, Goodness me'.

interrogative A sentence which consists of a question and in ModE has the order auxSV.

intransitive A verb which does not take an object, such as 'to go'.

justification The process of making the right hand margin of a page straight so that the page looks neat.

labial A sound made by blocking the airstream through closing the lips.

lengthening The change of a short vowel or consonant into a long one.

levelling The process of making different sounds coalesce under a single one.

lexical word A word which has semantic meaning, like 'boy', rather than a grammatical function such as 'the'.

lexicon The total number of words found in a given language.

lexis The items of vocabulary in a language.

liquid Traditionally includes both *r* and *l* sounds.

loan(word) A word borrowed in one language from another.

lowering The process of lowering the tongue so that a different vowel is produced lower in the mouth.

malapropism The use of a morpheme or a word incorrectly, as to say *dissent* instead of *consent*.

metathesis The process of changing the order of linguistic units often found in speech so that *brid* becomes *bird*.

Mischsprache A term used to describe written language which contains different dialect forms through various stages of copying.

modal Those auxiliaries like *may* and *will* which express mood, aspect or tense.

monophthong A single vowel sound as distinct from a **diphthong**; to **monophthongise** is to turn a diphthong into a monophthong.

monosyllable A word consisting of a single syllable.

mood The term used to embrace indicative, subjunctive and imperative.

morpheme The smallest distinctive unit of meaning in a grammar; a free morpheme is also a word by itself but a bound morpheme must be attached to another morpheme to form a word. Thus in *unkindness, un-* and *-ness* are bound morphemes, but *kind* is a free morpheme. **Morphology** includes the study of morphemes and the inventory of morphemes in a language.

multilingualism The ability to speak more than two languages competently or the situation where several languages are spoken in a community.

mutation The term used to refer to specific changes in language.

nasal Sounds formed by letting air escape through the nasal passage.

Neogrammarian A grammarian who accepted that sound rules were inflexible and uniform in their operation in a language; the concept is particularly associated with nineteenth-century historical linguists.

nominative In traditional grammar the case which represented the subject.

non-finite A part of the verb which by itself cannot form an independent verb group.

non-standard Linguistic forms which do not conform to people's understanding of what the standard is for their own language.

noun In traditional grammar that part of speech which is said to refer to person, place or thing.

noun group A word or words which together can act as the subject of a sentence; 'the little brown jug' is a noun group because it can act as a subject.

number The term which refers to quantity and is divided into **singular** (only one), **dual** (only two) and **plural** (more than one if no dual exists, otherwise more than two).

object In traditional grammar the object suffers the action of the verb so that in 'He hit her' *her* is the object or **direct** object; the **indirect** object fulfils the function of dative, so that 'He gave her the book' *her* is the indirect object because the book is given *to her*.

oblique Any case other than that expressing the subject.

open syllable A syllable ending in a vowel or in a bisyllabic word the first syllable when followed by a single consonant.

open syllable lengthening The change of short vowels to long vowels which occurred in the post-Conquest period when the short vowel was in an **open syllable**.

orthography The term used to describe a spelling, often the approved, system in a language.

palatal A consonant formed by restricting the air flow by placing the tongue at or near the hard palate. **Palatalisation** is the process of turning other consonants into palatals.

palatal umlaut The change occurring in the tenth and eleventh centuries whereby /e/ was raised to /i/ and /eo/ monophthongised and then raised to /i/, cf. ModE *right* with ModG *Recht*.

paradigm The pattern or system of inflections in a noun, adjective, pronoun or verb.

parataxis The term used to describe a succession of main clauses with no or few subordinate ones.

participle A non-finite part of the verb used as an adjective or as the head of a verb group after one or more auxiliaries. In ModE the present participle ends in -*ing*; the past participle has various endings, usually either -*en* or -*(e)d/t*.

part of speech In traditional grammar the various categories into which all words were divided, such as noun, adjective, etc. Their number was never fixed for English.

passive A clause in which the actor of the verb is not the grammatical subject: in 'John was killed by Mark' the actor of the verb is *Mark*, but *John* is the grammatical subject.

perfect The past form of the verb formed with the auxiliary *has/have*, or earlier also by part of the verb *to be*, and the past participle e.g. 'He has arrived'.

person In verb paradigms the persons include first (i.e. the speaker), second (the person addressed) or third (neither speaker nor person addressed); plurals are the same but with more than one person.

philology The name given to the study of language which focussed particularly on the historical development of languages with particular reference to sound change. Philology gave special emphasis to older stages of a language.

phoneme The minimal meaningful unit in the sound system of a language. A sound is meaningful if substituting another sound changes the meaning of a word, cf. 'pit' with 'bit'.

phonetics The study of the sounds which can be made by humans.

phonology The study of the sound system of a particular language.

phrasal conjunction A conjunction which consists of more than one word, e.g. 'in view of'.

phrasal verb A verb which consists of the head and a postposed adverbial preposition so that the two have a different meaning from the simple verb, e.g. 'to go off' compared with 'to go'.

pluperfect The verb tense formed by *had* and the past participle, e.g. 'He had arrived'.

polysyllable A word consisting of more than two syllables, e.g. 'admirable'.

post-modifier A group of words coming after the head of a noun group; in 'The House of Lords', *of Lords* is the post-modifier after the head *House.*

pre-determiner A linguistic item which comes before the determiner in the noun group; in 'all the best men', *all* is the pre-determiner before the determiner *the.*

predicate In traditional grammar that part of the clause other than the subject.

prefix A morpheme attached to the front of a word usually to alter its meaning, as *un-* does in *unwelcome.*

pre-modal Those verbs which became modals in English, but which were not full modals in the earlier history of the language.

pre-modifier That part of the noun group which comes before the head other than the determiner; in 'the blessed Virgin', *blessed* is a pre-modifier to the head *Virgin.* A pre-modifier is often the same as an adjective, but they are not identical.

preposition A word such as *to* or *from* which precedes a noun group and expresses the relationship of that group to the rest of the clause.

prescriptive Used of grammars which prescribe rules of usage rather than describe the data found in the language.

preterite The simple past tense without an auxiliary which expresses a completed action in the past without specific relevance to the time of utterance, e.g. 'He arrived yesterday'.

preterite-present Those verbs which turned their preterites into a present tense and formed new preterites; in English they are mostly the modals.

progressive The tense formed by a part of the verb 'to be' and the present participle to express an action in progress, e.g. 'He *is coming*'.

pronoun In traditional grammar a word class said to stand in place of a noun, so that 'He' can stand instead of 'the man' or 'that' instead of 'the train'.

propword The word 'one' which can be used instead of a noun, as in 'the big one'.

raising The process of raising a vowel in height so that, for example, a low vowel becomes a low-mid vowel.

Received Pronunciation That pronunciation with social status which is recommended by some as the correct and best pronunciation of English.

reduplication The process of repeating a sound or group of sounds in a word; this process cannot be seen in ModE, but in the past was used to form certain verb forms.

reflexive Verbs which have a personal pronoun or in ModE a reflexive pronoun as the object of a verb which refers to the same person as the subject.

register A variety of language which is employed in relation to the social environment in which it is used.

restrictive clause A relative clause which restricts the reference of the noun to which it refers and is not in Modern English enclosed within commas; a **non-restrictive** clause does not have this restriction. Thus 'Pilots who are foolish die young' restricts the sense to those pilots who are foolish, whereas 'Pilots, who are foolish, die young' implies that all pilots are foolish and die young.

resumptive Used to refer to a pronoun which is introduced into a clause even though the noun to which it refers is also in the same clause, as in 'That **man** over there, **he** looks crooked'.

retraction The opposite of **fronting**; the change of a front vowel to the equivalent back one.

Romance The Italic language family embracing in modern times all those languages derived from Latin.

rounded vowel A vowel formed with the lips rounded as the air issues out.

runes The early Germanic writing system; its alphabet is known as *futhark*.

schwa The central vowel /ə/ found in many unstressed syllables in English.

scriptorium The room used for copying manuscripts before the age of printing (pl. **scriptoria**).

smoothing The term used to describe the monophthongisation of diphthongs in the post-Conquest period.

sociolinguistics The study of language within its social use.

sound change The term used to express changes within a sound system, though the representation is schematised.

standard That variety which cuts across regional differences and has become institutionalised as the status variety within a country.

stop A consonant made by blocking the air stream completely for a moment.

stress The degree of force used to utter a syllable; where a high degree is used a syllable is said to be **stressed**, where not it is said to be **unstressed.**

strong noun/verb Terms used to describe particular paradigms of noun and verb; the name is arbitrary. Their opposites are **weak** nouns or verbs.

Structuralism The term used to describe the theory which sees language as consisting of systems and the study of language as focussing on the description of the structures.

subject The noun group which is usually the actor of the verb and in statements in Modern English precedes the verb.

subjunctive The mood which traditionally expressed a wish or a hypothetical statement, but it is hardly significant in Modern English, e.g. 'If I **were** you...'.

suffix A bound morpheme added to the end of a word, as -*ism* in *Structuralism*.

synchronic The study of language at one moment in time without reference to that language's past or future development.

syncope The term used to describe the elision of a syllable especially in the middle of a word, as in ModE *medicine*, which is usually pronounced as *med'cine*.

syndetic The term used to describe clauses which are joined together by conjunctions. Its opposite is *asyndetic*.

syntax The study of the grammatical relations of a language especially with words, groups and clauses.

synthetic A language which expresses its grammatical relations through inflections rather than through word order.

tense Traditionally used to indicate how verbs are related to different times (present, past, future) through the use of morphemes.

transitive A verb which takes a direct object.

triphthong Three vowel sounds in sequence, as in ModE *fire*.

umlaut See **mutation**

velar A sound produced when the back of the tongue is in contact with the soft palate or velum.

verb group One or more words which together make up the verb group which is normally the essential element of all clauses.

verb second/final Terms used to define languages from the position of the verb; when second the verb comes after the first element of the clause and when final it comes at the end of the clause.

voice A sound is said to be voiced if the vocal cords vibrate when it is pronounced; otherwise it is said to be **unvoiced**.

vowel A sound produced when there is no interruption of the air stream through the mouth. Vowels can be **long** or **short**, **rounded** or **unrounded**, and produced with the tongue at different heights or positions in the mouth.

vowel alternation See **ablaut**; also known as **gradation**.

zero relative A relative clause in which the relative pronoun is not expressed. 'The boy Ø *I love* is coming to tea'.

PHONETIC SCRIPT

A simplified system of phonetic symbols has been used in this book as detailed below. Only those symbols used in it are listed here. Phonetic symbols are used only when a sound is regarded as a phoneme and included within slashes, e.g. /o/, or is a specific sound rather than a phoneme and included in square brackets, e.g. [o].

Vowels and diphthongs

Vowels are mainly classified by the position of the tongue in the mouth: its height (high, mid high, mid low, and low) and which part of the tongue is used to form the vowels (front, central or back). Vowels can also be rounded; but unless rounding is specified it may be assumed that front vowels are unrounded. Back vowels are rounded. Length is indicated by a colon (:) following the equivalent short vowel; vowels and diphthongs are short unless they have this colon. Diphthongs are made up of two vowel sounds.

i	front high vowel
y	front high vowel with rounding
e	mid high front vowel
œ	mid high front vowel with rounding
ɛ	mid low front vowel
æ	low front vowel
a	low front vowel, but slightly further back than æ
ə	mid central vowel
u	high back vowel with rounding
ʊ	mid high vowel slightly further forward than *u* with rounding
o	mid high back vowel with rounding
ɔ	mid low back vowel with rounding
ʌ	mid low back vowel slightly further forward than ɔ
ɑ	low back vowel with rounding
ɒ	low back vowel slightly further forward than ɑ

Consonants

Consonants are formed through blocking or constricting the passage of air through the mouth and are classified mainly through the place of articulation and the level of blockage or constriction. Consonants can be voiced or unvoiced.

Stops with total blockage of the air stream

b	voiced labial
p	unvoiced labial
d	voiced alveolar
t	unvoiced alveolar

Affricates with complete blockage leading to constriction in the place of articulation

dʒ	voiced palato-alveolar
tʃ	unvoiced palato-alveolar

Fricatives with constriction at the place of articulation

v	voiced labiodental
f	unvoiced labiodental
z	voiced alveolar
s	unvoiced alveolar
ʒ	voiced palato-alveolar
ʃ	unvoiced palato-alveolar
j	voiced palatal
ç	unvoiced palatal
χ	unvoiced velar
ɣ	voiced velar
h	unvoiced glottal

Nasals

m	voiced labial
n	voiced alveolar
ŋ	voiced velar

Liquids

l	voiced alveolar
r	voiced alveolar trill

Index

GENERAL

abbreviation 101–2, 135, 162,
205, 221, 233, 241, 245, 265,
269, 281, 285, 296, 318, 323
Abingdon 87
ablative absolute 35
ablaut 66, 96
Academie Française 237
Academy, ideas about 22, 33,
246–7
Accedence 199
Adam 147
Addison, J. 254, 257, 262, 265–6,
268–9
Spectator 268–71
adjective 27, 31, 65, 96, 146–9,
155–6, 165–6, 178, 200, 234,
249, 261–2
comparative 147, 219, 260, 271
double 219, 260–1
demonstrative 98, 103, 121,
149, 221, 262
gender 65, 121
possessive 121, 165
strong 121
superlative 103, 121, 147, 165
weak 103, 121, 146, 165
administration 279
adverb 27, 67, 70, 99, 100, 146,
152, 155, 179, 200, 224, 226,
249, 261, 296, 321
adverbial 41, 97–8, 121, 156, 234
advertising 184, 267, 307,
317–18, 329, 331
Ælfric, abbot of Eynsham 18,
89–90, 101–5, 119, 128, 225
correction to texts 90
grammar 18, 89–90, 114
sermons 89, 128
Catholic Homilies, second
series 101–4, 113

Colloquy 90
Æthelberht, king of Kent 57, 86
Æthelflæd, Alfred's daughter
81–2
Æthelmær 89
Æthelred, king of Wessex 77
Æthelred, Mercian ealdorman 81
Æthelred the Unready, king of
England 105
Æthelwold, bishop of
Winchester 89–90, 104
Regularis concordia 89
affix 202, 228–9, 267, 326
Africa 34, 279, 282
Agincourt 11, 133, 174
Alcuin 82
Aldhelm 82
Alford, H., dean of Canterbury
278–9, 292–5, 301–2
Queen's English 279, 292, 301–2
Alfred, king of Wessex 3, 8–9,
18, 47, 76ff, 175
alliteration 95, 97, 119, 126–9,
168
alliterative revival 158, 168
allophones 210
alphabet
phonetic 25, 255
Roman 18
runic 17, 56–7
America, North 15, 34, 202, 214,
248, 265–6, 275, 277–9, 303–4,
310, 316, 319–20, 322–3, 328
Declaration of Independence
277
Americanism 5, 331
analogy 40, 258
Ancrene Wisse 21, 125, 129
Angles 3, 53–4
Anglo-Frisian 53

353

Anglo-Norman 111–13, 133–5,
    140–2, 205–6, 215
Anglo-Saxon Chronicle 18, 75,
    86ff, 111, 114–15
Anglo-Saxons 2–4, 17–18, 32–4,
    54–8, 64, 77, 80ff, 107–9, 201
Anjou, earl of 117
Anne, queen of England 236, 255
anthropology 310
apostrophe 207, 261–2, 269, 292,
    318
    Barclays Bank 318
Aquitaine 132–3
Areley Kings (Worcs) 117–18
Arthur 127
article 51, 70, 98, 120, 147, 149,
    165–6, 178, 200, 221, 234,
    249–50, 328
    position of 328
    suffixed 51
Ascham, R. 199–200
Asia 47, 282
Asiatic Researches 282
Asser, bishop of Sherbourne 84
Athelney 84
Athelstan, king of England 81–2
Atlantic 277–8
Augustan period 245, 272
Augustine of England 3, 56–7
Augustine, St, *Soliloquies* 86
Australia 279
auxiliaries 35, 99, 179, 220,
    222–6, 262–3, 329
    do 100–1, 152–3, 179, 223–4,
        226, 264, 294–6, 329–30
    gin 152–3
    grammaticalised 223–4, 264
    modal 99, 121, 151, 153, 220–3,
        263–4, 296
    pre-modals 99, 121, 152–3
Awdeley, J., *Fraternitie of
    Vacabondes* 192

back mutation 62 103
Bacon, F. 182
    Novum organum 221
Bailey, N., *Universal Dictionary*
    251–2
Barclays Bank 318

Battle of Maldon 105
Bayeux Tapestry 107
BBC 306–7
Bede 56, 69–72, 75, 82, 86
    Historia ecclesiastica 53, 69, 86
Bedfordshire 170
Beowulf 95, 97
Berkeley (Glos.) 142
Bernard St, of Clairvaux 134
Bernicia 56
Bible 51, 174, 186, 241, 245, 250,
    264, 274, 285, 294
    New Testament 250
    St Matthew 195
bilingualism 44, 109
Black English Vernacular 37
Blund, John 112
Bobbitt, Mrs 322
Boer War 300
Boethius, *De consolatione* 86
Boniface 82
borrowing 30, 41, 194–5, 227–8,
    242, 265, 322
Boswell, J. 240, 258
Bosworth, battle of 4
Bourchier, W. 180
Bourne (Lincs) 21
breaking/fracture 60–1, 72, 103
Bretigny, treaty of 133
Bretwalda 56
Britain 5, 13, 31, 53–5, 75–7, 81,
    203, 276–7, 300, 307–8, 310,
    316–20, 332–3
    immigration 307
Britons 53, 307
Browning, R. 14, 288
Brunanburh, battle of 82
Brutus 127
Bullokar, J., *English Expositor* 198
Bullokar, W. 190
Burgred, king of Mercia 81
Burgundy 89
Byrhtnoth, ealdorman 105
Byron, Lord 288

Cædmon 69
'Cædmon's Hymn' 18, 69ff, 76,
    82, 88
Cæsar, Julius 26

Calais 133
Calcutta, Asiatick Society 47
calque 97
Cambridge 142, 283, 286
Cameron, A. 114
Canada 279
Canute, king of England 33, 79,
    105–6
Caribbean 265
case 64–6, 152
    ablative 66
    accusative 52, 65ff, 90, 120, 264
    correct use 186
    dative 41, 65ff, 90, 126, 148–9,
        225
    double 148, 222
    ethic 226
    genitive 64, 97, 120, 148–9,
        218, 222, 234, 259–61, 292;
        with *of* 119–20, 148, 222,
        234
    group 148–9, 166, 222
    instrumental 66
    nominative 52, 63, 65ff.
    oblique 40–1, 63, 147, 165
causality 226
Cawdrey, R., *Table Alphabeticall*
    198
Caxton, W. 184, 187–8, 204
    Eneydos 184–5
    History of Troy 188
Celts 2, 17, 32, 55–6, 77, 94
Centre for Policy Studie s 317
Chad, St 76
Chambers, E. 251
Chancery 11, 138, 170, 176–8
    Chancery Standard (Type IV)
        171–80, 187, 204
Channel 109, 132, 137, 229
Chanson de Roland 110
Charles I 12
Charles II 12, 236–7, 246
Charles IV, king of France 132
Charles VI, king of France 174
charters 57, 111, 113, 252
Chaucer, G. 21, 112, 134, 142–4,
    147–50, 154, 158–9, 161–71,
    173, 176, 182–5, 187, 189,
    194–5, 215, 227

Canterbury Tales 112, 142–3,
    147–9, 152–7, 159, 161ff,
    176, 187, 210
    To Rosemounde 158
    Treatise on the Astrolabe 157
    Troilus and Criseyde 169
    Words to Adam 169
Cheke, Sir John 195, 202
Chester 78, 82, 123
Chesterfield, Lord 258
Christianity 3, 17, 30, 35, 56, 72,
    75, 94, 186, 284
    Celtic 56
    Roman 56
    church 57, 91, 106, 108–9, 174,
        186
    Catholic 186, 195, 236
    education and 286
    influence of 56
    of England 283–4
    Civil Service examination 288
clause 26, 28–9, 99–102, 226
    adverbial 166–7
    conditional 223
    interrogative 224
    main 25, 99, 167
    negative 224
    non-finite 121, 166–7
    relative 167, 270
    restrictive 167
    subordinate 25, 28, 98–102,
        121, 155, 226, 234, 302
clichés 285
Cobbett, W. 274–7, 279
    grammar 274–7, 291–2
Cold War 303–6
Coleridge, H. 290
Coleridge, S.T., *The Rime of the
    Ancient Mariner* 273
colonies, British 35, 229, 265,
    279, 285, 299, 307
Commonwealth 303
    puritan 236
communication 2–3, 16, 281, 309,
    319
    developments in 305ff
compensatory lengthening 63
complementary distribution 59,
    124

compound phrase 97
compounding 30, 96, 102, 158, 202
concord 146, 264, 275–6
conjunction 28, 70, 100, 102, 155–6, 167–8, 179, 200, 226, 234, 248–9, 302
co-ordinating 28, 102, 302
phrasal 28
subordinating 28–9
connotation 30, 159–60, 299
conquest 33–6, 105
Conservative government 16, 315
consonant 38ff, 49–50, 57, 78–9, 121ff, 139–40, 163–4, 215–17, 320
assimilation 38–9
changes 43
dental 66
double 59, 118, 125–6, 164, 206, 233, 292
fall of 38, 52, 73, 258
final 38, 73, 293, 321
fricatives 49–50, 59, 124
groups 39, 65, 121, 223–4, 259, 293, 321
initial *h* 37, 216, 259, 285, 293, 310–11, 321
lengthening 52
liquid 68, 124–5
nasal 25, 39, 68, 124–5
palatal 60, 78
stops 49
velar 60, 78
voice 44, 49–50, 58–9, 118, 124, 216
consonant shift
first 49–50
second 50
Continent 54, 59, 109, 133, 265, 282
co-ordination, syndetic 226
Coote, E., *English Schoolemaister* 190, 198, 200–1
copyright 273–4
Cornwall 55, 142
correctness 5, 12, 317
Cotgrave, R. 198

Crashaw, R. 255
Crécy, battle of 133
Critical Review 266
Cromwell, Oliver 236
Cromwell, Richard 236
Cumberland 82
Cura Pastoralis 83–6, 98
Cursor Mundi 136
Cynewulf 75–6, 83, 95

Dale, T., professor of English 287
Danelaw 78, 81, 93, 137
Danes 34–5, 73–8, 81–2, 92, 105–6, 142
Great Army 77
Darwinism 284
Davis, Professor N. 181
Deira 56
Denmark 106, 283
Derbyshire 75
Derwent, River 107
determiner 147–8, 262
Devon 170, 189
dialects 1, 15, 18, 34, 41, 115, 122, 130, 187, 252, 310, 320
Anglian 54, 63, 88, 91, 122
British 309
Cockney 314
eastern 116, 140–1, 210, 216
Kentish 54, 57, 61, 122, 137, 139, 187–8
Mercian 137
Midlands 42, 138–9, 142, 152, 210
central 170
east 116, 137
north-east 138
north-west 138
south-east 138, 154
south-west 137–8
mixed 145
northern 42, 71, 92, 116, 140–5, 151, 157, 162, 165, 190, 213, 216
Northumbrian 69ff, 88ff, 137–8
Old English 78
regional 14
Scots 141
Somerset 4

south-eastern 137–40
south-western 135–9
southern 116, 137, 140–5, 149,
     151, 154, 157, 162, 165, 188,
     204, 210, 213
  stage 188, 217
  Types I–III (London) 170–1
  west 116, 139
  west 129, 137, 139–40
Dickens, C. 288
dictionary 12, 21, 190, 196,
     198–9, 228, 243–4, 246, 250ff,
     310, 315
  American 11
  branding 243, 252, 255
  completeness in 251
  Latin 21
  new words 315
  Old English 17
  other varieties of English 290
  prescriptive 12, 255–6
  pronunciation 252
  quotations in 254–5, 291
  universal 251
diphthongs 24, 50, 57–60, 78–80,
     88, 118ff, 139–41, 209–12,
     214–15, 320
  general history 24
  new 24, 124
  simplification of 320
diphthongisation 61, 78, 88, 103,
     209, 258
documents 58, 110, 134–5, 145,
     177–8, 180, 182, 189, 206
  chancery 127–9
  diaries 11, 21, 205, 208
  letters 11, 22, 138, 189, 205
  official 111, 173
  personal 8, 173, 190, 205, 208,
     213, 257
Dogberry 191
Domesday Survey 109
Donatus 90, 200
Dorset 77
Dover 188
Dream of the Rood 18, 82
Dryden, J. 246, 255, 257, 261
Dunstan, archbishop of
     Canterbury 89

Durham 82
Dutch 53
Dyonise de Mountechensi 113

Eadred, king of England 81
Eadwig, king of England 89
Early English Text Society 284
East Anglia 54–6, 77–8, 138, 140,
     172–4, 210
Edgar, king of England 89, 91
Edinburgh 145, 305
Edmund, king of East Anglia 77
Edmund, king of England 81
education 9, 14–15, 33, 37, 217,
     238, 274, 280, 287, 297–8, 313
  Act of *1872* 287
  A-level English language 312
  Alfred's programme 83ff
  Board schools 298
  Bullock Report 317
  changes in 311
  comprehensive 311
  Cox Report 311
  grammar schools 169, 274–5,
     286–7, 310
  Leeds 275
  National Curriculum 16, 312,
     317
  Newbold Committee 316
  public schools 13, 286, 300,
     313
  teaching in schools 169
  universities 134, 136, 283–4,
     300, 310, 316, 323
Edward III 132–3
Edward the Confessor 106
Edward the Elder, king of
     Wessex 81–2
E.K. 195
Eleanor of Aquitaine, queen of
     England 132
Elbe 52
Eliot, T. S., *The Waste Land* 314
Elizabeth I 32
Ellis, A. 292
Elmet (Yorks) 55
Elyot, Sir Thomas 196
     Governor 188
Emma of Normandy 105–6

Empire
  British 14–15, 279, 305, 309, 313
  Scandinavian 105–6
encyclopaedia 252–4
England *passim*
  Anglo-Saxon 84, 93, 106
    division into four earldoms
      105–6
  north 42, 73–4, 77, 123, 140
  north-east 75
  north-west 77, 168
  political unity 33
  population make-up 107–8
  south 54, 77, 123, 139, 313
  south-east 16, 127, 319
  west 77, 127–8
English *passim*
  American 1, 15, 204, 299, 306,
    318, 329–30
  American influence on 318
  as second language 1, 305
  attitudes to 1ff, 168ff, 272, 279,
    315
  Australian 279, 318
  basic 37
  beginning of 2–3
  British 1, 15, 277–8, 299, 300,
    306, 320, 328–30
  Caribbean 318
  colloquial 226, 237, 272,294
  complaints about 182ff
  concept of 1ff, 312
  correct 12, 280, 302, 312–14,
    317
  Estuary 319, 321
  feminist influence on 315ff
  first professor of 287
  formal 21, 242
  Germanicness 31
  good 285, 313–16
  grammatical 317
  historical tradition 281, 184
  history of 2–3, 284, 286–7, 319
  immigrants 308
  Indian 13
  informal 242
  international education 305–6
  Jamaican 13
  King's/Queen's 278–9, 316

  lack of antiquity 184, 201–2
  language of business, science
    and scholarship 305ff
  modern 140, 144, 147–8, 155,
    162, 165, 167, 179, 213–4,
    225, 328
  national literature in 176
  nature of 1ff, 184
  Nigerian 310
  Oxford 316
  plain 187
  political correctness 315ff,
    326–7
  poverty of 194
  praise of 185, 291
  sources for 16ff
  spoken 314
  status of 182–4, 279
  teaching of 243, 249–50, 287–8
  Types I–IV 170–1
  varieties of 1, 4, 15, 57, 288,
    318, 332
  world language 1, 303–5, 312
  written 181, 294, 318
English Dialect Dictionary 290
Englishness 10
epic formulas 127
Erasmus, D. 182
Erminones 53
Essex 56, 320
etymology 11, 195–6, 203–5, 252,
    280–1, 286, 288–90
euphemism 267, 315–16
Europe 47, 229, 266, 306
  north-west 49
  western 17, 82, 303–4
European
  East 306
  West 9, 24, 266, 278
Evelyn, J. 246
Evesham 87
Exchequer 138
Exeter Book 115

Farman 116
feminism 315
Fielding, H. 273
first fronting 59–60
Fisher, J. 173

Fowler, H., *Modern English Usage* 314
Foxe, J., *Book of Martyrs* 244
France 11, 34, 108–12, 133, 142, 175, 236–7, 265, 278, 281
Île de 111
francien 111, 133
Fraunce, A., *Arcadian Rhetorike* 194
French 9–12, 20–2, 28–36, 91, 107ff, 114–19, 127, 132–3, 136–42, 150–65, 167, 170, 174, 178–82, 194, 201, 204, 210, 214–19, 229, 232–4, 237, 258, 265–6, 275, 299, 305, 328
    central 112
    use of 136
    varieties 112
Friesland 53
Frisian 53
Froissart, J. 181
front mutation, i/mutation 51, 61–2, 72–3, 88, 116–17, 122
functional shift 27, 41, 148, 158–9, 229–30, 323
Furnivall, F. 284, 290
futhark 17

Garrick, D. 258
Gascony 132–3
Gaul 94
Gawain and the Green Knight, Sir 168
gemmination 68–9
gender 64–6, 313
    feminine 64, 66
    grammatical 147
    masculine 64–6
    natural 64, 147
    neuter 64–6
Geneva 308
Geoffrey the Grammarian 196
Geoffrey of Monmouth, *Historia regum britanniae* 127
George I, II, III 236
Gerald of Wales 112–13
Germanic 2, 14, 17, 25, 30–1, 43, 48–54, 59–66, 78–9, 88, 94–7, 100, 159, 165, 178, 196, 201–2,

206, 217, 229, 232, 235, 244, 283, 294
East 51
North 50–3, 78–9
West 2–3, 31, 50–6, 60, 79, 103, 116
Germany 32, 36, 53, 281–3, 305
gerund 330
Gil, A., *Logonomia anglica* 210
glossaries 94, 136, 192. 196, 199–200
glosses 18, 94, 113
    Mercian 116
    post-Conquest 114
Godden, Malcolm 113
Godfrey Gobylyve 187
Godwine, earl of Wessex 105–6
Googe, B. 185
    Zodiake of Life 186
gospels 18,, 21
Gower, J. 21, 168, 171, 173, 185
grammar 11, 21–2, 89–90, 129, 196–200, 246, 275, 310
    logic in 5, 221, 261, 294
    mistakes in 243, 265, 285, 287
    prescriptive 248, 250, 294
    rules 5, 12, 199,43, 249, 256, 265, 285
    teaching of 199, 243, 280, 286–7, 312
    traditional 314
    universal 247–8, 280–2
grammarians 5, 218, 220, 247, 261, 282, 296–7, 301, 331
generative 44
great vowel shift 7, 205ff
graphs 18, 57ff, 101, 118, 205–8
    capitals 101, 167, 206–7, 256
    Caroline *g* 118, 126
    eth 58, 102, 118, 124, 146
    final *e* 147, 149, 164–5, 206, 233
    thorn 58, 101, 118, 124, 178
    wynn 58, 102, 117, 146
    yogh 58, 102, 118, 126, 178
Greene, R. 192
Gregory the Great, pope
    Cura Pastoralis 83
    Dialogues 86
Grimbold 84

Grimm, J. 43, 49, 283
Grimm's Law 43, 49–50, 284
Grumio 225
Gulf War, new words 322–4, 326
Guthrum, Danish leader 78
Guyenne 132

Hali meiðhad 129
Hampshire 54, 56
Hannoverians 236
Harman, T., *Caueat for commen cursetors* 192–4
Harold Godwinson, king of England 106–7
Harold hardrada, king of Norway 106
Harris, J., *Lexicon technicum* 251
Hart, J.
  Methode 190
  Orthographie 190
  Unreasonable Writing 207
Hastings, Battle of 10, 105–6
Hawes, S., *Pastime of Pleasure* 187
head (of noun/verb group) 147, 328
Henry II 117, 132, 138
Henry III 135
Henry IV (Duke of Lancaster) 11, 174, 181
Henry V 11, 133, 173–6, 179
Henry of Huntingdon, *Historia Anglorum* 114
heptarchy 56
Herder, J. 282
Herefordshire 129–31
Higden, R., *Polychronicon* 141–2
Hoccleve, T. 170–1
Hodges, R., *Special Help* 220
Holland 36, 53, 278
Holliband, C. 198
Hollywood 306
Holofernes 191
homographs 205
homophones 205, 241, 258
  homophonic clash 157
Hopkins, G. M. 288
Horatio 221
Hortus vocabulorum 196
Hotspur, Lady 192

humanism 182, 221
Humber 82, 106
Hundred Years War 133
Huntingdonshire 170
Hwicce 56
hypercorrection 38, 115–16, 118, 310
hypotaxis 28–9, 112, 155, 166–7

imperative 27 67, 98, 151, 155
Idley, P., *Idley's Instructions to his Son* 187
India 34, 47, 174, 265–6, 279, 282, 300, 306, 318
  Raj 174
indicative 67, 98, 119, 151
Ine, king of Wessex 86
infinitive 50, 62, 67, 99, 120–1, 144, 166–7, 179, 233–4, 261, 330
inflected 99, 120, 152
inflections 16, 26, 34, 48, 64, 71, 125, 135, 178, 218
  difference OE/ON 78–80
  fall of 6–7, 26–9, 42, 121, 125–7, 146–9, 151–2, 158
  levelling of 6–7
Ingvæones 53
inkhorn controversy 195, 228
intensifiers 148, 229, 296
interjection 200, 249, 281
Iona 75, 77
Ireland 1, 56, 202, 248
Isabella, queen of England 132
Istvæones 53
Italy 266

Jackson, M., Conservative minister 327
James II 36, 236
Japan 305–6
Jarrow 75
J.K. (?John Kersey) 251
Job 102
John of Cornwall 169
John the Saxon 84
Johnson, Dr Samuel 12, 238–9, 242–7, 251–60, 268, 274–5
  Dictionary 238, 252–6

Plan of a Dictionary 247, 252
Rambler 244
Jones, D. 313, 318
Jones, J., *Practical Phonography*
238
Jones, Sir William 47, 273, 282
Jonson, B. 261
Joyce, J.
Finnegans Wake 314
Portrait of the Artist 328
Jutes 53–6

Katherine of France, queen of
England 174
Kemble, J. 283
Kent 21, 54–7, 77, 137, 187–8, 192
North 321
Kipling, R. 288
Kristensson, Professor G. 145
Kuhn, S. 116

La¢amon, *Brut* 21, 127–8, 130,
158
Lancashire 82, 138
Lancastrian monarchy 11, 132,
173, 175
Langland, W., *Piers Plowman*
168, 170
language
AB language 129–30
analytic 218, 221
Arcadian 267
binary system 309
bureaucratic 111, 133–4, 328
business 267
change 5–6, 38ff, 42
and character 288
class 192, 210, 243, 274, 285,
288, 294–5, 298, 300, 313
colloquial 148, 192, 221
contemporary 284, 187
democratic 199
diachronic and synchronic
44–5, 261, 308–9
diversity 14
divine origin 280–1, 283–4
education 238–9, 283
familiar 228
fixing 246–7, 252, 255, 280

as fossil history 286
genius of 237
of gentlemen 240, 244
history 255, 281, 285
linguistic corpora 314
literature 133, 158, 186–7,
191–2, 200, 284, 288
and mind 280–1
morality 239, 245, 281, 284–7,
316
non-standard 38, 192, 288, 326
origin of 280–2, 284
in Parliament 279–80
polite 239ff, 244, 273
and politics 4–5, 245, 312
purification of 246, 252, 273,
281
rational 13
regulation 12–14, 36, 187, 249,
256
and religion 280–4
standard 7–11, 32
structure 14, 249, 275, 308, 311
study 14, 42, 280–4, 287, 308
synthetic 26
system 6, 44
of trade 229, 242, 298
universal 247
of vagabonds 22, 192–4, 243
vulgar 239, 244, 267
of young 307, 326
languages
African 299
Afrikaans 300
Albanian 48
American Indian 44, 266, 278,
299, 310
Arabic 229
Armenian 48
Avestan 48
Balto-Slavic 48
barbarous 285
Basque 47
Celtic 47–8, 55, 94, 110
classical 14–15, 40, 267, 274,
294
Danish 34, 51–2, 106
Dutch 31, 36, 52, 79, 212, 266,
300

languages – *continued*
  Eastern 282
  European 30, 47, 282, 215
  Finnish 47, 51
  Finno-Ugric 47
  Frisian 52
  Gaelic 48
  German 25, 31–2, 36, 52, 96,
    195, 219, 299, 305
  Gothic 47, 51–2, 73
  Greek 31, 36, 43, 47–8, 71, 97,
    194–6, 203–4, 227–9, 266,
    273–4, 286–7, 299
  Hellenic 48
  Hindi 174, 306
  Hittite 47
  Hungarian 47
  Indo-Iranian 48
  Icelandic 51
  Italian 26, 36, 266, 299
  Italic 48
  Japanese 306
  Lappish 51
  Mycenaean 48
  non-European 30, 229
  Norwegian 51
  Portugese 229, 266
  'primitive' 309
  Romance 26, 31, 217
  Russian 304
  Scandinavian 19, 30, 51, 91
  Sanskrit 43, 47–9, 273
  Spanish 15, 26, 32, 229, 266,
    299
  Swedish 51
  Welsh 48
Latin 2, 5, 9–10, 13, 17–20, 26–32,
    35–6, 43, 47–51, 55–7, 62,
    66–72, 76, 79, 82–3, 88- 102,
    110–16, 129, 132–5, 141,
    155–60, 164–7, 174, 180–6,
    190–204, 216–17, 221, 227–9,
    233–4, 237, 241–2, 247–51,
    267, 273–4, 294, 299,
    311–12
  classical 135, 182, 204
  grammar 13, 21, 89, 199, 221,
    264, 311
  learning 9, 82–3, 190

model for English 182, 275,
    311–12
  teaching 35, 286–7
  vulgar 134–5, 182
  writing 17
law 18, 57, 86, 97, 110–11, 181–2
  copyright law 273
  Salic law 132
Lay Subsidy Rolls 145
learning 9, 18, 82
  decay of 83
Leicestershire 75, 170
lexicon 37, 126, 229, 255
lexis *see* vocabulary
Life of St Chad 76, 83, 113
Lily, W., *Grammar* 199–200
Lincolnshire 178
Lindisfarne 75, 77
linguistics 16, 24, 38, 311–12,
    317
  development of 308–11
  historical 46, 288, 308
linguistic sign 309–10
literacy 274
literature, primacy of 284
loan-words 92ff, 102, 107, 112,
    116, 124, 127, 143, 156–8, 186,
    189, 194–5, 227–9, 237
Locke, J. 237, 247–8
Lollards (Wycliffites) 160, 169,
    174
London 10, 21, 42, 78, 138–9,
    144, 162, 165, 168, 170–5, 187,
    192, 203–5, 208–111, 214, 240,
    275–7, 290, 305
  Brewers Guild 175–6
  Chancery Lane 138
  English 11, 25, 137, 149, 151,
    157, 165, 188–90, 210–16,
    239, 242, 278
  University 313
  University College 283, 287
London Bridge 180
Low Countries 133
Lowth, Bishop 12, 248
  English Grammar 248–50
Lund 145
Lydgate, J. 185, 194, 227
Lyrical Ballads 13, 272

McIntosh, Professor A. 145–6
Macbeth 244
Mak, a shepherd 188
malaproprism 191, 228
Maldon 105
Malvern 168
Mankind 191
manuscripts 18–19, 57, 90, 110,
   127, 130, 145–6, 168, 176, 201
  Bodleian Library, Oxford
    Bodley 34 120
    Bodley 343 114
    Hatton 20 84
    Hatton 113–14 114
    Laud Misc. 636 117
  British Library
    Arundel 57 137
    Cleopatra B xiii 114
    Faustina A ix, x 114
    Vespasian D xiv 114
  Cambridge University Library
    Gg.3.28 101
    Kk.5.16 [Moore] 69
    Ii 1 33 114
  Corpus Christi, Cambridge
    MS 173 [Parker] 87–8
    MS 302, 303, 367 114
    MS 402 129
  National Library of Scotland,
    Edinburgh,
    19.2.1.[Auchinleck] 21, 170
  National Library of Wales,
    Aberyswyth, Peniarth
    392D [Hengwrt] 161
Marenbom, J., *English our
    English* 317
Marlborough, duke of 265
Marshall aid 303
Martin, B., *Lingua britannica* 252
Mary II, queen of England 36,
   236
Merchant Adventurers 36
Mercia 56, 75–8, 81–4, 116
Michael, Dan of Northgate,
   Ayenbite of Inwyt 137, 147
Michaelis, J., of Göttingen 282–3
Middle Ages 34, 36, 299
Middle English 4, 6–7, 113ff, 123,
   153–6, 159, 207, 212, 284

Middlesex 56
Midlands 54
  central 178
  east 116, 138, 140, 145
  north-east 20, 126
  west 20–1, 54, 75–6, 78,
   129–30, 145
Milton, J. 182
Mischsprache 19, 137, 146
Modern English *passim*
  early 4
  late 4
monasteries 57, 91, 108, 114, 136,
   186
  St Augustine's (Canterbury)
   137
  Cerne Abbas 89
  Cluny 89
  Eynsham 89
  Ghent 89
  Hyde Abbey 113
  St Mary's Abbey (Leicester)
   170
  Peterborough 114–15
  St Bertin (St Omer) 84
  Whitby 69
  Wigmore Abbey 129–31
  Benedictine reform 89
  destruction of 81
monasticism 88
  Carthusians 134
  Cistercians 134
monophthongisation 63, 88, 120,
   122
Mopsae 210
Morley, H. 287
morphemes 195, 325, 327
morphology 6, 17, 22, 40, 55, 80,
   103, 117, 143, 145, 149, 218,
   259–61, 282, 291–2
Mulcaster, R., *Elementarie* 195,
   198
multilingualism 44
Murray, J. A. H. 290–1
Murray, L., *English Grammar* 282,
   286

Napoleonic Wars 274, 299
Nash, T. 192

NATO 203, 323
negation 100, 154, 179, 223–4, 229, 297
  double 100, 226, 264–5, 297
Neighbours 318
neogrammarians 44–5, 308
New England 229
New English Dictionary [Oxford English Dictionary] 286–91, 298
newspapers 27, 33, 274, 285, 292, 295, 318, 322–3, 325, 327–8, 331–2
  Guardian 323
  provincial 292, 295
  stamp duty 274, 276
newsprint 274
Newton, I. 255
New World 184, 229, 299
New York 275
Nicholas of Guildford 127
Norfolk 190
Norman Conquest 4, 9–10, 17–20, 34, 104, 107ff, 111–14, 119–21, 125, 137, 202
  impact of 107ff
Normandy 107–10, 132
Normans 35, 108–11, 142
Northanger Abbey 256
North Sea 52–4, 105
Northamptonshire 75, 170
Northumbria 56, 73, 75–8, 82–3, 106
Norway 77, 106
Norwegian 34, 75
Nottinghamshire 75
noun 26–7, 40, 52, 61–2, 71, 80, 117, 121–3, 146–9, 152, 162, 165, 200, 222, 249, 281, 292, 324–5, 328–9
  group 70, 103, 147, 207, 221, 328
  number, plural 6, 40, 42, 117, 119, 125, 149, 166, 178, 218, 259, 292
  phrasal 229
  as pre-modifier 328–9
  strong 64
  verbal 152

weak 64, 125
novel 288, 300
number 64–5, 125

oaths 191
object 26, 28–9, 41, 52, 97, 100, 167
Oder 52
Offa, king of Mercia 56
Old English (Anglo-Saxon) 4, 6–7, 9, 19–20, 30, 40–2, 48–52, 59–104, 113–19, 127–9, 137–9, 147–56, 160–6, 244, 284, 288
Old French 3–4, 112, 235
Old Norse 52, 58, 78ff, 91ff, 116, 119–20, 126, 140, 143, 157, 167
Old Saxon 73
Old Scandinavian 3, 78
Oliphant, K., *Standard English* 285
open syllable lengthening 123ff, 165–6, 215
Orkneys 77
Orm (Ormin), *Ormulum* 21, 125–6, 140
Orosius 84
orthoepists 217
Orton, H. 145
Oswald 188
Oswald, bishop of Worcester 89
Owl and the Nightingale 21, 127
Oxford 142, 283, 286
  Provisions of 135, 138
  University Press 290
Oxford Dictionary of New Words 315

Pacific 34, 265, 299, 304
Paine, T. 274
palatal umlaut 88
palatalisation 60–1, 72, 78
Palsgrave, J., *Lesclarcissement* 196–8
pamphlets, journals 12, 265
Panini 47–8
parataxis 28, 99, 102
Paris 112
Parker, S., *Ecclesiastical Politics* 243

Parliament 136, 169, 172, 236–7
  convention 236
  House of Commons 174, 176,
    276, 279–80
participle 200
  past 50, 67, 96, 100, 150–1,
    165–6, 179, 220, 329
  present 67, 151–2, 179, 222,
    233, 296
Partridge, E. 238
Pastons 138, 180–1, 189–90
Peasants' Revolt 144
Pecock, R., bishop of Chichester
  170
Penrith 82
personal names 102, 143, 252
Petruccio 225
Peterborough Chronicle 86ff, 114ff,
  126, 132, 167
Philip VI of Valois, king of
  France 132
Phillips, E., *New World of Words*
  198, 252
Phillips, K., *Language and Class in
  Victorian England* 295
Philological Society 6, 284, 286,
  288–9
philology, new 283–4, 287, 308
Phoenix, The 115
phoneme 19, 42, 57, 125, 211,
  215–16
phonemic system 19–20
phonemicisation 125
phonetics 20, 292
phonology 25, 42ff, 55, 59ff, 78ff,
  88, 103, 121ff, 126, 129, 139,
  143, 146, 165ff, 208ff, 257–9,
  284
  differences OE/ON 78–80
phrase 95, 119, 329
place names 55, 57, 61, 79, 81,
  122, 145, 252
Plegmund, archbishop of
  Canterbury 84
poetic diction 272
poetry 11–14, 18, 21, 30, 41, 115,
  127–8, 147–9, 153, 161, 164–5,
  186, 208, 215, 222, 224, 260,
  272–3, 258, 294

Poitiers, Battle of 133
Poland 304
politeness 35, 38, 237–8, 242
Pope, A. 258, 261
Porson, W. 175
post-modifier 147, 262
Prayer Book 221
pre-Alfredian period 10, 56
pre-determiner 147–8
predicate 221
prefix 27, 29, 96, 119, 160, 191,
  229, 232, 325–8
pre-modifier 147, 167, 229–30,
  262, 325, 328–9
preposition 5, 28, 71, 90, 127,
  152, 158, 179, 200, 225, 248,
  263–4, 294
  adverbial 28, 126, 325
prepositional group 152, 167,
  230, 234
Prince Hal 192
printers 33, 184, 205–7, 256–7
  printing press 8, 11, 182, 204
  justification 205
Priscian 90, 200
Promptorium parvulorum of
  Geoffrey of Norfolk 196
pronoun 65, 146, 165, 200, 221,
  249, 264–5
  demonstrative 66, 149
  dual 66, 149
  indefinite 295
  interrogative 66, 331
  personal 35–6, 41, 65, 100,
    147–50, 165, 218, 234, 296,
    314–15, 331
    first singular 65, 165, 178
    second singular 65, 150, 178,
      219, 260, 292
    third singular 65, 120, 126,
      150, 167–8, 178–9, 218–19,
      260
    plural 34, 65, 80, 126, 168, 179
  possessive 70, 219
  predicative 150
  reflexive 225
  relative 154–5, 179, 226–7, 234,
    262
  zero 155, 227, 262, 270–1

pronunciation 2, 20, 33, 39–40,
122, 130, 141, 190, 205,
209–11, 233, 238, 240, 255,
258–9, 290–3, 298
advanced 211, 215
affected 237ff, 266
American 319–20
British 319–20
conservative 211, 215, 217
correct 252, 291, 293, 312–13
fashionable 208, 238–9
new 14
polite 192, 258
provincial 218, 240
social pressures on 191, 214,
293
spelling 36–7, 191, 203–4, 238,
292–3, 319
propword 148, 222, 295
Proto-Germanic 48–52, 73
Proto-Indo-European 14, 43,
47–51, 63, 96, 282, 284
Western 48
Eastern 48
psalters 18
pun 140, 258
Punch 300
punctuation 101, 117–18, 161–2,
207, 232, 241–2, 250, 256, 269,
301–2
Puritans 186–7, 195, 202, 224,
236–7, 242–3
Puttenham, G., *Arte of English
Poesie* 188–90, 194, 230–5

Quebec 112
question 264, 329
indirect 154
tag 329
wh- 224
yes/no 223
Quickly, Mistress 191

radio 16, 41
Ralegh, Sir Walter 189
Ralph Roister Doister 188
Rask, R. 283
Reason, Age of 12

received pronunciation 8, 20–1,
25, 291, 309, 313, 317–21
reduplication 66
Reform Bill 280
register 1, 4, 41, 158–50, 190ff,
247, 298, 300, 314, 326
Regularis concordia 89
renaissance, twelfth century 134
Respublica 188
Restoration 12, 236–7, 242–3,
246, 253, 264
drama 212, 262
retraction 60
revolution
American 273
French 13, 266, 273, 299
Glorious/Protestant 36, 236
Puritan 12
Rheims, archbishop of 84
rhetoric 12, 101, 162, 187, 194,
200, 202, 207, 221, 242
Rhine 52
rhyme 20, 127–8, 208, 213, 232,
258
rhythm 28
Richard II 11, 174, 181
Right Spelling 257
river names 55
Romans 52–3, 82, 94, 201
Roman historians 49
Romanticism 272, 299
Royal Society 246–7
committee on English 246
Rushworth Psalter 116
Russia 304
Ruthwell Cross 18, 82
Rynell, A. 93

Samuels, Professor M. 169–72
Saudi Arabia 322
Saussure, F. de, *Cours de
linguistique général* 308–10
Saxons 3, 53–6
Scandinavia 33, 52, 106
Scandinavians 4, 78
Schlegel, F. 282
Schleswig-Holstein 53
science 17, 37, 184, 229, 239, 246,
266–7, 299, 305

Scotland 1, 32, 55, 77, 181, 202, 240
scribal profile 146
sentence 221, 226, 250
  complex 226
  declarative 41, 224–5
Severn 127, 137
Shakespeare 26–7, 41, 191, 196, 215, 223, 228–30, 244, 261, 290
  Antony and Cleopatra 222
  Hamlet 221
  1 Henry IV 191, 223
  Henry V 191
  3 Henry VI 222
  Julius Caesar 261
  King Lear 188
  Love's Labour's Lost 191, 197
  Macbeth 255
  Merchant of Venice 226
  Much Ado About Nothing 191
  Taming of the Shrew 225
  Timon 26
  First Folio 11
  pastiche 314
Sheridan, T.
  General Dictionary 255
  Lectures on Elocution 240
Shetland 77
Shropshire 129–30
Sidney, Sir Philip 36, 186, 253
Signet Office 175–7, 179
Skeat, W. W. 279
Skelton, J., *Phyllyp Sparowe* 185
slang 300, 315, 323–6
Smart, B. H. 292
smoothing 63, 72, 81
society 256
  changes in 304–7
Society for Pure English 313, 316
sociolinguistics 114–15, 209–11, 310
South Africa 266
Soviet Union 303, 305
Spain 305
speakers 5, 38, 45
  non-native 8
  upper class 264
Spectator 262

speech 3, 16–17, 28, 44, 144, 164–5, 181, 189–90, 210, 298
  affected 210, 237–9, 266
  educated 211, 239, 265, 313, 320
  parts of 27, 90, 96, 148, 200, 291, 326
  polite 191, 210, 238, 242ff, 258, 273, 298
  primacy of 3
  as social marker 187
spelling 11–12, 21, 33–4, 38, 71–3, 115–19, 122, 126–30, 139, 143, 158, 162–4, 178- 81, 189, 201–6, 212–7, 232–3, 238–41, 256–7, 277, 291–2, 301, 319
  American 37, 277, 319
  correct 33, 38, 190, 201, 205, 252
  etymological 205–6
  lists 22
  reform 20, 203, 208, 246
  rules for 240–1
  traditional 190, 203
spelling books 251–2, 256
spelling system 11–12, 25, 129–30, 190, 206, 214, 269
  private and public 257
Spenser, E. 185–6
  Shepheardes calender 195
Sprat, T. 246
Stamford Bridge, Battle of 107
Standard English *passim*
  Old English 114–17, 125–32, 138
  spoken English 318, 322
  taught 239–40
standardisation 2, 7–11, 19–21, 33, 36, 42, 76–7, 103, 169, 172–4, 181, 201–4, 208, 221, 224, 242, 252, 255, 258
Statute of Pleading 169
Steele, R., *Spectator* 262
Stephen, king of England 117
Stockwood, J., *Accedence* 199
Stratford-atte-Bowe 112
stress 28, 39, 45, 50, 164–5, 217, 294, 319–20

Stuarts 236
subject 26, 29, 52, 97, 221, 314
  co-ordinate 120–1, 146
  dummy 100, 102, 121, 147, 225
subjunctive 29, 67, 98–9, 102,
    119–20, 151–3, 179, 222–3,
    263, 285, 294, 329
suffixes 96–7, 160–1, 191, 229,
    233, 267, 326–7
Surrey 21, 137
Survey of English Dialects 145
Sussex 56, 137
Sweden 305
Sweet, H. 6–7, 272
Sweyn, king of England 79
Swift, J. 213, 245–6, 323
  Proposal 245
syllable 165, 201, 252
  closed 206
  mono 125, 202
  open 124, 206
  poly 31
  stressed 59
  unstressed 25, 28, 39, 52, 117,
    119, 121, 125, 150, 205, 213,
    259, 320
syntax 2, 5, 16–17, 22, 33–4, 41–2,
    55, 69–70, 80, 102, 221, 242,
    261, 270, 295
  regulation 128

Tacitus 53
Tamworth 82
technology 37, 184, 229, 266, 299,
    305
television 16, 41
tense 152
  compound 152
  future 222
  historic present 153–4, 167, 263
  perfect 152, 222, 263, 295–6
  pluperfect 152, 222, 263
  present 50, 62, 67, 151–2, 219,
    222, 261
    second singular 61, 151, 219,
      223
    third singular 6, 61, 117, 151,
      166, 179, 219–20, 233–4,
      261

plural 117, 166, 179
preterite 6, 26, 50, 67, 98, 103,
    119–20, 150–2, 166, 220,
    222, 261–3, 295
progressive 100, 152, 263, 296–7
Thackeray, W. M., *Book of Snobs*
    300
Thames 137, 319
Thatcher, M. 322
Thomas, T., *Dictionarium* 198
Thorpe, B. 283
Tilney, H 256
Tom Brown's Schooldays 297
Tooke, H., *Diversions of Purley*
    280–2, 284
Tory 245, 275
Tostig Godwinson, earl of
    Northumbria 106
Towneley Cycle, *Second
    Shepherd's Play* 188
trade 34–6
translation 28, 35, 67, 76ff, 83ff,
    90, 94–5, 99–100, 113, 133,
    135, 184, 199, 200
transitivity 225
travel, increase in 288, 305
Trench, R. C. archbishop of
    Dublin 286–7, 290, 292
  English Past and Present 286
  On the Study of Words 286
Trevisa, J. 141–2, 144, 169
Trollope, A. 297
Tudor monarchs 4

Uganda 307
Ulfilas 51
United Kingdom 14, 307, 332
United States of America 1, 15,
    303, 318
usage 5, 12, 22, 237–9, 242–3,
    249, 252, 255, 264–5, 273, 277
    279, 282–3, 291
  American 278, 329, 331
  best 314
  class 232, 295, 313
  colloquial 237, 327–8
  polite 237ff, 240, 252, 254, 268,
    291
  upper class 295, 297

Utilitarians 281

variety 4, 22, 45, 188, 217, 309–10
 charters 18
 formal 14, 22, 160
 informal 22, 160
 legal 18
 non-British 303, 319, 332
 non-standard 14, 290–1, 313,
  332
 regional 1, 187ff, 303, 313
 religious 18
 science 18
 slang 192
Vedic hymns 47
verb 26–7, 30, 41, 66ff, 80,
  96–102, 121–3, 146, 150–2,
  179, 200, 219–26, 249, 281,
  296, 331
 active 29
 auxiliary 35, 67, 97, 119, 167
 bisyllabic 39
 completice 100
 group 157–8
 impersonal 41, 100, 147, 152,
  224–5
 intransitive 152, 225, 264
 lexical 29
 nouns from 324
 passive 29–30, 35, 225, 297, 302
 phrasal 27, 29, 126, 157, 225,
  230, 234–5, 268, 302, 324–5,
  330
 preterite-present 67, 71, 99, 119
 reflexive 100, 152, 225, 330
 simple 29
 strong 41, 66–8, 150ff, 220
 transitive 264, 295
 weak 41, 66,68–9, 150–1, 220
 see also tense
verb-final 25
verb-second 25
Verner, K. 43
Verner's Law 50–1, 67
Vikings 4, 8, 19, 33–4, 52, 75–7,
  82–3, 91–2
Virginia 229
vocabulary 2, 16–17, 30–1, 34–5,
  42, 55, 72, 80, 90, 102–3, 127,

159, 167, 184, 200, 234–5, 240,
  265, 298ff, 302, 322
 acronyms 323–4
 change in 22
 common core 228, 282
 demise of Latin 225
 enlargement of 37, 35, 71, 94,
  160, 191, 235, 270
 Latinate 12, 31, 35, 71, 94, 160,
  191, 235, 270
 poetic 128
 purist 195
 regional 243, 251
 regulation 12, 228
 Saxon 12
 specialised 160
 standardised 90–1
 taboo 325
 technical 91, 228
 traditional 95, 119, 158, 160
 transparency of 30–1, 227, 242,
  248
 vulgar 251–2
 see also word
Vortigern 53
vowel 57, 78–80, 88, 122ff,
  139–41, 208–9, 258–9, 320–1
 contraction 63
 doubling 143, 164, 206
 fall of 39
 lengthening of 121
 levelling of 6, 25, 50–1
 long 24, 57, 209–12
 quality 24, 58, 121, 126
 short 57, 212
 shortening 121–2
 system 50, 59, 122, 208
 unstressed 6, 39, 98, 119
Vulgaria 199
Vulgarities of Speech Corrected 297

Wace 127
Wærferth, bishop of Worcester
  84, 86, 98
Wales 1
Walker, J. 255–6, 258
Walter of Bibbesworth, *Tretiz de
  langage* 113, 136
Wanderer, The 98

Warsaw Pact 303–4
Wash 82, 123
Watts, Dr 275
Waverley Annals 114
Webster, Noah 15, 37, 277ff
  American Spelling Book 277
  American Dictionary 277
Wedmore, treaty of 78
Wessex 9, 56, 73, 78, 81–2, 84, 92,
    175
West Indies 318
Westminster 138, 177
Westmoreland 82
West Saxon 9–10, 62–5, 76–7,
    81–4, 88, 91–3, 115–17, 122,
    137
  kingdom of 81–4, 93
  late 90, 103, 105
  standard 60, 105
Whig 245–6
Whitby, Synod of 56
Wight, Isle of 54, 56
Wilberforce, W. 280
Wilkins, J., *Philosophical
    Language* 247, 280
William the Conqueror, duke of
    Normandy and king of
    England 107–8, 138
William III and Mary II 36, 236
Wilson, T., *Arte of rhetorique* 194
Winchester 9, 89–90, 138
  new minster 106
  Synod of 89
  school of 89–91, 101
Worcester 108, 130
  scribe 'tremulous hand' 114,
    128
Worcester fragments 128–9
word 17, 228–9
  acceptable 12
  Anglo-Saxon 31, 116, 160
  archaic 37, 116, 127–9, 194–5,
    232, 251, 291
  blends 322–3
  clipping 245, 285, 323
  colloquial 268, 290–1, 310, 325
  compound 30, 102–3, 119, 194,
    229, 322, 328
  derivative 229

dialectal 290–1
doublets 228, 235
foreign 251, 285, 299
fossilised 37
four-letter 325
grammatical 28, 71, 248
Greek 21
hard 21, 200–1, 252
Latinate 20, 31, 168, 191,
    195–6, 199, 227, 251, 267,
    285, 315, 326
lexical 71, 248
medical 229, 325
morality in 288
new 13, 30, 35, 42, 93–4, 195–6,
    198, 228, 314–15, 322
obsolesence 38, 116, 127, 158,
    160, 252, 291
Scandinavian 52, 80–1
seafaring 36, 266
slang 290, 298, 300–1, 325
technical 94, 157, 232, 328
three syllable 39
see also vocabulary
word formation 30, 160, 229, 322
word maps 22
word order 25–6, 28, 34, 41, 70,
    97–9, 120–1, 146, 158, 166–7,
    223–4, 234, 294, 331
  inversion, subject-verb 121,
    146, 224
Wordsworth, W. 14, 272
World War
  First 13, 15, 303–5
  Second 27, 303, 305, 307,
    318
Wrenn, C. L. 87
Wright, J. 290
writing 2–3, 8–9, 16–20, 35–7,
    56–7, 93, 189, 221, 239, 284,
    298
  primacy of 254, 284, 309
  system 20, 37, 224–27, 212,
    126, 130, 146, 165, 172–3,
    317
Writing Scholar's Companion
    240–1
Wyld, H. C. 313
Wynkyn de Worde 196

Yonge, Sir William 258
York 62, 78, 141–2
Yorkist monarchy 4

Yorkshire 82, 138

Zutphen 36

ENGLISH WORDS

Note: Whatever their form in this book, words are normally listed in the index under the lemma and spelling the word would have in a dictionary of Modern English since this will enable the historical development of words to be traced. If the word is not extant in Modern English, the form quoted is given. All graphs are modernised, even for those words which retain their earlier form.

aardvark 300
a(n) 98, 216, 263
aback 255
abalienate 259
aband 255
abbot 178
abominable 204
about 152, 251
academy 217
achieve 206
acre 49–50
add 233, 269–70
admonish 203
adultery 203
aelda 72
affect 223–4, 266
aflemde 116
again 171, 178
ageism 327
agriculture 50
ain't 297–8
alderman 87
all 87, 147, 214
all-powerful 230
almighty 71
alpaca 266
alright 38
also 143
alter 233
alteration 233, 270
American 277
am't 221
ancient 214
and 148, 170, 178, 234, 261, 302
Angelcynn 119

anger 151, 216
angostura 266
Anjou 122
ansyne 103
any 148, 170, 178, 234, 261
apache 299
apostasy 292
appeal 25
appear 178
appendage 266
April 164, 168
army 119
arrive 270
as 234
ascendant 157
ascension 157
assure 159
at 118, 152, 179, 225
attrit 323
aunt 214
author 204
avalanche 299
avaunt 159
aversion 270
Avon 55
ayatollah 322

bait 79
baksheesh 266
balewen 129
balls-up 324
bar 257
barn 72, 91
bath 257
bathos 267

BBC
be 87, 90, 99, 120, 143, 166, 179,
    220–1, 224,227, 234, 263–4,
    294–7, 301, 329
-by 235
beam 122
bear 68, 150, 259
because 28–9, 156, 227, 234
bee 149
beginning
beige 216
below par 267
benefit 292
berry 206
between 179
bilious 266
biographee 327
bivouac 266
black-out 324
blaxploitation 322
blissful 164
blood 214
boatswain 79
bobbitt 322
bodily 31
bog-up 325
bolt 321
book 64, 126, 206
boomerang 299
booze 325
borough 94, 119
both 93, 143–4, 157, 261
both . . . and 99
bottle up 27
bowl 257
bramble 40
break 212, 96
breakout 325
breath 164, 214
brest 79
Bretwalas 79
bright 216
brill 326
broad 184
broadloid 323
brother 49–51
brown-out 324
bryce
brynige 116

build 297
bungalow 266
burn 79
bury 25, 139
bush 213
but 28, 178, 234, 295

café 299
calf 257
call 157
calm 257
can 178, 296
cannon 259
car 259
care 6
caribou 266
carve 68
cashew 266
cast 39
castle 39, 119
catch 213
cattle 112
ceaster 61
centre 278
cephalick symptoms 268
chance 214, 258
change 269
chastisement 294
chattel 112
cheese 62
cheque 278
chiffon 299
child 40, 119
child-abuse 329
chill 158
chimney 241
China 25
chipmunk 299
choose 96, 122
chord 255
Christ 29, 102
    Christ his 218, 250
Christmas 39
church 58, 78–9, 91, 140, 149
churl 61
chutney 300
cicerone 266
clause 214
claw 124

clean 122, 160
clerk 213
cliché 299
client 158, 316
climb 41
clip-on 325
clique 265
closing 270
cloth 293
cnapa 9164
cobble 230
cocktail 300
collect 158
come 6, 26, 58, 62, 100, 220
commandeer 300
commentary 229
common 184, 268
communism 326
complete 251
comptroller 204
compulsory 294
concorde 323
confound 233
considering that 28
contradiction 158
contribute 320
controversy 45, 217, 294
cool 326
cope with 330
cor anglais 299
cord 256
cornucopia 50
corporal 31
corps 266
cough 140
could 178, 204
countryside 227
county 168
courage 164, 168
couth 164, 167, 327
cove 194
cow 149
coxcomb 266
coyote 299
crack 326
crag 213
crampon 299
creep 67
cripple 315–16

crop 164
cross 293
cupboard 294
custom 233, 235
customer 316
cyre 96
cythere 91

dagger 196
daliance 158
dance 196
dare 296
darling
daunt 159
day 52, 60, 78, 88, 118
de-air 326
death 214
debt 130, 191, 203
defeatist 327
delay 330
delectable 217
dentist 50
departure 215
depôt 266
Derby 213
de-skill 326
despicable 294
destroy 140
destruction 27
dew 214
dialects 321
dictionary 30
different 5, 8
dinghy 300
diocese 158
disabled 316
disadvantaged 316
disconfirm 326
disfiguring 270
distant 168
disuse 302
divorcee 327
do 100, 177, 152–3, 179, 220,
    223–4, 226, 232, 257, 261, 264,
    297, 321, 329
don't 297
doubt 191, 203
dough 49, 124, 140
dramsoc 323

drat 212
draw 124
dream 39
drihten 71–2, 128
drought 162
drown 270
dry 124
duchess 257
dun 244, 255
duty 293

each 125, 148
earl 60, 119
eat up 234
ecstasy 292
edge 58, 126
eek 162–4
eight 51
emanate 266
embellish 184
end 69
endebyrdnysse 103
enfilade 266
engender 158, 166, 168
England 119
enhance 158
entune 158
enthusiasm 143–4
entreat(ment/y) 267
epaulette 299
equal 158
equinoctial 157
exam 285
exchange 233
executor 158
existence 267
expense 323
explain 25
extravaganza 266
eye 164

fair 148
fambles 194
family 39
famous 168
fan 125
fanatic 294
fantasia 266
fantasy 204

far 168
fare 62, 68, 126
-forth 127
fart 159
fascism 326
fast 261
fasten 39
father 49, 71, 257
fault 140, 204, 233
fellow 158, 206, 300
feminism 327
feorh 63
feorþsiþ 129
ferian 69
ferly 148
fern 259
fertile 293
feather 93
fey 128
fierd 118–19
fight 118
figure 233
filmsoc 323
find 68
fin de siècle 299
fir 259
fire 117, 259
fish and chips 318
fix 326
fixture 323
flee 268
flit 126
flood 211, 214
flotilla 266
flour 259
flower 162–4, 167–8
fly 268
foe 149
foldu 71
folk 168
fonne 143
fool 211
football-speak 327
forbear 233, 235
forfeit 159
forget 157
forleosan 50
forlorn 50
formidable 294

formula 40
forthfyrde 115
for thaem the 102, 156
for to 179
forward 119
forweorthan 96
fowl 124, 162
fox 140
fra 119
fraternal 50
freedom 327
freely 155
fremman 69
Friday 257
friendly 155
full 148
fundie 315
funk 268
funny 327
fur 259
fuss 268

gage 112
gainrising 195
galantyne 158
gan 194
garderobe 112
garrynge grisbayting 142
gazelle 300
gecladod 96
gelathung 91
general 251
geneva 266
genius 269
genteel 298
gentleman 298
gersum 116
get 157, 297. 329
gewinnan 96
giefu 65
gift 178, 323
gin (n) 266
gin (v) 152–3
give 6, 68, 140, 168, 178
    up 302
go 152, 166–7, 220, 233, 329
    forth 127
    into 234
God 212

gold 321
goldfaet 129
good 211
gospel 97
government 321
grand 39
grant 178
great 212, 258, 326
ground 160
groundwrought 195
gruntled 328
guarantee 112
guillotine 299

hale 143–4
half 39
halfpenny 294
hammer 158
hand 213
handbag 322
handicapped 315
handkerchief 39
hands off 269
hang 268
hangover 325
hant 221
happen 225, 269
harrynge 142
hatan 68
have 68, 99, 103, 125, 143, 166–7,
    220–1, 261, 263, 295–7, 329
have to 223
hawk 158
he 65, 70, 87, 234, 315
headbanger 315
heath 164
heaven 71–2, 125
heed 234
help 68, 119, 151, 166
Henry 122
her 295
herbarium 267
hers 150, 219, 295
heterosexism 327
hickory 266
hill 139
him 87–8, 120
his 70, 103, 150, 167, 218, 250,
    260, 295

hold 120, 123
holiday 122
holy 71, 119, 166
honest 259
honour 257, 278
horn 49–50
horse 149, 259
horticulture 50
hospital 230
hospitalise 327
housecarl 116
how 331
humanity 315
humour 270
humvee 324
hunderder 195
hunt 159
hunting 152
husband 293
hwaethere 99

I 147, 149, 165, 178, 187–8, 331
idea 293
if 103, 178, 223
ilk 171, 221
ill 143–4
imperfect 184
impi 300
in 179
incarnate 191
indaba 300
inertia 267
ingenious 268
ingenuous 268
in order that 28
input 325
inspire 166, 168
interior 328
intermezzo 299
Ipswich 293
island 204
issue 159
it 65, 100, 126, 147, 178, 218, 225, 234
its 218–191, 260, 295, 318

jest 159
jocund 158
join 233, 258

kapellmeister 299
kayak 266
keep 69
kick 324
    in 324
    off 324
    up 324
kindergarten 299
king 118
kiwi 299
knave 259
knife 244, 255, 259
knight 88
know 68
koala 299

laager 300
laboratory 319
labour 160
lady 159, 298
lady-chapel 218
lamb 217
lamentable 294
land 121, 165, 178
landlady 39
langsum 103
lasso 299
laugh 216
lavatory 319
law 93
lay 264, 268
lean-to 325
learn 96
learner 96
left-overs 325
leitmotiv 299
lemman 159–60
leorningcniht 91
less 79
let 52
liberate 327
licour 162–4, 168
lie 233, 264, 268
life 267
light 63
line 258
lingerie 299
listen 217
live-in 325

loaf 63
logic 252
loin 258
London 55
long 165, 167
loose 79, 292
loot 300
loquacity 270
lord 63
lose 67, 292
lousy 325
love-in 324
low 93

mace 125
machine 278
maecti 71
maeg 87
maid 125
make 123, 166, 212, 268
  cheer 158
  fair 184
  up 234
maker 235
malady 198
malicious 201
man 40, 62, 64, 139, 298, 315
mankind 72, 315
manoeuvre 265
man-of-war 230
manred 119
mansion 157
many 148, 178, 234
March 168
Marxism 326
mass 94
maté 266
may 29, 103, 234, 296
maybe 159
maze 125
me 107, 331
means 249–50
meat 260
medicine 291, 294
meerkat 300
meet 121, 206, 211, 233, 258
melody 164
menu 299
merchant 259

merry 25, 139
mescal 299
methinks 41, 100, 225
metud 52
micel 118
Michael Jackson-speak 327
middungeard 71–2
might 296
mine 150, 178, 219
misanthrope 266
mob 245
modgidanc 72
modig 91
more 123, 219, 259–60
morgenleoht 97
most 219, 260
mother tongue 148
mouse 62, 118
much 170, 178
music 256, 278
must 297
mutual 268
my 149–50, 178, 219
myself 331–2

name 6, 65
nap 212
nathe 126
NATO 323
nave 259
nawab 266
Nazism 326
ne 154
near 63
neck 157
need 296
neither 171, 226
neolaecan 63
neuter 158
new 214, 267
night 162, 178
niman 80, 119
noon 94
not 154, 171, 178–9, 226
notice 269
nought 154, 171
novel 267
nucleus 267
nygle 194

obey 259
observer 25
of 28, 120, 152, 166, 234
oferhygd 91
ofermod 91
often 217, 291, 293, 319–20
offer 94
ofslean 27, 128
ointment 158
old 103, 171
on 90, 179, 263
one 98, 139, 148, 221–2, 295
oneself 301
ongean 90, 103
only 265
operation 157
Ormskirk 79
other 118
ought 295
　to 295
our 178, 234
ours 150, 219
outbreak 325
outlaw 116
outrage 159
out-tonk 325–6
over 90
overcome 117
owe 124

pacifist 327
pampas 266
pannam 194
pant 220
parliament 204
part 269
pass 258
passenger 316
past 258
peace 119
pear 212
penknife 59, 125
people 168
perceive 31, 308
perestroika 322
perfect 158
person 298
pewter 140
phang 26

pharynx 267
phlox 267
physical 31
physically challenged 316
physiognomy 245
pick-me-up 324
pick up 324
pierce 166–8
pilgrimage 164
pint 258
pirate 30
pizzicato 299
please 226
pleasure 216, 233
plough 124
point 140, 258
polite 271
polo 300
poor 327
possible 245
pray-in 324
prick 162–4, 166
pride 91
prima donna 299
prince 158
priesthood 97
profess 159
project 320
proper 331
psalm 158
pueblo 299
pull 213
pure 160
purree 300
put 143
　in 325
pyjamas 300

quagmire 321
quango 323–4
queen 118
quinine 299
quote 140, 293
quick 103

rabbat 233, 235
radio 27
rather 264
real 331

redistribute 328
regroup 328
reinvent 328
remember 152
retrain 328
rhyme 203–4
rhythm 204
rice 118
rich 327
ride 40, 67, 150, 152
right 103, 178, 180
rococo 299
roe 143
room 269
root 168
rucksack 299
rude 184
run 164–7
rural 227

sacerhad 94
sad 327
saegenga 97
saerinc 30
sahte 118–20, 126
saint 158, 168
salmon 39
salt 321
same 221, 260
sammtale & sahhte 126
sandbag 322
sarong 299
say 69, 88. 103, 140, 188, 215, 233
SCAA 323
scene 205
scepen 72
school 94
schooner 266
scop 72, 94
screw-up 325
scudbuster 322
scudstud 322
sea 30, 215
sealmscop 84
seat 211
see 31, 50–1, 60, 63, 168, 205, 308
seeing life 267
seek 162–5, 212

self 170, 221
sell-by 325
senseless 191
sergeant 259
servant 213
set off 268
seven 103
sex offender 329
shant 221
shake 159
shall 71–2, 143–4, 153, 178, 180, 220–2, 263, 296
shampoo 266
sharp 142
she 65, 119, 126, 150, 315
sheep 40, 61, 65
ship 58, 65
shire 168
shirt 78
shoe 149
shorter 215
should 39, 118–20, 171, 178, 204, 263, 296, 330
shove 67, 220
sib 119
sick 165
simile 158
simple 184
sin 216
sing 216, 220
sit in 324
skerry 78
skirt 78
skuit 323
skypper 194
slave 188
slavery 327
slay 27
sleep 151, 166
sleet 159
slitting 142
snob 300
snow 88, 124
so 70, 140, 147, 215
soldier servant 230
sole 215
some 148, 321
son 91, 119
soothly 187

soprano 266
sore 217
sort 188
sortie 266
soul 215
sovereign 232
sow 124
spastic 316
speak 62, 68, 103, 212
speciality 319
specially 165
speech 233
spick and span 268
spire 158
spite 216
sporting 267
springbok 266
staff, stave 123
stampede 299
state 258
stead 170
steak 212
stimulus 267
stone 6, 40, 42, 65, 79–80
strand 165, 167
strange 168
stricter 201
student 316
style 256
such 170, 178
sun 164, 206
superstition 244
support 159
suppress 233
surplus 233
suspect 191
Sussex 54
swain 79
swear 217, 220
sweet 165
swin-in 324
swink 160
swithe 118, 139
swive 159
swollen 293
sword 140, 217
syllable 233
syththan 102

tail 215
take 80, 116, 119, 321
take-away 325
tale 215
talk 220
tapioca 266
tapster 96
teacher guidance 329
teach-in 324
teenage vandalism 329
tell 321
termination 270
terracotta 266
terrain 266
tha 66, 70–2, 149, 156
Thames 55
that 66, 99, 139, 149, 154–6, 162,
    167, 179, 221, 226–7, 234,
    261–2, 270–1
the 66, 119, 148–9, 178
theatre 203
their 34, 126, 150, 168, 178
theirs 150, 219
them 34, 126, 150, 168, 178
then 179
theow 93
there 273
therefore 156
thereof 259
these 66, 149
they 34, 65, 126, 150, 157, 171,
    179, 315
thief 206
thilke 171
thine 150, 219
thing 149
this 66, 149, 221, 328
thonne 156
thorp 49
those 66, 149
thou 35, 219, 260
though 79, 99, 157, 171
thrall 93
three 49–50
throne 203
throng 159
through 90
throwere 91
Thursday 93

thy 159
tiadae 71
til 72
time and tide 95
to 234, 292
todaelde 119
too 232, 292
tongue 270
tooth 49–50
top 205
  score 323
toslean 27
totem 266
town 30
traught 328
traveller 278
trek 300
trespass 159
tricolour 299
trinity 50
triptych 267
trousseau 299
tsetse 300
Tuesday 293
turn 269
two 217

unalyfedlic 103
uncouth 164, 327
undergrad 323
unDutch 328
unfreedom 327
universal 251
unkindest 261
unless 234
unnbedenn & unnbonedd 126
unpoor 327
Unprofor 324
unrad 116
unraed 116
untid 116
up 115
uplandish 144
urban 30
urbanise 327
used to 295
usell 126
usual 235

vain 302
van 125
vein 168
victuals 203, 294
vineyard 294
virtue 168
vision 216
vulgar 233

waft 321
wag 213
wage 112
waistcoat 291
walk 7, 40, 270
walk-about 325
wallah 266
wand 213
wander 321
want 270
war 115
ward 72
wardrobe 112
warrant 112
watch 213
way 88
Wednesday 291
weep 151
well 148
  known 168
wench 159
wend 103, 166
weofod 91
weorthan 50, 96, 99, 118
wergild 97
Wessex 54
what 66, 115, 331
whelk 204
when 28, 156, 167
whereof 234
which 125, 154, 167, 178–9,
  226–7, 234, 262, 270, 285
while 156, 171
white-out 324
Whitsun 38
who 66, 154–5, 217, 226–7, 262,
  264, 270, 285, 314, 331
whole 204, 217, 321
whose 154, 226, 262
wicked 326

Wight 88
will 29, 99, 153, 171, 178–9, 207,
    222, 263–4, 296
Winchester 55
win 96
window 157
wing 93
winter 149
witan 87
with 90, 162, 264
wlafferynge 142
Woden 79
wolf 79
woman 298
wombat 299
wonder 225
wonderfully 270
word 30, 40, 64, 115
wordhord 30
world 171
worm 79, 125
worry 321
wot 143

would 178, 204, 263, 296
wright 159
write 220
wrong 233
wurtscipe 118

yard 49–50, 78
ye 219, 260
year 61, 149
yell 159
yield 61
ymbe 90
yon(der) 221, 261
York 62
you 35, 178, 219, 260
young 61, 118, 162
your 178, 234
yours 150, 219
ythes gewealc 97
ythlad 97

Zeitgeist 299
Zephirus 164, 168